EASY GARDENS FOR THE SOUTH

By Harvey Cotten, Pamela Crawford, and Barbara Pleasant

For any southerner who has ever killed a plant!

Where to Buy "Easy Gardens for the South"

The book is available through many garden centers and book sellers. It is also available through www.amazon.com. To locate your nearest source or place an order with the publisher, contact us at:

Color Garden Publishing, 3575 S. Ocean Blvd., Suite 202, South Palm Beach, FL 33480
Phone: 561-371-2719
Web site: www.easygardencolor.com, www.pamela-crawford.com
Email: info@easygardencolor.com

Credits:

Authors: Harvey Cotten, Pamela Crawford, and Barbara Pleasant
Managing Editor: Barbara Hadsell
Cover Design and Graphic Design: Elaine Weber Designs, Inc. (www.ewdlogos.com)
Proofreader: Barbara Iderosa, Best Editing Service, Wellington, Florida
Horticultural Consultant: Bill Funkhouser
Researcher: Tammy Brogan and Sheila Allen
Bargain Gardening Consultant: Joan Ahrens

Printing: Asianprinting.com, Korea

Published by Color Garden, Inc., South Palm Beach, GA. First printing: 2009
Library of Congress Catalog Card Number pending

ISBN 10: 0-9712220-7-X
ISBN 13: 978-0-9712220-7-6

This book is not designed as a source to the possible toxicity of each plant. Do not eat any plant in this book and teach your children to never eat any plant unless you can find it in the produce department of your grocery store.

Cover photos: 'Catalina Midnight Blue' torenia, 'Big Sky Twilight' coneflower, and 'Patriot Firewagon' lantana from Proven Winners.

Title page photo and the photo on this page from the home of Mrs. Bill Taylor, Jr. in Louisville, Mississippi.

Contents

Easy Plants and Symbols

What are Easy Plants?

This book includes many plant profiles, which are descriptions of the plants. Large profiles take up two pages. Here is the criteria for double-page profiles:

- Ability to withstand climate conditions in the south, including warming trends and moisture extremes
- Attractive appearance with trimming three times a year or less
- Consistent behavior for at least two years in multiple locations
- Ability to adapt to a variety of urban and suburban situations
- Plants of various heights and environmental tolerances to provide a complete plant palette for many residences and commercial establishments.

To further evaluate the plants, we put them on a spreadsheet and classified them by how many times a year they had to be touched. The easiest plants are designated by a blue ribbon, next easiest by a red ribbon (defined on pages 12 to 13). It is amazing to see how many southern plants only need care once or twice a year!

At the end of each chapter (chapters two to four), we include smaller profiles of other plants that deserve mention.

Each double-page plant profile includes symbols at the top of the page to make it easier to determine key characteristics of the plant without having to read a lot of text.

- The butterfly and hummingbird symbols denote the plants whose flowers produce nectar for butterflies or hummingbirds.
- The bird symbol denotes the plants that provide either shelter or food for birds.
- The flower (dogwood) symbol indicates plants that are native to the south, defined as growing in the south before Columbus discovered America.
- The 'Lives on Rainwater' symbol refers to those plants that live on natural rainwater without any supplemental irrigation. We surveyed hundreds of county extension agents throughout the south regarding water use of southern plants to gain this information.
- 'Average Weeks of Color' refers to the number of weeks that plant has either flowers or colorful leaves
- The deer symbol refers to those plants that are almost never eaten by deer. Deer will eat anything when they are starving, but they like some plants more than others. In addition to plants that are almost never damaged, we have further classified the plants as 'Frequently damaged,' 'Often damaged,' or 'Seldom damaged.' Those classifications appear in the left sidebar under 'Cautions.'

Trial Gardens

Pamela Crawford has been extensively testing plants at both university and private trial gardens since 1988. Harvey Cotten has been testing plants at Huntsville Botanical Garden (Huntsville, Alabama) for about the same time period. Both of their goals have been similar: to find superior plants for the south that give the most color for the longest period of time with the least amount of care. This book is a compilation of knowledge gained from each of these authors' extensive plant trial experience, along with a lifetime of gardening experience in the south from Barbara Pleasant (see author biographies in the inside, back cover).

Georgia Trial Gardens

Pamela Crawford's trial gardens in Canton, Georgia, test the easy, colorful plants and low water gardening methods she writes books about. She has worked with annuals, perennials, and shrubs, testing both new varieties and old favorites. Pamela has tested more than 13,000 plants in her quest for color that is quite well adapted both to our changing climate and busy lifestyles.

Her gardens are primarily watered from rainwater collected from the roof (*see pages 40 to 43*).

Huntsville Botanical Garden

The Huntsville Botanical Garden (butterfly house, left) is relatively young garden in Huntsville, Alabama. 2008 marked the 20th anniversary for this garden. With a garden built by volunteers and supported by a small, permanent horticulture staff, finding and utilizing those superior plants that would provide the most color and the best visual displays with the easiest of care is always top of mind. As a botanical garden they are expected to have the rare and unusual for their visitors to see, but they know that the whole garden can not be designed in this fashion. The bulk of the botanical displays must follow the tenets promoted in this book - simple, colorful, and low water. The Garden also provides an educational resource for its members, volunteers and visitors to see which plants are not only surviving the changing climactic conditions but actually thriving in them.

The Huntsville Botanical Garden has a wonderful relationship with many of the top wholesale growers and plant breeders in the southeast. As the Garden's visitation has steadily grown over the years (topping 325,000 in 2008) plant breeders and growers realize that a partnership with the Garden to "trial" new introductions to see how they will perform in the landscape is beneficial to all. Research efforts at the Garden include looking at what plants perform best in their changing climate without a lot of care and maintenance. Other efforts involve identifying more heat-tolerant peonies for southern gardens. This book has afforded a great opportunity to record much of what they have discovered and share it with their southern friends.

Photo Credits

All photos by Pamela Crawford except for the following: Aceshot 1: Burning bush, p. 262. Albert Mednelewski: Grape hyacinth, p. 190. Allan Armitage: Baptisia in sidebar, p. 114. An Nguyen, Baptisia, large photo, p. 114. Ann Kitzman: White pine, p. 309. Antique Rose Emporium: 'Mutabilis' rose, p. 16, 247; 'New Dawn' rose, p. 17, 247;

Bailey Nursery: Smoke tree, p. 17; spiraea, p. 22, 51; daylily, p. 99, 171, 215; grass, p. 140; 'Sugar White' iris, p. 151; 'Joe Pye' weed, p. 152; obedient plant, p. 190; winterberry, p. 222; honeysuckle 'John Clayton,' p. 224; spiraea, large, p. 248, 249; witch hazel, p. 258; quince, p. 264; Virginia sweetspire and wintercreeper, p. 265; ginko, p. 286; smoke trees, small, p. 306; smoke tree, large, p. 307; ash, river birch, p. 308; white oak, crabapple, fringe tree, pin oak, p. 309; poplar, weeping willow, p. 311; 'Endless Summer' hydrangeas, p. 228. Ball Horticulture: Ice plant, p.14, 51; hibiscus, salvia, p. 15-16; 'Profusion' zinnia, p. 24; hibiscus, p. 29; angelonia on p. 56; pansies on p. 63, 78, 79, 83; vinca, hibiscus pp. 98, 99; Jacob's coat, p. 104, coneflowers, p. 121, hibiscus, pp. 144-145; small ice plants, p. 148; ice plant, p. 149; salvia, p. 154, 163; hibiscus, p. 161; large salvias, p. 172-173; small scabiosa, p. 176; gaura, p. 189; Browyn Photo: Walnut, p. 311.

Candace Garber: Crocosmia, p. 14; spiraea, p. 15; Japanese maple, p. 17, 50; viburnums, redbud, p. 17, 22, 51; scabiosa, p. 50, 187; angelonia, p. 51, scabiosa, p.81, 214, 243; portulcace, p. 105;Joe Pye weed, p. 153; phlox under tree, p. 164, small salvias, p. 172; large scabiosa, p. 177, 178; large azaleas, p. 202; winterberry, p. 221; spiraea, p. 251; viburnums, p. 252-255; sweet pepper, p. 264; maple, large, p. 294; top, left maple and bottom, green maple on p. 295; redbuds, p. 304; spiraea, p. 307. Casa Flora: Ferns on pages 14, 27, 50, 132, 133. Chamblee Roses: 'Home Run' rose, p. 16, 24. Conard Pyle, Rob Cardillo: 'Knock Out' rose, p. 16, 50, 109, 167, 177, 183, 197, 210, 225, 243, 244, 245, 28. Syl Arena, double and rainbow 'Knock Out' roses, p. 245, p. 307.

Dagmar Schneider: Witch hazel. p. 16, 17 and small one on 259. Dwight Smith: crocosmia, p. 124. Encore Azaleas: large photo, p. 200. Flowerwood: White azalea, p. 20, 209; Japanese boxwood, p. 205; maple leaf, p. 294. Gail Johnson: Sycamore, p. 311. Gardener's Confidence Collection (courtesy of): © Michael Dirr, crapemytle, p. 117, 129, 169, 195, 197, 214-215, © Pure Red Creative, Mini Penney Hydrangea, p. 49. © Jim Midcap, 'Ever Red Sunset' loropetalum, p. 275. Gene Joiner: Pindo palm, p. 309.

Harvey Cotten: Crapemyrtle, p. 10; amsonia, aster, p. 14; switch grass, lenten rose, baptisia, American boxwood, p. 15; muhly grass, switch grass, hydrangea Annabelle, juniper 'Grey Owl,' abelia, wax myrtle, page 16; American holly, oakleaf hydrangea, wax myrtle, arborvitae, Chinese elm, bald cypress, oaks, maples, p. 17; abelia, roses, magnolias, p. 20; bald cypress, chinese elm, hawthorn, willow oak, 'Grey Owl' juniper, 'Parsons' juniper, p. 22; abelia, American holly, dwarf yaupon holly, naked ladies lily, wax myrtle, p. 22; lenten rose, p. 27; Joe Pye weed, p. 29; hydrangea, p.31and 32; butterflies on pp. 44 and 49; abelia, p. 50; aster, crapemyrtle, lily, p. 55; hyacinth bean, p. 103; amsonia, p. 110, 111, 253; asters, p. 112,113; baptisia, p. 115; rudbeckia, p. 116; crocosmia, p. 125; muhly grass, p. 139; switch grass, p. 141; Joe Pye weed, p. 152; magic lily, small, p. 160; magic lily, p. 161; phlox, p. 166; small salvia, p. 174; sedums, p. 178; asters, p. 179; loropetalum, p. 193; abelia, p.194, 195; phlox, p. 195; amsonia, p. 201, 210, 225; boxwoods, small, p. 204; boxwood hedge, p. 205; juniper, p. 213; crapemyrtle, p. 214; holly, p. 220; inkberry, p. 221, two small hollies, p. 222; American holly, p. 223; hydrangeas, p. 226-227 and 230-232; junipers, p. 238; parson's and 'Grey Owl' juniper, p. 239; spiraea, loropetalum, p. 248; wax myrtles, p. 255-256; witch hazel, p. 258, Jackson vine, p. 263; leatherleaf, p. 265; arborvitaes, p. 268; crapemyrtle, abelia, p. 275; crapemyrtle, p. 277; bald cypress, p.278-279; wax myrtle, p. 279; dogwood, p. 280; Chinese elms, p. 284-285; hawthorns, p. 288; abelia, p. 289; hollies, p. 290; 'Moonfire' and 'Oshi Beni' maples on p. 295; maples, p. 296; maples in fall, p. 297; oaks, p. 299; red redbud leaves, p. 305.

©ivanastar: Redbud close up, p. 305. Jackson & Perkins: 'Fairy' rose, p. 247. Jill Lang: Coreopsis, p. 122, 145, 153, 185, 207, 233. Joan Brookwell: Cherry laurel, p. 308; Water oak, p. 309. KBR Photos: Coreopsis, p. 123; black-eyed Susans, large, p. 116. Leighton Photography & Imaging; Spider lily, p 15, 162. Leu Botanical Gardens: Camellias, p. 208. Magdalena Bujack: Anemone, p. 188. Martin Anderson: Wisteria, p. 265. Martin Heaney: Viburnum flower, p. 265. Marty Metcalf: 'Karl Foerster' grass, p. 141. © McCorkle Nursery (courtesy of): Carolina jessamine, 'Lady Banks' rose, p. 17; loropetalum, p. 20, 21; boxwood, p. 21; kerria, p. 22, 27, 51, 111, 165; Carolina jessamine, large photos, p. 210-211; hydrangea, p. 161; kerria, p. 201, 240-241; boxwood (large), p. 204; 'Mini Penny' and 'Midnight Duchess' hydrangeas, p. 228; 'Little Rose Dawn' and 'Ever Red' loropetalum, p. 242; 'Lady Banks' rose, p. 246, 247; ginko, p. 28. Novalis: Amaryllis, angel's trumpet, p.188. Missouri Botanical Garden PlantFinder: Black gum, p. 308, Becky Homan; loblolly pine, p. 309, Chris Starbuck. Paul Marcus: Loquat, p. 309.

Park Seed: Ginkgo, p. 17; zinnia, p. 85, salvia 'Fairy Queen,' p.86; zinnias, p. 100-101; hosta, p. 147; 'Goldbound' and James Dickenson' irises, p. 151; zinnia, p. 154, 175; lenten rose, small, p. 156; stokesia 'Purple Pixie' and 'Peachies Pink,' p. 182; salvia, p. 191; butterfly bush flowers, p. 206; Carolina jessamine 'Margarita,' p. 210; honeysuckle 'Harlequin,' p. 224; 'Ivory Tower' yucca, p. 260; ginko (small) p. 286; 'Golden Full Moon' and red maples, p. 295. Patricia Davies: Coreopsis, p. 122. PDSI: Cleyera, p. 16 and 17; honeysuckle, p. 22; cleyera, p. 27; stokesia, p. 182; snowflake, p. 191; aucuba, p. 199; little leaf boxwood, p. 205; cleyera, Japanese yew, p. 212-213, 257, 259, 268; honeysuckle 'Mardi Gras' and 'Trumpet,' p. 224; indian hawthorn, p. 234; plum yew, cleyera, p. 236; 'Anthony Waterer' and gold mound spiraea, p. 250. Peder Digra: Sumac, p. 264. Pencho Hristov Tihov: Hawthorn, p. 289. Proven Winners: Torenia, elephant ear, p. 14; heuchera, Persian shield, butterfly bush, p. 15, 83, 95; elephant ear, heuchera, p. 27; angelonia, p. 84, coneflower, p. 87; butterfly bush, p. 89; sweet potato, p. 94, 95; torenia, p. 96, 97; hydrangea, p. 87; butterfly bush, heuchera, hosta, p. 50, lantana, butterfly bush, and coneflower on p. 75, 77, 81; cuphea, butterfly bush, p.101; Euphorbia 'Diamond Frost,' p. 103; coneflowers, p. 120, 173, 177; butterfly bush, coneflowers p. 121; elephant ear, p. 130; heucheras, hostas, p. 142-143, 146; butterfly bush, p. 145, 186; Persian shield, p. 147; candytuft, p. 188; foxglove, p. 189; *Miscanthus,* p. 190; rose of Sharons, p. 196; hosta, p. 199; butterfly bush (shrub form), p. 206; butterfly bush, coneflowers, p. 207; torenia, p. 229; hydrangea, 233; spiraea 'Snowstorm', p. 250; hosta, p. 301.

Reike Photos: Sweet gum, p. 311. Robert H. Mohlenbrock @ USDA-NRCS PLANTS Database / USDA SCS. 1991. Southern wetland flora: Field office guide to plant species. South National Technical Center, Fort Worth: American wisteria, p. 265. Ronnie Howard, hummingbird, p. 134. Rose Smith: black-eyed Susans, p. 117. Rosetta-hidek: Spider lily, p. 163. RT Images: Photinia, p. 262. Sam Aronov: Witch hazel, large one, p. 259. Scheeper's Bulbs: Lily, p. 79, Irises, p. 115, daffodils, pp. 126-127; iris, p. 150; lilies, p. 158; iris, p. 216. Sharon Day: Red hot poker plant, p. 170; dianthus, p. 189. sochgirl: Trillium, p. 191. Stephen van Horn: Hummingbird, p.11. Steve Huddleston: Shumard oak, p. 22, 298; rosemary, p. 264; yaupon holly tree, p. 290; leaves and berries, p. 291;

Tim Mainiero: Ice plant, p. 148. Tesslar, Tropicana canna p. 118. Texas A&M University: 'Carefree Beauty' rose, p.247. W. Woyke: Crocus, p. 89. Wayside Gardens: Abelia 'Kalaidascope,' p. 195. www.derekfell.com, Carolina silverbell, p. 17, 51, 270, 271; lenten roses on pp. 156-157, 241; magic lily, large, p. 160; phlox, large, p. 164; stokesia, large, p. 182; smoke tree, p. 306. www.rainpillow.com, photos on p. 42. Yuriv Chertok: Canary Island date palm, p. 309.

Climate and Acknowledgments

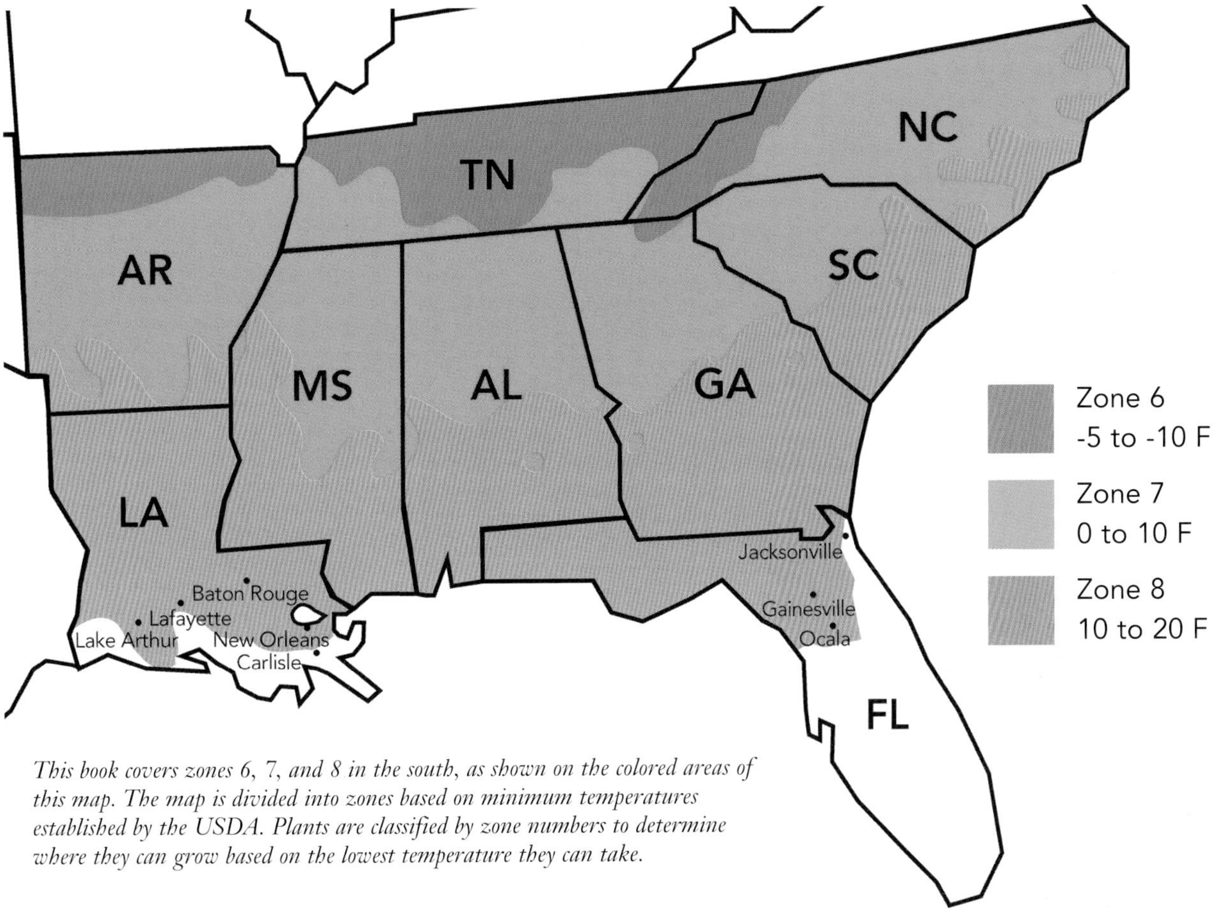

AR
TN
NC
SC
MS
AL
GA
LA
FL
Baton Rouge
Lafayette
Lake Arthur
New Orleans
Carlisle
Jacksonville
Gainesville
Ocala

Zone 6
-5 to -10 F

Zone 7
0 to 10 F

Zone 8
10 to 20 F

This book covers zones 6, 7, and 8 in the south, as shown on the colored areas of this map. The map is divided into zones based on minimum temperatures established by the USDA. Plants are classified by zone numbers to determine where they can grow based on the lowest temperature they can take.

Contributors

Mark Arena, *Horticulturist*, Moncks Corner, South Carolina
Judie Bicknell, *Master Gardener*, Woodstock, Georgia
Beth Bolles, *Escambia County Extension Office*, Cantonment, Florida
Jennifer Davidson, *City Extension Agent*, Columbus, Georgia
Becky Griffin, *Master Gardener*, Canton, Georgia
Tony Glover, *Regional Extension Agent*, Birmingham, Alabama
Hayes Jackson, *Urban Regional Extension Agent*, Alabama Cooperative Extension System
Dr. Kerry A. Johnson, *Area Horticulture Agent*, Lucedale, Mississippi
James Morgan, *County Extension Agent*, Dougherty County (Georgia) Cooperative Extension
Pam Raines, *Master Gardener*, Woodstock, Georgia
Ken Rudisell, *Horticultural Agent*, Bay County Extension Office, Panama City, Florida
Stephanie Toelle, *Horticultural Agent*, Duval County Extension Office, Jacksonville, Florida

Thank You

Barbara Hadsell

Elaine Golob Weber

We want to thank Barbara Hadsell, Pamela Crawford's assistant. She worked tirelessly on making this book a reality.

Elaine Weber, the graphic designer, worked enthusiastically with Pamela on some very tight deadlines. She showed great patience with her last-minute requests.

Chapter 1

Easy Basics for Sustainable Gardening

It's time to learn a new way of gardening in the south. Our temperatures are rising while our rainfall amounts are falling. Bees are disappearing, and butterflies are diminishing. We are all concerned that the activities of man might actually be harming our environment.

At the same time, people are busier than ever, and few have time to devote to maintenance-intensive landscapes. Budgets are stretched to the limit. The purpose of this book is to show plants and gardening techniques that help our environment and fit into our busy, budget-driven lifestyles.

These photos show our Georgia trial gardens - before and after. We use the principals in this chapter to plant and maintain our gardens in an environmentally responsible way. The water came from our roof, which we cover in this chapter. We also used quite a few easy shortcuts you will learn about in this chapter that will save you time and effort. Skim this chapter before putting your first plant in the ground. It will save you a lot of time, money, and trouble – and make gardening a lot easier for you. Look for easy instructions on these key sustainable principles.

✿ Choose plants that can take our changing climate. The plants in this book adapt to warmer temperatures as well as the rainy years that are forecast for our future. Quite a few breezed through our recent drought with no irrigation at all!
✿ Learn how to grow healthy plants naturally by placing them in the right spot, preparing the soil, planting, and watering in a way that keeps the plant healthy. Healthy plants resist pests and use less water.
✿ Learn which plants bloom the longest, so your butterflies will have enough food.
✿ Learn which grass saves you time and uses the least amount of water.
✿ Learn how to keep your plants healthy with natural compost and mulching as well as which fertilizers are best for the environment.
✿ Learn how to save water and how to use water from your roof to water your plants. This information will free you from city water bills and water restrictions.
✿ Learn about the latest plants. Breeders are working to produce plants that bloom longer and require less care than before. Some are worth the money, and others aren't. Make it a habit to take this book with you to your garden center, so you can check out the plants BEFORE you buy them!

(Above and left): Our Georgia trial gardens include many side-planted container gardens, as shown here. These baskets and column kits are available from www.kinsmangarden.com. That web site also shows quick videos of the planting and installation of these containers and columns.

Seven Worst Gardening Mistakes

1. Buying the Wrong Plants

Most beginners buy plants that don't meet their expectations simply because they don't understand the plant's flowering habits - or that the plant is an erratic performer. Take this book with you to your garden center. If you stick to the blue ribbon plants described on pages 12 to 17, you will have a great chance of success with tough plants that are well-adapted to the southern environment. Most plants you see in your garden center will be described in this book, with both good and bad qualities. It' s much better to know how they grow before you buy them. See pages 24-25 for more plant shopping tips.

2. Planting in Areas with Poor Drainage

Most plants that are grown in soil that is constantly wet die pretty quickly. Drainage problems are the major cause of wet spots in the garden. See pages 28 and 29 to learn how to check your soil as well as how to fix it. If you can't fix your drainage problems, these pages tell you what plants are most likely to make it, as well as which ones are the worst for wet spots.

3. Buying the Wrong Fertilizer

Several times, we have killed plants by using fertilizers. One of our first lawns died from over fertilization. An entire garden done by a local landscaping company died because the popular, slow-release fertilizer they used released all three month's worth of nutrients at once. Water causes the fertilizer to activate, and we had a lot of rain. No one wants to kill plants because of such a routine occurrence! See pages 46 to 48 for information regarding good, easy fertilizers.

4. Watering Incorrectly

Plants need quite a bit of water right after they are planted, particularly if you plant in spring or summer. If they don't get enough in the beginning, they can die. If you give them too much later, they can also die. Read pages 34 to 37 to learn how to water easily and efficiently.

5. Piling Soil Around the Stem of the Plant

If soil or organic mulch comes into contact with the stem of many plants, the stem rots, killing the plant. It is quite easy to avoid this plight by simply planting the plants a little higher. To help retain water, most people put organic mulch on top of the soil after they have planted. Learn to pull the mulch away from the trunk or stem when you are mulching. Learn how to plant properly on pages 32 and 33.

6. Spacing Plants Incorrectly

Each plant requires a certain amount of space to grow properly. If you plant them too close together, they won't grow properly, nor will they flower profusely. If you plant them too close to your house, they will eventually have to be removed. See the individual plant profiles in chapters two, three, and four to find the proper spacing for each plant.

7. Planting in the Wrong Amount of Light

Different plants need different amounts of light. A petunia likes sun, while a hosta likes shade. But how much sun is enough for sun plants? The rule of thumb is at least four to six hours of direct sun a day. In other words, if your petunia just gets two hours of sun, with shade the rest of the day, it will not do well. For your shade-only plants, if they are left in the sun, the leaves and flowers will burn. Of the two, shade plants are more complicated to place than sun plants. See pages 26 and 27 for more information on shade gardening.

Six Tips that Benefit the Environment

1. Learn the Latest Water Saving Methods

You will learn about many plants that breezed through our recent droughts with nothing but rainwater. You'll find them in chapters two, three and four, with the symbol stating 'Lives on Rainwater' in the green band on the top of the right-hand pages. Plant them in late fall, when you won't need much water to establish them. Use these for your main planting areas. If you want more diversity, plant thirstier plants in separate areas that can easily be watered with the water you collect from your roof, air conditioner, or shower. Use Bermuda grass or the most drought-tolerant grass for your climate zone. Bermuda lived fine through the worst droughts the south has ever seen, although it did turn brown when it went without water for periods of three weeks or more. Read pages 38 to 43 to learn lots more ways to save water.

2. Appreciate Our Wonderful Native Plants

The south is loaded with fabulous native plants, many of which flower beautifully, like native azaleas and dogwoods. You'll find them in chapters two, three, and four with the symbol of the dogwood flower in the right-hand, green bar that runs along the top of each page. Appreciate natives both for their natural fit in the environment as well as their cultural significance. Understand, however, that all natives are not necessarily low water plants. Our surveys showed that native azaleas, mountain laurels, and dogwoods were among the plants that suffered most in the recent droughts. Many native plants, like azaleas, are native to areas near streams, where they have frequent moisture. Other natives, like eastern red cedar, is quite adaptive to different moisture levels, taking rainy periods or droughts equally as well.

3. Look for Plants That Can Adapt to Our Changing Environment

The temperatures in the south have risen substantially since 1990. We have also had historic droughts. The climate scientists tell us to prepare for more heat, as well as water extremes (drought years alternated with years of high rainfall). Look for plants that can adapt to these changes. Crapemytle, for example, does fine if the temperature goes up a few degrees. It can also take high rainfall years as well as droughts. This book is loaded with plants that are ready for our new environment.

4. Use Environmentally-friendly Fertilizers and Pesticides

We have all read about links between toxic chemicals and disease. In addition to health risks, many fertilizers are contaminating our ground water. Learn how to use environmentally-friendly fertilizers and pesticides on pages 44 to 47.

5. Attract Butterflies and Hummingbirds to Your Garden

Butterflies are diminishing in this country, which is one of the first signs of environmental problems. It it easy to attract both butterflies and hummingbirds by simply planting the flowers that offer the nectars they drink. Look for the butterfly and/or hummingbird symbols on the top right portion of the plant profile to find the best plants for butterflies and hummingbirds.

6. Attract Birds to Your Garden

Recent reports have shown our songbird population diminishing. Plant trees and shrubs that provide both nesting spots and food for birds. Look for the bird symbol on the top right page of the plant profiles in chapters two to five to find plants that are friendly to birds

Blue Ribbon Means Easy!

The easiest, blue ribbon plants require no more than one chore from you per year, in addition to proper planting, watering, and fertilization. Although wc discuss many other plants in this book, wc recommend that beginners or serial plant killers stick to the blue ribbon plants until they have some successful growing experiences.

Characteristics of the Blue Ribbon Perennials, Shrubs, Vines, & Trees

- Require touching (trimming, deadheading, etc) no more than once a year
- Are very well adjusted to the southern climate (drought years as well as years with normal or above normal rainfall).
- Fare well with little susceptibility to pests
- Have an established record (they've been around for enough years to fully understand it's requirements).
- Need water (at the most) once or twice a week after the establishment period (see pages 34 to 35). Many blue ribbon plants need no supplemental irrigation at all.

Left to right: 'Miss Huff' lantana, crapemyrtle, and 'Homestead Purple' verbena are all blue ribbon plants.

Characteristics of the Blue Ribbon Annuals

- Perform the same way every year (dependable).
- Require little to no trimming
- Are very well adjusted to the southern environment, including high heat and humidity
- Live a long life (at least the five to six months of your growing season)
- Fare well with little susceptibility to pests
- Have an established record (they've been around for enough years to fully understand their requirements).
- Bloom continuously for a minimum of five to six months (except for cacti, bromeliads, and plants used primarily for leaf color).
- Need water, at the most, once or twice a week after they are established.

2ND Red Ribbon, Almost as Easy

Red ribbon plants are not far behind the blue ribbon plants in overall performance. The only difference is that red ribbon plants require more care - up to three chores per year, if they are planted, watered, and fertilized correctly. Some may have susceptibility to pests and require occasional deadheading. Red ribbon plants may be watered up to twice a week.

Characteristics of the Red Ribbon Perennials, Shrubs, Vines & Trees

- Require touching (trimming, deadheading, etc.) no more than three times per year
- Are very well adjusted to the southern climate (years with droughts as well as normal or above normal rainfall).
- Have an established record (they've been around for enough years to fully understand their requirements).
- Need water, at the most, once or twice a week.

Above: Hydrangeas are red ribbon plants because they require more water than blue ribbon plants. Home of Mrs. Melba Pearson, Louisville, Mississippi.

Left: Hydrangeas at the home of John and Carol Mitchell, Louisville, Mississippi.

Characteristics of the Red Ribbon Annuals

- Perform the same way every year (dependable).
- Adjust well to most climates
- Require trimming every month or so
- Have a long lifespan, at least the four to six months of our growing season
- May have some susceptibility to pests
- Have an established record (it takes many years on the market for a plant to be a reliable success).
- Bloom continuously for a minimum of five to six months (except for cacti and bromeliads or plants used primarily for leaf color).

Plants Arranged by Size

This photo chart (four pages) includes all the plants covered in this book on the large, two-page plant profiles. These are some of the best plants in the south. Use this chart for planning, so you can see at once all the plants that fit a certain environment. This chart is organized by size because size is the first criteria you normally have for an area. The page numbers refer to the plant profiles. The plants in the small profiles at the end of chapters two to four are not included in these charts.

UNDER 1'

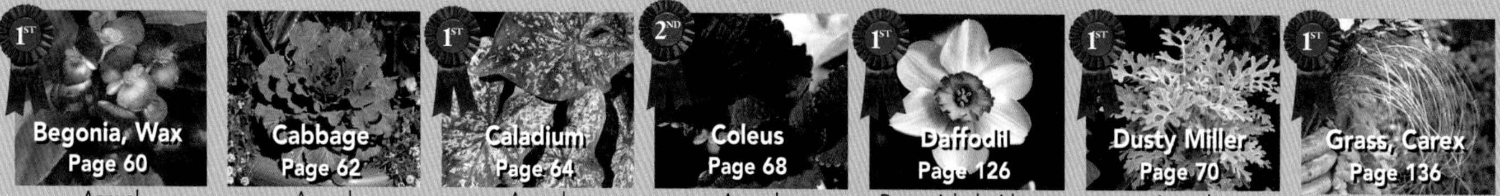

1ST
Begonia, Wax
Page 60
Cabbage
Page 62
1ST
Caladium
Page 64
2ND
Coleus
Page 68
1ST
Daffodil
Page 126
1ST
Dusty Miller
Page 70
1ST
Grass, Carex
Page 136

Annual / Medium water / Medium shade - sun

Annual / Medium water / Light shade - sun

Annual / Medium - high water / Medium shade - sun

Annual / Medium - high water / Medium shade - sun

Perennial, deciduous / **Very low water** / Sun

Annual / Medium water / Light shade - sun

Perennial / Low water / Light shade - sun

1ST
Grass, Liriope
Page 137
1ST
Grass, Mondo
Page 137
1ST
Ice Plant
Page 148
1ST
Iris
Page 152
1ST
Ivy
Page 218
1ST
Pachysandra
Page 219
1ST
Pansy
Page 78

Perennial, evergreen / Low water / Dense shade - sun

Perennial, evergreen / Low water / Dense - medium shade

Perennial, deciduous / **Very low water** / Sun

Perennial, deciduous / Medium water / Light shade - sun

Vine, evergreen / **Very low water** / Dense - light shade

Vine, evergreen / Low water / Dense - medium shade

Annual / Medium water / Light shade - sun

Petunia
Page 84
1ST
Purple Heart
Page 168
1ST
Scaevola
Page 90
Snapdragon
Page 92
Sweet Potato
Page 94
1ST
Torenia
Page 96
1ST
Verbena
'Homestead
Purple'
Page 184

Annual / Medium water / Light shade - sun

Perennial, deciduous / Low water / Light shade - sun

Annual / Medium water / Light shade - sun

Annual / Medium water / Sun

Annual / Medium water / Light shade - sun

Annual / Medium water / Medium shade - sun

Perennial, deciduous / Low water / Light shade - sun

1ST
Vinca, Periwinkle
Page 98
1ST
Vinca Vine
Page 219
1ST
Zinnia 'Profusion
Series'
Page 100

Annual / Low water / Sun

Vine, evergreen / Low water / Medium - light shade

Annual / Medium water / Sun

1' TO 3'

1ST
Abelia
Page 194
1ST
Agastache
Page 108
1ST
Amsonia
Page 110
1ST
Angelonia
Page 56
1ST
Aster
'Purple Dome'
Page 112
1ST
Azalea,
Evergreen
1ST
Begonia
'Dragon Wing'
Page 58

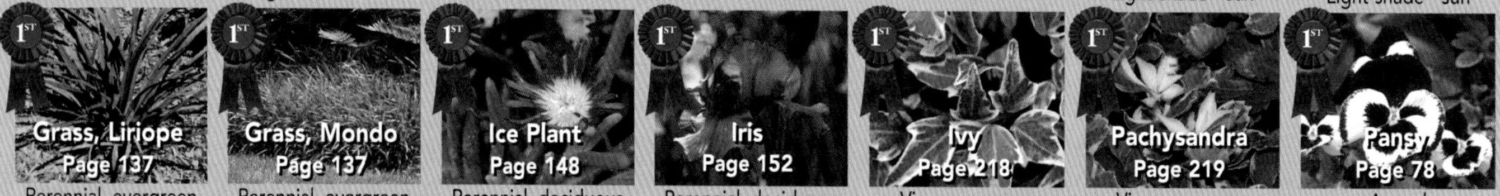

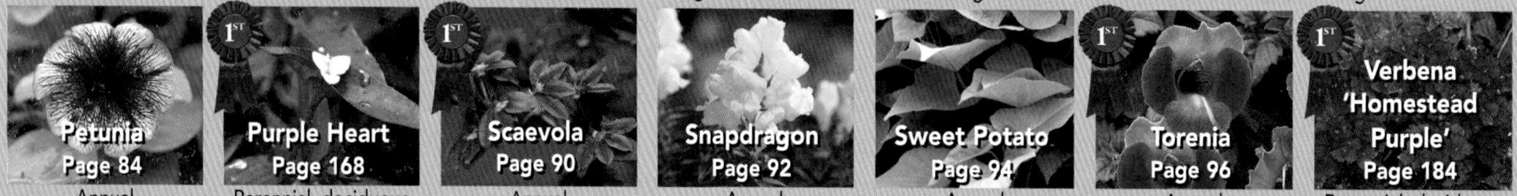

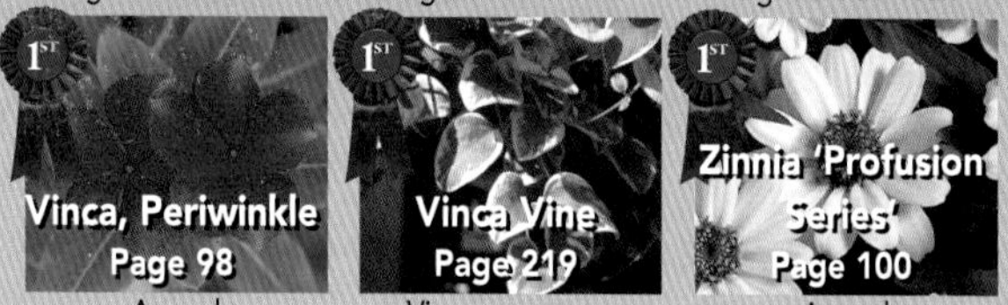

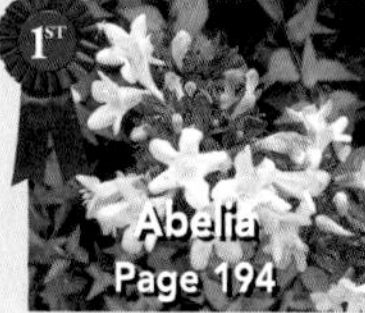

Shrub, evergreen / **Very low water** / Light shade - sun

Perennial, deciduous / Low water / Sun

Perennial, deciduous / Medium water / Light shade - sun

Annual / Medium water / Light shade - sun

Perennial, deciduous / Low water / Light shade - sun

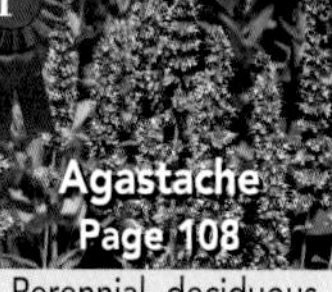

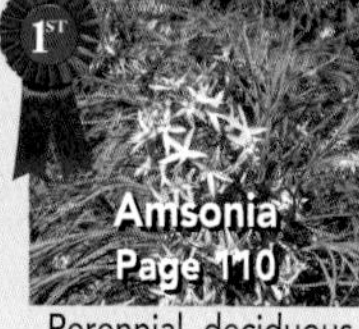

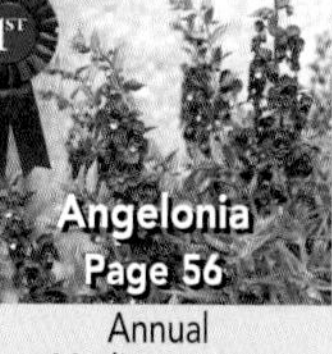

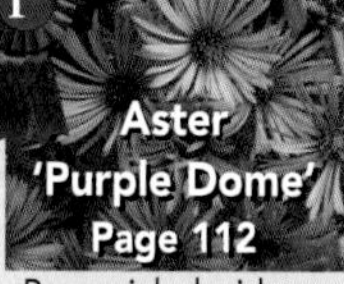

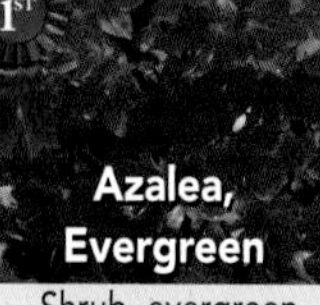

Shrub, evergreen / Medium water / Light shade - sun

Annual / Medium water / Medium to light shade

Black-Eyed Susan
Page 116
1ST
Boxwood,
English
Page 204
1ST
Boxwood,
'Little Leaf'
Page 204
1ST
Caladium
Page 64
Canna Lily
Page 118
Cleome
Page 66
2ND
Coleus
Page 68

Perennial, deciduous / Low water / Light shade - sun

Shrub, evergreen / Low water / Light shade - sun

Shrub, evergreen / Low water / Light shade - sun

Annual / Medium - high water / Medium shade - sun

Annual / Medium water / Sun

Annual / Medium water / Light shade - sun

Annual / Medium - high water / Medium shade - sun

Coneflower
Page 120
1ST
Coreopsis
Page 122
1ST
Crocosmia
Page 124
1ST
Daffodil
Page 126
1ST
Daylily
Page 128
1ST
Elephant Ear
Page 130
1ST
Fern, Autumn
Page 132

Perennial, deciduous / Low water / Light shade - sun

Perennial, deciduous / Low water / Sun

Perennial, deciduous / Low water / Light shade - sun

Perennial, deciduous / **Very low water** / Sun

Perennial, deciduous / Low water / Sun

Perennial, deciduous / Medium water / Medium shade - sun

Perennial, evergreen / Medium water / Medium to light shade

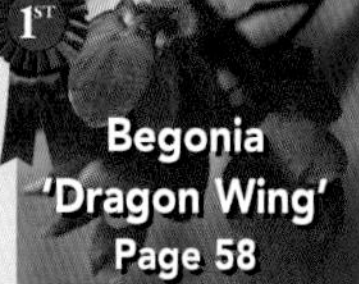

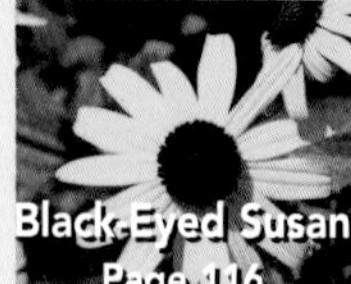

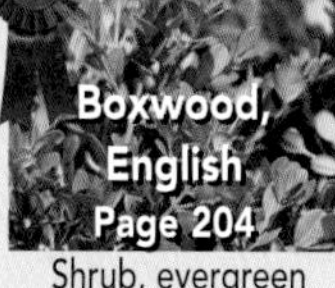

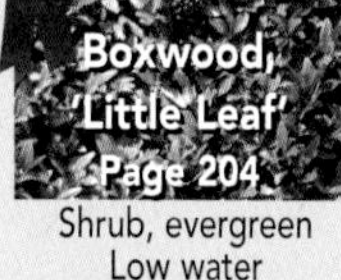

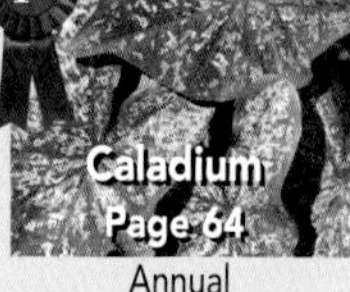

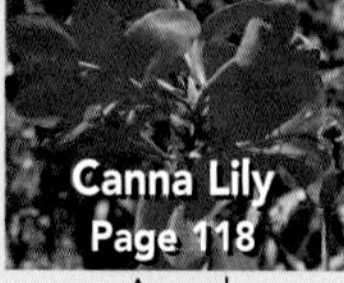

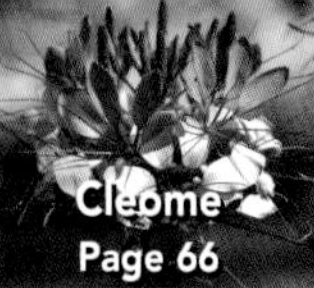

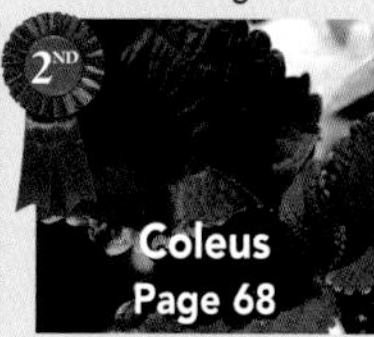

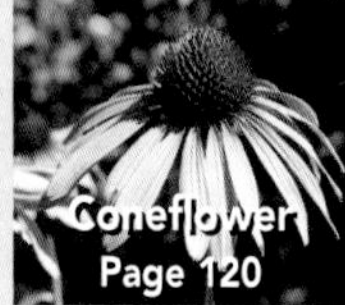

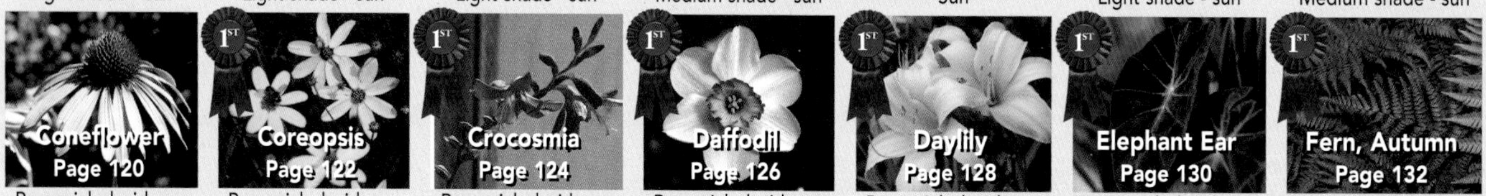

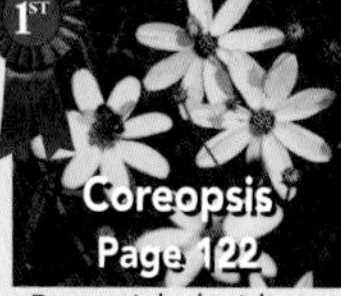

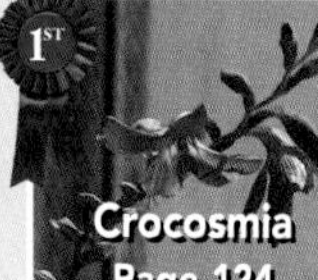

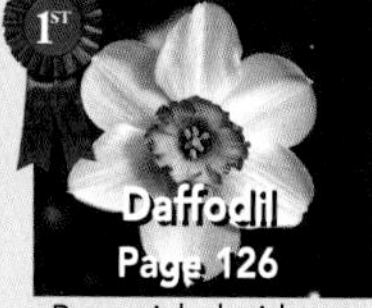

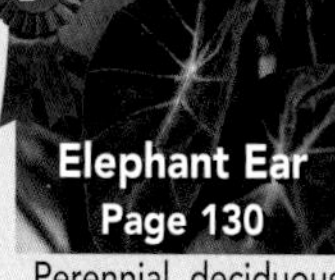

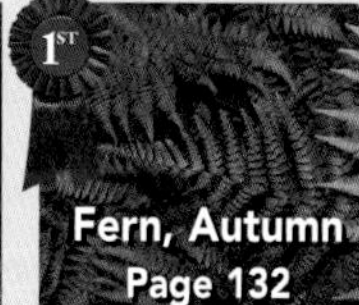

1' TO 3', (continued from previous page)

Plant	Page	Award	Type	Water	Light
Fern, Cinnamon	Page 132	1ST	Perennial, deciduous	Medium water	Dense - medium shade
Fern, Painted	Page 132	1ST	Perennial, deciduous	Medium water	Dense - medium shade
Grass, 'Feather Reed'	Page 141	1ST	Perennial	**Very low water**	Light shade - sun
Grass, Acorus	Page 137	1ST	Perennial, evergreen	Low water	Light shade - sun
Grass, 'Hameln' Fountain	Page 138	1ST	Perennial, evergreen	**Very low water**	Light shade - sun
Grass, Liriope	Page 137	1ST	Perennial, evergreen	Low water	Dense shade - sun
Grass, Purple Fountain	Page 139	1ST	Annual	**Very low water**	Light shade - sun
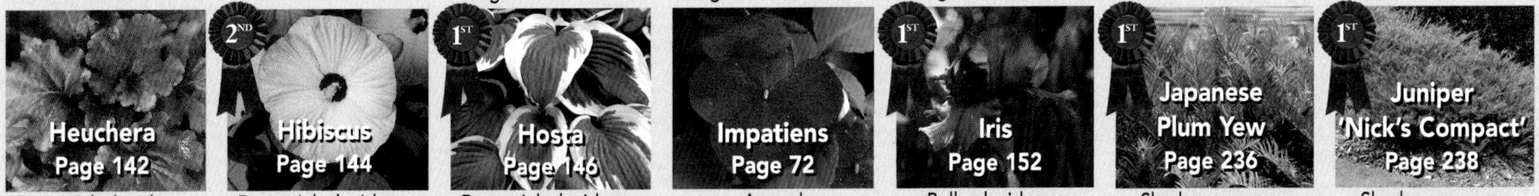 Heuchera	Page 142		Perennial, deciduous	Medium water	Light shade
Hibiscus	Page 144	2ND	Perennial, deciduous	Medium water	Light shade - sun
Hosta	Page 146	1ST	Perennial, deciduous	Medium water	Medium - light shade
Impatiens	Page 72		Annual	High water	Medium - light shade
Iris	Page 152	1ST	Bulb, deciduous	Medium water	Light shade - sun
Japanese Plum Yew	Page 236	1ST	Shrub, evergreen	Low water	Light shade - sun
Juniper 'Nick's Compact'	Page 238	1ST	Shrub, evergreen	**Very low water**	Sun
Juniper 'Parsons'	Page 238	1ST	Shrub, evergreen	**Very low water**	Sun
Lantana	Page 74	1ST	Annual,	Low water	Sun
Lenten Rose	Page 156	1ST	Perennial, evergreen	Low water	Medium - light shade
Lily, Asiatic	Page 158	1ST	Bulb, deciduous	Medium water	Light shade - sun
Lily, Naked Ladies	Page 160	1ST	Bulb, deciduous	**Very low water**	Light shade
Lily, Oriental	Page 158	1ST	Bulb, deciduous	Medium water	Light shade - sun
Lily, Spider	Page 162	1ST	Bulb, deciduous	Low water	Light shade
Loropetalum	Page 238	1ST	Shrub, evergreen	**Very low water**	Light shade - sun
Melampodium	Page 76	1ST	Annual	Medium water	Light shade - sun
Palm, Needle	Page 300	1ST	Tree, deciduous	**Very low water**	Light shade - sun
Persian Shield	Page 82	1ST	Annual	High water	Medium shade - sun
Phlox, Woodland	Page 164	1ST	Perennial	Low water	Medium - light shade
Rose, 'Fairy'	Page 247	2ND	Shrub	Low water	Light shade - sun
Salvia, Blue	Page 86	1ST	Annual	Medium water	Light shade - sun
 Scabiosa	Page 176		Perennial, deciduous	Medium water	Sun
Sedum	Page 178	2ND	Perennial, deciduous	**Very low water**	Light shade - sun
Snapdragon	Page 92		Annual	Medium water	Sun
Spanish Bluebells	Page 180	1ST	Bulb, deciduous	Low water	Light shade
Spiraea, 'Gold Mound'	Page 250	1ST	Shrub, deciduous	Low water	Light shade - sun
Stokesia	Page 182		Perennial, deciduous	Low water	Light shade - sun
Yarrow	Page 186	1ST	Perennial, deciduous	Low water	Sun
Yucca	Page 260	1ST	Shrub, evergreen	**Very low water**	Light shade - sun

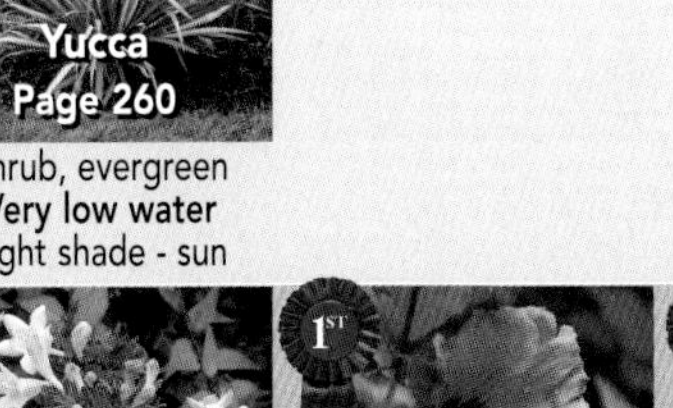

3' TO 6'

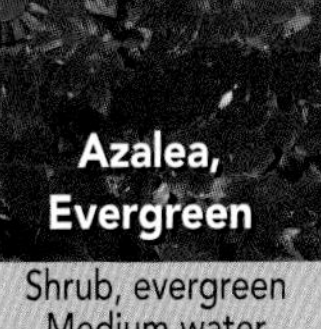

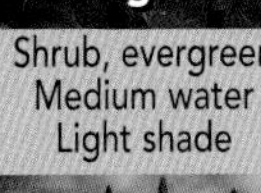

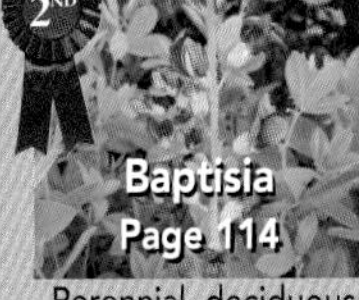

Plant	Page	Award	Type	Water	Light
Abelia	Page 194	1ST	Shrub, evergreen	**Very low water**	Light shade - sun
Althea, Rose of Sharon	Page 196	1ST	Shrub, evergreen	Low water	Sun
Aucuba	Page 198	1ST	Shrub, evergreen	Low water	Dense - medium shade
Azalea, Evergreen		1ST	Shrub, evergreen	Medium water	Light shade
Baptisia	Page 114	2ND	Perennial, deciduous	Medium water	Sun
Boxwood, American	Page 204	1ST	Shrub, evergreen	Low water	Light shade - sun
Boxwood, Japanese	Page 204	1ST	Shrub, evergreen	Low water	Light shade - sun
Boxwood, Korean	Page 204	1ST	Shrub, evergreen	Low water	Light shade - sun
Butterfly Bush	Page 206	1ST	Shrub, deciduous	Low water	Sun
Canna	Page 118		Perennial, deciduous	Medium water	Sun
Cleome	Page 66		Annual	Medium - high water	Light shade - sun
Crapemyrtle, Shrub	Page 214	1ST	Shrub, deciduous	**Very low water**	Sun
Elephant Ears	Page 130	1ST	Perennial, deciduous	Medium water	Medium shade - sun
Fern, Cinnamon	Page 132	1ST	Perennial, deciduous	Medium water	Medium - light shade

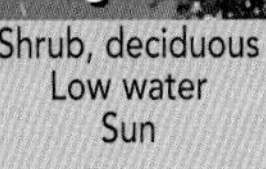

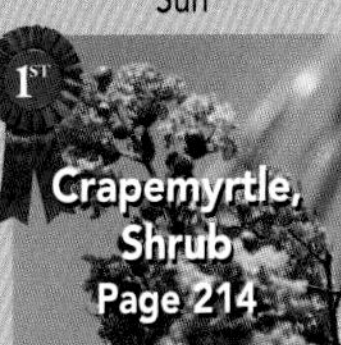

Plants Arranged by Size

3' TO 6' (continued from previous page)

Annual or perennial
Medium - low water
Medium shade - sun

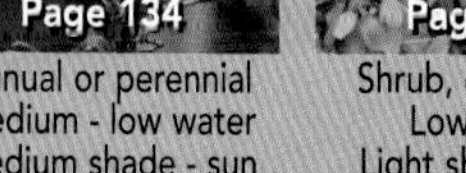

Shrub, deciduous
Low water
Light shade - sun

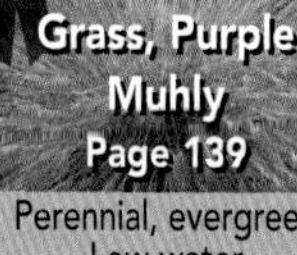

Perennial, evergreen
Low water
Light shade - sun

Perennial
Very low water
Light shade - sun

Perennial, deciduous
Medium water
Light shade - sun

Shrub, deciduous
Medium water
Light shade

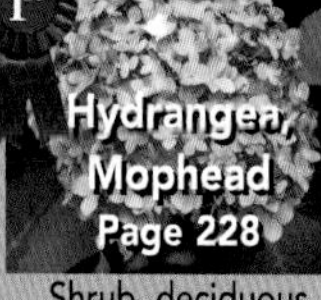

Shrub, deciduous
Medium water
Light shade

Shrub, deciduous
Medium water
Light shade

Shrub, evergreen
Very low water
Light shade - sun

Perennial, deciduous
Low water
Light shade - sun

Shrub, evergreen
Very low water
Sun

Shrub, evergreen
Very low water
Sun

Shrub, evergreen
Very low water
Sun

Shrub, deciduous
Very low water
Medium - light shade

Perennial, deciduous
Very low water
Sun

Bulb, deciduous
Medium water
Light shade - sun

Shrub, evergreen
Very low water
Light shade - sun

Tree, deciduous
Very low water
Light shade - sun

Perennial, deciduous
Medium water
Light shade - sun

Perennial, deciduous
Low water
Sun

Shrub, deciduous
Low water
Light shade - sun

Shrub
Low water
Light shade - sun

Shrub
Low water
Light shade - sun

Shrub, deciduous
Low water
Light shade - sun

Perennial, deciduous
Low water
Light shade - sun

Perennial, deciduous
Medium water
Sun

6' TO 10'

Shrub, evergreen
Very low water
Light shade - sun

Shrub, evergreen
Low water
Sun

Shrub, evergreen
Low water
Dense - medium shade

Shrub, deciduous
Low water
Light shade

Shrub, evergreen
Medium water
Light shade

Shrub, deciduous
Low water
Sun

Shrub, evergreen
Low water
Light shade

Tree, deciduous
Low water
Sun

Shrub, evergreen
Low water
Medium shade - sun

Shrub, deciduous
Very low water
Sun

Perennial, deciduous
Medium water
Medium shade - sun

Perennial
Very low water
Light shade - sun

Shrub, deciduous
Medium water
Light shade

Shrub, deciduous
Medium water
Light shade

Shrub, evergreen
Very low water
Sun

Shrub, evergreen
Very low water
Light shade - sun

Tree, evergreen
Very low water
Light shade - sun

Shrub
Low water
Light shade - sun

Shrub, deciduous
Low water
Light shade - sun

Shrub, deciduous
Very low water
Light shade - sun

Shrub, deciduous
Low water
Light shade - sun

Shrub, deciduous
Very low water
Medium shade - sun

Shrub, deciduous
Low water
Light shade - sun

10′ TO 15′

Azalea, Deciduous Page 202

Shrub, deciduous
Low water
Light shade

Camellia Page 208

Shrub, evergreen
Low water
Light shade

Chaste Tree Page 272

Tree, deciduous
Low water
Sun

Cleyera Page 212

Shrub, evergreen
Low water
Medium shade - sun

Crapemyrtle Page 212

Tree, deciduous
Very low water
Sun

Holly, American Page 223

Shrub/tree, evergreen
Very low water
Light shade

Hydrangea, Oakleaf Page 230

Shrub, deciduous
Medium water
Light shade

Loropetalum Page 238

Shrub, evergreen
Very low water
Light shade - sun

Maple, Japanese Page 294

Tree, deciduous
Medium water
Light shade - sun

Viburnum, 'Chinese Snowball' Page 252

Shrub, deciduous
Very low water
Light shade - sun

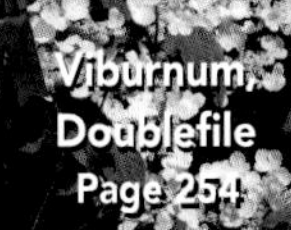

Viburnum, Doublefile Page 254

Shrub, deciduous
Low water
Light shade - sun

Wax Myrtle Page 256

Shrub, deciduous
Very low water
Medium shade - sun

Witch Hazel Page 258

Shrub, deciduous
Low water
Light shade - sun

Yaupon Holly Page 290

Tree, evergreen
Very low water
Light shade - sun

15′ TO 25′

Arborvitae Page 268

Tree, evergreen
Low water
Sun

Carolina Silverbell Page 270

Tree, deciduous
Low water
Light shade - sun

Crapemyrtle Tree Page 274

Tree, deciduous
Very low water
Sun

Dogwood Page 280

Tree, deciduous
Medium water
Light shade - sun

Eastern Red Cedar Page 282

Tree, evergreen
Very low water
Sun

Holly, American Page 223

Shrub/tree, evergreen
Very low water
Light shade

Magnolia, Little Gem Page 293

Tree evergreen
Very low water
Light shade

Palm, Sabal Page 301

Tree, evergreen
Very low water
Sun

Palm, Windmill Page 301

Tree, evergreen
Very low water
Light shade - sun

Redbud Page 304

Tree, deciduous
Very low water
Light shade - sun

Smoke Tree Page 306

Tree, deciduous
Very low water
Sun

Yaupon Holly Page 290

Tree, evergreen
Very low water
Light shade - sun

25′ PLUS

Arborvitae Page 268

Tree, evergreen
Low water
Sun

Bald Cypress Page 278

Tree, deciduous
Very low water
Sun

Chinese Elm Page 284

Tree, deciduous
Very low water
Sun

Chinese Pistache Page 302

Tree, deciduous
Low water
Light shade - sun

Cryptomeria Page 276

Tree, evergreen
Medium water
Light shade - sun

Dogwood Page 280

Tree, deciduous
Medium water
Light shade - sun

Eastern Red Cedar Page 282

Tree, evergreen
Very low water
Sun

Ginkgo Page 286

Tree, deciduous
Low water
Sun

Hawthorn Page 288

Tree, deciduous
Very low water
Light shade - sun

Holly, American Page 223

Shrub/tree, evergreen
Very low water
Light shade

Magnolia, Southern Page 292

Tree, evergreen
Very low water
Light shade - sun

Maple, Red Page 296

Tree, deciduous
Low water
Light shade - sun

Maple, Sugar Page 296

Tree, deciduous
Low water
Light shade - sun

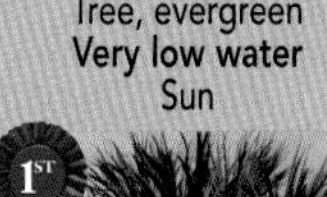

Palm, Sabal Page 301

Tree, evergreen
Very low water
Sun

Shumard Oak Page 298

Tree, deciduous
Very low water
Light shade - sun

Willow Oak Page 298

Tree, deciduous
Very low water
Light shade - sun

VINES

Carolina Jessamine Page 210

Vine, evergreen
Low water
Light shade - sun

Honeysuckle Page 224

Vine, deciduous
Very low water
Light shade - sun

Ivy Page 218

Vine, evergreen
Very low water
Dense - light shade

Pachysandra Page 219

Vine, evergreen
Low water
Dense - light shade

Rose, 'Lady Banks' Page 246

Climber or Vine
Low water
Light shade - sun

Rose, 'New Dawn' Page 247

Climber or Vine
Low water
Light shade - sun

Vinca Page 219

Vine, evergreen
Low water
Light - medium shade

Grass: Ten Key Points

Grass requires more maintenance than any other plant in this book. Water, cutting, fertilizing and spraying are frequent tasks. Here are some tips to make it easier:

✿ Mow with a good, sharp blade. Get it sharpened at a hardware store or do it yourself with a rasp. A blunt, cutting blade tears the grass blades, resulting in brown spots.

✿ Watering grass too often or not enough is one of the most common gardening mistakes. Apply half an inch each time you water. Place a coffee can in the grass before you turn on the sprinklers and turn them off when the cup has half an inch of water in it.

✿ No grass grows in medium to dense shade. Fescue, St. Augustine, centipede, zoysia grow in light shade. Bermuda needs full sun, at least six hours per day.

✿ Like most plants, different grasses tolerate cold differently.

✿ Bermuda is the best grass for drought tolerance in zones 7 to 9b. It takes lots of water and fertilizer to make it look like a golf course but looks quite good with less frequent waterings.

✿ Zoysia is the easiest of the warm-season grasses for zones 7 to 9b. Since zoysia grows so slowly, it is difficult to get an established lawn with seed. You are better off buying sod, but understand that zoysia sod will be more expensive than Bermuda sod. It grows slower than Bermuda, however, so you don't have to cut it as much. Zoysia uses a little more water than Bermuda.

✿ Bermuda, St. Augustine, centipede, and zoysia grass all go dormant and turn brown or yellow from late fall to spring.

✿ Fescue stays green all year in zones 6 and 7. It struggles in the heat of zone 8. However, it looks at its worst in July and August.

✿ Rye grass is primarily used to overseed warm-season grasses that turn brown in the winter. It is somewhat tricky to use and may damage your permanent grass.

✿ Blue grass is frequently used in zone 6. For information on bluegrass, see http://www.american-lawns.com/grasses/bluegrass_ky.html.

We use Bermuda grass at our trial gardens in Georgia because it requires less water than the other southern grasses. Although it requires water twice a week to make it look like a golf course, it looks good with weekly watering and pretty good with water every two weeks. The color dulls when it hasn't had water in about a month, but it recovers shortly after the first rain.

This is the best grass to use if you ever have total outdoor watering bans in your area (zones 7 to 9b). It can live through the worst of them!

Six Southern Grasses

Bermuda

Easiest and most drought tolerant. Lots of water and fertilizer to make it look like a golf course, but it won't die in an extreme situation, although it will turn brown. Tolerates no shade whatsoever.

Light: Full sun
Water: Best drought tolerance. To keep it perfect, water 1/2 inch twice a week. Looks fine with once a week and pretty good with water every 2 weeks. Color dulls in about a month without water, but it recovers with the next rain.
Hardiness: Zones 7 to 9b
Pests: Rare, if you water correctly. Cut down on water and fertilizer if you see brown patches.
Cutting: Requires frequent mowing. Cut it high at 2 inches every week. If you cut more than 1/3 of it at once, expect browning.
Fertilization: Low. Once a year in spring.
Green Period: From the last frost of spring to the first frost of fall.

Zoysia

Good, tough, very wear tolerant. Grows slower than Bermuda, so you don't have to mow it as much. Takes more shade than Bermuda. More expensive but better grass than Bermuda. Difficult to seed because of its slow growth, so you have to use sod.

Light: Light shade to full sun
Water: Good drought tolerance, but shows stress after 2 to 3 weeks.
Hardiness: Zones 7 to 9b
Pests: Rare. Brown patch
Cutting: Cut it high at 2 inches every 7 to 10 days.
Fertilization: Low. Once a year in spring.
Green Period: From the last frost of spring to the first frost of fall.

Centipede

Good, low maintenance grass for zones 7 to 9B. Often available only as seed. Similar to St. Augustine, but finer textured. Low fertilization requirements.

Light: Light shade to full sun
Water: Good drought tolerance, but shows stress after 2 to 3 weeks.
Hardiness: Zones 7 to 9b
Pests: Rare. Chinch bugs occasionally in coastal areas. Brown patch.
Cutting: Cut it high at 2 inches every 7 to 10 days.
Fertilization: Low. Once a year in spring.
Green Period: From the last frost of spring to the first frost of fall.

Fescue

Best, cool-season grass for zones 6 and 7. Struggles in zone 8. Doesn't fill in quickly after a problem, like brown patch. Stays green all year but looks at its worst in July and August.

Light: Light shade to full sun
Water: 1/2 to 1 inch per week. Browns much faster without water than zoysia or Bermuda. Visible effects in 2 weeks.
Hardiness: Zones 6 and 7
Pests: Brown patch, usually in June. Cut back on water and fertilization.
Cutting: Cut it high at 3 inches weekly.
Fertilization: March and September. Follow instructions on bag carefully.
Green Period: All year but suffers in summer.

St. Augustine

Coarse-textured; fairly high water requirements. Tolerates more heat than the rest. Good color. Zones 8 to 11.

Light: Light shade to full sun
Water: Fairly high. Needs 1 inch per week in sandy soils, 1/2 inch in clay. Shows drought stress easily by browning.
Hardiness: Zones 8 to 11
Pests: Lots, including chinch bugs, webworms, army worms, and more.
Cutting: Cut it very high at 3 to 4 inches every 10 to 14 days.
Fertilization: Yearly in spring when in clay soil. Again in June in sandy soil.
Green Period: From the last frost of spring to the first frost of fall.

Rye

Comes in annual or perennial forms. Most often used as temporary, winter grass over-seeding permanent grasses that turn brown in winter. A bit tricky to use. Sometimes damages your permanent grass.

Light: Light shade to full sun
Water: 1/2 to 1 inch per week
Hardiness: Zones 6 and 7a for perennial, all the south for annual.
Pests: Brown patch
Cutting: Cut it high at 2 1/2 or 3 inches weekly.
Fertilization: March and September for perennial grass; September only for annual grass. Follow instructions on bag carefully.
Green Period: All year but suffers in summer.

Easy Hedges and Screens

For easy edges, use evergreen plants with dense forms that don't require much trimming. The following lists are excellent choices. And, don't forget color! Many of these plants either have colored leaves or flowers. See page 21 for tips on saving money when you buy plants.

Small Hedges, 1 to 4 Feet

'Rose Creek' Abelia

1' to 4'

- Abelia, 'Rose Creek' (light shade - sun)
- Azalea, dwarf (light shade)
- Boxwood (light shade - sun)
- Holly (light shade - sun)
- Loropetalum, smaller cultivars (light shade - sun)

Loropetalum

Medium Hedges, 4 to 12 Feet

'Knock Out' Rose

4' to 8'

- Abelia, larger varieties (light shade - sun)
- Aucuba (dense to medium shade)
- Azalea (light shade)
- Boxwood (light shade - sun)
- Camelia (light shade)
- Cleyera (medium shade, light shade, sun)
- Holly (light shade - sun)
- Loropetalum (light shade - sun)
- 'Knock Out' rose (light shade - sun)
- Wax Myrtle, dwarf (light shade - sun)

8' to 12'

- Arborvitae (sun)
- Camelia (light shade)
- Cleyera (medium shade, light shade, sun)
- Cryptomeria (light shade - sun)
- Eastern red cedar (light shade - sun)
- Holly (light shade - sun)
- Loropetalum (light shade - sun)
- Wax myrtle (light shade - sun)
- Yaupon holly (light shade - sun)

Tall Hedges, 12 feet plus

Southern Magnolia

12' to 25'

- Arborvitae (sun)
- Cryptomeria (light shade - sun)
- Eastern red cedar (light shade - sun)
- Holly (light shade - sun)
- Magnolia, 'Little Gem' (light shade - sun)
- Wax myrtle (light shade - sun)

25' Plus

- Arborvitae (sun)
- Cryptomeria (light shade - sun)
- Eastern red cedar (light shade - sun)
- Holly (light shade - sun)
- Magnolia, southern (light shade - sun)

Cryptomeria

Low hedges are often used for geometric gardens. Boxwood (left and above) is a good choice for these hedges because it grows densely and slowly. Holly is less expensive than boxwood, but grows faster, so it requires more frequent trimming.

Loropetalum (right and below) comes in many different sizes, so be sure the variety you choose fits your space. They flower for part of the season, but the leaves retain their color all year, making this one of the few southern plants that offers color for 365 days per year.

Loropetalum hedges require very little care.

Easiest Plants in this Book

All of the 127 blue ribbon plants in this book are easy, but which are the easiest of the bunch? And which can live on rainwater? The plants on these two pages combine both very low water and very low care requirements. Granted, things can change. The south could turn into a desert. New plant diseases could wipe out whole species. Who knows what the future will bring? But for now, these are the best bets for serial plant killers, people who don't want to do much work, and people who live in areas with little water.

Maintenance Time: Almost Nothing

About the only way you can kill these trees is to plant them incorrectly (see pages 32 to 33) or give them poor drainage (see pages 28 to 29). They grow well in almost any soil, live on rainwater, and seldom need trimming. These nine are not currently susceptible to any serious pests or diseases.

Most of theses trees lose their leaves once a year, which requires raking if you have grass underneath them. Why not forgoe the grass? Plant easy, low water shrubs underneath, and just mulch for groundcover. This way, you don't even have to rake the leaves, unless they fall on your drive or walk.

Remember that trees can cut your power bills by 50 percent if you shade 50 percent of your roof.

60' - 80' tall
Full sun

40' - 50' tall
Full sun

20' - 30' tall
Light shade - sun

15' - 20' tall
Light shade - sun

20' - 30' tall
Light shade - sun

50' - 75' tall
Light shade - sun

50' - 60' tall
Light shade - sun

50' - 70' tall
Light shade - sun

20' - 25' tall
Light shade - sun

Maintenance Time: About One Minute Per Year

We have had junipers in our trial gardens for about three years. We have never touched them - no water, no fertilizer, no trimming, no spraying. The only reason you might need a minute a year for your junipers is to fertilize them if your soil needs it. The only way you can kill junipers (other than running them over with your car) is to plant them in a location with poor drainage. See pages 28 to 29 for information about how to avoid that.

6" - 8" tall
Sun

3' tall
Sun

4' - 6' tall
Sun

2' tall
Sun

6' tall
Sun

No Irrigation,* Little Care

Maintenance Time: About Two Minutes Per Year

These plants are incredibly easy and only require about two minutes of care a year, either fertilization or trimming. And, like the other plants on these two pages, they live on rainwater after establishment except in the most extreme conditions. Many of these plants have long bloom periods. Abelia blooms for about six months and crapemyrtle for about two to three months. See the individual plant profiles for more information.

Abelia: 3′ to 10′ tall, Light shade - sun

Crapemyrtle: 3′ - 25′ tall, Sun

European Fan Palm: 5′ - 10′ tall, Light shade - sun

Holly, American: 12′ - 30′ tall, Light shade - sun

Holly, Dwarf Yaupon: 2′ - 5′ tall, Light shade - sun

Honeysuckle: 10′ - 20′ tall, Light shade - sun

Japanese Kerria: 4′ - 6′ tall, Light shade - sun

Smoke Tree: 8′ - 12′ tall, Sun

Yucca: 2′ - 3′ tall, Light shade - sun

Maintenance Time: About Five Minutes Per Year

These plants are also incredibly easy, only requiring about five minutes of care a year, either for fertilization or trimming. And, like the other plants on these two pages, they live on rainwater after establishment except in the most extreme conditions. Loropetalum is the only plant in this book that has color all year (from its leaves). Lantana 'Miss Huff' blooms for about five months per year. Spiraea and 'Chinese Snowball' viburnum are traffic-stopping plants that look like they would require tons of maintenance, but they don't. See the individual plant profiles for more information.

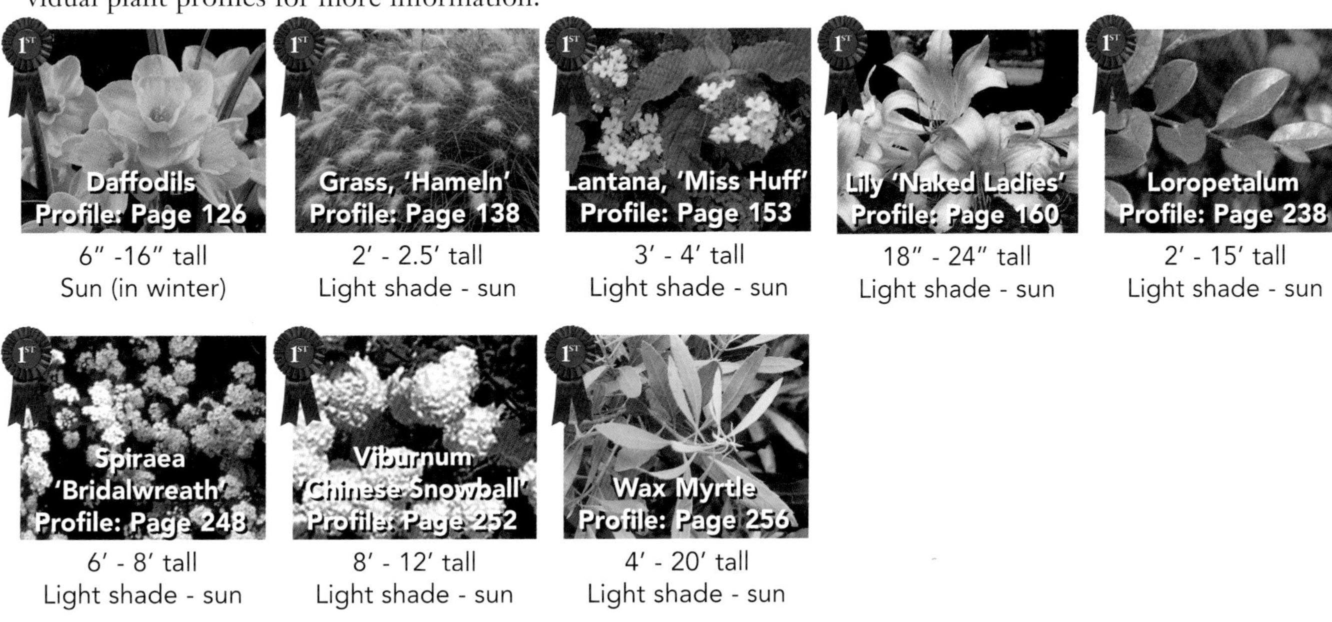

Daffodils: 6″ -16″ tall, Sun (in winter)

Grass, 'Hameln': 2′ - 2.5′ tall, Light shade - sun

Lantana, 'Miss Huff': 3′ - 4′ tall, Light shade - sun

Lily 'Naked Ladies': 18″ - 24″ tall, Light shade - sun

Loropetalum: 2′ - 15′ tall, Light shade - sun

Spiraea 'Bridalwreath': 6′ - 8′ tall, Light shade - sun

Viburnum 'Chinese Snowball': 8′ - 12′ tall, Light shade - sun

Wax Myrtle: 4′ - 20′ tall, Light shade - sun

Lives on rainwater after establishment in all but the most extreme conditions.

Take This Book with You...

BUDGET GARDENING TIPS: SAVE MONEY ON PLANTS

✿ Buy the smallest size you can. A shrub in a one-gallon pot costs about 1/3 as much as the same shrub in a 3 gallon pot.

✿ Buy annuals in multi-packs. We like the 18 packs the best. The roots of the plants are about three inches across. The same plant in a four inch pot is at least twice as much money! And it only takes about a week for the smaller plants to grow as large as the more expensive ones!

✿ Seeds are the cheapest way to buy new plants. Buy and old book from a used book supplier called 'Park's Success with Seeds' by Ann Reilly. It will only cost a few dollars and is the best book we know for fast and easy success with seeds.

✿ In each individual plant profile (chapters 2 to 4), we explain how to propagate the plant. In most instances, it's easy! Learn how to root cuttings, and you will have a gorgeous garden for nothing!

✿ Trade with your neighbors. Have everyone divide their perennials, trade with each other at a block party, and color your neighborhood!

✿ Look for local gardening events. Often, home growers sell plants really cheaply.

✿ Abandoned properties that are scheduled to be cleared can be great places to find plants. Be sure to get permission from the owner. Check with your local city hall to find out how to find the owner's name.

✿ Space plants correctly. Each plant profile (chapter 2 to 4) tells you the proper spacing. If you plant them too close, you waste a lot of money. For example, it takes 4 times as many plants for 1 foot spacing than for 2 foot spacing.

Take this book with you when you go to garden centers. After seeing a plant that interests you, check the index to find the appropriate pages. The information can save you a lot of time, frustration, and money. This book not only covers the great plants but also describes many of the not-so-great ones as well. We don't want you to make the same mistakes we did!

Some Plants Won't Meet Your Expectations

Pamela Crawford (one of the authors of this book) purchased gerber daisies, thinking they would bloom throughout her growing season, or at least six months or so. Not so. They bloomed for a month and never even set another bud. She thought she had done something wrong until she found out that gerber daisies are supposed to only bloom for a month. Had she known that, she would have bought one plant instead of the six she planted in a container for $4 each!

But the label didn't say how long the plant bloomed, and the garden center lady told her she thought they bloomed for months. She was wrong.

She had the same experience with the kalanchoe. It looked great the day she planted it but only stayed in bloom for about a month.

Many garden center personnel are encyclopedias of plant knowledge. Others are novices in gardening.

The hardest information to find is how long the plant blooms. So take this book with you. The plant you are looking for may not be here, but chances are it will.

If you see a plant you like that is not in this book, by all means ask the garden center personnel. Be sure to ask if they have any personal experience with the plant.

Name Confusion

Zinnias are widely planted in the south. Some (right, top) look great in the pot at the garden center but are very susceptible to disease and won't look very good in your garden for long.

On the other hand, 'Profusion' zinnias (right, bottom) are blue ribbon plants, and are labeled with their name at the garden centers. They have consistently bloomed for six month periods in our trial gardens with no care other than water! Take this book with you so you can check out all the plants you buy before you plant them!

When You Shop for Plants.

Great Plants That are Hit or Miss

One of the most popular annuals in the south are petunias. We tried eight different varieties of trailing petunias in our Georgia trial gardens, and they all did beautifully. We've had great luck with some of the Wave petunias from Pan American Seed as well as the Supertunias from Proven Winners (shown left, at one of their growing facilities in Vancouver).

So, why aren't they blue ribbon plants? Several reasons:

- Many petunias sold today are unnamed. The label just says 'Petunia.' Quite a few of these died on us. We're afraid if we class them as the best of the best, you might end up with one of these bad ones and be quite disappointed.

Many other blue ribbon plants are also sold as unnamed plants, but the species are so strong that all of them do well. Wax begonias and impatiens are both examples of this - they are almost foolproof - named or unnamed.

- One of the most important criteria for blue ribbon annuals is at least a four to six month lifespan. Most petunias won't last that long, particularly if the weather is quite hot.

Erratic Performers

Calibrachoa, or million bells, is one of the hottest and prettiest plants in container gardening. However, when they are good, they are very, very good; but when they are bad, they are awful!

We're not sure why. Probably, some of the new ones haven't been tried in certain climates and might not like it there. Eventually, they will sort themselves out.

We frequently use calibrachoa in our Georgia trial gardens because we really like the plant. Sometimes, it is fantastic, other times not.

Once again, take this book with you to your garden center so you will have a better shot at assessing your risk with certain plants. In many instances, they are so inexpensive that cost is not an issue. However, it is important that both new gardeners and serial plant killers have successful gardening experiences. So, stick with the blue ribbon plants if you fall into either of those categories.

New Plants

New plants as well as new cultivars and varieties of old plants are showing up by the thousands. Between our test garden in Georgia and Huntsville Botanical Garden, we have tested many of these new plants. Many are really superior to older varieties - more flowers, longer bloom period, etc. Others are not so great. We have written about lots of them in chapters two to five. Take this book with you to make plant shopping much easier.

Understand Light

Different plants need different amounts of light. A petunia likes sun, while a hosta likes shade. But how much sun is enough for sun plants? The rule of thumb is at least four to six hours of direct sun per day for sun plants. In other words, if your petunia just gets two hours of sun with shade the rest of the day, it will not do well.

If you put a plant (that just likes shade) in the sun, the leaves and flowers will burn. And, shade is more complicated than sun. It's pretty easy to tell whether your area is in sun; but, shade is trickier. Many plants are quite sensitive to varying degrees of shade - light, medium, and dense. Sit in the same location you are considering for a plant and look around.

Light Shade

Light shade is often characterized by morning sun and afternoon shade. Many plants do well in light shade. If you are under trees, try this exersize to determine if you are in light shade. Look up, and you will see about 20-30% leaves and the rest sky. The trees are planted farther apart in light shade than in medium shade. Look down, and notice many types of plants growing. Look around, and see many patches of sky from any direction.

Plants that grow well in light shade also thrive in part-sun, part-shade situations - provided the sun is in the morning hours. If your area gets sun all afternoon, choose plants that tolerate full sun.

Medium Shade

Look up, and you will see medium shade from trees. Look for about 50% or more of sky. Look down, and see ferns or other shade plants growing. Look around, and see more trees but not much open sky on the south or west sides. Sun from the south or west is strong and too much for most medium shade plants.

Fewer plants grow in medium shade than light shade, but your choices are still wide enough to make a great, colorful garden.

Dense Shade

Look up, and you will see the dense shade of very thick trees or the roof of a building. Less than 30% of the sky is visible. Look down and see almost nothing growing, except possibly a few weeds. Look all around, and you will still see very little sky but rather more thickly-leafed trees or buildings.

Many plants thrive in light to medium shade. Dense shade, however, is a difficult situation. Most flowering plants require more light than dense shade provides.

Easy Shade Plants

Plants for light shade are easy to find - over half the plants in this book thrive in light shade. Azaleas and hydrangeas love that light condition. Finding plants for medium to dense shade is more difficult than for light shade. Here are some good shrub, groundcover, and perennial choices.

Dense Shade Perennials, Groundcovers, and Shrubs

Aucuba
Profile: Page 198

Fern, Holly
Profile: Page 132

Fern, Painted
Profile: Page 132

Grass, Liriope
Profile: Page 137

Grass, Mondo
Profile: Page 137

Ivy
Profile: Page 218

Pachysandra
Profile: Page 219

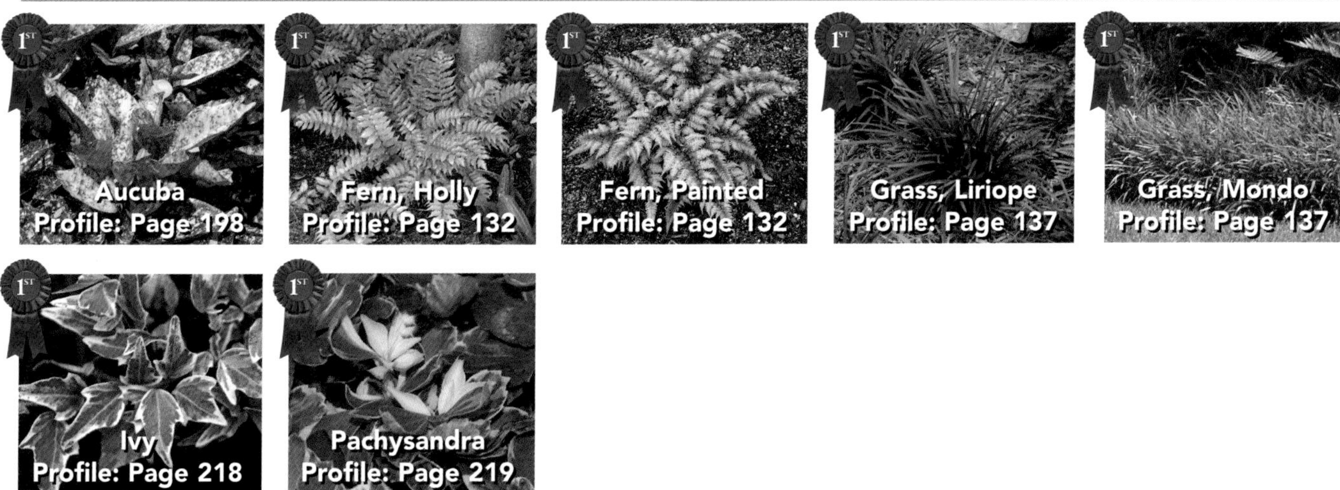

Medium Shade Perennials, Groundcovers, and Shrubs

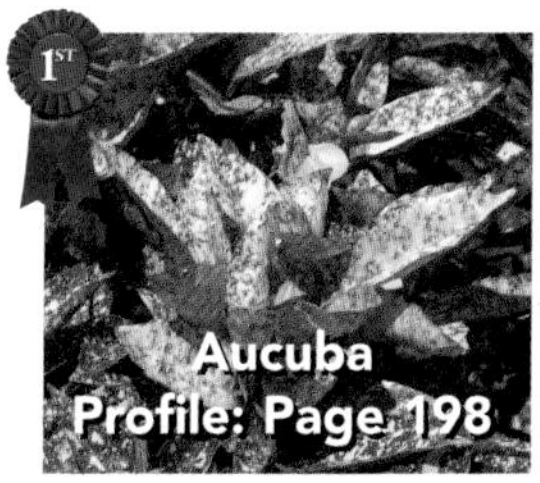
Aucuba
Profile: Page 198

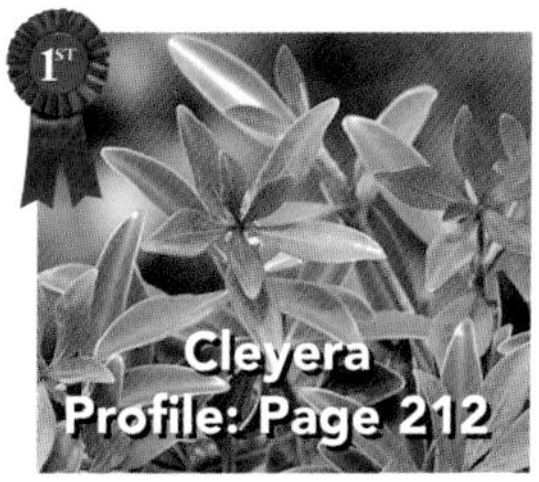
Cleyera
Profile: Page 212

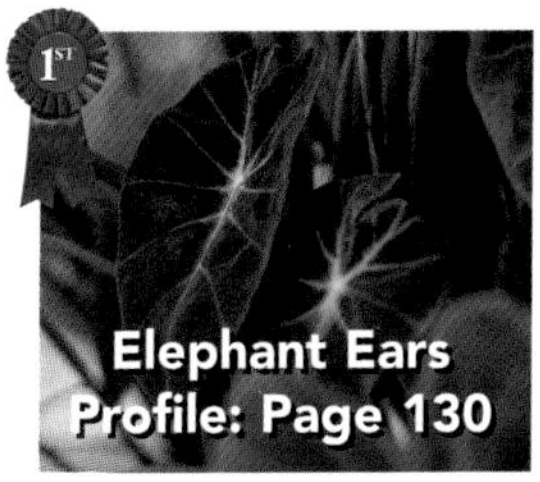
Elephant Ears
Profile: Page 130

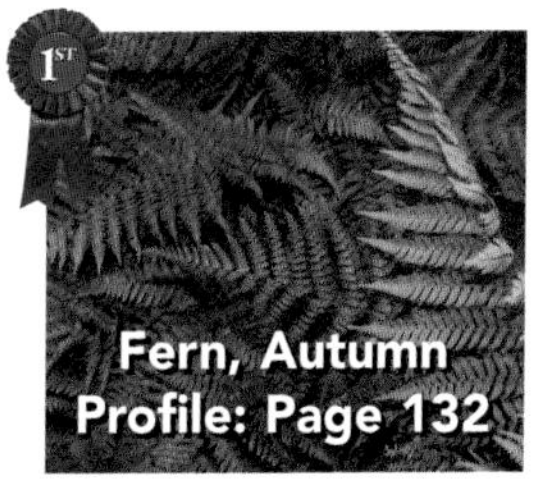
Fern, Autumn
Profile: Page 132

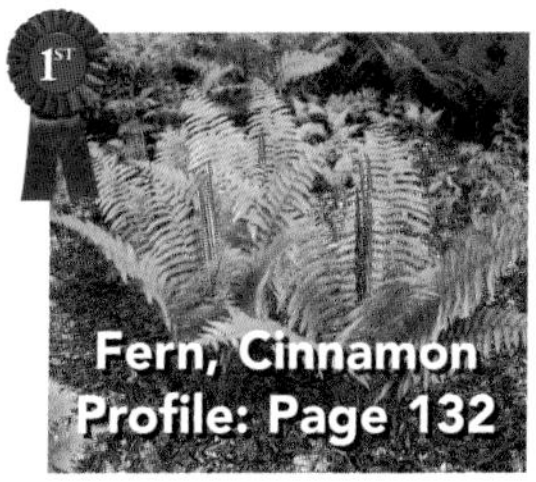
Fern, Cinnamon
Profile: Page 132

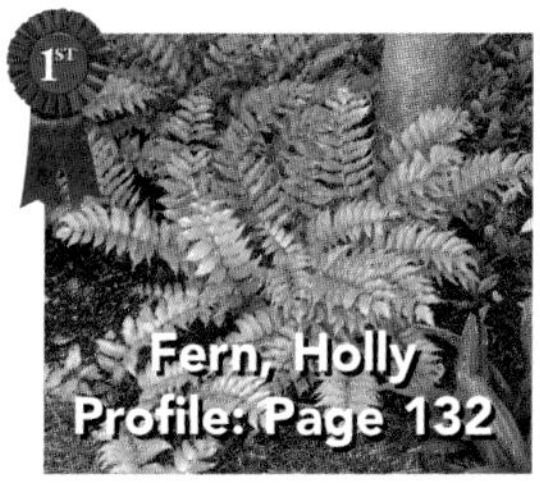
Fern, Holly
Profile: Page 132

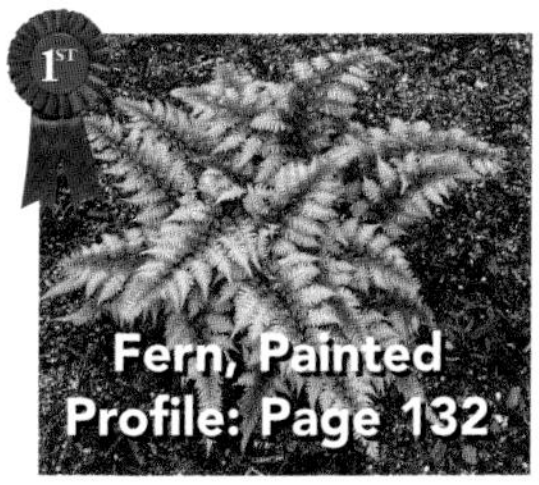
Fern, Painted
Profile: Page 132

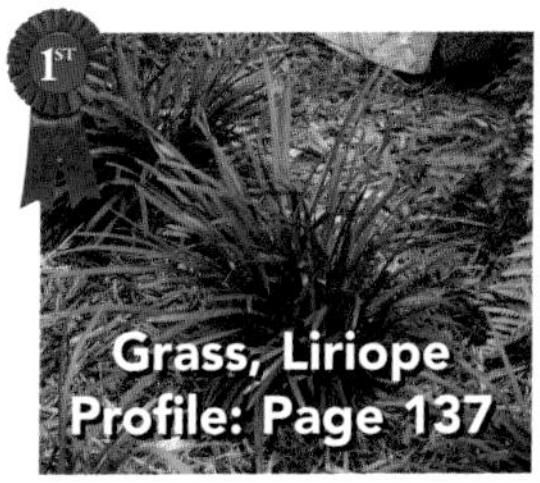
Grass, Liriope
Profile: Page 137

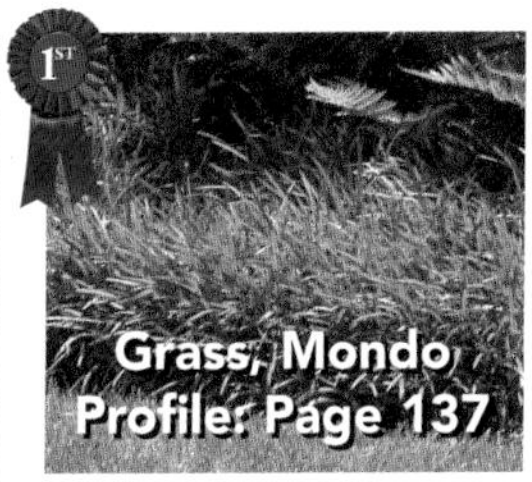
Grass, Mondo
Profile: Page 137

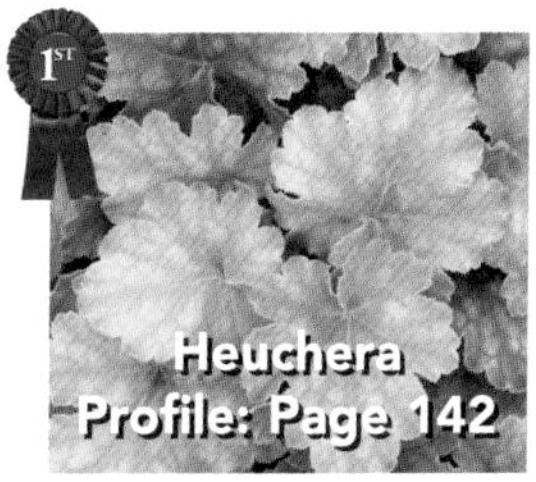
Heuchera
Profile: Page 142

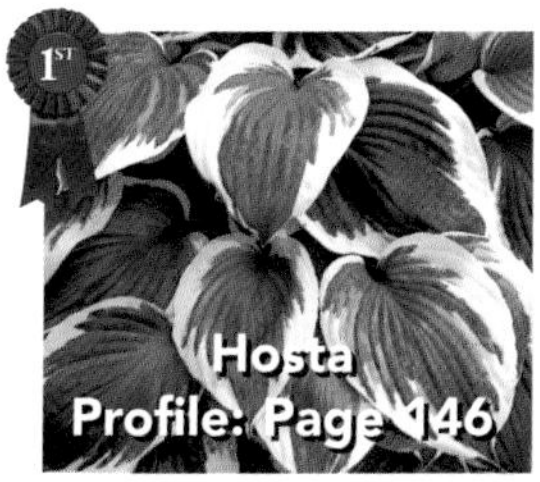
Hosta
Profile: Page 146

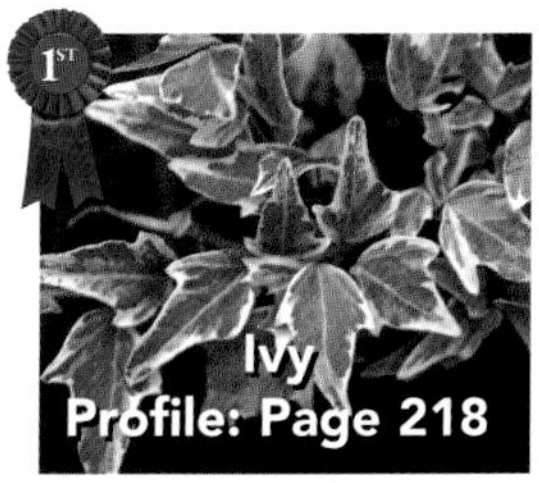
Ivy
Profile: Page 218

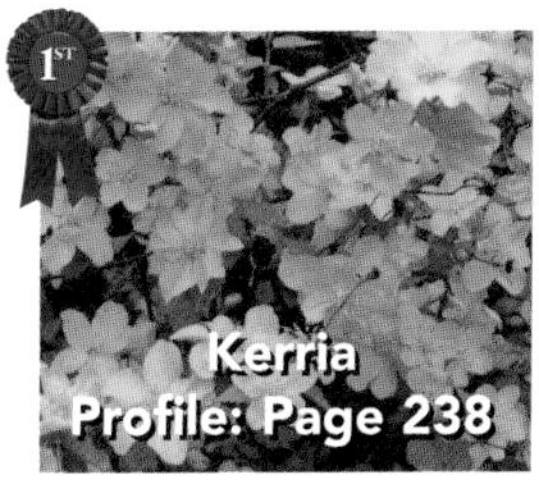
Kerria
Profile: Page 238

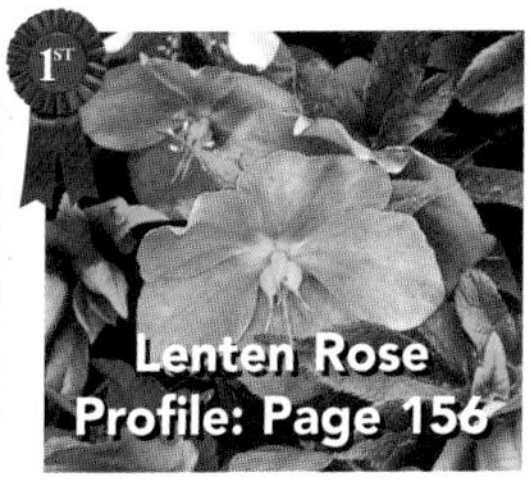
Lenten Rose
Profile: Page 156

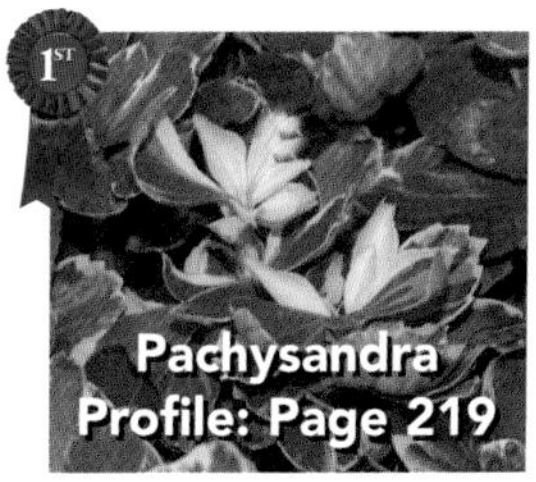
Pachysandra
Profile: Page 219

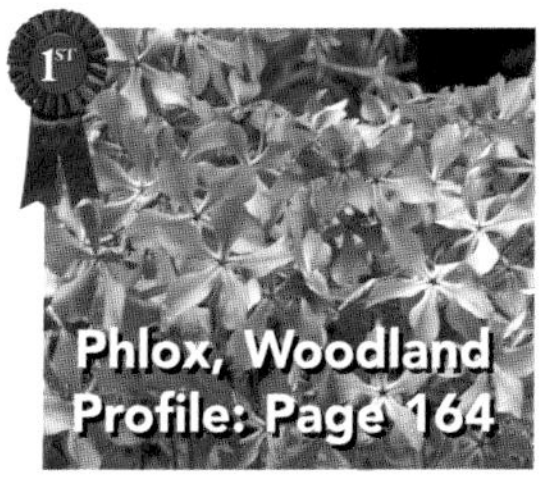
Phlox, Woodland
Profile: Page 164

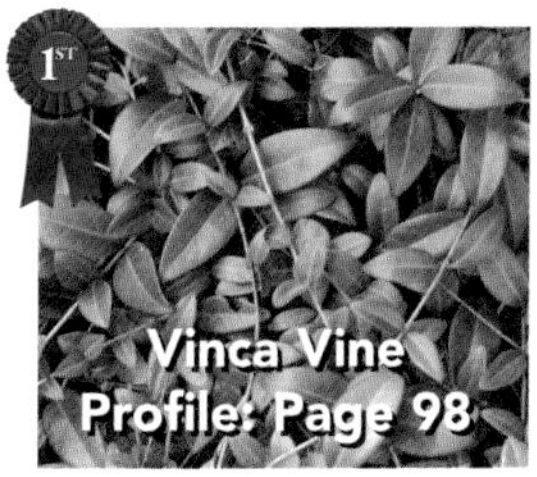
Vinca Vine
Profile: Page 98

Check Drainage Before Planting

Bad Drainage Usually Kills Plants

Planting in a bed that drains poorly is one of the easiest ways to kill a plant. Compacted soil can keep a plant's root system from growing. Without a good root system, the plant will never be able to live without a ton of water, and many will die.

Areas Most Likely to Have Drainage Problems

✿ 'Bathtubs' are areas in between the house and the walk. Since the walk often interrupts the drainage pattern, these areas are among the first you need to check. They often drain poorly.

✿ Any area that could have had heavy equipment running over the soil. Heavy equipment can compact the soil, making it hard. Roots cannot grow well into hard, concrete-like soil.

✿ Any area of clay soil. Since clay is such a dense soil, it doesn't take much to cause it to drain poorly.

An Easy Way to Check Your Drainage

Check your drainage by digging a hole about two feet square by one foot deep. Does the soil you removed look really hard? Fill the hole with water. If it hasn't drained in 12 hours, you have a drainage problem.

Fixing Drainage Problems

✿ Till your soil to a depth of 8 to 12 inches. Try the drainage test again.

✿ If it still doesn't drain, you may have a hardpan, or concrete-like shelf under your soil. A deep auger can loosen it up. Or, you can punch holes through it with a shovel to give the water a way out, like the drainage holes in flower pots.

✿ Coarse-textured soil amendments, like gravel and pine bark added to the top of the soil and tilled down to a 12" depth, also helps drainage. Don't use sand. Clay plus sand makes concrete.

✿ Ask for advice if you don't know what to do. Many garden centers and nurseries know how to solve drainage problems. Look for the nurseries that have heavy equipment. It might cost less than you think to hire a machine and an operator for an hour or so to fix your problem.

✿ French drains can be dug and filled with gravel. Once again, get a professional opinion before going to the trouble and expense of installing a French drain.

Plants for Wet Spots

If you cannot fix your drainage problem, and the water stays in your test hole for 24 hours, you need to call in professionals for help. However, if it drains in between 12 and 24 hours, there are some plants the might work. Here are your best bets.

Best Plants for Wet Spots (or Areas of Poor Drainage)

Joe Pye weed

- Bald cypress
- Canna
- Carolina jessamine
- Elephant ear
- Fern
- Grass, *Acorus*
- Hibiscus
- Holly, inkberry
- Holly, winterberry
- Holly, yaupon
- Honeysuckle
- Jackson vine
- Joe Pye weed
- Magnolia, 'Little Gem'
- Magnolia, southern
- Maple, red
- Oak, willow
- Palm, sable
- Salvia 'Black and Blue' and 'Argentine Skies'
- Wax myrtle

Hibiscus 'Luna Pink Swirl'

Worst Plants for Wet Spots

Dogwood tree

- Aucuba
- Azalea, evergreen
- Boxwood
- Camellia
- Cryptomeria
- Daffodil
- Dogwood
- Eastern Red Cedar
- Grass, feather reed 'Karl Foerster'
- Grass, purple muhly
- Grass, switch
- Heuchera
- Holly, American
- Holly, Chinese
- Holly, dwarf yaupon
- Holly, Fosters
- Holly, Japanese
- Holly, Nellie Stevens
- Hosta
- Ice plant
- Iris (except Louisiana iris)
- Japanese plum yew
- Juniper
- Pachysandra
- Phlox
- Red hot poker plant
- Sedum
- Smoke tree
- Spanish bluebell
- Yucca

Preparation

Identifying Your Soil

There are many different types of soil in the south - from clay to sand to loam - as well as many combinations of the three. If your soil is orange, it is clay. If you don't know what type of soil you have, call your county extension and ask the master gardeners. Also, ask them for instructions on soil amendments to add to your soil before planting. Since clay is the most common soil in the south, here are instructions for clay.

Beautiful gardens are easily grown in clay soil if it is properly prepared. Garden: Mrs. Bill Taylor, Jr., Louisville, Mississippi.

Preparing Clay for Planting Beds

Most annuals and perennials don't do well at all when planted in straight clay or sand. It is better to prepare an entire planting bed instead of preparing one hole at a time. Beds in clay are better raised somewhat to encourage drainage. If possible, plan to raise the level of the bed about three inches by adding soil amendments. If that's not possible, remove the top three inches of the clay so the level of the finished bed will remain at the same level it was before the preparation. Add three inches of soil amendments and till it in so that it is thoroughly blended in with the existing soil.

Organic amendments - like compost, peat moss, pine bark, and manure - come from living things (see pages 48 for compost instructions). They improve both water and nutrient retention of the soil. They also allow for more aeration, which helps roots grow healthy and strong. Organics help to provide a healthy environment for beneficial organisms, like earthworms. Inorganic amendments come from things that were never alive, like gravel, perlite, or vermiculite. Inorganic amendments are used strictly to improve drainage. They have little nutritional value.

Many garden centers have their own mixes of soil amendments that work well in your area that are sold by the cubic yard. These amendments are mixes: products that increase drainage mixed with products that add to the nutrient content. If the salesperson has had quite a bit of landscape experience and appears quite knowledgeable, use his/her recommendation. If not, you can buy bags of soil conditioner. It is critical that you use the right products. You need something to make the soil drain better as well as something to add organics. Don't use sand in an attempt to make the soil drain better because sand and clay make concrete!

After adding the soil amendments, blend them into the existing clay with a tiller, fork, or shovel. Blending them well into the soil underneath is very important. If you don't, water will pass through the amendments and stop on top of the clay. You will have created a bathtub instead of a planting bed, and many plants will drown.

We recommend planting shrubs in beds instead of in single holes in the middle of grass. However, trees are often planted alone. We do not add amendments for these holes. See page 33, 'Planting Single Trees or Shrubs from Containers,' for preparation instructions.

Plants That Do Well in Unimproved Clay

Many university studies have found that shrubs and trees don't need organics incorporated into the top layer of soil because their roots quickly outgrow them. Here is a list of shrubs, vines, and trees that we think have a good chance of doing well in unimproved clay, provided it is loosened up quite a bit and not compacted.

Panicle hydrangeas are one of the shrubs that can be planted in unimproved clay.

Shrubs

Althea, Rose of Sharon
Butterfly bush
Crapemyrtle
Forsythia
Holly
Hydrangea, panicle
Spiraea, bridlewreath
Viburnum, Chinese snowball
Viburnum, doublefile
Wax myrtle

Trees

Arborvitae
Bald cypress
Carolina silverbell
Chaste tree, Vitex
Chinese elm
Chinese pistachio
Crapemyrtle
Cryptomeria
Eastern red cedar
Ginkgo
Hawthorn
Holly
Magnolia
Maple
Palms, European fan, needle, sabal, and windmill
Redbud
Oak
Smoke tree

Vines

Carolina jessamine
Honeysuckle

Preparing Soil for Grass

Grass requires drainage, so check out if your soil is compacted, and how much. If it feels hard, it is best to till the top six inches. This can be quite hard work, but it will ensure the health of your grass. Add an inch of top soil or organics, and blend it into the top three inches of soil. Rake the bed to remove clods, rocks, etc., so you can have a smooth bed. This raking is time-consuming but necessary. Avoid creating 'birdbaths' (small, low spots that collect water).

If you are planting grass at a new house, the soil could be really compacted and almost impossible to till by hand. Check with a local garden center or landscaper to find out what they would charge to do the work with a machine. It could be worth it in the long run.

Planting

When to Plant

It is best to plant shrubs, trees, and perennials in fall or winter because they require less water during these cooler periods. Also, cooler temperatures are less stressful for the plants than summer heat. The roots of plants installed in fall continue to develop most of the winter, even when the tops of the plants aren't growing. However, most garden centers sell perennials and blooming shrubs when they are flowering, which could be June. You can plant most plants from containers anytime, but it will take more water to establish them. Annuals, some bulbs, and some other plants can't be planted in fall or winter. Check each individual plant profile for specifics.

Spacing the Plants Appropriately

Spacing plants appropriately is very important. We have the proper spacing listed on each individual plant profile. Plants need room for their roots to expand as well as room for their branches to grow long enough to bloom or fruit. They also need to be far enough away from a building to allow for cleaning and painting. Understand the mature plant size (also detailed in the plant profiles), and place the plant so it will be two to three feet away from a building when it is mature.

Space plants according to their mature size to reduce competition for water. Overcrowding increases the need for water in that area. It may also increase bugs and diseases.

If you follow proper spacing guidelines, your garden may appear bare on planting day. Fill in with annuals for the first season if this open space bothers you.

These panicle hydrangeas should be planted six to eight feet on center (from center to center). With new plants fresh from the nursery, the bed may look bare but the proper spacing will pay off in the long run. If these hydrangeas are planted closer together, they would never look this good. Photo from Huntsville Botanical Garden

Planting Trees or Large, Single Shrubs from Containers

Since tree and shrub roots quickly grow beyond your soil amendments, most soils (including clay) are not amended prior to planting individual trees or shrubs. Dig a hole three to four times the width of the root ball, to a depth of one inch less than the height of the pot. We use a tape measure to make this faster. Loosen up the soil that has been removed. It could be quite solid, especially if you are in a new home. Heavy equipment driving over clay will turn it quite hard. Since roots have a hard time growing through that, loosen up the removed soil so that it has a good, soft consistency. If it is not loosened up, the tree will have a hard time growing into the existing soil. (See page 28 for info on checking and fixing drainage problems.)

Do not add organic matter to the holes of large shrubs or trees. It acts as a sponge, absorbing all the water. The roots of the plants have more trouble growing away from the sponge. Roots can also suffocate in wet, waterlogged soil, which is a leading cause of plant death in the south.

Remove the plant from its container. If the roots are growing in a circular shape around the root ball, rake your hand up the side to loosen them up. Set the plant in the middle of the hole and check to see that it is at the right depth. The top of the root ball should be one inch above the level of the surrounding soil. Fill in around the root ball half way up to the top. Water thoroughly until you see no more bubbles coming up from the bottom. Fill in to the top of the hole, and water again. Fill in where the soil settles. The goal is to remove any air bubbles from the soil.

Be sure the root ball is slightly out of the ground, and no soil is piled up around the stem (a really fast way to kill your tree!). Fertilize if it is spring or summer with the slow-release product described on page 47. Do not fertilize in fall or winter. Mulch according to the instructions on page 38.

Planting Balled and Burlapped Trees

Planting balled and burlapped trees is exactly like planting trees from containers (as described above) except for handling the burlap. Do not remove it because it keeps the roots together and naturally rots in the soil after planting. Set the tree in the hole with the burlap intact. Cut the twine or string, so you can fold back the burlap on top of the plant to see the location of the top of the root ball is, as well as where the trunk comes out of the ground. Proceed with filling around the roots the same way you would with a containerized tree (see previous page).

Planting Annuals, Perennials, and Shrubs in Prepared Beds

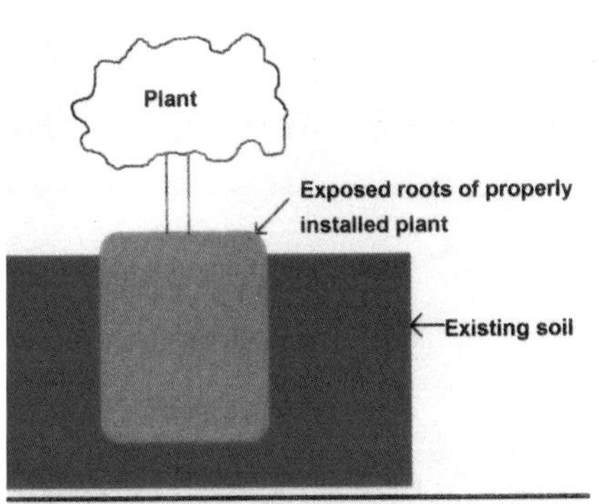

After your soil is prepared, planting is fairly easy, if your soil is soft. If it is rocky, digging can be difficult, so sharpen the edge of your shovel (with an electric grinder sold at home improvement stores) or rent a mechanical digging tool. Dig a hole slightly wider and one inch shallower than the root ball. Take the plant out of the pot. If any roots are circling, loosen them slightly, so they can grow straight into the soil and not in a circle. This step is very important, especially for annuals. Their roots are often so tight, the root ball looks white! If they are not loosened, the plant won't grow much. Place the plant in the hole. Fill in the sides with the same soil. Do not put any additional soil on top of the root ball. It should be slightly out of the ground, as shown in the diagram. The major cause of plant death is planting the plant too deep. Soil piled up on top of the root ball and covering the stem can kill the plant. Water the plant, so the soil is settled in the hole and there are no air pockets. If you see bubbles coming from the soil you used to fill in around the roots, there are still air pockets.

Establishment Watering

Plants need lots of water right after they are planted. That water is called establishment watering. Most plants store water in their roots. Since their roots are small when they are in nursery containers, they need more water until the roots can grow large enough to store more.

Observe Your Garden Carefully for Its First Growing Season

Recently installed plants need frequent, deep watering to establish their roots in the ground. The watering schedule depends upon the plants' environment. Shade gardens require half the water of sun gardens. Windy gardens require more water than calm gardens. Plants require much more water if planted in summer than if planted in fall.

Your plants will tell you when they need water. Observe them carefully for their first growing season. If a plant is wilting, it needs water. If the soil feels dry when you insert your finger, it needs water. Plants that are grown in containers are usually grown in a different soil than your garden soil. They can quickly dehydrate if you plant them in clay. The clay can absorb the water in the potting soil quickly. The clay is damp, but your plant is wilted. Push your finger into the potting mix, and give it water if it is dry. After about two weeks, the roots will begin growing into the clay, and the water needs will be somewhat reduced. But the plant will still need extra water for the remainder of that growing season.

Field-grown trees present another problem. These are trees that were grown in the ground in a tree farm. Their roots are cut, so they can be transplanted into your landscape. They require more water than containerized plants because their root balls are larger (often two to three feet in depth), and they have been through the trauma of having their roots cut. They will need more water than smaller plants because the water needs to be absorbed deeper into the soil. They won't need water as frequently as a small, container plant, however, because their soil will be similar to the one you are planting in, and the water will not be sucked out of the rootball into the surrounding soil.

How Much Water to Apply

On the average, you'll need to apply enough water to soak into the soil to a depth of six to eight inches. That will take different amounts of time depending on your watering method. Slow watering directly on the soil is better than a fast hit with the hose because the roots have more time to absorb water if it is applied slowly. It takes about 45 minutes for our drip irrigation system to apply that much water. Since watering systems vary greatly in their application time, you need to see how long yours takes to apply that much water.

Deep watering is very important. It encourages deep, healthy root growth. A common mistake is to give too little water with each watering. The plants will never be their best unless their roots are encouraged to grow deeply.

New Fall Plantings: How Often to Water

Water the plants right after planting. Mulch well. Most of the time, that's all you have to do if you plant in November because the temperatures are cool, and it usually rains every week or so. The plants aren't using that much water, but be sure to check them closely. If the temperatures rise to the 70's and it doesn't rain for a while, the plants will dry out and could die. Put your finger in the soil around the roots. If it feels dry, water it. The most Huntsville Botanical Garden has ever had to water is once or twice after planting in November. However, the south is getting warmer, so be sure to check your new plants weekly.

Fall Planting Saves A Lot of Water

New Summer Plantings: How Often to Water

Plants installed in fall need the least amount of water to establish, and those planted in summer need the most. The first two weeks is the most critical period. The roots have not left their root ball, and they might need water twice a day until they do, which takes about two weeks. That is unusual, however. The most we have ever watered in clay soil was every two days and once a day in sand. However, remember to observe your plants closely during this critical period. The need for water will diminish during the second two week period, and will continue to diminish for the remainder of the season. Expect to have to water about twice a week from the second week until the end of the season.

This bed mixes plants with low or very low water requirements. They need frequent watering immediately after planting if they are planted in summer, less if planted in fall. Once they are established, they need only occasional water to supplement the rainfall. Plants include crapemyrtle, daylilies, purple heart, lantana, and coneflower. This garden is at the home of Mrs. Bill Taylor, Jr. in Louisville, Mississippi.

Watering the Established Garden

Overwatering is the gravest error gardeners commit. This common practice shortens a plant's life, causes disease, and increases the maintenance requirements of each plant. Root rot is the biggest problem for plants in clay soil. Also, the plant grows faster with more water and, therefore, needs more trimming. The growth is often leggy because the plant is frantically trying to figure out where to store all this water; thus, long stems result. Overwatered plants also require more fertilizer than properly watered plants because the water washes the fertilizer through the soil.

Different Plants Need Different Amounts of Water

Different kinds of plants have different watering needs. Each plant profile (chapters two through four) tells you how often the plant needs water during the growing season. Most people don't water much in winter, unless you have planted annuals, like pansies.

Native plants have differing water needs, just like plants from other places. It is a common misconception that native plants tolerate drought better than non-natives. Some natives, like magnolia trees, are very drought tolerant. Others, like dogwoods, show quite a bit of damage in a drought. Many plants native to the south live near streams, like native azaleas. They are accustomed to relatively damp soil and can't adapt to sites that are continually dry. Bald cypress, on the other hand, is a native that adapts to both wet and dry. We have included water needs of each plant, as well as classifying them as high, medium, low, or very low water users.

It is easier to water a garden that has beds with plants that have similar water needs. Many use the 'no irrigation' plants as the mainstay of their garden and put higher water plants together in a small, highly visible location.

These flowers are impatiens, which are some of the thirstiest flowers used in the south. They are easy to water if they are kept in a small area, such as in this gazebo at the home of Mrs. Bill Taylor, Jr. in Louisville, Mississippi.

How Often to Water

Annuals, like these petunias, require more frequent watering than more permanent plantings.

It is best to water plants when they need it rather than putting them on a set schedule. Here are some tips:

✿ Wait until the plant shows you it needs water. Most plants show they need water by wilting or turning a pale grayish-green color.

✿ Watering too frequently causes the plants root to develop only close to the surface. Your goal should be working to grow large, deep roots on the plants, so they have large areas to store water in times of drought.

✿ Water at night or early morning to avoid water loss to evaporation.

✿ Grass turns a dull, bluish-gray color when it needs water. If you can see your footprints after walking on it, then you should water.

✿ Watering frequency depends on many environmental factors.

- Plants in shade require about one third as much water as those in sun
- Plants in clay soil require much less water than those planted in sand.
- Plants need more water when temperatures are higher.
- Plants need more water if it is windy.

✿ Shrubs, vines, and trees generally have larger root systems than perennials, so they may not need water as often.

How Much to Water

✿ Water deeply to encourage deep root growth. Check your soil to see how long it takes to penetrate to a depth of six to eight inches.

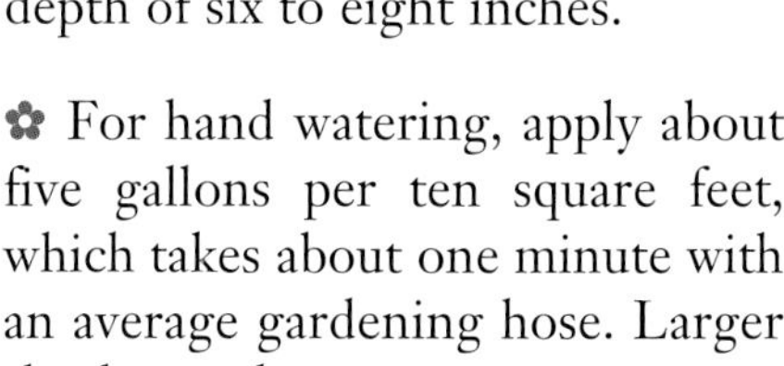

✿ For hand watering, apply about five gallons per ten square feet, which takes about one minute with an average gardening hose. Larger shrubs need more.

✿ For grass, apply one half inch per time. Never more than twice a week in summer and once a week in spring and fall usually suffices. If you water more, your grass will never grow a healthy enough root system to look its best. Put a coffee can in the grass and see how long your sprinklers take to fill it up to half an inch.

Water containers until a steady stream flows from the bottom. Since they require frequent watering, we have them hooked up to a drip irrigation system that gets watered automatically from our rainwater collection system. Containers and posts from www.kinsmangarden.com.

12 Easy Tips for Saving Water

1. Set Up Different Areas for Plants with Different Water Needs

✿ Plant high-water plants, like annuals, in one area, so it's easier to water them. Since annuals are short-lived, they never have a chance to develop root systems large enough to store much water, so they need frequent watering. Moisture-retaining polymers can be mixed in with the soil when planting annuals. They reduce the water needs of these small plants. Be sure to follow the instructions, or they can harm your plants. These polymers don't work for larger plants because their roots quickly outgrow the area with the polymers.

✿ Place plants according to their water needs - very low water (no irrigation after establishment), low water, medium, or high water use. Temporary irrigation can be used for all the very low water use areas because you should only need it during the eight to ten week establishment period. Or, if you plant in late fall, they won't even need that much water for establishment.

✿ Use plants that don't need irrigation for the majority of your plants. Use drip irrigation lines for smaller areas with higher water use plants.

2. Mulch

Mulch does a great job of holding moisture in the soil as well as preventing weeds and adding organic matter to keep your plants healthier. Here are some tips (see page 49 for sources of free mulch):

✿ Apply three inches of mulch on top of the soil after planting. Take care not to pile it up around the stem (or trunk) of the plant because wet mulch can rot a trunk. Keep it completely away from trunks and stems. Use your hands to pull it two to three inches away from trunks as you are applying it.

✿ Pine straw is very attractive but doesn't insulate the soil as well as finer mulches, like ground up pine bark or hardwood mulch. Pine bark is the most popular mulch in most of the south.

3. Reduce Areas of Grass

Grass uses more water than any other plant in your garden (unless you plant impatiens in full sun!). It also needs a lot of care - cutting, aerating, etc. Areas of grass are shrinking in newer landscapes. Landscape designers and architects are installing a much higher percentage of beds and a lower percentage of grass. Some areas of the country, like Las Vegas, are actually paying people one dollar per square foot to take grass out!

4. Water Your Plants Only When They are Thirsty!

Don't set your sprinkler timer to water whether the plants are thirsty or not! Most plants show they need water by wilting or turning a pale, grayish-green color. Or, push your finger into your soil (down a few inches) and see if it feels dry.

✿ Buy a rain gauge, so you can easily see how much rain actually falls in your garden. If you get half an inch of rain or more, it gives your plants a good watering. If it is only a sprinkle, it doesn't do much good.

✿ Install a rain sensor on your sprinkler system. These sensors keep the system from operating when it is raining. Soil moisture sensors are quite a bit more sophisticated. They measure the moisture content of the soil and turn on your sprinklers only when the soil is dry. University studies are giving these moisture sensors rave reviews for saving water.

5. Create Shade

Shady areas can be 20 degrees cooler than sunny spots. Plants need MUCH less water in shade than in sun. We have been amazed at how little water shade containers need compared to their sun counterparts. This window box needed water about once a week. It is large (36" side-planted, from www.kinsmangarden.com), and we used potting mix that included moisture-retaining granules.

The sun baskets that were near this window box needed water every day! That means this shade container required SEVEN TIMES less water than those in direct sun!

6. Plant Low Water Plants

Many of the plants in this book need minimal to no water from you after they are established. They are well-adapted to the south and can take the south's rainfall as well. Many desert plants grow on almost no water, but will die in the 30 to 60 inches of annual rainfall that exists in the south.

7. Use Drip Irrigation

Drip irrigation waters the roots of the plants instead of spraying water up in the air, like traditional irrigation systems. They are suitable for beds and containers but not for grass. Drip systems use 20 to 70 percent less water than traditional irrigation systems. See page 43 for more information.

8. Plant in Fall Rather Than Spring or Summer

Gardens planted in November need very little water to establish. The same garden planted in July could require water every other day (or sometimes every day) for many weeks. See pages 34 to 35 for more information.

9. Space Plants Appropriately

Space plants according to their mature size to reduce competition for water. Overcrowding increases the need for water in that area. It also increases bugs and diseases.

10. Collect the Rainwater that Falls on Your Roof

48,000 gallons of water come off the average southern roof each year. That's a lot of water! See pages 40 to 43 for more information.

11. Take Care When Planting Under Trees

The root systems of trees are quite large, generally extending three times the diameter of the drip line (the outer diameter of the leaves). If you plant shrubs or groundcovers under these trees, there may not be enough room for all of the roots. Since roots store water, the smaller plants may suffer.

12. Fertilize Correctly

Healthy plants use less water than unhealthy ones. Learn to use slow release fertilizers that send nutrients slowly to the plant roots rather than liquids or granular products that can overdose your plant on chemicals. Overfertilization causes plants to either get sick or go into hypergrowth, using more water than they need.

Rainwater Collection Systems

In the fall of 2007 (we remember that day like most remember 9/11), the water was turned off for most of north Georgia landscaping. No irrigation was allowed at all. We were in a complete state of panic. Should we move? How could we possibly continue our trial gardens with no water? Since we were constantly planting new plants to test, how could they survive our hot summers right after they were planted? We knew we could install a well, but water from wells was under the same restrictions as city water in Florida. We figured it was just a matter of time before Georgia included well water in the restrictions.

We found a solution that is becoming more and more popular in southern gardens with frequent, severe water restrictions. Collect the rainwater from your roof and use it to water your garden. Our new system works beautifully, and allows us to grow whatvever we like (other than grass) with just rainwater!

They Work Quite Simply

Pipes are connected to your roof gutters. The water goes through the pipes to a tank. The water can either flow by gravity or sump pumps to the tank.

Collecting rainwater from roofs has been a common practice for centuries in areas of low rainfall, like Australia, Israel, and Bermuda.

The color of the tank is important. It needs to be a dark color to reduce bacteria formation and algae build up.

Getting Water Out of the Tank

Small tanks, like rainbarrels, are often hooked up to a hose, with gravity forcing the water out of the hose. Some small tanks and most larger tanks use a pump to get the water to its destination.

48,000 Gallons per Year Comes Off an Average Roof!

Rainwater collection systems can easily collect enough water to take care of most residential planted beds but not enough for the average amount of grass. Lots of water comes off the average roof. One inch of rain from 1600 square feet of roof yields about 960 gallons of water! Multiply that by 50 inches per year rainfall, and you get 48,000 gallons of water! That is plenty of water for all your landscape needs.

We had two big surprises from our roof water collection system: how quickly the tank filled and how quickly it was used by our garden! We learned quite a bit about how to manage a garden (using only the water collected from our roof) that includes both our beds and containers. We are sharing our knowledge with you.

Some considerations are: How large of an area do you want to irrigate? How big of a tank can you afford? Where will you store the tank? How will you get the water from the tank to your plants?

Solutions for Limited Water

Tank Prices

Tanks vary from about $50 to tens of thousands of dollars, depending on size. Rainbarrels are the smallest tanks we have seen. They hold about 50 gallons of water and are usually hooked directly to the bottom of a gutter. They are very inexpensive ($30 to $100); some people use plastic trash cans to capture rain. Home improvement stores sell small, submersible pumps to go inside rainbarrels to give you more water pressure.

Most homeowners who want more water capacity are installing tanks in the 200 to 2500 gallon range. You need the tank, a pump, and a filter. Many do-it-yourself systems are available from home improvement stores, hardware stores, and garden centers. Online systems are also available. A company called Brae is advertising do-it-yourself systems ranging from $780 to $1449 for a 1100 gallon tank (includes tank, pump, and filter).

If you want to hire someone to do the whole thing, it's easy to find. We used Green Water Systems (Canton, Georgia, 678-395-7138, www.greenwatersystemsusa.com) for our tanks and David Roach (Woodstock, Georgia, 404-391-1628) for the drip irrigation system. Cost for tanks installed range from about $1000 to over $10,000, depending on the size of the tank and the complexity of the installation.

Tanks can be kept above or below ground. Below-ground tanks are more expensive. You cannot bury a standard, above ground tank because it will collapse under ground. Underground tanks need to be reinforced with steel or concrete. It is also expensive to bury them. However, since most people expect many parts of the south to have water problems for quite a while, they are becoming more and more popular.

What Size Tank Do You Need for Your Garden?

You need to size your tank based on the most water you might need, which occurs at the hottest part of summer. The south can go for up to four weeks without rain in July or August, so you'll need a tank that can store a four week water supply.

Since so many factors influence water use (sun or shade, types of plants, soil type, wind, watering system, temperature, etc.) it is impossible to say for sure what size you would need. Water pressure and the type of irrigation emitter also influences the amount of water it takes to cover a bed. Ask your tank supplier for recommendations. However, we can share with you what we learned - as well as give you ideas for the ideal, low water garden. We only use drip irrigation in our beds because it uses 20 to 50 percent less water than pop-up systems and it is easier for us to install and adapt to new planting schemes. Let's look at three different scenarios that all have drip irrigation systems.

Low water garden: Mainly shrubs and low water perennials that are well spaced (go by the spacing on the individual plant profiles). Maximum water needs: about every 10 days in the hottest days of summer.

Medium water garden: Many shrubs and perennials that are listed as medium water use, once again, properly spaced. Maximum water needs: about every 7 days in the hottest days of summer.

High water garden: Annuals that are closely planted and need water twice a week

Garden size	Tank size: Low Water	Tank Size: Medium Water	Tank Size: High Water
100 square feet	150 - 200 gallons	200 - 250 gallons	400 - 500 gallons
250 square feet	375 - 450 gallons	500 - 625 gallons	1000 - 1250 gallons
500 square feet	750 - 950 gallons	1000 - 1250 gallons	2000 - 2500 gallons
1000 square feet	1500 - 1875 gallons	2000 - 2500 gallons	4000 - 5000 gallons

Rainwater Collection Systems

Collecting Water from AC's, Showers, Washing Machines, etc.

We connected our water tanks to everything we could. Here are the results:

✿ First, we connected our air conditioners the wrong way. A hose ran off the ac unit into the ground. We pulled the hose up to the top of the tank and left it there. The next day, our air conditioner stopped working. The repairman told us the water had backed up and shut off the system. We then ran it into a hole in the ground with a sump pump to pump it up into the tank. We didn't get much water from the air conditioners, possibly because the units were new and very efficient.

✿ Our washing machine and dishwasher were also new, water saving models. They only use about five gallons per run. Since connecting them to the tank involved putting a hole in the wall, we decided it wasn't worth it. We had also heard that people ran into problems with the water coming from washing machines because of the high concentration of soap. One lady was watering her roses strictly with water from her washer and the soap killed the roses.

✿ The shower is the best source we found other than rainwater. Our plumber connected one shower to our largest tank. Since the tank was 2500 gallons, we weren't worried about the small amount of soap that came out of the shower. We noticed a bump in the water level of the tank every time we took a shower!

Where to Store the Tank

1

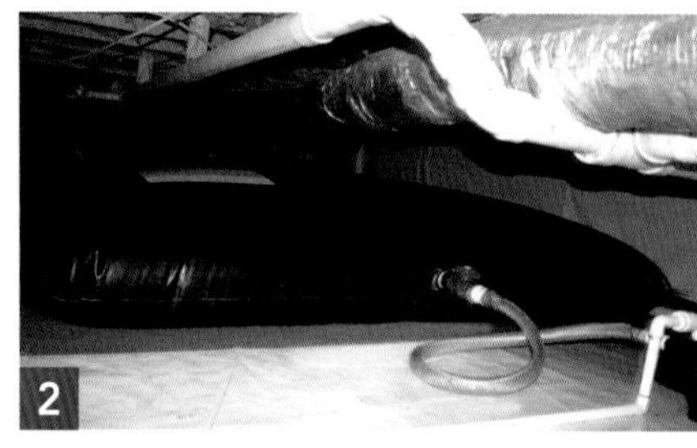
2

3

4

✿ Many homeowners on small, exposed lots are having their tanks buried, which is expensive, but the best way to hide them (tanks need to be reinforced with concrete or steel in order to keep from collapsing if they are going to be buried underground). Here are some other ideas for tank placement.

1. One of the tanks from our Georgia trial gardens is shown above, left. It is a 650 gallon tank. We stored it in an out-of-the-way utility area that also holds our air conditioning units. It has a submersible pump inside that pushes the water through the sprinkler system.

2. A 'Rainwater Pillow' (www.rainwaterpillow.com) is stored in the crawl space under a house.

3. Another 'Rainwater Pillow' is stored under a deck.

4. A rain barrel that is actually an old wine barrel is connected to a gutter. It sits out front of an old building, and is used to water their container gardens. A hose hooks up to the outlet.

Drip Irrigation Systems

Our first sprinkler system in our Georgia trial gardens was a traditional system that included heads that popped out of the ground. When the water problems started, we decided to switch to a drip system because they use less water. Our sprinkler man suggested we leave the old system in the ground and put a drip system on top of the ground in the beds. It was much easier to do it that way. We left the regular sprinklers in case we ever decide to water the grass. All of the beds and containers in our Georgia trial gardens are now hooked up to drip irrigation systems that feed off our rainwater tanks. We have been thrilled with the results.

How Drip Systems differ from Traditional Sprinklers

Drip systems emit water slowly, and directly to the roots of the plants instead of spraying water up in the air. They are used in beds and containers, but not on grass. There are many different types of emitters. We had our Georgia trial garden system designed by Rainbird Corporation (www.rainbird.com). We were extremely happy with the results. We had tried others products but had problems with difficulty of installation.

All of the containers in our Georgia trial gardens are hooked up to drip irrigation. Thirty containers can be watered with the flick of a switch! The container and column shown right from www.kinsmangarden.com

Advantages of Drip Systems

- Use 20 to 50 percent less water than traditional systems
- Since water doesn't hit the leaves of the plants, you'll have fewer leaf diseases
- The drip lines can go on top of the ground (hidden by mulch), making it much easier to install or move than underground systems.
- Drip systems are particularly useful for container gardens. We have quite a few container gardens, enough to require an hour of hand watering a day in the heat of summer. Once we had them hooked up to the drip system, they were watered automatically. Drip systems are also quite easy to hook up to container gardens - either from a hose or from a water tank.

Maintaining Your Garden

Healthy Pest Control

Many of the plants in this book don't attract any bugs that will harm the plant, so don't make the mistake of using toxic chemicals just to keep bugs from arriving. Many common garden pesticides are quite toxic to people and pets, so take great care before using them. Here are some tips for minimizing pesticide use:

✿ Healthy plants don't get as many pests as weak plants, just like people. Weak people are more likely to get sick than strong, healthy people. So, keep your plants healthy with the proper amount of water, fertilizer, and mulch.

✿ If you see holes in the leaves, let them alone for a while. Many bugs will take a few nibbles out of a plant and then abandon it for another, especially if the plant is healthy.

✿ Plants are particularly vulnerable to pests immediately after planting. They are in a weakened state and actually send out signals that attract pests. If you see bugs on the plants, they are normally very easy to remove. Aphids, for example, are clustered on the ends of the branches, eating the new growth. They look like little dots. Simply remove them by cutting the tip of the plant off and throwing it away. If they return, spray the plant with something that will make it taste bad to bugs but won't hurt the plant, like pure soap, garlic or pepper. None of these will kill birds, butterflies, pets, or people! Garden centers sell sprays with these natural products as their base.

✿ If you see holes in the leaves but cannot see the bug, they are probably snails, slugs, or caterpillars. Most stay hidden in the daytime, feeding only at night. If you can see the caterpillar, take a photo and have your county extension office identify it. If it is a butterfly caterpillar, you might want to leave it alone. It won't kill the plant, just eat some leaves (sometimes, quite a few leaves)!

If the damage becomes severe, take the leaves to the garden center or your county extension office so they can tell you what kind of bug or disease is doing the damage. Once you know the cause, ask them for the least-toxic remedy. If you buy a pesticide, look it up on the internet prior to using it to find out the risks. Also, the internet is a great source for natural remedies for pests and diseases. Check out www.gardeninsects.com for beneficial insects.

✿ The only really bad pest we have in our Georgia trial gardens is the Japanese beetle, which comes in May and stay until late June or early July. We made a big mistake when we first saw them: we bought Japanese beetle traps. They attracted the entire Japanese beetle population of north Georgia to our gardens! After three years, we no longer spray our beetles. They leave in June or July anyway, so we put up with some holes in the leaves of some plants. The only plants we had that were almost completely ruined by the beetles were hollyhocks, which we removed. They took quite a bit of our sweet potato vines as well. Our 'Knock Out' roses were quite chewed up in June, but recovered quickly in July after the beetles left.

Weeding: Some Time-Saving Tips

Weeds are always a problem, but particularly right after planting. Soil has been disturbed, which uncovers every weed seed in the area. And, water is being applied heavily. The new plantings have lots of space in between, which gives weeds room to grow. Here are some tips for saving time with your weeding chores:

✿ There are two classes of herbicides - pre-emergent herbicides and post-emergent. Look for products you trust, as many herbicides are toxic. More safe, natural products are coming on the market all the time. Many home-brew recipes for healthy weed killers are showing up. Check out http://www.garden-counselor-lawn-care.com/vinegar-weed-killer.html for some great ideas.

✿ Pre-emergent herbicides inhibit weed seeds from germinating. You spray (or broadcast) them on top of the mulch after planting The do not hurt the existing plants. They simpy inhibit weed seeds from germinating. There are many different types on the market. Follow the instructions closely. This type of herbicide can cut your weeding chores down by 70 percent. You need to re-apply them, however, so be sure to follow the instructions. Proper timing of the application is critical.

✿ Post-emergent herbicides are made up of two types: selective and not selective. Selective herbicides kill the targeted species like dandelions in a Bermuda lawn (Weed-B-Gon). Non-selective herbicides kill everything they touch - Glyphosate (Round-up) being the most common product. Spray in the early morning, when the wind is down. Herbicide drift (herbicide that hits plants you don't want to kill) is a common problem. Be sure to check out the dangers of any herbicide before using it.

✿ Weeds that sprout close to plants must be removed by hand.

✿ Mulch can greatly decrease weeding.

✿ Spacing your plants so they will eventually grow together without leaving much light on the ground is another way to combat weeds.

✿ Many weed cloths are on the market. Do not use plastic that will not let water through because it will not allow water to get through to the roots of the plants. Do not use weed cloth under mulch if you want the mulch to break down to add organic matter to the soil. If weed cloth is placed under paths or other areas that are not planted, the mulch or gravel must be thick enough to cover it.

✿ Boiling water will kill most weeds in your garden. Just fill up your tea kettle, boil some water, and pour away! Be careful to avoid the good plants with the hot water!

BUDGET GARDENING TIPS: FREE WEED CONTROL

✿ Newspapers, cardboard, or brown paper bags cut down on weeds until they disintegrate. Put them on top of the soil, wet them down (so they don't take water out of the soil), and cover them up with mulch.

CHEAP PEST CONTROL

✿ Before applying any home-made sprays to an entire plant, test one leaf to be sure the spray doesn't hurt the plant. Spray the top and bottom of one leaf and flower, and wait 24 hours. If no damage shows on the plant, spray the entire thing. Be sure to spray the tops and bottoms of the leaves.

✿ Soap and water works on aphids, mealybugs, mists, and some scale and thrips. Mix one tablespoon Ivory liquid in a gallon of water.

✿ Slugs and snails are attracted to beer. Sink a small can in the garden (so the top is level with the soil), and fill it with beer. The slugs and snails will drown in it.

✿ Salt spray works on spider mites. Mix two tablespoons of salt in a gallon of water.

✿ Make the leaves or flowers of the plant taste bad to any bug who tries to eat it. Mix some garlic cloves and hot peppers in your blender in a cup of water.

✿ For fungus and mildew, mix a tablespoon of baking soda and three tablespoons of vegetable oil in a gallon of water.

Fertilizer

General Information

Plants need 16 elements to grow. In ideal conditions, all of these elements come from nature. Picture a natural forest. Leaves fall from the trees and break down into organic matter that is constantly feeding the roots of the plants. Contrast that with a residential garden. Since plant roots grow out three times the diameter of the plant itself, much of their roots are covered with grass, houses, walkways, and driveways. So, we fertilize to give the plants the nutrients they need. There are many, different kinds of fertilizers on the market.

✿ Grass fertilizers are different from the fertilizer you will use on the rest of your plants. Buy a brand name you trust. Follow the instructions very carefully. It is easy to put too much and kill the grass. Also, check to see if the fertilizer stains, so you will be careful around hardscape. See page 19 to learn how often to feed your grass.

✿ Liquid fertilizers (usually come in powder form that is used with a hose-end sprayer) are good for the plants but not much else. They need to be applied with great frequency, like every two weeks. This frequent application is hard on you as well as your groundwater. The liquid goes into the groundwater and has been banned in some areas.

✿ Granular fertilizers also have drawbacks. They need to be applied less than liquids but more than slow-release fertilizers. Many of them stain hardscapes. Some are also quite harsh and capable of burning plants.

✿ Slow release fertilizers are best. They are milder, and most don't burn plants. The nutrients are released slowly, so they don't ruin your groundwater. And they don't have to be applied as frequently as the rest, making it easier for you as well.

✿ Organic fertilizers are made from things that were once living. This does not mean they are perfect, however. Some, like Milorganite, can easily burn plants. We used it generously around the edge of our planting beds one year to repel deer, and all the plants along the edge died! However, you can build up the nutrients in your soil over time by using organics. See pages 48 and 49 for information.

Fertilizer Tips

✿ Avoid placing harsh, granular fertilizers in planting holes. They can damage plant roots.

✿ Testing your soil is the best gauge of the need for fertilizer. It is important that you keep your soil healthy, because healthy plants store water more efficiently, therefore needing less water.

✿ Use slow release fertilizers to get a more uniform, water-efficient growth rate. They also decrease plant burn.

✿ Avoid overfertilization, which can cause plants to grow too quickly. Hyper growth can cause lanky, miss-shapen plants that require more water. Excess nitrogen present in many granular and liquid fertilizers is the primary culprit here.

✿ Fertilization frequency depends on the type of plant and the type of fertilizer used. For easy gardening, use a slow-release product that only has to be applied once a year (like the one recommended on the next page).

✿ Early spring is the best time to fertilize.

Best Slow Release Fertilizer: For Containers, Annuals, & Perennials

We have killed many plants with fertilizer and also have been through other fertilizers that simply didn't make the grade. They included some but not all of the elements a plant needs. Weird, hard-to-diagnose nutritional deficiencies developed that were time consuming, annoying, and definitely not easy.

Plants are like people - they need lots of different nutrients to keep them alive. If you have a vitamin deficiency, you might get quite sick. Same thing for a plant. Learn to read the fertilizer label to make sure it includes ***all*** the nutrients your plants need.

Most fertilizers include nitrogen, phosphorus (phosphate), and potassium (potash). Most, including some of the best-selling brands, don't include the micronutrients that plants need. ***So look for boron, copper, iron, manganese, and magnesium as well. Do not buy a slow-release product that doesn't include these micronutrients, or your plants could suffer later.***

We have only found one fertilizer that works perfectly every time. And it is forgiving. If you use too much, it doesn't burn the plants. It also is excellent for the environment, winning the 2005 Gulf Guardian Award from the EPA Gulf of Mexico Program Partnership.

This fertilizer is slow-release, meaning its little pellets release the nutrients over a period of time. It is a great improvement over the liquids you apply weekly with a hose sprayer! However, there are many slow-release products on the market. We have tested every one we could get our hands on, and none come close to this one. Some either don't last as long or don't have all the nutrients plants need. Others release all their nutrients at once if there is a lot of rain, burning the plants.

This fertilizer lasts nine months in 'average' conditions. If you see the plants yellowing a bit, just add some more. Sprinkle it on top of the potting mix, following the instructions on the label.

We recommend this fertilizer for all your container, annual, and perennial plantings. We use it on all our shrubs as well.

Signs that Plants Need Fertilizer

- The best method is to get a soil nutrient test through your county extension office.

- Abnormal leaf color is usually a sign of nutrient deficiency, although it is also symptomatic of some plant diseases.

- If all the leaves are lighter green than normal, the plant probably has a nitrogen deficiency.

Organic Fertilizer and Mulch

Differences between Chemical and Organic Fertilizers

✿ Chemical fertilizers can include any and all nutrients a plant needs to grow. Organic fertilizers either have primarily only one element or more in very low levels.

✿ Organic fertilizers are usually slow-release, which is good. However, they take quite a while to work. The idea behind organics is to slowly improve the structure of the soil, not provide quick nutrients. So, if your plants need nutrients quickly, like annuals or plants in container gardens, we recommend the chemical fertilizer shown on page 47. It has both slow and fast-acting elements, and it includes all 16 elements your plants need to grow. Plus, it is not an environmental threat.

✿ Organic fertilizers are free from many sources. All chemical fertilizers cost money.

✿ The long term effects of organics are excellent, in that they can greatly diminish the amount of chemicals needed in your yard.

✿ Learn about any organic fertilizer prior to using it, so that understand specific risks and benefits. Go to www.cdcg.org/goOrganic.html for more info.

Composting: Free Soil & Fertilizer from Kitchen and Garden Waste

✿ Composting is using garden and kitchen waste to create healthy soil. See www.guvswd.org/compost for complete instructions.

✿ You'll need a place to store your compost. We just have a waste pile in our backyard. Some people construct two chicken wire boxes next to their house. One box for new waste (which requires time to break down and turn into soil), and the other is for the compost that is ready to use. Many fancy, compost bins are for sale at garden centers and through online suppliers.

✿ It takes certain microorganisms to turn your leaves into soil. These microorganisms are present in green waste, like grass clippings or fruit and vegetable waste. Layer green waste with dry waste like leaves. Add water and mix it together occasionally. If it is not breaking down and turning into soil, buy a compost starter at your garden center.

✿ Some composters keep turning the waste to be sure it is well mixed. It will get quite hot (150 degrees), and turning helps that process work evenly. Other composters just leave the pile alone for a year or two and let nature do the work.

✿ Use compost as an amendment for new planting beds (see pages 30 to 31 for instructions) or to spread around existing plants in your beds. Organic gardeners use compost instead of chemical fertilizers.

✿ Wear gloves and long-sleeved shirts when handling compost to keep from getting bacterial infections.

✿ University of Minnesota reports that there have been rare cases of compost piles catching on fire, without anyone lighting a match. No documented cases have been reported on compost piles under seven feet tall.

✿ Avoid putting weeds in your compost pile. Weed seeds could end up in your finished compost!

✿ Avoid putting in meat or dairy products, pet manure, fats, or oils.

Building Up Your Soil Naturally

The Role of Organic Mulch

✿ Mulch is discussed on page 38. Organic mulch acts much like leaves in a forest. It breaks down into the nutrients your plants need to grow. Apply it at least once a year.

Manure

✿ Livestock manure (sheep, cattle, horses, pigs, chickens) provides nutrients to the soil that plants need to grow. It also helps the water holding capacity of the soil.

✿ Use only what you need, as manure contains nitrates that can leach into the groundwater. Take your soil to your local county extension office for testing before applying manure.

✿ Weed seeds are common in free manure (other than chicken droppings). Purchased manure has probably been sterilized, meaning no weed seeds.

✿ Chicken manure has the most nutrients, but also is the 'hottest,' burning plants (more than the rest) unless it has been composted.

Homemade Fertilizer

✿ Coffee grounds are wonderful for acid loving plants, like azaleas and roses. Just sprinkle the grounds on the soil around the plants. In addition to being acidic, coffee grounds include nitrogen, magnesium, and potassium, all essential elements for plant growth.

BUDGET GARDENING TIPS:

FREE MULCH

✿ Rake the pine straw in your yard and sweep it from your street. Check with your neighbors to see if you can rake up their pine straw as well.

✿ Some tree companies give away chipped wood. Look them up in the yellow pages and ask. If you see a tree company chipping up trees in your neighborhood, ask them if they will dump it at your house.

✿ Some counties will deliver free mulch. Call and ask. Be sure to ask how much they deliver so that you'll know if you have room for it.

✿ Free mulch is not sterilized like many sold mulches, so you might get weed seeds. Also, fresh tree mulch needs to age for six months to a year before you can use it on your garden.

FREE FERTILIZER

✿ Look in the yellow pages for stables. Call and ask them if they have any manure they want hauled away, or if they know anyone who does.

✿ Manure must be aged six to twelve months because it burns plants when it is fresh.

✿ Only use manure from herbivores, like horses, chickens and cows. Manure from meat eaters, like dogs and cats, can contain unwanted bacteria.

Color Your Garden!

Easiest Colorful Plants

✿ The easiest, colorful plants are shown on pages 22 and 23.

✿ Shrubs, trees, and vines are the easiest sources of color on the whole. Most don't require either deadheading (removing dead flowers) or dividing, which is the norm with perennials. Some don't require any care at all for years!

✿ Annuals offer the most color for a long time (five to seven months for blue ribbon annuals), but they have to be replaced each year.

✿ Perennials offer color from two weeks to five months. Many require deadheading (removing of dead flowers) to look good. Most require dividing every three to five years. Some exceptions to both of those rules are 'Miss Huff' lantana, 'Homestead Purple' verbena, purple queen, agastache, baptisia, heuchera, hibiscus, hostas, lenten roses, and woodland phlox. These eleven perennials are the easiest of all, but all of them require at least one cutback per year. Although that quick chore might seem easy to most gardeners, some shrubs, vines, and trees don't even require that.

✿ Bulbs are perennials with short but very intense bloom periods, adding more color impact than other perennials. They are worth planting to give that traffic-stopping impact that many of us are looking for. Most are easy to grow. Use different bulbs in clumps throughout your garden, where they show extremely well when blooming but hide when they are not in flower.

Perennials, Shrubs, Vines, and Trees with the Longest Color Period

These plants offer color from leaves or flowers for more than five months each year. If you really like color, use them as the main plants in your garden, accenting with plants that have shorter color seasons.

Perennials, Shrubs, Vines, and Trees with the Strongest Color Impact

These plants are the traffic-stoppers - with more color impact than any other reasonably easy plant for the south. Most plants with a lot of color impact don't bloom for long. These average two to four weeks of flowers, except for the crapemytle (two to four months) and the Joe Pye weed (one to two months). Use these plants to accent a garden loaded with longer bloomers.

- 1ST Aster 'Purple Dome' Profile: Page 112
- 1ST Azaleas Profile: Page 200
- 1ST Carolina Silverbell Profile: Page 270
- 1ST Chaste Tree Profile: Page 272
- 1ST Crapemyrtle Profiles: Pages 214 & 274
- 1ST Daffodils Profile: Page 126
- 1ST Dogwood Profile: Page 280
- 1ST Forsythia Profile: Page 216
- 1ST Hydrangea Profiles: Pages 226 - 233
- 2ND Ice Plant Profile: Page 148
- 1ST Iris Profile: Page 152
- 1ST Joe Pye Weed Profile: Page 150
- 1ST Kerria Profile: Page 238
- 1ST Lilies Profiles: Pages 158 - 163
- 1ST Phlox, Woodland Profile: Page 164
- 1ST Redbud Profile: Page 304
- 2ND Sedum Profile: Page 178
- 1ST Spiraea 'Bridalwreath' Profile: Page 248
- 1ST Viburnum 'Chinese Snowball' Profile: Page 252
- 1ST Viburnum 'Doublefile' Profile: Page 254

Rebloomers

Encore Azalea Profile: Page 202

Plant breeders have been quite busy recently producing new plants that bloom more than the originals. New daylilies, azaleas, irises, hydrangeas, and many more flowering plants now bloom longer than their ancestors. Look for plants labeled 'rebloomers' and you will be pleasantly surprised!

'Mini Penny' Reblooming Hydrangea Profile: Page 228

Seasonal Gardens

Most of our southern plants are seasonal bloomers. Luckily, the temperate climate of the south proves mild enough to produce blooms for twelve months each year. The color calendar on the next four pages organizes the plants by season. Have fun planting seasonal gardens, one for each of our four seasons. Since each garden will have lots of plants blooming at the same time, the effect is quite spectacular!

Color Calendar

This listing shows plants that are likely to have color during a particular month, either from leaves or flowers. Oak trees, for example, don't have significant flower color, but have nice leaf color in fall, so they are listed as fall color. The timing of both leaf color and flower color varies throughout the south, depending primarily on temperature, which varies from year to year. Azaleas can bloom for about two weeks, beginning either in March or April, depending on how far north you live. So, if you see azaleas listed in both April and May, it doesn't mean they bloom the whole time. See the individual plant profiles for more exact information.

January

Aucuba
Camellia
Daffodils
Loropetalum
Witch hazel
Yucca

February

Aucuba
Camellia
Daffodils
Lenten Rose
Loropetalum
Witch hazel
Yucca

March

Aucuba
Azalea, deciduous
Azalea, evergreen
Camellia
Daffodils
Dogwood
Forsythia
Iris
Kerria
Lenten rose
Lily, Asiatic
Loropetalum
Phlox, woodland
Redbud
Witch hazel
Yucca

April

Amsonia
Aucuba
Azalea, deciduous
Azalea, evergreen
Baptisia
Camellia
Carolina silverbell
Carolina jessamine
Daffodils
Dogwood
Forsythia
Hawthorn
Heuchera
Honeysuckle
Hosta
Indian hawthorne
Iris
Kerria
Lenten rose
Lily, Asiatic and oriental
Loropetalum
Maple, Japanese
Phlox, woodland
Redbud
Rose
Smoke tree
Spanish bluebells
Spiraea, bridlewreath
Spriaea, gold mound
Viburnum, Chinese snowball
Viburnum, doublefile
Yucca

May

Abelia
Agastache
Amsonia
Aucuba
Azalea, deciduous
Azalea, evergreen
Baptisia
Canna
Carolina silverbell
Coneflower
Hawthorn
Heuchera
Hibiscus
Hosta
Hydrangea, mophead
Ice plant
Lily, Asiatic and oriental
Loropetalum
Maple, Japanese
Phlox, woodland
Purple heart
Roses
Scabiosa
Smoke tree
Spanish bluebells
Spiraea, bridlewreath
Spiraea, gold mound
Stokesia
Yucca

June

Abelia
Agastache
Althea, rose of Sharon
Aucuba
Azalea, deciduous
Black-eyed Susan
Butterfly bush
Canna
Chaste tree (vitex)
Coneflower
Coreopsis
Crocosmia
Daylily
Heuchera
Hibiscus
Hosta
Hydrangea, Annabelle
Hydrangea, mophead
Hydrangea, oakleaf
Ice plant
Lily, naked ladies, magic
Lantana 'Miss Huff'
Loropetalum
Magnolia
Maple, Japanese
Phlox 'David'
Purple heart
Red hot poker plant
Roses
Salvia
Scabiosa
Smoke tree
Stokesia
Verbena 'Homestead Purple'
Yarrow
Yucca

Perennials, Shrubs, Vines, & Trees

July

Abelia
Agastache
Althea, rose of Sharon
Aucuba
Azalea, deciduous
Black-eyed Susan
Butterfly bush
Canna
Chaste tree
Coneflower
Coreopsis
Crapemyrtle
Crocosmia
Daylily
Heuchera
Hibiscus
Hosta
Hydrangea, Annabelle
Hydrangea, oakleaf, panicle
Hydrangea, mophead (rebloomers)
Lantana 'Miss Huff'
Lily, naked lady or magic
Lily, oriental
Loropetalum
Magnolia
Maple, Japanese
Phlox 'David'
Purple heart
Red hot poker plant
Roses
Salvia
Scabiosa
Smoke tree
Verbena 'Homestead Purple'
Yarrow
Yucca

August

Abelia
Agastache
Althea, rose of Sharon
Aucuba
Black-eyed Susan
Butterfly bush
Canna
Chaste tree (vitex)
Coneflower
Coreopsis
Crapemyrtle
Crocosmia
Daylily
Heuchera
Hibiscus
Hosta
Hydrangea, mophead (rebloomers)
Hydrangea, oakleaf
Hydrangea, panicle
Joe Pye weed
Lantana 'Miss Huff'
Lily, naked ladies or magic
Lily, oriental and spider
Loropetalum
Magnolia
Maple, Japanese
Purple heart
Roses
Salvia
Scabiosa
Sedum 'Autumn Joy'
Smoke tree
Verbena 'Homestead Purple'
Yarrow
Yucca

September

Abelia
Agastache
Aucuba
Azalea, rebloomer
Black-eyed Susan
Butterfly bush
Canna
Chaste tree (vitex)
Coreopsis
Crapemyrtle
Daylily
Heuchera
Hibiscus
Hosta
Hydrangea, Annabelle
Hydrangea, mophead (rebloomers)
Hydrangea, panicle
Joe Pye weed
Lantana 'Miss Huff'
Lily, naked ladies or magic
Lily, spider
Loropetalum
Magnolia
Maple, Japanese
Purple heart
Roses
Salvia
Scabiosa
Sedum
Smoke tree
Verbena 'Homestead Purple'
Yucca

October (including fall leaf color)

Abelia
Aster 'Purple Dome'
Aucuba
Azalea, rebloomer
Bald cypress
Butterfly bush
Camellia
Chinese elm
Chinese pistachio
Coreopsis
Crapemyrtle
Dogwood
Ginkgo
Hawthorn
Heuchera
Hibiscus
Hosta
Hydrangea, Annabelle
Hydrangea, mophead (rebloomers)
Hydrangea, panicle
Lantana 'Miss Huff'
Lily, spider
Loropetalum
Maple, Japanese
Oak, shumard and willow
Phlox 'David'
Purple heart
Red maple
Roses
Salvia
Scabiosa
Sedum 'Autumn Joy'
Smoke tree
Verbena 'Homestead Purple'
Yucca

November (including fall leaf color)

Abelia
American holly (berries)
Aster 'Purple Dome'
Aucuba
Bald cypress
Butterfly bush
Camellia
Chinese elm
Chinese pistachio
Crapemyrtle
Dogwood
Foster's holly (berries)
Ginkgo
Hawthorn
Hydrangea, Annabelle
Hydrangea, panicle
Loropetalum
Maple, Japanese
Nellie Stevens holly (berries)
Oak, shumard and willow
Red maple
Rose
Salvia
Sedum 'Autumn Joy'
Smoke tree
Verbena 'Homestead Purple'
Winterberry (berries)
Witch hazel
Yaupon holly (berries)
Yucca

December

Aucuba
Camellia
Daffodil
Loropetalum
Witch hazel
Yucca

Chapter 2

Annuals

Annuals are plants that just last one season. Why buy annuals when you could have perennials or shrubs that live much longer?

✿ Annuals have a much higher percentage of color than most flowering perennials or shrubs.

✿ Annuals bloom quite a bit longer than most perennials or shrubs. Azaleas, for example, are gorgeous in bloom but only flower for about two weeks. Even the re-blooming azaleas bloom for only about four weeks. Expect 28 to 31 weeks of blooms from most of the annuals in this chapter.

✿ Annuals are quite a bit less expensive than perennials or shrubs.

✿ Annuals are fun! And who can resist stopping at a garden center in spring and loading up the trunk with beautiful flowers? Many cost less than a dollar!

Annuals bloom all year in most of the south, with summer annuals lasting for about five or six months and winter annuals the same.

Be sure to take this book with you when you shop for annuals. Many annuals are for sale that don't last an entire season. Look them up in this book, so you know what to expect before you buy them!

Above: Butterfly on a lantana blossom

Left: Our Georgia trial gardens in August, showing many of our highest performing annuals. Lantana is planted on the ground. The yellow lantana on the left conceals a large container planted with red dragon wing begonias and golden shrimp plants. The basket on the column (from www.kinsmangarden.com) is planted with a croton as the centerpiece and is surrounded by coleus, sweet potato vines, and some blanket petunias at the end of their bloom cycle. Go to www.easygardencolor.com to see a series of three-minute videos about Pamela (one of our authors) installing a column and planting one of these side-planted containers.

1ST Angelonia

CHARACTERISTICS

Plant Type: Tropical perennial, grown as annual.

Average Size: About 18 to 30 inches tall by 8 to 12 inches wide, depending on variety and growing conditions. 'Serena' angelonia grows to about 18 inches tall by 12 inches wide in the south.

Growth Rate: Fast

Leaf: Narrow, pointed, dark green

Flower: Small flowers resembling orchids clustered on long spikes.

Lifespan: 4 to 7 months

Origin: Mexico and West Indies

Spacing: About 8 to 12 inches on center (measure from the center of each plant). Closer in containers.

Cautions: None known

Colors: Purple, pink, white, and purple-pink bicolors.

1. Serena angelonia, light purple
2. Serena angelonia, medium purple
3. Serena angelonia, white

Angelonia is one of the best annuals for southern summers. It easily meets the blue ribbon* requirement of blooming all season long with no additional care other than water.

'Serena' angelonia does beautifully planted in the ground or in containers

Many different angelonias have been released in the last ten years. Some have not done well for us. The 'Serena' series has done incredibly well, blooming for the entire growing season in our trial gardens with very little care. Plant the Serenas when danger of frost is over, and don't touch them for the entire growing season - other than periodic watering.

Regional Differences: Angelonia grows well throughout the south.

Color Period: Spring to fall, continuously. Plants often bloom a little less in very wet summers.

Buying Tips: Angelonias are generally easy to find in your garden centers in spring and summer. We look for the 'Serena' series since it has done well for us in the past. If the label just says 'Angelonia,' see if the colors are similar to the ones shown to the left. If so, it is probably the 'Serena' series.

**Blue ribbon plants are defined on page 12. For blue ribbon performance, follow the planting and maintenance guidelines on pages 28 to 49.*

Companions: Angelonia is a great plant for mixed flower gardens because its texture is quite different from most other plants. Mixing plants with different flower textures for example, spiky angelonia with round petunias, makes each flower type stand out better. Some high-performing, round flowers that bloom the same time as angelonia include pentas, lantana, and petunias.

'Serena' angelonia with some companion plants

Dwarf Pentas are great companions for angelonia because the flowers are a different shape, and they are slightly shorter, working well as a mid layer. Pentas don't bloom continuously, like angelonia, but bloom for most of the summer. Both thrive in full sun to light shade and are very easy to grow.

Lantana makes a gorgeous front border for angelonia, with red pentas planted in between the two. Lantana blooms all spring, summer, and fall - like the angelonia. And, mixing red, purple and yellow creates wonderful color impact. Look for the low-growing lantanas like, 'New Gold,' so it won't grow taller than the angelonia. Stick to full sun only for this combination.

Petunias, particularly the 'Wave' series, work well with angelonia both in the ground as well as in containers. Try purple angelonia bordered with bright pink or red petunias in full sun. Also, combine these two in containers with angelonia in the center and petunias, particularly trailing 'Wave' petunias, planted around the edge.

GROWING CONDITIONS

Light: Light shade to full sun

Water: Medium after establishment. Likes water once or twice a week during the growing season, depending on its environment. Requires more water when grown in containers.

Soil: For the garden, plant in any fertile, well-drained soil that has been enriched with organic matter. Use only good-quality potting mix for containers. See page 30 for specific instructions on soil preparation.

Hardiness: Use as an annual in above freezing temperatures. Some have reported angelonia growing as a perennial in zones 9 and 10. We have tried it in zone 10, and it only lived about 6 months.

Propagation: Seed, rooted cuttings.

Pest Problems: Rare

PLANTING & MAINTENANCE

When to Plant: Spring or summer

Trimming: The 'Serena' series makes it through the summer without a trim. Taller varieties start falling over mid summer. Should this occur, shear them back by one-third to restore their form and encourage a late flush of fresh blossoms.

Fertilization: Use the fertilizer described on page 47 only on planting day.

UNIVERSITY AWARDS

2007: Mississippi Medallion ('Serena').

2002, 2004, 2005, 2007: Top 10 from North Carolina State University ('AngelMist Spreading Pink,' 'AngelMist Dark Pink,' 'AngelMist Lavender Stripe' and 'AngelMist Light Pink').

1ST Begonia, Dragon Wing

CHARACTERISTICS

Plant Type: Annual

Average Size: About 12 to 18 inches tall by 8 to 12 inches wide.

Growth Rate: Medium

Leaf: Dark, glossy green. About 3 inches long by 1 1/2 inches wide. Shaped like a wing.

Flower: Hanging clusters that measure about 4 inches across.

Lifespan: 6 to 12 months but won't take freezes. Easily lasts for an entire southern growing season.

Origin: Begonias are native to the new world tropics. This one is a hybrid.

Spacing: About 12 inches on center (measure from the center of each plant). Closer in containers.

Cautions: Irritant, if eaten, which can result in breathing difficulties. Seldom damaged by deer.

Colors: Red or pink

UNIVERSITY AWARDS

1998: Exceptional performance winner from North Carolina State University.

2002: Mississippi Medallion Winner.

2000: Top 10 from North Carolina State University.

2005: University of Georgia Gold Medal Winner.

1. Pink dragon wing begonia
2. Red dragon wing begonia

Dragon wing begonias are one of the best annuals for southern gardens - in light or medium shade. They rate a blue ribbon* because they bloom all season long, with no attention other than water.

Dragon wings grow beautifully planted in the ground or in containers

Dragon wing begonias are quickly becoming one of the most valuable sources of garden color in the south. Plant them when danger of frost is over, and don't touch them for the entire growing season - other than periodic watering. They are beautiful in shade or sun gardens, with a high percentage of color, low water requirements, and a distinctive appearance. Dragon wings are larger and showier than wax begonias but share the begonia habit of a long bloom period with very little care.

Regional Differences: Dragon wing begonias do well throughout the south

Color Period: Spring, summer, and fall - continuously. They keep blooming until the first freeze.

Buying Tips: Good dragon wing begonias are simple to find at your local garden center. We have bought many that are simply labeled 'Dragon Wing Begonias,' and all have done extremely well. They look gorgeous in the larger, gallon nursery pots. However, they don't look spectacular in smaller, four inch nursery pots. Don't hesitate to buy them in small containers, however, because they will fill out before you know it. Also, be sure to look for dark green leaves and red or pink flowers, like the ones shown left. Lots of angel wing begonias (with spotted leaves and lighter flowers) are for sale with similar characteristics, but they don't bloom anywhere near as long.

**Blue ribbon plants are defined on page 12. For blue ribbon performance, follow the planting and maintenance guidelines on pages 28 to 49.*

Companions: Pink dragon wings work well with pastel colors. Either pink or red dragon wings look wonderful with white. Both also do quite well paired with bright colors - particularly yellow, blue, and purple. Try either color with the bright plants shown below - planted either in the ground or in containers.

Dragon wing begonias with some companion plants

Trailing Torenia makes a great border for dragon wings. It is frequently sold in hanging baskets but also thrives when planted in the ground. The purple color is a perfect contrast to the red begonia. Plant this combination in light shade to partial sun, but in a location where they get a break from afternoon sun in the heat of summer.

Golden Shrimp Plant is one of the best companions for dragon wings because both the flower color and shape are different. Plant the shrimp plants behind the shorter dragon wings because the dragon wings are easier to trim if they grow taller than the shrimps. Shrimp plants last all season, like the dragon wings, and require no care other than water, if planted correctly. Plant this combination in light shade to some sun but in a location where they get some break from afternoon sun in the heat of summer.

'Dark Star' Coleus is another purple plant that thrives either in the ground or in containers - bordering dragon wing begonias. This coleus lasted for the entire growing season in our trial gardens. Plant this combination in light shade to full sun but in a location where they get some break from afternoon sun in the heat of summer.

GROWING CONDITIONS

Light: Medium to light shade. Takes full sun in early summer and fall, but suffers with this much light in the middle of summer. We have put them in full sun in the hottest part summer; we had to put up with some blotches appearing on the leaves and the green color bleaching out a bit.

Water: Medium after establishment. Likes water once or twice a week during the growing season, depending on its environment. Requires more water when grown in containers. See pages 34 to 37 for more information

Soil: For the garden, plant in any fertile, well-drained soil that has been enriched with organic matter. Use only good-quality potting mix for containers. See page 30 for specific instructions on soil preparation.

Hardiness: Use as an annual. Takes temperatures down to 32 degrees.

Propagation: Cuttings

Pest Problems: Rare. We have never had a problem in over 10 years of trials. However, if the leaves or stems develop brown spots or slimy areas, the plant has fungus. Cut down on water. Spray with a fungicide only if it becomes severe. If holes appear in the leaves, it is from caterpillars or snails.

PLANTING & MAINTENANCE

When to Plant: Spring is ideal, so you can enjoy the plants for the entire growing season. However, the plants can be planted anytime the temperatures are over 32 degrees.

Trimming: None needed unless they grow taller than you like. Pinch them back anytime this occurs.

Fertilization: Use the fertilizer described on page 47 only on planting day.

Begonia, Wax

1ST

CHARACTERISTICS

Plant Type: Annual

Average Size: About 8 inches tall by 8 inches wide.

Growth Rate: Medium

Leaf: Rounded, glossy green or bronze leaves, 1 to 2 inches long and wide.

Flower: Hundreds of small, open-centered blossoms.

Lifespan: 4 to 7 months

Origin: Brazil

Spacing: About 8 inches on center (measure from the center of each plant). Closer in containers.

Cautions: Irritant, if eaten which can result in breathing difficulties. Seldom damaged by deer.

Colors: White, red, or pink flowers on green or bronze leaves.

1. *White wax begonia*
2. *Pink wax begonia*
3. *Red wax begonia*
4. *'Cherry Blossom' double wax begonia (which performed beautifully in our trials).*

Wax begonias are one of the best annuals for southern gardens - in sun or shade. They rate a blue ribbon* because they bloom all season long, with no attention other than water.

Red and pink wax begonias with silver dusty miller planted in front

Wax begonias bloom constantly, from early spring until the first freeze takes them down. Their constancy of color is truly remarkable as is their ability to adapt to sun or partial shade. Wax begonias also transition beautifully from cool to hot weather and back to cool weather again in the fall. Plants grow into rounded mounds that always look neat with very little care. Wax begonias are small enough to use as edging plants along walkways, and they are unsurpassed for unifying flower beds planted with a number of different flowers.

Regional Differences: Wax begonias are easy to grow throughout the south. In zone nine, they often continue to bloom well into early winter.

Color Period: Late spring to late fall, blooming constantly

Buying Tips: Good wax begonias are one of the easiest annuals to find at your local garden center. We have bought many that are simply labeled 'Wax Begonias,' and all have done extremely well. If you need quite a few, look for them in the money-saving eighteen packs.

**Blue ribbon plants are defined on page 12. For blue ribbon performance, follow the planting and maintenance guidelines on pages 28 to 49.*

Botanical Name: *Begonia x semperflorens-cultorum*
Family: Begoniaceae

Companions: Wax begonias are truly go-with-everything flowers. Their neat, mounded form brings discipline to the scene when sprawling, informal plants – like cleomes – are used as background plants. They work in formal gardens as well. Try the pink begonias with the plants shown below - planted either in the ground or in containers.

Wax begonias with some companion plants

White Begonias are one of the best annuals to use for borders of pink begonias or any other flowers in your garden. They work with all colors and last the entire season with no care other than water, if they are planted correctly.

Persian Shield can be added for a dramatic color accent with pink and white begonias. Alternate the two colors of begonias as a border around the Persian shield, either in a container or in the ground. This combination lasts all season, from spring to the first frost of fall. Plant them in full sun to light shade.

Pink and White Caladiums are a natural companion for begonias. Use begonias that coordinate with the colors in the caladium leaves. Plant the begonias as the border because they are smaller than the caladiums. Most caladium cultivars require shade, but some newer ones take sun. Generally, the thick-leafed varieties take more sun than the thinner-leafed types. Either works well with the light requirements of wax begonias.

GROWING CONDITIONS

Light: Light shade to full sun.

Water: Medium after establishment. Likes water once or twice a week during the growing season, depending on its environment. Requires more water in containers.

Soil: For the garden, plant in any fertile, well-drained soil that has been enriched with organic matter. Use only good-quality potting mix for containers. See page 30 for specific instructions on soil preparation.

Hardiness: If you cover plants to protect them through light frosts in fall, they will continue to bloom until the first hard freeze kills the plants.

Propagation: Seeds or cuttings

Pest Problems: Rare. Root rot can develop if plants are kept too wet.

PLANTING & MAINTENANCE

When to Plant: Spring or summer

Trimming: Should plants become leggy in late summer, shearing them back by 1/3 to restore their form and encourage a late flush of fresh blossoms.

Fertilization: Use the fertilizer described on page 47 only on planting day.

UNIVERSITY AWARDS

1991, 1992, 1997: Exceptional performance winner from North Carolina State University ('Ambassador Rose Blush,' 'Inferno Red,' 'Eureka Bronze Rose,' 'Stara Clara Rose,' and 'Rio Pink').

2006: Top 10 from North Carolina State University ('Emperor Pink,' 'Emporer Rose,' 'Braveheart Rose Bicolor').

Cabbages or Kale, Ornamental

CHARACTERISTICS

Plant Type: Annual

Average Size: About 8 to 12 inches tall by equally as wide.

Growth Rate: Medium

Leaf: Large, cabbage-type leaves with curled or frilled edges.

Flower: Yellow flowers in spring; grown primarily for foliage.

Lifespan: 4 to 7 months

Origin: North Africa and Europe

Spacing: About 10 inches on center (measure from the center of each plant). Closer in containers.

Cautions: Leaves are edible and often used for garnishes, but they are not as flavorful as those of culinary kale. Occasionally eaten by deer.

Colors: White, red, pink, or purple

1. *Cabbages get their color during cool weather. When you buy them in fall, they look grey.*
2. *As the temperatures cool, their leaves turn beautiful colors, like this white one...*
3. *...or this purple one.*

Ornamental cabbages and kale are two of the best sources for color when the temperatures cool. Plant them in fall, and enjoy until the temperatures drop to about twenty degrees. They miss a ribbon because of their temperature limitations as well as the fact that they are newcomers to the south.

Cabbages are planted in the side holes of a side-planted basket from www.kinsmangarden.com. Juncus grass and pansies are planted in the top.

Ornamental cabbages and kale join pansies and violas as the stars of winter gardens in the south. They make wonderful companions for these flowers but won't last through the low temperatures that both pansies and violas can handle. Plant them in a warm spot (south side of your home or on a sheltered patio), and you can enjoy them for most of the winter with little to no care other than occasional water. Cabbages do quite well in containers but feel the cold more, showing damage at about 25 degrees. Most grow well in the ground until the temperatures dip into the low 20's.

Regional Differences: Shows damage in the ground when the temperatures dip into the low 20's. In containers, shows damage at about 25 degrees.

Color Period: Cabbage leaves need cool weather to show leaf color. Expect to buy them in fall with dull, gray leaves that quickly begin to color with the first cold spell. Cabbages flower in spring with large, yellow spikes. Some people like the flowers, and some don't. Cut them off if they bother you.

Buying Tips: We have only used these plants for two years in our trial gardens. All of them have done well, but there are many more we haven't yet tried.

Companions: Mix cabbages with other plants that have color in winter, like snapdragons, dusty miller, violas, and pansies. Since violas and pansies bloom longer than the others, they are the highest performing flower companions for cabbages. Both violas and pansies show some damage when temperatures drop into the low 20's, but they recover quickly and keep blooming until early summer.

Choose companions you like for the different-colored ornamental cabbages. Here are some ideas for the purple ones.

Ornamental cabbages with some companion plants

Yellow Violas are great companions for cabbages because they will bloom the entire time the cabbages thrive - and yellow is a great companion for purple. Use violas if you plant the cabbages in a partial shade situation because they take shade better than pansies. The violas grow shorter than the pansies, so use them as a border.

Red Pansies contrast well with purple cabbages. Use them in sun. For maximum color impact, plant the cabbages with both red and yellow flowers. Pansies grow shorter than cabbages, so use them as a border.

Light Purple Pansies provide a quieter combination than the bright red and yellow. Add some pink for a gentle contrast. The pansies will bloom the entire time the cabbages thrive. Pansies grow shorter than cabbages, so use them as a border in sunny situations.

GROWING CONDITIONS

Light: Light shade to full sun. Plants need 6 hours of sun daily to develop the best leaf color.

Water: Medium in warm weather, low in cool weather. We seldom water our cabbages in winter. Take care to check the dryness of the soil if a hard cold spell is forecast, however. Severe cold spells frequently dry out the soil, so water before one arrives.

Soil: For the garden, plant in any fertile, well-drained soil that has been enriched with organic matter. Use only good-quality potting mix for containers. See page 30 for specific instructions on soil preparation.

Hardiness: Do best in temperatures ranging from 20 to 60 degrees in the ground; 25 degree minimum in containers.

Propagation: Seeds

Pest Problems: Caterpillars occasionally. We have never had a pest in our trial gardens.

PLANTING & MAINTENANCE

When to Plant: Fall. For winter hardiness, plant early enough in fall (early to mid-September) for the plants to establish themselves before the cold arrives.

Trimming: None generally needed. Trim the flowers off in spring if you don't like them.

Fertilization: Use the fertilizer described on page 47 only on planting day.

UNIVERSITY AWARDS

2001: Top 10 from North Carolina State University (Kale 'Flamingo Plumes').

2002: Top 10 from North Carolina State University (Kale 'Flamingo Plumes,' 'White Peacock' and Coral Prince').

1ST

Caladium

Caladiums are one of the best choices for annual leaf color for southern gardens - in sun or shade. They rate a blue ribbon* because they bloom all season long, with no attention other than water.

CHARACTERISTICS

Plant Type: Tropical perennial tuber, grown as an annual.

Average Size: 8 to 20 inches tall, 10 to 14 inches wide. Be sure to know the mature size of the variety you buy so you can use it appropriately.

Growth Rate: Medium

Leaf: Large heart- or lance-shaped leaves, splashed with red, pink, white and green; often with contrasting veins.

Flower: Insignificant, finger-shaped spikes.

Lifespan: 6 to 7 months

Origin: South America

Spacing: About 8 to 12 inches on center (measure from the center of each plant).

Cautions: Poisonous, if eaten; sap may irritate skin. Occasionally damaged by deer.

Colors: Red, pink, white, or green

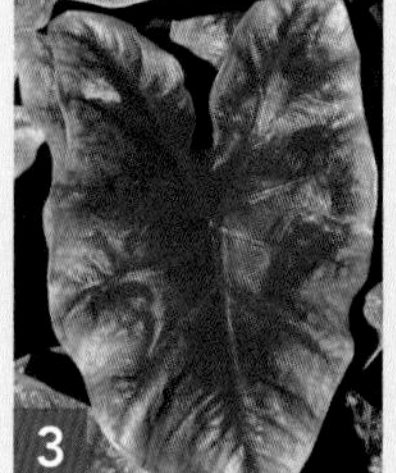

1. *Caladium 'Candidum'*
2. *Caladium 'Carolyn Whorton'*
3. *Caladium 'Frieda Hemple'*
4. *Caladium 'White Queen'*

White caladiums surrounding Miscanthus grass

Caladiums have been popular throughout the south for generations. Plant them when the temperatures have warmed into the 70's, and don't touch them for the entire growing season - other than periodic watering and removing a brown leaf or two. Even in the very hot weather that is typical of southern summers, caladiums appear cool and elegant. Traditionally used only in shade gardens, some new cultivars do equally as well in sun.

Regional Differences: Caladiums need temperatures above 70 degrees to grow. In zones eight and nine, the knobby tubers can be planted directly in the ground in spring. In zones six and seven, begin with purchased plants, or start the tubers inside to give them a head start on summer.

Color Period: The flowers are insignificant, but the plants will produce a nice show of colorful leaves about six weeks after planting tubers, or by early summer. With good care, they will keep their handsome good looks until nights cool down in the fall.

Buying Tips: All caladiums we have planted, regardless of the name on the tag, have done well for us. However, they come in a wide variety of sizes, from eight to 20 inches tall. Be sure you know the height of the ones you are buying. While garden centers are ideal choices for purchasing caladium plants, a huge variety of tubers can be purchased online or from catalogs. Tubers are generally fresher when purchased directly from a grower.

**Blue ribbon plants are defined on page 12. For blue ribbon performance, follow the planting and maintenance guidelines on pages 28 to 49.*

Companions: Since wide- and narrow-leafed plants show well next to each other, combine caladiums with the narrowest leaves you can find, as shown with the grasses, left. The narrow leaves of the grass really accentuate the large leaves of the caladiums.

Caladiums make excellent centerpieces for container gardens. Whether you use them in the ground or in containers, mix them with leaves or flowers that coordinate with the leaf patterns as shown in the examples below.

Caladiums with some companion plants

Wax Begonias form nice borders for caladiums because they bloom the entire time the caladiums thrive. Although these begonias are shorter than most caladiums, check the caladium label to be sure the variety you are buying grows over 12 inches tall, so it will remain taller than the begonias. Choose the color of the begonia flower to coordinate with the leaf of the caladium. Since wax begonias take sun or shade, they will do well with either sun or shade caladiums.

Lime Coleus works well as a mid layer, in between the caladiums and the begonias. Once again, coordinate the coleus color with the caladium leaf. Be sure the caladiums are on the tall side, at least 18 inches tall.

Pink Torenia coordinates well bordering this caladium in sun (if the caladium take sun) to light shade. Although torenia doesn't last quite as long as the begonias, the combination looks terrific!

GROWING CONDITIONS

Light: Most cultivars require shade, but some newer ones take sun.

Water: Medium in shade and high in sun. Ideal water is twice a week in shade and three to four times a week in sun (after establishment). Requires more water when grown in containers.

Soil: For the garden, plant in any fertile, well-drained soil that has been enriched with organic matter. Use only good-quality potting mix for containers.

Hardiness: Grows wherever temperatures stay about 70 degrees for a few months.

Propagation: Tubers

Pest Problems: Slugs and snails may cause light damage.

PLANTING & MAINTENANCE

When to Plant: Plant tubers or plants after soil temperatures have risen above 60 degrees.

Trimming: Occasional, if at all. Clip off any old leaves that bend over and lose their color, if you like. Some people don't like the look of the flowers and clip them off as well.

Fertilization: Use the fertilizer described on page 47 .

PLANTING & STORING TUBERS

Planting: Place the knobby side up, and cover with 1 inch of soil. After the summer season, dig them up when temperatures dip into the 50's. Leave the leaves on the tubers, as well as a small amount of soil around them.

Storage: Let them dry out in a warm, dry location. Place them on dry wood shavings or sphagnum moss, and don't let the tubers touch each other. Clean off the leaves and soil in about 3 to 4 weeks. Cut the leaves gently, leaving some of the base attached to the tuber. Store in a cool, dry location for the winter, and don't let the tubers touch each other.

Cleome

CHARACTERISTICS

Plant Type: Annual that often reseeds itself.

Average Size: Old fashioned cleomes grow to about 4 feet tall by 2 feet wide. The 'Sparkler' series tops out at about 2 feet tall by 18 inches wide. 'Linde Armstrong' is the smallest, about 16 inches tall.

Growth Rate: Fast

Leaf: Green leaves consisting of 5 to 7 pointed leaflets. Short spines are often present where leaves attach to main stems.

Flower: Rounded clusters of delicate, open blossoms borne at stem tips.

Lifespan: 4 to 7 months

Origin: Brazil and Argentina

Spacing: About 10 inches on center for the smaller ones and 18 inches on center for the larger ones (measure from the center of each plant). Closer in containers.

Cautions: The large, old fashioned varieties have an unpleasant scent. Seldom damaged by deer.

Colors: Pink, mauve, white, rose, or lavender.

'Serena' angelonias are planted on either side of these cleomes in this side-planted window box from www.kinsmangarden.com. Scaevola and wax begonias are planted in the side holes and along the edge.

Cleomes are easy to grow but don't bloom as long as the four to six month minimum we require for annuals to get a ribbon. However, the smaller varieties are worth growing for the distinctive appearance of the flowers.

Cleomes bordered by impatiens

Use of cleomes in the garden has greatly increased recently due to the introduction of new, smaller, and more compact varieties. Old cleomes are large and lanky, seeding freely in the garden. While some might welcome the new plants produced by these seeds, others consider them a weed. Old cleomes also have the annoying habit of falling apart halfway through the summer. The new cleomes are smaller and much better mannered, seldom popping up the next year. Most cleomes sold in garden centers are the new, smaller varieties. The 'Sparkler' series did incredibly well in our Georgia trial gardens but only bloomed for a few months - not as long at the annuals in this chapter that were awarded ribbons.

Regional Differences: Cleome grows well throughout the region. In zones seven through nine, the old variety needs partial shade, but cleome can adapt to full sun in zone six. Smaller cleomes take full sun throughout the south.

Color Period: Early summer to fall, if deadheaded regularly. We never have had time to deadhead the cleomes in our trial gardens, where they have bloomed on and off for about half of the growing season.

Buying Tips: Be sure to check the size that is printed on the tag. If it states that the plant grows any taller than two feet, it is probably one of the older, pain-in-the-neck varieties.

Companions: Finding companions for cleomes is great fun and easiest to do at the garden center. Put a cleome in your cart, and wheel it around to see other flowers that look good with it. Use your eyes to see which combinations make you smile! Be sure to take this book with you, so you can check out the characteristics of the flowers you like.

Cleomes are such complex flowers that they look best with simple companions, like the petunias, salvia, and pentas shown below.

Cleomes with some companion plants

Pink Petunias are great companions for cleomes, working well as a front border. Since there are so many colors of petunias at the garden centers in spring, choose the one that looks best with your color of cleomes.

Purple Salvia work well as a mid layer, in between the petunias and the cleomes. The vertical flower shape contrasts with both other flowers. Plant them in sun to light shade, so all the flowers do well.

Purple Pentas are another good choice for a mid layer cleome companion. They are one of the best flowers for attracting butterflies. Check the tag on the pentas to be sure the variety stays smaller than your cleomes.

GROWING CONDITIONS

Light: Light shade to full sun.

Water: Medium. Healthy cleomes can tolerate drought, but flower production is best when plants receive enough water to soak the roots at least once a week. Requires more water when grown in containers.

Soil: For the garden, plant in any fertile, well-drained soil that has been enriched with organic matter. Use only good-quality potting mix for containers. See page 30 for specific instructions on soil preparation.

Hardiness: Annual that grows in the summer throughout the country.

Propagation: Seeds for the older varieties. Some new ones grow from cuttings.

Pest Problems: Very rare

PLANTING & MAINTENANCE

When to Plant: Spring or summer

Trimming: New, smaller varieties do not require trimming but benefit from removing the old blooms, if you have time. The old, large varieties need a mid summer trimming. Use sharp pruning shears to cut back stem tips after the flowers fade, which keeps the plants from using their energy to produce long, stringy seed pods and encourages them to develop bud-bearing branches. Some gardeners let their cleome go until late summer and then prune back the plants by one-half their size. This is a good practice if you want your plants to reseed.

Fertilization: Use the fertilizer described on page 47 only on planting day.

2ND Coleus

CHARACTERISTICS

Plant Type: Annual

Average Size: 6 to 36 inches tall, depending on variety.

Growth Rate: Fast

Leaf: Intricately variegated leaves vary in shape, with some quite thin and thread-like, others broad and oval, and many with curled or frilled edges.

Flower: Spikes of pale blue flowers are usually clipped off to encourage production of leaves.

Lifespan: 4 to 7 months

Origin: Tropical areas of Mediterranean region.

Spacing: About 8 to 18 inches on center (measure from the center of each plant), depending on cultivar. Closer in containers.

Cautions: Seldom damaged by deer.

Colors: Burgundy, lime green, chartreuse, pink, purple, and white, in endless combinations.

1. *'Defiance' coleus*
2. *'Gay's Delight' coleus*
3. *'Dark Star' coleus*
4. *'Crime Scene' coleus*

In field trials throughout the south, coleus is the top-rated summer annual for long-season color. However, it requires more water than most annuals. Just misses a blue ribbon* because it needs monthly pinching.

These three layers of coleus demonstrate the height differences of various cultivars. The back layer is 'Mississippi Summer Sun;' middle layer, 'Giant Webfoot;' border, 'Wizard Golden' coleus. Layering like this is difficult unless you know the mature height of each coleus used.

Coleus are one of the most popular annuals in the south. Their tolerance for heat, coupled with long lifespan, have ranked them as a top annual for southern growing conditions. However, most seed-grown coleus (like the 'Wizard' series) don't last as long as coleus grown from cuttings. And coleus like more water than southern droughts and water restrictions can sometimes handle. Traditionally thought of as shade plants, their tolerance for sun has greatly increased with new varieties.

Regional Differences: Coleus grow well throughout the south.

Color Period: Continuous until the temperatures drop to 40 degrees. Coleus are grown for their colorful leaves, which are more abundant when flower spikes are clipped off as soon as they appear. Most varieties grown from cuttings flower much less than those grown from seed.

Buying Tips: Coleus are fast growers, so buying smaller plants pays off. Since coleus vary from six to 36 inches tall, it helps if the plant tags in the garden centers include the height, so you know how to design with them.

**Red ribbon plants are defined on page 13. For red ribbon performance, follow the planting and maintenance guidelines on pages 28 to 49.*

Companions: Coleus come in so many different colors and sizes that you will never run out of neat ways to use them. A popular approach is to combine two varieties - one chartreuse and one dark red or purple - to form a tapestry of high contrast color. For neon color, try the combination shown below.

Coleus with some companion plants

Dragon Wing Begonia not only blooms nonstop all season, but also looks great with this red and yellow coleus. Plant the coleus as a border for the dragon wings, or use it as a side planting, with the dragon wing as the centerpiece in a container.

Golden Shrimp Plant (above, center) blooms constantly all season in light to medium shade. The yellow flowers coordinate perfectly with the yellow in the coleus leaf. Since the shrimp plant gets taller than the coleus, use the coleus as the border. Be sure to buy shrimp plants whose flower is identical to the one shown above. There are many others in the garden centers, and none did anywhere near as well as this one in our trials.

Persian Shield (above, right) can be added to this bright mix, and you could stop traffic in your neighborhood! Use all of them in a container, or plant them in the ground. For a dynamite garden accent planting, alternate three each of begonias, shrimp plants, and Persian shield, and border all of them with coleus. Be sure to use dragon wing begonias and not wax begonias because the wax begonias don't grow tall enough for a coleus border.

GROWING CONDITIONS

Light: Full sun to nearly full shade, depending on cultivar. Check plant tags for light preferences.

Water: High in sun, medium in shade. To save time, install a soaker hose in beds planted with coleus. In summer, plants need water three times a week in sun and once or twice a week in shade. Requires more water when grown in containers.

Soil: For the garden, plant in any fertile, well-drained soil that has been enriched with organic matter. Use only good-quality potting mix for containers.

Hardiness: Shows cold damage at about 40 degrees.

Propagation: Seeds or cuttings

Pest Problems: Most coleus are pest free, but very wet soil can cause root rot problems. We have never had a pest problem in our trial gardens.

PLANTING & MAINTENANCE

When to Plant: Spring, summer, or fall. It makes the most sense to plant in spring, so you can enjoy them longer!

Trimming: Clip off flower spikes when they appear if you have time. Should plants become leggy, shearing them back by 1/3 their size will quickly increase bushiness. We pinch the tips of our coleus about once a month.

Fertilization: Use the fertilizer described on page 47 only on planting day.

UNIVERSITY AWARDS

2000: Georgia Gold Medal Winner (10 to 15 sun cultivars).

2002, 2006: Mississippi Medallion Winner ('Mississippi Summer Sun' and 'Kong' Coleus).

1ST Dusty Miller

CHARACTERISTICS

Plant Type: Perennial grown as hardy annual.

Average Size: 8 to 12 inches tall, equally as wide.

Growth Rate: Medium

Leaf: Deeply-cut, gray leaves covered with fine, felt-like hairs.

Flower: Small clusters of yellow flowers develop on year-old plants, but they usually are removed.

Lifespan: 4 to 7 months. Occasionally lives up to one year.

Origin: Mediterranean region

Spacing: About 8 inches on center (measure from the center of each plant). Closer in containers.

Cautions: All parts of the plant are poisonous if eaten. Seldom damaged by deer.

Colors: Grown for its frosty, gray leaves.

1. Close up of flower
2. Dusty miller works well as a border for these blue salvia and pink wax begonias.

An easy annual that makes most flowers look better. Sometimes lives longer than just one season. Tolerant of frost. Dusty miller rates a blue ribbon.*

Dusty miller planted around Miscanthus grass

All flowers are pretty, but many look even prettier when grown in the company of plants that provide strong contrast in color and texture, which is exactly what you get with dusty miller. The gentle, gray leaves flatter bright reds and deep pinks, making them appear sharper, and they also amplify blues beautifully. True go-with-everything plants, dusty miller does an amazing job of separating masses of different-colored flowers. When used as an edging, dusty miller makes a bed look like it is trimmed with lace.

Dusty miller needs contrasting companions to look good. It doesn't work well when planted alone.

Regional Differences: Dusty miller is easy to grow in zones six and seven in summer; in winter, it does well in zone eight. In very warm, rainy years, it may be troubled by root rot diseases.

Color Period: Dusty miller rarely blooms unless the plants have wintered over in the garden. Year-old plants bloom in early summer.

Buying Tips: All the dusty millers we have purchased have done well, regardless of the other names on the tags.

**Blue ribbon plants are defined on page 12. For blue ribbon performance, follow the planting and maintenance guidelines on pages 28 to 49.*

Companions: It is hard to name a flower that does not partner well with dusty miller, but some make such fantastic bedfellows that they should be high on your list of choices. Use plants that are quite different from dusty miller. The grass (shown on the opposite page) looks good with dusty miller because its leaves are such different sizes and shapes. Also, the grey color really sets off hot pinks and purples. Try dusty miller as an annual accent for a perennial garden featuring those colors, as shown below.

Dusty miller with some companion plants

Use 'Homestead Purple' Verbena (above, left) as a border for dusty miller. It blooms on and off all summer and returns year after year.

Pink Dragon Wing Begonias (above, center) can be added as the tallest plant in this perennial/annual grouping. The begonias grow about two to three feet tall and bloom from spring until the first frost of fall.

Purple Heart (above, right) is possibly the best perennial companion for dusty miller because its color contrasts so beautifully, and it keeps its color from spring until the first frost of fall. Border dusty miller with the shorter-growing purple heart.

To combine them all, plant the begonias as the tallest plants, bordered by dusty miller. Alternate groups of three verbena with groups of three purple heart as the border. Since two of these four plants are perennials, they will last for many years to come.

GROWING CONDITIONS

Light: Light shade to full sun.

Water: Medium after establishment. Likes water once or twice a week during the growing season, depending on its environment. Requires more water when grown in containers. See pages 34 to 37 for more information.

Soil: For the garden, plant in any fertile, well-drained soil that has been enriched with organic matter. Use only good-quality potting mix for containers. See page 30 for specific instructions on soil preparation.

Hardiness: Dependably hardy in Zones 8 to 10, and often hardy in Zone 7 when grown in a protected place. Although some lucky people have dusty miller that has lasted them for years, that's the exception rather than the rule.

Propagation: Seeds, though they are very tiny and slow to grow. Stem cuttings will root with the help of rooting powder.

Pest Problems: Root knot nematodes can stunt the growth of dusty miller.

PLANTING & MAINTENANCE

When to Plant: Set out plants in early spring, after danger of frost has passed.

Trimming: When buds rise up on overwintered plants, you may want to clip them off. The flowers are not showy, and plants that have bloomed usually deteriorate quickly.

Fertilization: Use the fertilizer described on page 47 only on planting day.

2ND Impatiens

CHARACTERISTICS

Plant Type: Annual

Average Size: About 12 to 18 inches tall by equally as wide.

Growth Rate: Fast

Leaf: Rounded with a point on the end. Medium green or variegated. About 1 inch long by equally as wide in regular impatiens. New Guineas can be twice as large.

Flower: Regular impatiens measure about 1 1/2 inches wide. New Guineas are about twice as large.

Lifespan: 4 to 7 months

Origin: Africa

Spacing: About 12 inches on center (measure from the center of each plant). Closer in containers.

Cautions: None known

Colors: Many shades of red, purple, peach, orange, and white. Most impatiens have green leaves, but many New Guineas feature darker-colored or variegated leaves.

1. Double pink impatiens
2. 'Little Lizzy' orange impatiens
3. New Guinea lipstick impatiens
4. Regular 'Blue Pearl' impatiens

Impatiens are the most popular bedding plant in the world but are too thirsty for most southern gardeners to plant extensively. However, they are great for containers, especially the New Guinea and 'Little Lizzy' series.

New Guinea impatiens surrounding a bromeliad. Container from www.campaniainternational.com.

In our Georgia trial gardens, we no longer plant impatiens in the ground but do use a few in containers, where they excel. The New Guinea impatiens, which feature larger leaves and flowers than the regular impatiens, are one of the most colorful plants in the world and use the least water of any impatiens. We only had to water them twice a week in large, shade containers for an entire summer. The 'Little Lizzy' series is smaller than regular impatiens and is also more colorful in containers. And don't forget the double impatiens, which are one of the most beautiful flowers for containers that are viewed from up close

For shade color in the ground, try dragon wing or wax begonias instead of the more thirsty impatiens.

Regional Differences: No differences throughout the south

Color Period: Late spring to late fall, blooming constantly

Buying Tips: Regular impatiens are one of the easiest plants to find in the garden centers in spring. New Guineas and double impatiens are also showing up everywhere. 'Little Lizzies' are harder to find. All the impatiens we have purchased have done well for us, regardless of the name on the tag.

**Red ribbon plants are defined on page 13. For red ribbon performance, follow the planting and maintenance guidelines on pages 28 to 49.*

Companions: One of our favorite designs with any of the impatiens is to alternate jewel-toned flowers - orange, red, purple, or hot pink. Both these container designs feature alternating orange, purple, and red New Guinea impatiens. In the container shown left, the colors coordinate with the primary intensity of the bromeliad used in the center. The container shown below features white begonias and pink caladiums, which quiet down the wild colors of the impatiens.

Impatiens with some companion plants

Begonias (above, left) are one of the best annuals to use for shady areas. They tone down the intensity of the bright impatiens flowers.

Caladiums (above, center) are an excellent choice for centerpieces of shady container gardens. They contrast well with the other plants in this group because their leaves are so much larger.

Put them all together in a 16 inch, side-planted basket (#ZGBS16) on a 36" border column (ZGBC36) from www.kinsmangarden.com. First, the impatiens are planted through the side holes in the basket. Second, the caladium is planted in the center. Third, the begonias are tucked in along the edge. The basket is mounted on a wooden post that is sunk into the garden itself. See the Kinsman web site for short videos showing this technique.

GROWING CONDITIONS

Light: Medium to light shade. Some New Guineas, called 'Sunpatiens,' take more sun.

Water: High. Regular impatiens need daily water in light shade in the ground during the hottest time of summer. New Guineas need less. We have watered them as little as twice a week in large containers in shade.

Soil: For the garden, plant in any fertile, well-drained soil that has been enriched with organic matter. Use only good-quality potting mix for containers.

Hardiness: Very sensitive to the slightest frost.

Propagation: Seeds or cuttings

Pest Problems: Fungus, slugs, Japanese beetles.

PLANTING & MAINTENANCE

When to Plant: Spring or summer

Trimming: Should plants become leggy in late summer, shearing them back by 1/3 will restore their form and encourage a late flush of fresh blossoms.

Fertilization: Use the fertilizer described on page 47 only on planting day.

UNIVERSITY AWARDS

1991, 1993, 1996, 1997, 2000, 2001: Awards from North Carolina State University to the following:

Regular impatiens: *'Impulse Bright Eye,' 'Accent Lilac,' 'Super Elfin Melon and White Improved,' 'Accent Red.'*

New Guinea impatiens: *'Paradise Aruba,' 'Super Sonic Scarlet,' 'Celebration'* series, many colors, *'Ovation Hot Lava,' 'Harmony Pink and Magenta.'*

Double impatiens: *'Tioga Hot Pink.'*

1ST Lantana

CHARACTERISTICS

Plant Type: Tropical perennial used as an annual in the south.

Average Size: Varies by variety, from 12 to 36 inches high by 12 to 24 inches wide.

Growth Rate: Fast

Leaf: Medium green, serrated, and pointed. About 1 inch long by 1/2 inch wide.

Flower: Clusters of tiny flowers forming larger flowers of about 1 to 2 inches inches across.

Lifespan: 6 to 7 months for annual lantana. 'Miss Huff' is a perennial lantana that lives for many years but doesn't start blooming until mid summer.

Origin: Tropical America

Spacing: About 14 to 20 inches on center (measure from the center of each plant). Closer in containers.

Cautions: Poisonous to humans, dogs, and livestock. Can cause serious illness or death. Almost never damaged by deer.

Colors: White, red, pink, yellow, purple, or orange.

1. *'Landmark Rose Glow Improved' lantana*
2. *'Landmark White' lantana*
3. *'Landmark Flame Improved Red' lantana*
4. *Lantana montividensis, a cool-weather bloomer.*

If you can only choose just have one annual, make it lantana. Unstoppable garden color from early summer to fall. This heat lover practically grows itself, blooms like crazy, and requires very little maintenance. It rates a blue ribbon* and is one of the butterflies' favorite foods.

'New Gold' is a low growing lantana that is covered with blooms all season long.

One year, we planted eight varieties (all from Ball Horticulture) of annual lantana in our Georgia trial gardens to see which ones did the best. We were quite surprised to see that all of them did equally as well. The next year, we tried several Proven Winners varieties, including the 'Patriot' series. All of them outperformed any other annual that summer, blooming constantly with very little care. And, we had hundreds of butterflies! These were drought years, however, so we didn't have to worry about too much water. Lantana doesn't do as well in wet years. Lantana is also available as a perennial ('Miss Huff' lantana, page 154), but it doesn't start blooming until mid summer, whereas annual lantana starts in April.

Regional Differences: Does equally well throughout the south in dry years

Color Period: Most lantana bloom heavily, non-stop from April until the first frost. Purple lantana, however, flowers more in cool months, shutting down for a good bit of the hottest part of summer.

Buying Tips: Since the height of lantana varies from one to three feet, check the plant tag at your garden center to be sure the selection fits your space. With larger lantanas, you can space them farther apart than most other annuals, saving you money in your annual beds.

**Blue ribbon plants are defined on page 12. For blue ribbon performance, follow the planting and maintenance guidelines on pages 28 to 49.*

Companions: Lantanas are excellent color accents for perennial gardens. Most perennials don't bloom anywhere near as long as lantana, so adding lantana ensures constant color in your bed. And, if you use perennials that also attract butterflies, like the ones shown below, you will attract clouds of them!

Lantana 'Patriot Firewagon' with some companion plants

Yarrow (above, left) is an easy perennial companion for lantana. Yellow yarrow lights up a garden for about two to three months in summer and contrasts wonderfully with this 'Patriot Firewagon' lantana. Yarrow grows to about three feet tall, so place it where it shows up with the size of lantana you choose. This lantana grows to about two feet tall, so it fits well in front of the yarrow.

'Purple Butterfly' Bush (above, center) can be added for a dramatic color accent with the yarrow and lantana. Most of the newer, compact butterfly bushes, like this 'Purple Emporer,' grow to about four feet tall, so put it in the center or back of the bed surrounded by the yarrow and lantana. It, too, blooms for about two months in summer.

'Big Sky After Midnight' Coneflower (above, right) is a great, pinkish purple color that contrasts well with the other flowers in this grouping. It grows to about 18 inches tall, so place it so that it shows well with the lantana. This coneflower blooms at about the same time as the yarrow and butterfly bush.

GROWING CONDITIONS

Light: Full sun

Water: Low after establishment. Likes water every week or two during the growing season, depending on its environment. Requires more water when grown in containers. See pages 34 to 37 for more information.

Soil: For the garden, plant in any fertile, well-drained soil that has been enriched with organic matter. Use only good-quality potting mix for containers.

Hardiness: Lantana used as an annual in the south (zones 6 to 8) grows as a short-term perennial (living for about a year) in zones 9 to 10. There is perennial lantana called 'Miss Huff' (page 154) for zones 6 to 8, but it doesn't start blooming until about July.

Propagation: Cuttings

Pest Problems: If brown spots appear on the leaves, it is a fungus. These spots are routine, especially in the summer. If possible, cut back on water. Spray only if they become quite severe.

PLANTING & MAINTENANCE

When to Plant: Spring and summer.

Trimming: Accept lantana as an informal plant, if you are looking for low maintenance. We never trimmed ours in Georgia.

Fertilization: Use the fertilizer described on page 47 only on planting day.

UNIVERSITY AWARDS

1995: Gold Medal Winner from University of Georgia.

1996, 2003, 2006: Mississippi Medallion Winner.

2006, 2007: Top 10 from North Carolina State University

Melampodium

1ST

One of the top annuals for sun and heat. Thrives from spring until frost with almost no care. Rates a blue ribbon* because of its long bloom period and ease of care.

Melampodiums are informal plants but look quite neat with a formal, clipped border.

If your plans for any sunny spot call for bright yellow, melampodium should be a top contender. Although the flowers are small, they appear so abundantly and continuously that the plants are always gloriously clad with deer-resistant color. You can start with bedding plants, but melampodium is also easy to sow from seed. As long as the soil is warm, melampodium seeds sprout quickly and begin blooming in a few short weeks. They reseed themselves, too, and volunteer seedlings are easy to dig and move to wherever you want them to grow and bloom. The taller varieties tend to fall over in mid summer, which isn't visible if they are planted in a mass, but shows quite a bit in containers or in formal borders. Stick to the smaller varieties if compact form is needed.

Regional Differences: Melampodium grows well throughout the south.

Color Period: Early summer to fall, continuously

Buying Tips: Since melampodiums vary from 10 to 36 inches tall, be sure to check the plant tag at your garden center (or the description in the seed catalog) to be sure the selection fits your space.

**Blue ribbon plants are defined on page 12. For blue ribbon performance, follow the planting and maintenance guidelines on pages 28 to 49.*

CHARACTERISTICS

Plant Type: Annual

Average Size: We have purchased many unnamed melampodium (tag just says 'Melampodium'), and they all grew to about 12 to 18 inches tall by 12 inches wide. 'Derby,' 'Golden Globe,' 'Sunflake Gold,' 'Lemon Delight' and 'Million Gold' are dwarfs of about 12 inches tall and equally as wide. 'Showstar' is about 24 inches tall and equally as wide. 'Medallion' can grow to 36 inches tall.

Growth Rate: Fast

Leaf: Medium green leaves, 2 to 3 inches long.

Flower: Inch-wide, yellow daisies with yellow centers.

Lifespan: 4 to 7 months

Origin: Tropical America

Spacing: About 10 inches on center for the dwarfs; up to 2 feet on center for the largest varieties (measure from the center of one plant to the center of another). Closer in containers.

Cautions: Reseeds. We have had just a few reseed in our trial gardens, but have heard reports of massive reseeding in other gardens, becoming a nuisance. Seldom damaged by deer.

Colors: Light yellow or gold, depending on variety.

BUDGET GARDENING TIP

Melampodium are really easy to grow from seeds. You can sow them directly in your garden, and they sprout in 7 to 10 days. The plants also show up again next year in your garden (although not necessarily where you want them!), because they reseed naturally. Some consider these new plants nuisances, but budget gardeners love free plants and move them wherever they like!

Companions: Think of melampodium as a basic piece in your color garden's wardrobe. The list of garden allies is long indeed and includes sun lovers from agastache to zinnia. A packet of seeds can quickly and inexpensively fill a large space for a mass planting, which is beautiful when edged with 'Blue Wave' petunias.

Melampodium mixes equally as well with annuals and perennials. Try the combination below for a mix of each.

'Sunflake Gold' melampodium with some companion plants

'Patriot Firewagon' Lantana (above, left) is a terrific companion for melampodium. It is the brightest lantana we tried, doing incredibly well in a long, hot summer and growing to about two feet tall. Plant it along the side of tall melampodium or behind shorter ones.

'Blue Fortune' Agastache (above, center) is one of the longest blooming of the easy southern perennials and looks great with melampodium. Since it reaches three feet tall, plant the melampodium in front of the taller agastache.

'Twilight' Coneflower (above, right) is a perennial with a fairly long bloom period that likes sun and reaches about two feet tall. Use the most common melampodiums as a border for this flower.

To combine them all, alternate the agastache with lantana. Plant the coneflowers along the sides and border all of them with melampodium.

GROWING CONDITIONS

Light: Light shade to full sun

Water: Medium after establishment. Likes water once or twice a week during the growing season, depending on its environment. See pages 34 to 37 for more information.

Soil: For the garden, plant in any fertile, well-drained soil that has been enriched with organic matter. Use only good-quality potting mix for containers. See page 30 for specific instructions on soil preparation.

Hardiness: Cannot tolerate frost

Propagation: Seeds

Pest Problems: We never had any pests in our trial gardens. However, large insects, including blister beetles and grasshoppers, occasionally chew the foliage, but they seldom weaken these vigorous plants.

PLANTING & MAINTENANCE

When to Plant: Spring or summer

Trimming: None needed

Fertilization: Use the fertilizer described on page 47 only on planting day.

UNIVERSITY AWARDS

1997: Mississippi Medallion Winner.

Pansies and Violas

1ST

CHARACTERISTICS

Plant Type: Hardy annual

Average Size: 6 inches tall and equally wide.

Growth Rate: Medium

Leaf: Dark green, scalloped leaves on short stems that stay close to the ground.

Flower: Pansy and viola flowers range from 3/4 to 4 inches wide. In any size, pansy blooms are comprised of 5 overlapping petals. Viola blossoms are slightly smaller than most pansies.

Lifespan: 6 to 7 months

Origin: Europe

Spacing: About 6 to 8 inches on center (measure from the center of each plant). Closer in containers.

Cautions: Commonly used as edible flowers. Frequently damaged by deer.

Colors: White, yellow, blue, pink, purple, orange, red, and many bicolors.

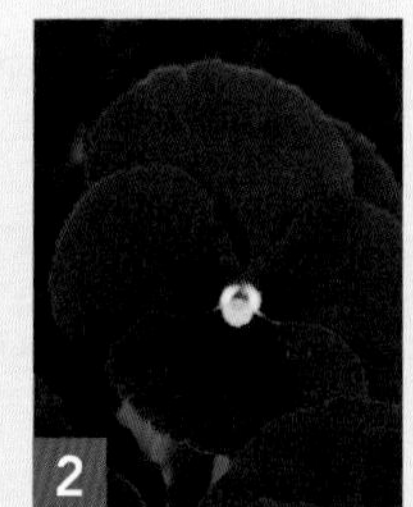

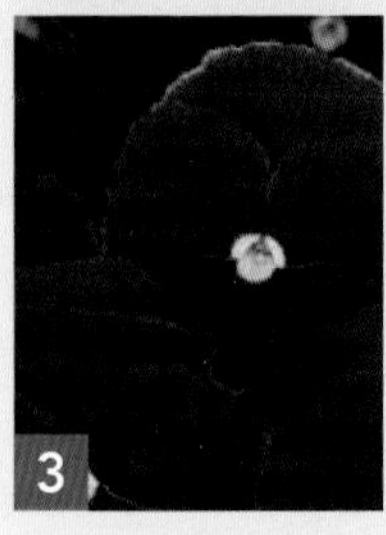

1. *'Sorbet Blue Heaven' viola*
2. *'Matrix Blue Blotch' pansy*
3. *'Matrix Rose' pansy*
4. *'Sorbet Yellow Delight' viola*

Cold tolerant and easy to please, pansies are one of the best flowers to plant for the fall-to-spring season. They rate a blue ribbon* because of their high performance and ease of care.

Pansies do well planted in containers or in the ground. However, they feel the cold more in containers. Photo from Gibbs Gardens in Ball Ground, Georgia.

Pansies and violas love winter in the south and are the most popular annual for our cool months. They are grown primarily as winter annuals in the south and spring annuals in the north. Pansies and violas come in either solid colors or with blotches in the center. The solid ones show up better from a distance. Pansies with smaller flowers generally bloom more than those with larger blooms.

Violas are closely related, but their performance is different. They generally recover from extreme cold faster than pansies and bloom in much less light. Violas have smaller flowers that are not as impressive as pansies when seen from a distance.

Regional Differences: Throughout the south, pansies and violas are easily grown from fall through spring.

Bloom Time: Most of the fall, winter, and spring. Although they stop blooming and don't look too happy when temperatures drop to the mid-twenties, they bounce back at the first hint of warmth.

Buying Tips: We have grown many different kinds of pansies and violas and never had a problem, so have a great time when they roll into the garden centers in fall!

**Blue ribbon plants are defined on page 12. For blue ribbon performance, follow the planting and maintenance guidelines on pages 33 to 46.*

Companions: Pansies and violas are great partners for dianthus, dusty miller, and miniature snapdragons, but none of these flowers bloom as long as pansies and violas. Pansies and violas often come in mixes of colors that are professionally chosen for good design. You can't go wrong choosing one of these mixes.

Pansies' and violas' long bloom period includes late winter and early spring, when few other annuals flower. Try them with other shrubs and bulbs that bloom at the same time.

'Matrix Blue Blotch' pansies and some companion plants

Iris (above, left) blooms for about two weeks from early to late spring, depending on the cultivar you choose. Since both its flowers and leaves are quite different from pansies, it makes a great companion.

Forsythia (above, center) is a great shrub companion for pansies because it blooms in late winter or early spring. Its yellow flowers contrast well with blue or purple pansies. Since it gets quite tall, plant the pansies as the front border.

Asiatic Lilies (above, right) bloom for a few weeks from late spring to early summer, so they would take over for tall bloomers after the iris and forsythia have stopped blooming.

To put it all together, plant forsythia as the tallest layer; alternate clumps of Asiatic lilies and iris in front, as the middle layer; border with the pansies From February to May, two or three out of four of the plants should flower at the same time.

GROWING CONDITIONS

Light: Full sun for pansies. Violas grow in medium shade to full sun.

Water: Medium. Supplemental water is often needed after planting in fall, when dry weather often prevails. After Thanksgiving, winter rains are usually sufficient for pansies. However, cold spells often dry out plants, so water before really cold weather threatens, if the soil is dry. Requires more water when grown in containers.

Soil: For the garden, plant in any fertile, well-drained soil that has been enriched with organic matter. Use only good-quality potting mix for containers. See page 30 for specific instructions on soil preparation.

Hardiness: Violas and pansies are winter hardy to zone 5.

Propagation: Seeds

Pest Problems: Rare. Root rot can develop if plants are kept too wet.

PLANTING & MAINTENANCE

When to Plant: Pansies grow best when they develop good roots before soil temperatures drop into the 40's. Plant in early October.

Trimming: You don't have to remove the dead blooms from pansies but doing so will help the plants bloom longer and stronger. Pull up plants in June because they cannot tolerate hot weather.

Fertilization: Use the fertilizer described on page 47 only on planting day.

UNIVERSITY AWARDS

2000: Mississippi Medallion Winner (Panola 'Panache').

2001, 2002, 2006, 2007, 2008: Top 10 Winner for North Carolina State University. Many different varieties of both pansies and violas.

Pentas

CHARACTERISTICS

Plant Type: Tropical perennial grown as an annual.

Average Size: 1 to 4 feet tall by 1 to 2 feet wide, depending on variety.

Growth Rate: Medium

Leaf: Dark green leaves with pointed tips; prominent leaf veins give the leaves a quilted texture.

Flower: Rounded clusters of star-shaped, 5-petaled flowers.

Lifespan: 4 to 7 months. Larger varieties usually outlive dwarfs.

Origin: Tropical Africa

Spacing: Set dwarf plants 12 inches on center (measure from the center of each plant); mid sized varieties do well with 18 inch spacing. Grow tall varieties as specimen plants, as they grow to the size of bushy 3 to 4 foot tall shrubs. Place closer in containers.

Cautions: Seldom damaged by deer.

Colors: Red, pink, lilac, lavender, purple, and white.

1. *Pentas 'Butterfly Deep Pink'*
2. *Pentas 'Butterfly White'*
3. *Pentas 'Butterfly Rose Deep'*

Pentas take all the heat the south has to offer and are one of the favorite foods of both butterflies and hummingbirds. Although they don't rate a ribbon because they don't bloom constantly for the whole summer, they are definitely worth planting for the butterflies.

Pentas 'Butterfly Deep Pink'

The original pentas were shrubs that grew to four feet tall in tropical areas. Since they bloomed continuously and took heat well, hybridizers began working to get a more compact plant. The results are seen all over southern garden centers as they have become quite popular. The new varieties, particularly the dwarfs, have lost some of the strength of their taller ancestors, however. They are a little more susceptible to fungus and don't bloom continuously. However, even the dwarfs bloom about 75 percent of the time and attract butterflies and hummingbirds like crazy. Pentas are well worth planting in areas with long, hot summers.

Regional Differences: No regional differences

Bloom Time: Spring, summer, and fall; about 75 percent of the time for the smaller ones. The larger ones bloom continuously.

Buying Tips: If you are lucky, you might see some of the old-fashioned, red pentas in your garden centers. They bloom dependably all summer but get up to four feet tall. More likely, you will see the 'Butterfly' series, which gets about 16 inches tall and blooms on and off from spring until fall.

**Blue ribbon plants are defined on page 12. For blue ribbon performance, follow the planting and maintenance guidelines on pages 33 to 46.*

Companions: Phenomenal plants for attracting butterflies and hummingbirds, pentas partner perfectly with other butterfly magnets, such as butterfly bush, lantana, salvia, and zinnias. For clouds of butterflies, plant the combinations shown below.

Pentas 'Butterfly Deep Pink' and some companion plants

Scabiosa (above, left) is a small (12 to 18 inches tall) perennial that is one of the best for butterflies, particularly right after it goes into bloom. It blooms for two to four months, starting in May. Plant it as a border for mid sized pentas.

Add a Purple Butterfly Bush (above, center) for another butterfly favorite. Most of the newer, compact butterfly bushes, like this 'Peacock Butterfly,' grow to about four feet tall, so put it in the center or back of the bed, surrounded by the pentas, scabiosa, and lantana. It blooms for about two months in summer.

Lantana (above, right) has attracted more butterflies to our Georgia trial garden than any other plant. The annual variety will flower from spring until fall. The pink and yellow one (shown) usually grows to about two feet tall, but check the plant tag to be sure.

To put it all together, plant the butterfly bush as the tallest layer, the pentas and lantana (side by side) as the mid layer, and border with the scabiosa.

GROWING CONDITIONS

Light: Full sun to light shade

Water: Medium after establishment. Likes water once or twice a week during the growing season, depending on its environment. Requires more water when grown in containers. See pages 33 to 37 for more information.

Soil: For the garden, plant in any fertile, well-drained soil that has been enriched with organic matter. Use only good-quality potting mix for containers. See page 30 for specific instructions on soil preparation.

Hardiness: Easily killed by hard freezes.

Propagation: Seeds or cuttings

Pest Problems: Powdery mildew sometimes causes white patches to form on the leaves. It weakens but does not kill the plants.

PLANTING & MAINTENANCE

When to Plant: Spring or summer

Trimming: Most pentas currently sold in garden centers don't need trimming because they have a dense form and only grow about 18 to 24 inches tall. Removing the dead flowers increases the blooming, however. Taller pentas might become leggy in late summer. If this happens, shearing them back by 1/3 will restore their form and encourage a late flush of fresh blossoms.

Fertilization: Use the fertilizer described on page 47 only on planting day.

UNIVERSITY AWARDS

1999: Georgia Gold Metal Winner ('Nova' pentas).

2001: Mississippi Medallion Winner ('Butterfly' pentas).

Persian Shield

1ST

CHARACTERISTICS

Plant Type: Tropical perennial grown as an annual.

Average Size: About 2 to 3 feet tall by 2 feet wide. Smaller in containers.

Growth Rate: Medium

Leaf: 2 to 4 inch long pointed leaves with serrated edges, reddish purple beneath and purple above, with dark green leaf veins.

Flower: Small blue flowers occur primarily on year-old plants that survive winter; not showy. Grow this one for the leaf color.

Lifespan: 6 to 7 months. Does not look good after that, regardless of how warm it is.

Origin: Burma

Spacing: About 18 inches on center (measure from the center of each plant). Closer in containers.

Cautions: Poisonous to some. Do not eat this plant.

Colors: Purple

Persian shield makes a great centerpiece for container gardens. Red wax begonias, 'Dark Star' coleus, and Lysimachia 'Outback Sunset' are planted along the edge and through the side holes of this side-planted hanging basket. 16" double Imperial planter (#ZGIPD16) from www.kinsmangarden.com

Persian shield is possibly the most beautiful foliage plant in the world. Its purple leaves are almost iridescent. Tolerant of heat, it rates a blue ribbon* because of its long lifespan and ease of care. It is hard to believe a plant this beautiful is actually easy to grow! It even produces lots of color in shade.

Persian shield with lime coleus and 'Blue Pearl' impatiens planted in front

Easy to grow, Persian shield was named a Georgia Gold Medal winner in 1999. It thrives in our hot, humid southern summers in shade and takes sun in all but the hottest (over 100 degrees) days. Since it is too large to use for borders, plant it as an accent in the garden, as shown above, or as the centerpiece of a container, as shown left.

Persian shield is supposed to be a perennial in the tropics. However, we tried it in areas that don't freeze, and it still only lived for about six to seven months.

Regional Differences: None

Bloom Time: Grow Persian shield for its leaf color instead of its insignificant and seldom-seen flowers. Its leaves offer color anytime temperatures stay above 32 degrees.

Buying Tips: Persian shield is getting more popular in garden centers. We have used hundreds of them over a number of years, and they all have done well, so this is an easy one to shop for. Anyone you see should do quite well in your garden!

**Blue ribbon plants are defined on page 12. For blue ribbon performance, follow the planting and maintenance guidelines on pages 33 to 46.*

Companions: Persian shield is quite versatile, looking great with a variety of different colors. Red dragon wing begonias and golden shrimp plants combine with the purple for a traffic-stopping combination. Pale pink flowers, like wax begonias, also look good with Persian shield, particularly if silver dusty miller is added to the mix. Or, pair it with lime green and different shades of purple, as shown below.

Persian shield and some companion plants

Gomphrena (above, left) is an annual that comes in different shades of purple that coordinate well with Persian shield. Most stay shorter than the Persian shield and bloom for much of the summer in sun to light shade. They make an excellent border for Persian shield.

'Gay's Delight' Coleus (above, center) has lime green leaves with dark purple veins. It looks like it was custom made for Persian shield! It grows to about two feet tall when planted in the ground- the same size as Persian shield - so it works very well planted on either side of it. This coleus grows well in sun to light shade.

Double Petunias (above, right) come with either double or single flowers. They grow to about six inches tall in sun or cascade over the edge of a container. Plant them as a front border for the Persian shield.

Put them all together as a color accent in the garden by placing the Persian shield in the center, with a few coleus on either side. Border the taller plants with either gomphrena or petunias.

GROWING CONDITIONS

Light: Medium shade to full sun. Prefers some break from full sun when the temperatures exceed 95 degrees.

Water: High after establishment. Likes water two to four times a week during the growing season, depending on its environment. Requires more water in containers. See pages 33 to 37 for more information.

Soil: For the garden, plant in any fertile, well-drained soil that has been enriched with organic matter. Use only good-quality potting mix for containers. See page 30 for specific instructions on soil preparation.

Hardiness: Survives a slight freeze, but only lives about 6 or 7 months - even in warm weather. Treat this plant like a summer annual.

Propagation: Cuttings. You can increase your supply of plants by pinching off 4 inch long stem tips, stripping off the leaves from all but the tip, and rooting them in damp potting mix.

Pest Problems: Rare. Root rot can be a problem in cold soil.

PLANTING & MAINTENANCE

When to Plant: Spring or summer

Trimming: Should plants become leggy, trim them back by half their size. They generally don't need trimming when planted in containers but need it occasionally when planted in the ground. The warmer the season, the more trimming they require.

Fertilization: Use the fertilizer described on page 47 only on planting day.

Petunia

CHARACTERISTICS

Plant Type: Annual

Average Size: 6 to 12 inches tall, 6 to 24 inches wide, depending on variety.

Growth Rate: Medium

Leaf: Slightly hairy, medium green leaves, about 2 inches long and 1 inch wide.

Flower: Open trumpets, often with contrasting throats. Flower size ranges from 1 inch wide in mini-petunias to 4 inches wide in varieties with very large flowers. Singles and doubles.

Lifespan: 3 to 7 months

Origin: South Africa

Spacing: Plant mini-petunias 8 inches apart, regular multiflora petunias (such as 'Celebrity' or 'Madness') 10 inches apart, and spreading 'Wave' petunias 15 to 18 inches apart.

Cautions: Leaves are poisonous if eaten. Seldom damaged by deer.

Colors: White, pink, purple, red, yellow, and many bicolors.

1. *'Double Wave Purple'*
2. *'Supertunia Royal Velvet'*
3. *'Easy Wave White'*
4. *'Double Wave Blue Vein'*

Versatile petunias can be employed as edgings, groundcovers, or mass plantings, and they are outstanding in containers. However, you need to know how to shop for the good ones.

'Ramblin Rose' petunias

Some petunias do fantastically well in the south, and others don't. You really need to know how to shop for this one. We seldom lost a named variety, but we lost fifty percent of the 'orphans,' the ones that just say 'Petunia' and nothing else on the label. We had particularly good results with 'Wave' petunias, 'Supertunias,' 'Suncatcher' petunias, and 'Blanket' petunias.

The only petunia that lived through an entire, seven month, growing season in our Georgia trial gardens was the 'Wave' petunia. But the others are worth planting because they add so much beauty to both containers and gardens planted in the ground. Petunias have some of the largest flowers of any annual commonly planted in the south, and contrast well either with smaller flowers or flowers of different shapes.

Regional Differences: Vigorous, heat-resistant varieties are trustworthy summer flowers throughout zones six through nine in the south.

Bloom Time: Late spring, until the first frost in fall. Most varieties lasted about five months, with the 'Wave' petunias lasting up to seven months.

Buying Tips: Avoid petunias that only say 'Petunia' on the label. Most of them died in our Georgia trial gardens. Look for named varieties, like 'Wave' petunias, 'Supertunias,' 'Suncatcher' petunias and, 'Blanket' petunias.

**Blue ribbon plants are defined on page 12. For blue ribbon performance, follow the planting and maintenance guidelines on pages 33 to 46.*

Companions: Petunias work particularly well with flowers and foliage of different sizes and shapes, such as spiky angelonia or tiny- flowered torenia. 'Profusion' zinnias are also good companions because their flower is shaped differently from the petunias.

Petunias and some companion plants

Upright Torenia (above, left) are annuals with flowers much smaller than those of petunias, so the two look good together. Use petunias to border the taller torenia.

White Angelonia (above, center) is an excellent companion for petunias because the spiky angelonia flower contrasts so well with the round petunia flower. Use the angelonia as the centerpiece of a container surrounded by alternated torenia and petunias, or plant them in the garden in layers.

'Pink Profusion' Zinnias (above, right) are another tough companion for petunias. Use the petunias to border the taller zinnias.

Put them all together by planting the angelonia as the tallest layer. Alternate the zinnias and torenia as the mid layer, and border them with petunias.

GROWING CONDITIONS

Light: Light shade to full sun

Water: Medium after establishment. Likes water once or twice a week during the growing season, depending on its environment. Requires more water when grown in containers.

Soil: For the garden, plant in any fertile, well-drained soil that has been enriched with organic matter. Use only good-quality potting mix for containers.

Hardiness: Plants tolerate light frosts but not hard freezes.

Propagation: Seeds or cuttings

Pest Problems: Stem rot is sometimes a problem with selections that bloom red. Few insect pests bother petunias. Very wet weather can cause blossoms to mold, but this does not hurt the plants.

PLANTING & MAINTENANCE

When to Plant: Spring or summer

Trimming: Removing dead flowers is not really necessary, but it helps keep the plants looking neat and encourages heavy flowering. For weary-looking plants, shear back by half their size in late July. They will come back into bloom in a few weeks.

Fertilization: Use the fertilizer described on page 47 only on planting day.

UNIVERSITY AWARDS

1996: Georgia Gold Medal Winner ('Purple Wave' series).

2000: Mississippi Medallion Winner ('Wave' series).

1995, 1998, 2001, 2002, 2005, 2006, 2007: Exceptional Performance Winner and Top 10 Award from North Carolina State University. Many different varieties.

Salvia, Blue

1ST

CHARACTERISTICS

Plant Type: Annual that occasionally grows for more than one season. A common misconception is that this plant is a perennial in the south, although it occasionally lasts for more than one season.

Average Size: About 18 inches tall by 12 inches wide.

Growth Rate: Medium

Leaf: Medium green and pointed. About 1 1/2 inches long by 1/3 inch wide.

Flower: Blue spike, about 5 inches tall.

Lifespan: 4 to 6 months

Origin: New Mexico, Mexico, and Texas.

Spacing: About 8 to 12 inches on center (measure from the center of each plant). Closer in containers.

Cautions: Almost never damaged by deer.

Colors: Blue and bicolored blue and white.

1. *Blue salvia*
2. *Salvia 'Fairy Queen', which has blue and white flowers.*

Beautiful blue flowers well adapted to southern heat. Rates a blue ribbon* because of its long bloom period with very little care. Plant it in spring, and add nothing but water until the first freeze of winter.

Blue salvia planted in between yellow marigolds and red salvia

Annual blue salvia is one of the best annuals for the south. It lasts for most of the growing season with no care other than water, and it's not a particularly thirsty plant. There are many perennial salvias in garden centers, some of which actually come back another year, but most don't. We have grown this salvia for two years in our Georgia trial gardens, and it died in the winter both times.

Look for one labeled 'Victoria Blue,' which won a Mississippi Medallion award in 1998. We have had excellent luck with this one as well as any other blue annual salvia we have picked up at our local garden centers.

Regional Differences: Grows well throughout the south

Bloom Time: Spring till fall, for about four to six months

Buying Tips: Good blue salvia is usually available at most southern garden centers in spring. Be sure it is an annual, because blue salvias also come in perennial forms that get twice as large. See pages 172 to 175 to learn more about the perennial salvias.

**Blue ribbon plants are defined on page 12. For blue ribbon performance, follow the planting and maintenance guidelines on pages 33 to 46.*

Attracts Butterflies | Attracts Hummingbirds | Avg. Weeks of Color | Resists Deer

Botanical Name: *Salvia farinacea*

Family: Lamiaceae

Companions: Combine blue salvia with other light-textured plants for a country garden look. Lantana, coneflower, and yarrow are ideal, and this grouping combines both annuals and perennials.

Blue salvia and some companion plants

Yellow Lantana (above, left) is the perfect border for blue salvia, either in the ground or in containers. Look for the 'New Gold' series, which stays lower than blue salvia. Both love sun and bloom their hearts out from spring until the first frost of fall.

'Twilight' Coneflower (above, center) is a perennial with a fairly long bloom period that likes sun and reaches about two feet tall. Use the salvia alongside this perennial. If your local garden center doesn't have this coneflower, you can order it online.

Yarrow (above, right) is an easy perennial companion for blue salvia. Yellow yarrow lights up a garden for about two to three months in summer and contrasts wonderfully with the spiky flowered salvia. Yarrow grows to about three feet tall, so place it behind the smaller salvia.

Put them all together by alternating the yarrow and coneflower as the tallest layer. Plant the blue salvia as the mid layer, and border with yellow lantana.

GROWING CONDITIONS

Light: Light shade to full sun

Water: Medium after establishment. Likes water once or twice a week during the growing season, depending on its environment. Requires more water when grown in containers. See pages 34 to 37 for more information.

Soil: For the garden, plant in any fertile, well-drained soil that has been enriched with organic matter. Use only good-quality potting mix for containers. See page 30 for specific instructions on soil preparation.

Hardiness: Occasionally hardy in zone 8, but for no more than a year or two. This plant is best used as an annual that is replaced each spring.

Propagation: Seeds or cuttings

Pest Problems: None serious

PLANTING & MAINTENANCE

When to Plant: Spring or summer

Trimming: Removing dead blooms increases flowering - if you have time for it.

Fertilization: Use the fertilizer described on page 47 only on planting day.

UNIVERSITY AWARDS

1998: Mississippi Medallion Winner ('Victoria' salvia).

1995: Exceptional Performance Winner from North Carolina State University ('Rhea' salvia).

Salvia splendens, Scarlet sage

CHARACTERISTICS

Plant Type: Annual

Average Size: About 8 inches tall by 8 inches wide.

Growth Rate: Medium

Leaf: Medium green and pointed. About 1 3/4 inches long.

Flower: Showy spike, about 5 inches tall.

Lifespan: 5 to 6 months

Origin: Brazil

Spacing: About 8 to 12 inches on center (measure from the center of each plant). Closer in containers.

Cautions: Almost never damaged by deer.

Colors: Many shades of red, peach, white, and purple.

1. *Salvia 'Red Hot Sally'*
2. *Salvia 'Vista Purple'*
3. *Salvia 'Vista Lavender'*
4. *Salvia 'Hotline Violet'*

Versatile, carefree flowers enrich the garden with fresh colors and upright form. Blooms for most of the season but requires frequent deadheading, which keeps them from rating a ribbon. Extremely easy to grow. Excellent choice for good color impact.

Mixed colors of salvia with yellow marigolds and silver dusty miller

This salvia is an annual that is most commonly seen in red. Its colors have expanded, however, to include many shades of purple, peach, and white. Annual salvia requires removal of dead flowers every week or so but makes up for this by being a favorite food of hummingbirds. Try some in a window box to attract these birds up close. The spiky texture of the flowers makes it an excellent choice for containers.

This annual salvia is one of the most dependable annuals for southern gardens.

Regional Differences: Salvia splendens does equally well throughout the south.

Bloom Time: From spring until fall, continuously. They lose some color with their mid-to-late summer trim, but not for long.

Buying Tips: Good red salvia is usually easy to find in garden centers in spring. We have purchased thousands over a multi-year period, and all have done equally as well. Purples, whites, and peaches are sometimes harder to find than the red.

**Blue ribbon plants are defined on page 12. For blue ribbon performance, follow the planting and maintenance guidelines on pages 33 to 46.*

Botanical Name: *Salvia splendens*

Family: Lamiaceae

Companions: One of the most effective ways to use this salvia is to mix the different colors together. Sometimes you can find mixed trays for sale in the garden center. These mixes (sometimes called 'Vista Mix') give great color impact to the garden. However, since the mixes are hard to find, try the red with these easy-to-find flowers.

Red salvia and some companion plants

Yellow Lantana (left, top) is the perfect border for red salvia, either in the ground or in containers. Look for the 'New Gold' series, which stays lower than red salvia. Both love sun and bloom their hearts out from spring until the first frost of fall.

'Peacock' Butterfly Bush (left, center) is smaller and more compact than the common butterfly bush, measuring about four feet tall by four feet wide. It blooms for several months in the summer and is ideal planted in the center of a bed with a salvia border. If you can't find this one at your local garden center, order it online.

Dark Blue Petunias (left, bottom) contrast well with red salvia, both in color and shape. Border your salvia with this rich, blue color. This combination does equally as well in containers or in the ground.

Put them all together by planting the butterfly bush in the center of the bed. Alternate the three smaller plants (salvia, petunias, and lantana) as a border. This mixed flower border looks better if you plant more than one row.

GROWING CONDITIONS

Light: Light shade to full sun

Water: Medium after establishment. Likes water once or twice a week during the growing season, depending on its environment. Requires more water when grown in containers. See pages 34 to 37 for more information.

Soil: For the garden, plant in any fertile, well-drained soil that has been enriched with organic matter. Use only good-quality potting mix for containers. See page 30 for specific instructions on soil preparation.

Hardiness: Cannot tolerate frost

Propagation: Seeds

Pest Problems: We never have had a pest on our salvias.

PLANTING & MAINTENANCE

When to Plant: Spring or summer

Trimming: When the flowers turn white, trim them off. This prolongs the blooming of the plants.

Fertilization: Use the fertilizer described on page 47 only on planting day.

UNIVERSITY AWARDS

1994, 1995: Exceptional Performance Winner from North Carolina State University ('Cover Girl,' 'Sizzles Lavender').

Scaevola, Fan Flower

1ST

CHARACTERISTICS

Plant Type: Tropical perennial used as an annual in the south.

Average Size: About 6 inches tall by 12 to 18 inches wide.

Growth Rate: Medium

Leaf: Medium green, oblong, and pointed.

Flower: Small flowers shaped like a fan.

Lifespan: Lives for an entire growing season in the south.

Origin: Australia

Spacing: About 12 inches on center (measure from the center of each plant). Closer in containers.

Cautions: Rabbits love them!

Colors: Blue or white

1. *Scaevola 'Whirlwind Blue'*
2. *Scaevola 'Whirlwind White'*

Excellent annual for southern gardens. Blooms all season with very little care. Butterflies love it! Blue ribbon* plant because of its long bloom period and ease of care.

Scaevola is a fabulous container plant, never failing in over six years of trials in our test gardens. It blooms all spring, summer, and fall, never taking a break. Scaevola is a bit pickier about performing well when planted in the ground, however. If it is a year of average or below average rainfall (20 to 50 inches), scaevola does incredibly well. But, it cannot take either too much rain (60 inches plus) or poor drainage when planted in the ground. Scaevola also takes heat beautifully. It breezed through a ten day run of 100 degree plus temperatures in our Georgia trial gardens.

Scaevola takes longer to get going than most other annuals. Don't expect it to grow and thrive until it has been planted for about three weeks. We have noticed it going into a wilt shortly after planting, even if the soil is moist. Don't give it extra water (unless it stays in a wilt for more than a day or two) and it will perk up shortly.

Regional Differences: Does equally well throughout the south

Bloom Time: Spring through fall, continuously

Buying Tips: We have never had any problems with scaevola. Every one we have bought (several different cultivars) has excelled in our gardens.

**Blue ribbon plants are defined on page 12. For blue ribbon performance, follow the planting and maintenance guidelines on pages 33 to 46.*

Botanical Name: *Scaevola aemula*
Family: Goodeniaceae

Companions: Blue scaevola needs bright companions if it is to be viewed from a distance. Yellow melampodium and red salvia are ideal companions for distance viewing. Or, blue and yellow works well together, like blue scaevola and yellow lantana.

However, if you are planting scaevola in a location to be viewed from up close, try using other shapes of blue flowers accented with leaf color, as shown below.

Blue scaevola and some companion plants

Blue Salvia (above, left) looks good with scaevola if some leaf color is added to punch it up a bit. Plant the salvia as the largest layer and border it with scaevola.

'Dark Star' Coleus (above, center) can be added on either side of the salvia. Lime coleus will look good with the grouping as well.

Dark Blue Petunias (above, right) work well in a container planting when added to the other plants shown above. Plant the salvia in the middle and some coleus on either side. Alternate the scaevola and the petunias around the edge of the container. Place the container in light shade to full sun.

GROWING CONDITIONS

Light: Sun to light shade

Water: Medium. Once or twice a week after establishment. Requires more water in containers.

Soil: For the garden, plant in any fertile, well-drained soil that has been enriched with organic matter. Use only good-quality potting mix for containers. See page 30 for specific instructions on soil preparation.

Hardiness: Not tolerant of freezes

Propagation: Seeds or cuttings

Pest Problems: No serious insect or disease problems.

PLANTING & MAINTENANCE

When to Plant: Spring or summer

Trimming: None required

Fertilization: Use the fertilizer described on page 47 only on planting day.

UNIVERSITY AWARDS

1997: Mississippi Medallion Winner ('New Wonder Scaevola').

1997: Georgia Gold Medal Winner.

Our favorite scaevola container combines it with salvia and creeping jenny. Container and column from www.kinsmangarden.com.

Snapdragon

CHARACTERISTICS

Plant Type: Annual

Average Size: 6 to 36 inches tall, depending on variety, and 10 to 14 inches wide.

Growth Rate: Slow in fall, fast in spring.

Leaf: Green, oval leaves with pointed tips clothe the base of the plants.

Flower: Vertical spikes of delicate flowers that open from the bottom upward.

Lifespan: 2 to 6 months

Origin: Mediterranean region

Spacing: About 8 to 12 inches on center (measure from the center of each plant). Closer in containers.

Cautions: Seldom damaged by deer.

Colors: White, yellow, red, pink, peach, and bicolors.

Charming, old-fashioned flowers for the fall-to-spring garden. Plant this one in fall. Removal of dead flowers required on tall varieties, which takes some time.

Tall snapdragons bordered by impatiens

Of all the flowers you can plant in fall for bloom in spring, snapdragons are the only ones that have an upright growth habit. They typically stay low through the winter and then explode with new growth as the weather warms in spring. The tall spikes make excellent cut flowers, and secondary spikes emerge after the first flower spike is removed.

Snapdragons come in a wide variety of sizes, from six inch dwarfs to three feet tall mid to background plants. We have been very happy with the ease of growth of the small ones. They offer a useful carpet of high-impact color and are excellent choices in areas where low stature is required. The tall ones are spectacular, with tall, spire-like flowers that look like the kind of flower that would never grow in the south. However, the tall ones require deadheading (removing of dead flowers), which takes time.

Regional Differences: In zone nine, snapdragons often bloom sporadically throughout the winter. In zones seven and eight, modest blooms often appear in fall, and these are best removed to help plants conserve their energy. In zone six, snapdragons planted in a protected spot with a warm south or west exposure survive winter's cold and bloom in mid to late spring.

Bloom Time: See 'Regional Differences,' above

Buying Tips: We have never had bad luck with snapdragons. Every one we have bought (several different cultivars) has excelled in our gardens.

**Blue ribbon plants are defined on page 12. For blue ribbon performance, follow the planting and maintenance guidelines on pages 33 to 46.*

Companions: Snapdragons look great with spring bulbs, particularly irises. They also work with other cool-weather flowers, like pansies. Mix tall snaps (over 16" tall) with different colored pansies and add some evergreen grasses, like 'Dwarf White Striped Sweet Flag,' for a textural change, as shown below .

White snapdragons and some companion plants

Pansy 'Panola Rose' (above, top) will stay in bloom for most of the late fall, winter, and spring. Plant it as a border for snapdragons.

Dwarf White Striped Sweet Flag Grass (above, center) grows to about 15 inches tall and is evergreen. Plant it as a mid layer between the pansies and the taller snapdragons.

Pansy 'Matrix Deep Blue Blotch' (above, bottom) gives the final touch to this red, white, and blue color scheme. Alternate it with the rose pansies along the border.

Put them all together by planting the tall snapdragons in the center of the bed. Border it with the two colors of pansies, alternated. Plant the grass as a mid sized layer, in between the snapdragons and the pansies. Plant all of them in fall. The pansies and grasses will stay for most of the fall, winter, and spring, with the snapdragons blooming in fall, going dormant for the winter, and re-appearing in spring.

GROWING CONDITIONS

Light: Full sun or at least 6 hours of direct sun each day. When grown in reduced light, flower spikes will curve toward the sun.

Water: Medium. Water twice weekly after planting in fall, when dry weather usually prevails. Winter and spring rains are usually sufficient for snapdragons, but check the soil before cold spells to be sure the flowers don't go into the cold, dry weather with dry soil.

Soil: For the garden, plant in any fertile, well-drained soil that has been enriched with organic matter. Use only good-quality potting mix for containers. See page 30 for specific instructions on soil preparation.

Hardiness: Always hardy in zone 8, provided the plants are well-rooted when cold weather arrives. In zones 6 and 7, plants rest through the winter and re-appear in spring. They bloom now and again in winter during warm spells.

Propagation: Seeds or cuttings

Pest Problems: Rare

PLANTING & MAINTENANCE

When to Plant: Plant in fall with enough time for the plants to become well rooted before the really cold weather comes. October is ideal.

Trimming: Should plants become leggy in late summer, shearing them back by one-third will restore their form and encourage a late flush of fresh blossoms.

Fertilization: Use the fertilizer described on page 47 only on planting day.

Sweet Potato Vine

CHARACTERISTICS

Plant Type: Tuberous, tropical perennial grown as an annual.

Average Size: Vines grow 3 to 8 feet long, depending on variety.

Growth Rate: Fast

Leaf: Leaf shapes include either heart shapes, pointed palmate leaves, and one variety, 'Sweet Caroline,' has deeply cut leaves.

Flower: Insignificant; usually does not bloom on most varieties. A few have attractive flowers.

Lifespan: Lasts for one, full growing season in the south because it won't tolerate freezes.

Origin: Tropical America

Spacing: About 12 to 18 inches on center (measure from the center of each plant). Closer in containers.

Cautions: Seldom damaged by deer.

Colors: Leaf colors include chartreuse, lime green, bronze, burgundy, and green with pink variegation.

1. 'Tricolor' sweet potato
2. 'Sweet Caroline Blackie'
3. 'Sweet Caroline Bronze'
4. 'Marguerite' sweet potato

Calling sweet potato vines easy might be a stretch because they grow too fast and attract insects. However, some new ones are much easier than their predecessors. Vibrant foliage stays lush from early summer to fall. Excellent heat-proof foliage to mix with vigorous summer flowers.

Sweet potato vines are most often used in containers. This window box (#ZWBS30 from kinsmangarden.com) features a Juncus grass as the centerpiece, surrounded by 'Dark Star' coleus, red wax begonias, and 'Black Heart' sweet potato vine.

Sweet potato vines tolerate heat extremely well and are not as thirsty as many other annuals. They are extremely easy to grow if you know what kind to buy and can put up with some holes in the leaves. We found the plants with heart-shaped leaves (like the leaves shown above) grew like Jack-in-the-beanstalk and required frequent trimming. The ones shaped more like a maple leaf (see photo 2, left) grew much slower and were much easier to control, particularly the 'Sweet Caroline' variety. The lime and purple grew at about the same rate. The pink ones grew quite a bit slower but were not as dependable as the lime and purple ones.

Regional Differences: None

Bloom Time: Occasionally, vines may produce small, morning glory-type flowers in late summer. Breeders are working on sweet potato vines that bloom more freely.

Buying Tips: Easy to find in the spring. Look for the ones with the maple-shaped leaves (see photos two and three, left) for the easiest ones to care for.

**Blue ribbon plants are defined on page 12. For blue ribbon performance, follow the planting and maintenance guidelines on pages 33 to 46.*

Botanical Name: *Ipomoea batatas*
Family: Convolvulaceae

Companions: Combine sweet potatoes with other plants that coordinate with the individual leaf colors. For a traffic-stopping color accent, plant lime green sweet potato with bright red and purple, as shown below.

'Marguerite' sweet potato and some companion plants

Dragon Wing Begonias (above, left) are one of the brightest red flowers and contrasts well with the lime green sweet potato. It grows taller than the sweet potato, so plant as the tallest layer, surrounded by sweet potato.

Persian Shield (above, center) can be added for a dramatic color accent with the red begonias. Alternate the two taller plants, and border with the sweet potato.

'Defiance' Coleus (above, right) contrasts really well with lime sweet potato.

Put them all together in a container by using the Persian shield in the center, with a dragon wing begonia planted on either side. Alternate the 'Defiance' coleus and the lime sweet potato vines around the edge. Plant this mix in spring in a container 16" wide or larger (with top-quality potting mix and the fertilizer shown on page 47) and it will last you all season, until the first frost of fall. Expect to trim the sweet potato a few times, as well as pinch the tips off the coleus monthly. Place your container in light shade, or morning sun with afternoon shade, for best results.

GROWING CONDITIONS

Light: Full sun to partial afternoon shade.

Water: Medium after establishment. Likes water once or twice a week during the growing season, depending on its environment. More water in containers.

Soil: For the garden, plant in any fertile, well-drained soil that has been enriched with organic matter. Use only good-quality potting mix for containers.

Hardiness: Vines die when exposed to frost. Tubers must be stored above 55 degrees through the winter.

Propagation: Rooted cuttings, slips that grow from tubers.

Pest Problems: Flea beetles sometimes make pinholes in leaves; various June bugs may casually eat the leaves, too, particularly Japanese beetles. Deer love sweet potato vine foliage.

PLANTING & MAINTENANCE

When to Plant: Set out plants in late spring, after the soil has warmed. Tubers can be saved through winter in a warm, dry place and then planted in a warm bed in spring. "Slips" that grow from the tubers are easily transplanted to new beds or containers when they are 6 inches long.

Trimming: Stems can be trimmed back any time to control their spread. You can increase your supply of plants by rooting 4 inch long stem tips in damp potting soil.

Fertilization: Use the fertilizer described on page 47 only on planting day.

UNIVERSITY AWARDS

2001: Georgia Gold Metal Winner ('Blackie,' 'Marguerite,' 'Tricolor').

Torenia, Wishbone Flower

1ST

CHARACTERISTICS

Plant Type: Annual

Average Size: Upright torenia, about 8 to 12 inches tall by 8 to 10 inches wide. Trailing torenia grows only 2 to 6 inches tall by about 12 inches wide.

Growth Rate: Medium

Leaf: Medium green. About 3/4 inch long.

Flower: Small flower that resembles a tiny pansy.

Lifespan: 3 to 4 months for the upright forms. The trailing form lasts the entire spring, summer, and fall growing season.

Origin: Vietnam

Spacing: About 8 inches on center for the upright forms and 12 inches for the trailing forms (measure from the center of each plant). Closer in containers.

Cautions: The upright form reseeds somewhat. We have never found the reseeding excessive.

Colors: Blue, purple, white, red, burgundy, and combinations. Yellow centers on many.

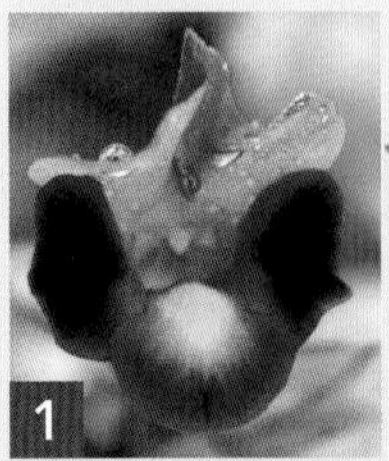

1. *'Clown Blue'*
2. *'Clown Burgundy'*
3. *'Summer Wave Amethyst'*
4. *'Summer Wave Blue'*

Trailing torenia is one of the best performing annuals in our trials, blooming from spring until the first frost of fall with very little care. Easily wins a blue ribbon.*

Torenia 'Summer Wave Large Violet' torenia is the best performer of our torenia trials. It does equally as well planted in containers or in the ground.

Torenia is a relatively new plant that deserves more use in southern gardens. There are two main types: upright (we tested the 'Clown' series) and trailing (we tested the 'Summer Wave' series). The 'Clown' series did acceptably well, taking the early summer heat with ease but giving out in August. We still use it because of its beauty and shade tolerance. The trailing type did very well, lasting from spring until the first frost of fall, with no care other than water.

Regional Differences: Torenia do equally well throughout the south. The trailing types are short-term perennials in the sub tropics (zones ten to eleven), lasting for up to a year.

Bloom Time: Late spring to late fall

Buying Tips: Upright torenia is often sold in four inch pots or multipacks. You may need to look up at the hanging baskets for the trailing torenia.

**Blue ribbon plants are defined on page 12. For blue ribbon performance, follow the planting and maintenance guidelines on pages 33 to 46.*

Botanical Name: *Torenia fournieri*

Family: Scrophulariaceae

Companions: Torenias make great borders for most plants that bloom in spring, summer, or fall. For a long-blooming garden, pair it with the shrubs and perennials shown below. If you can't find any of them at your local garden center, there are lots of internet suppliers.

'Summer Wave Large Violet' torenia and some companion plants

Phlox 'David' (above, top) is a perennial phlox that did better than any other phlox in the trials at Huntsville Botanical Garden because of its mildew resistance. It grows to about three feet tall and blooms for about two months (June and July) each summer. Trailing torenia is a great border for this phlox.

'Let's Dance Starlight' Hydrangea (above, center) is one of the newer, reblooming hydrangeas that flowers for about three months in summer, June through August. Again, trailing torenia is a gorgeous border for this shrub.

'Stella d'Oro' Daylily (above, bottom) is one of the longest blooming perennial daylilies, blooming for up to three months each summer. Torenia is an ideal border for daylilies.

Put them all together for a long blooming garden by planting the hydrangea as the tallest layer, surrounded by clumps of phlox and daylilies. Plant the torenia as a border.

GROWING CONDITIONS

Light: Medium shade to full sun

Water: Medium after establishment. Likes water once or twice a week during the growing season, depending on its environment. See pages 34 to 37 for more information. Requires more water when grown in containers.

Soil: For the garden, plant in any fertile, well-drained soil that has been enriched with organic matter. Use only good-quality potting mix for containers. See page 30 for specific instructions on soil preparation.

Hardiness: Not tolerant of even cool (45 degree) temperatures.

Propagation: Seeds or cuttings, depending on variety.

Pest Problems: Rare

PLANTING & MAINTENANCE

When to Plant: Spring or summer

Trimming: None required

Fertilization: Use the fertilizer described on page 47 only on planting day.

UNIVERSITY AWARDS

2004: Top 10 Winner from North Carolina State University ('Catalina Blue').

Vinca, Periwinkle

1ST

CHARACTERISTICS

Plant Type: Annual

Average Size: 9 to 14 inches tall, 12 to 24 inches wide, depending on variety.

Growth Rate: Fast

Leaf: Glossy, dark green, oblong leaves with prominent central leaf veins.

Flower: Flat blossoms to 2 inches across, often with contrasting eyes.

Lifespan: 5 to 6 months

Origin: Madagascar

Spacing: About 10 inches on center (measure from the center of each plant). Closer in containers.

Cautions: Poisonous. Do not eat this plant. Seldom damaged by deer.

Colors: White, red, purple, or pink flowers.

1. Vinca 'Cooler Raspberry'
2. Vinca 'Cooler Icy Pink'
3. Vinca 'Cooler Peppermint'
4. Vinca 'Cooler Rose Hot'

Heat-tolerant plants that withstand drought, making vinca a top choice for beds that bake in summer sun. Easily rates a blue ribbon* if they have excellent drainage.

Mixed vincas in a bed

Whether you call this amazing flower vinca or periwinkle, it will earn high ratings in your garden, as it consistently does in university field trials throughout the south. Vincas take heat and drought very well, but not too much rain. Average southern summers are fine, but when the rainfall exceeds 60 or so inches per year, they suffer.

Vincas often reseed in the garden, but the offspring of hybrid plants are seldom as vigorous or colorful as their parents. It is best to pull them out.

Vincas are very easy to grow, outlasting most annuals in the south with no care - other than occasional watering - after proper planting and fertilization.

Regional Differences: Annual vincas grow well throughout the south

Bloom Time: Mid June until the first fall frost, continuously

Buying Tips: Extremely easy to find at the garden centers in spring and summer. All we bought did quite well, provided it didn't rain too much.

**Blue ribbon plants are defined on page 12. For blue ribbon performance, follow the planting and maintenance guidelines on pages 33 to 46.*

Companions: Perwinkles are great companions for any other annuals that like sun in this chapter. They also make great accents in perennial beds. Try hot pink periwinkles with the perennials shown below and you will have about five months of color in your bed.

Vinca 'Cooler Rose Hot' and some companion plants

Luna Hibiscus (above, left) is an excellent perennial companion for vinca. It reaches about two to three feet tall and blooms from July until September. Its flowers are huge, up to seven inches across, which contrasts well with the smaller vinca flowers. Use the vinca as a border for the hibiscus.

'Stella d'Oro' Daylily (above, center) is one of the longest blooming perennial daylilies, blooming for up to three months each summer. They reach about 18 to 24 inches tall. Vinca is an ideal border for daylilies.

Purple Heart (above, right) is another perennial companion for vinca. They have color for the entire spring, summer, and fall growing season, and reach about a foot tall - the same as most vincas. Alternate clumps of vinca and purple heart for a low border for perennials.

Put them all together for a long blooming garden by planting the hibiscus as the tallest layer and the daylilies in the middle. Alternate clumps of vinca and purple heart as a border.

GROWING CONDITIONS

Light: Full sun, at least 6 hours per day.

Water: Medium to low. Water twice weekly for the first month after planting. Once established, vincas can get by with weekly water, provided they are mulched. Requires more water in containers.

Soil: For the garden, plant in any fertile, well-drained soil that has been enriched with organic matter. Use only good-quality potting mix for containers. See page 30 for specific instructions on soil preparation.

Hardiness: Not tolerant of frosts

Propagation: Seeds

Pest Problems: Root rot can develop if plants are kept too wet.

PLANTING & MAINTENANCE

When to Plant: Spring or summer

Trimming: None needed

Fertilization: Use the fertilizer described on page 47 only on planting day.

UNIVERSITY AWARDS

2007: Mississippi Medallion Winner ('Titan' vinca).

1993, 1994, 1996, 2004, 2007: Awards from North Carolina State University ('Blue Pearl,' 'Heatwave Burgundy,' 'Heatwave Grape,' Heatwave Peach,' 'Jaio Scarlet Eye,' 'Titan Blush,' 'Peppermint Cooler,' 'Icy Pink Cooler,' Pretty in Rose,' 'Hot Streak Salmon').

1ST Zinnia 'Profusion'

CHARACTERISTICS

Plant Type: Annual

Average Size: About 12 to 16 inches tall by 12 inches wide.

Growth Rate: Fast

Leaf: Oval medium green leaves with pointed tips.

Flower: Open, daisy-like flowers, about 1 1/2 to 2 inches across.

Lifespan: 4 to 7 months

Origin: Mexico

Spacing: About 12 inches on center (measure from the center of each plant). Closer in containers.

Cautions: Seldom damaged by deer.

Colors: White, red, pink, peach, and orange.

1. 'Profusion Apricot' zinnia
2. 'Profusion Cherry' zinnia
3. 'Profusion Deep Apricot' zinnia
4. 'Profusion Fire' zinnia

While most zinnias are prone to diseases in the south, the 'Profusion' series breezes through the worst extremes of drought, humidity, and heat the south has to offer. Winners of the coveted All-America selection prize. Blue ribbon winner* because of their long, all season bloom period with very little care.

'Profusion Coral Pink' zinnias

Many different kinds of zinnias have been grown in the south, most of which are taller than the small, 'Profusion' series. But the 'Profusion' series out performs them all because it doesn't get the diseases (mildew) that plaque most other zinnias in the south. These small zinnias are not only trouble free, but they also bloom so heavily that they give a great color impact either close up or from a distance. Another benefit of these easy plants is that they keep blooming their hearts out even when you don't remove the faded flowers.

Regional Differences: No differences throughout the south

Bloom Time: Late spring to late fall, blooming constantly

Buying Tips: These zinnias are fairly easy to find in garden centers, as are many other kinds of zinnias. The 'Profusion' series will not look as glamorous as many other zinnias because the flowers are smaller. But, you will be happier in the long run with these smaller zinnias because of better performance. Another small-flowered zinnia (*Zinnia angustifolia* or *linearis*) with tiny leaves blooms as well as the 'Profusion,' but its color doesn't show up as well. Check the plant tag at the garden center and be sure it says 'Profusion' zinnia.

**Blue ribbon plants are defined on page 12. For blue ribbon performance, follow the planting and maintenance guidelines on pages 33 to 46.*

Botanical Name: *Zinnia x hybrid*
Family: Asteraceae

Companions: 'Profusion' zinnias work well as borders for most shrubs and perennials. For a country garden look, mix them with perennial salvias and lantana. Or, try the combination of annuals and shrubs shown below.

'Profusion White' zinnias and some companion plants

Lantana makes a great companion for 'Profusion' zinnias because it blooms at the same time. Low-growing lantanas like, this 'New Gold,' grow about the same size as the zinnia, so alternate them for a country garden border. Stick to full sun only for this combination.

Add a Purple Butterfly Bush (above, center) for a dramatic color accent with the zinnias and lantana. Most of the newer, compact butterfly bushes, like this 'Purple Emperor,' grow to about four feet tall, so put it in the center or back of the bed, surrounded by the zinnia and lantana. It blooms for about two months in summer.

'Totally Tempted' Cuphea (above, right) grows to about the same height as the lantana and zinnia. Alternate these three, smaller plants as a border in front of the taller butterfly bush. Two rows of this border look much better than just one.

GROWING CONDITIONS

Light: Full sun to partial afternoon shade.

Water: Medium. Zinnias can tolerate drought but grow best when they receive water twice a week. More often in containers.

Soil: For the garden, plant in any fertile, well-drained soil that has been enriched with organic matter. Use only good-quality potting mix for containers. See page 30 for specific instructions on soil preparation.

Hardiness: Cannot tolerate frost

Propagation: Grows easily from seeds.

Pest Problems: None known

PLANTING & MAINTENANCE

When to Plant: Spring or summer

Trimming: None needed. Removing dead flowers will result in a few more blooms.

Fertilization: Use the fertilizer described on page 47 only on planting day.

UNIVERSITY AWARDS

2006: Mississippi Medallion Winner ('Profusion Apricot and Fire').

1997: Exceptional performance Winner from North Carolina State University ('Profusion Orange').

Other Annuals that Deserve Mention

Ageranthemum
Ageranthemum frutescens 'Butterfly'

This daisy-like flower is gorgeous when in bloom, but only in spring and fall. It doesn't take the southern summer heat. Full sun. 12 inches tall. Medium water.

Ageratum
Ageratum houstonianum

Primarily useful for its interesting texture and pretty color. It will stop blooming periodically, taking rests for brief periods. Prefers sun. About 8 to 10 inches tall. Lives for about three months. Medium water.

Allysum
Lobularia maritima

This cool-weather plant looks great in spring and fall. Won't take summer heat. Grow it in full sun in temperatures that range from 36 to 85 degrees. About 4 inches tall. Medium water.

Anthurium
Anthurium spp.

Usually sold with the houseplants. Blooms all season in dense to medium shade. Takes no sun at all. Some have success with it as a house plant in winter, but hard to grow inside. 12 to 18 inches tall. Low water.

Begonia, Rex
Begonia rex-cultorum

Used for their striking leaf patterns in shade. Doesn't like the heat of summer, but sometimes lasts the whole season. Frequently used as a house plant. 4 to 12 inches tall. Shade. Medium water.

Begonia, Tuberous
Begonia tuberoso

Do well in areas that have cool, dry summers. They have not done well for long in our southern gardens because of the heat. 4 to 12 inches tall. Shade. Medium water.

Blue Daze
Evolvulus glomeratus

We used this plant a lot in containers until discovering trailing torenia, which performs much better. Warm weather plant, but it stops blooming from time to time. Light shade to full sun. Lives about 6 months. Low water.

Calibrachoa or Million Bells
Calibrachoa x

We have had erratic results with this plant. Some have done quite well while others die quickly. New ones coming on the market all the time, so better plants probably exist. Plant in sun in spring or summer. Medium water.

Celosia
Celosia spp.

We've had mixed results with these plants. Some have lasted 6 months, while others have struggled to make it 2 months. Generally, taller varieties have did better than dwarfs. 6 to 20 inches tall. Sun. Medium water.

Copper Leaf
Acalypha spp.

Excellent tropical shrub used as an annual in the south. Used primarily for leaf color. Many varieties available. All the different ones we have tried did very well. Light shade to full sun. 2 to 8 feet tall in the tropics. Medium water.

Cosmos
Cosmos spp.

Summer annual that reseeds freely. Gorgeous flowers, but the plants don't stay in bloom continuously for the whole season. Lasts about 3 months. About 18 inches tall. Sun. Low water.

Croton
Codiaeum variegatum

An excellent tropical shrub used as an annual in the south. Lasts from spring until fall. Overwinters well in a garage if you give it light and occasional water (weekly). Medium shade to full sun. 1 to 4 feet tall. Low water.

Blue and red ribbon plants are defined on page 12 to 13.

Cuphea 'Totally Tempted'
Cuphea llavea

New hybrid of a plant called bat face cuphea. Takes heat well. Bloomed on and off during spring, summer, and fall. Full sun. 2 feet tall by 15 inches wide. Low water.

Diascia
Diascia spp.

We were quite impressed by the Diascia 'Miracle' in spring and fall. It bloomed quite well in temperatures ranging from 45 to 90 degrees. 8 inches tall. Sun. Medium water.

Dichondra 'Silver Falls'
Dichondra argenta 'Silver Falls'

A fabulous silver vine that is one of the best container plants for southern summers. It requires almost no care and gives incredible performance. Lasts from spring to fall. Light shade to full sun. Trails down as far as 8 feet. Low water.

Diplademia
Mandevilla spp.

Blooms all spring and summer, even in high temperatures. Treat it like an annual and it will require nothing but water and fertilizer! Full sun. 12 to 18 inches tall. Medium water.

Dracaena
Dracaena spp.

One of the most common indoor plants. They work well outdoors provided they are protected from frost. Really easy. Lasts all season and overwinters well indoors. Dense to light shade. 1 to 30 feet tall. Low water.

Duranta 'Gold Mound'
Duranta erecta 'Gold Mound'

An excellent, lime-green foliage plant that breezes through the hottest summer the south has to offer. Full sun. 8 inches tall. Low water.

Euphorbia 'Diamond Frost'
Euphorbia 'Diamond Frost'

We have had only one season's experience with this wildly popular plant. It did quite well, but only lasted about 3 months. We will definitely try this one again. Light shade to sun. 12 to 18 inches tall. Low water.

Geranium
Pelargonium spp.

Extremely popular plant that rates a red ribbon because it looks better if the dead flowers are removed. Having more problems with heat as the south gets hotter. Light shade to full sun. 12 to 14 inches tall. Low water.

Gerber Daisy
Gerbera jamesonii

Lovely but very short-lived plant. Only lives and blooms for about a month. Some people have good luck with it as a perennial, but we never have. 12 inches tall. Sun. Medium water.

Gomphrena
Gomphrena globosa

Excellent summer annual that adds an interesting texture to the garden. We've had good luck with it. Blooms for most of the growing season. Full sun. 8 to 18 inches tall. Low water.

Grass, Fiber Optic
Scirpus cernuus

Features tiny, grass-like leaves with minute yellow spikes on the tips of each leaf, giving the illusion of a fiber optic lamp. Did very well in our containers. Extremely easy. Medium to light shade. 6 to 8 inches tall. Low water.

Hyacinth Bean
Dolichos lablab

A fast grower, hyacinth vines will twine on any type of trellis, or you can let them ramble over a stump. Blooms from late summer to early fall. Easy to grow. 4 to 6 feet tall. Sun. Medium water.

Other Annuals that Deserve Mention

Iresine or Bloodleaf
Iresine 'Blazin Rose'

Gorgeous leaves in this mounding plant that did fairly well but only lived for 3 months in containers. Did better in spring than during the heat of summer Light shade to full sun. 12 to 18 inches tall. Medium water.

Joseph's Coat
Alternanthera spp.

An up-and-coming plant that is getting rave reviews throughout the south because of its heat tolerance. Use for leaf color. Full sun. Different varieties range from 4 to 20 inches tall. Low water.

Kalanchoe
Kalanchoe blossfeldiana

Usually sold with the house plants. Beautiful, succulent plant that flowers in shade. Only lasts about a month, however. Sun or shade. 8 inches tall. Low water.

Licorice Plant
Helichrysum petiolare

Did well in our containers but developed some mildew by the end of summer (didn't show much). Lasted 6 months. Great color for containers. Light shade to sun. 8 to 12 inches tall. Low water.

Lobelia
Lobelia spp.

One of our favorite container plants for cooler seasons like spring and fall. Not for the heat of summer. About 6 inches tall. Sun to light shade. Medium water.

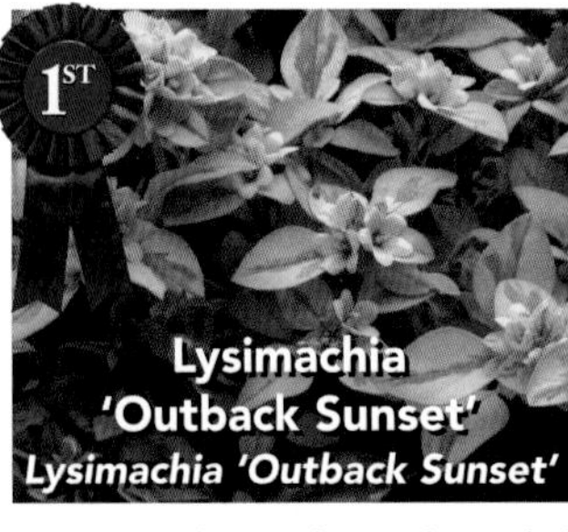

Lysimachia 'Outback Sunset'
Lysimachia 'Outback Sunset'

Semi-trailing plant that did very well in our container trials. Didn't bloom all summer, but the leaf color lasted. Takes some sun, but does better in medium to light shade. Grows about 8 inches down the sides of a pot. Medium water.

Mandevilla Vine
Mandevilla spp.

A tropical vine that does very well in hot, southern summers as an annual. Bright, pink flowers on a fast-growing vine. Grows about 10 to 12 feet long. Full sun. Medium water.

Marigold
Tagetes spp.

Very popular southern annual, but only lasted a few months in our gardens. Melampodium is a much better yellow annual. Full sun. 6 to 30 inches tall. Medium water.

Mint, Variegated
Plectranthus coleoides 'Variegata'

Fabulous container plant. Lasts all season, from spring until the first frost of fall. Trails 36 inches down the sides of a container, but slowly. Medium to light shade. Medium water.

Mona Lavendar
Plectranthus x plepalila

Great plant for cool weather blooms. Flowers in spring and fall, but not in summer. Medium shade to full sun in cooler weather, but burns up in summer sun. 18 inches tall. Medium water.

Morning Glory
Ipomoea purpurea

Planted in spring, this vine become a wall of foliage when grown in a wire or chain-link fence. Blooms open daily, and flowering often continues beyond the first fall frost. Sun. Medium Water

Osteospermum
Osteospermum spp.

Short, 2 month bloom period in spring, but gorgeous when flowering. 12 inches tall. Some lucky gardeners have luck with them as perennials. Not so for us! Sun. Medium water.

Blue and red ribbon plants are defined on page 12 to 13.

Perilla Magilla
Perilla frutescens 'Magilla'

Great plant that is very similar to coleus. Rates a red ribbon because it looks better with monthly pinching. Lasts all spring, summer, and fall in the south. Medium to light shade. 2 to 4 feet tall. Medium water.

Phlox
Phlox spp.

The best annual phlox in our trials is 'Phlox Intensia' that blooms for most of the season. Perennial phlox are covered in chapter 3. Full sun. 12 to 14 inches tall. Medium water.

Phormium
Phormium spp

Phormium or flax is an excellent, blue ribbon plant. Extremely easy. Likes temperatures from 40 to over 100. Overwinter it inside with bright light. Light shade to full sun outdoors. 2 feet tall. Low water.

Plumbago
Plumbago auriculata

Plumbago is a great perennial in the ground in zones 9 to 11 that is taking off as an easy, southern annual. Blooms for most of the spring, summer, and fall. Full sun. 2 to 3 feet tall. Low water.

Portulaca, Moss Rose
Portulaca grandiflora

Although this tough plant requires little water, it only blooms on and off throughout the hot season. The flowers close for up to half of each day. 4 inches tall. Full sun. Low water.

Purslane
Portulaca oleracea

Similar to moss rose, but the flowers are a little smaller and the leaves are larger. Like moss rose, the flowers close for part of every day. 3 to 6 inches tall. Full sun. Low water.

Salvia 'Indigo Spires'
Salvia 'Indigo Spires'

Shrub salvia that grows extremely well as an annual. Informal plant that flops over some. 3 feet tall by at least 4 feet wide, so give it space. Returns as a perennial is some parts of the south. Light shade to full sun. Medium water.

Shrimp Plant, Golden
Pachystachys lutea

Excellent plant that blooms most of spring, summer, and fall. Buy one that looks like this photo, because others did not do as well in our trials. Medium to light shade. 18 to 24 inches tall. Medium water.

Sunflower
Helianthus spp.

Wonderful but short lived summer annual. Look for varieties that rebloom. Easy to grow from seed and a lot of fun for children. 1 to 12 feet tall. Full sun. Medium water.

Syngonium
Syngonium spp.

Commonly-used as a houseplant for generations. It is easy to grow and many new types are introduced each year. Dense to light shade. Slow growing, viney plant. Medium water.

Verbena, Annual
Verbena spp.

Trailing annual verbena averaged lasting about 3 months each summer. The upright form died in about a month. See page 184 for profile of perennial verbena Sun. Medium water.

Vinca 'Illumination'
Vinca 'Illumination'

Excellent, long trailer that lasts a whole season with no care other than water! Use it with darker colors, like purple coleus, for contrast. Medium to light shade. Medium water.

Chapter 3

Perennials

✿ Perennials are plants that come back to life year after year, usually following a winter rest. They do not need to be replanted each spring, which saves time and money.

✿ Most perennials are deciduous, meaning they die back in winter. However, some (like lenten rose, autumn ferns, some grasses, and heucheras) are evergreen.

✿ Perennials generally have soft stems that die back with the leaves in winter. Shrubs have hard, woody stems that do not die back, even if they lose their leaves.

✿ Perennials don't bloom as long as annuals. And, they usually do not have as much color impact. However, by combining perennials with other perennials or shrubs that bloom at the same time, major color impact can be achieved with plants that don't require yearly replacement.

✿ Perennials generally need more water than shrubs, vines, or trees because their roots don't grow as large. However, we have included quite a few low water perennials in this chapter.

✿ Perennials in this chapter are basically easy to grow. All of them require at least one trimming a year. Many look better with deadheading (removal of dead flowers) but don't require it. Most have a longer flowering period if you have time to do this chore.

✿ Dividing is another maintenance chore common to most perennials, either to rejuvenate the clump or to get more plants. Some perennials require division every few years and others don't. Each plant profile gives details for that plant.

Above: White crapemyrtles with daylilies planted below

Left: This garden at the home of Mrs. Melba Pearson from Louisville, Mississippi, features shrubs, annuals, and perennials. The dark-colored shrubs in the background are loropetalum. Perennials include daylilies, canna lilies, and purple heart. The pink vincas are annuals.

1ST Agastache, Hummingbird Mint

CHARACTERISTICS

Plant Type: Deciduous perennial (dies back in winter).

Average Size: 36 inches tall and 18 inches wide.

Growth Rate: Medium

Leaf: Slightly-fuzzy, green leaves have a minty licorice scent when crushed.

Flower: Tall, upright spikes studded with numerous tiny flowers that attract bees and butterflies.

Origin: Native species, such as *A. foeniculum*, crossed with others.

Spacing: About 18 inches on center (measure from the center of each plant). In three years, a single plant will form a 2 foot wide clump.

Cautions: Attracts bees, but almost never eaten by deer.

Colors: Flowers are lavender-blue, pink, or coral.

UNIVERSITY AWARDS

2004: Georgia Gold Medal Winners include 'Apricot Sunrise,' 'Firebird,' 'Tutti Frutti,' and 'Blue Fortune.'

1. *Agastache 'Blue Fortune'*
2. *Agastache 'Tutti Frutti'*
3. *Agastache 'Acapulco'*

Agastache is a great butterfly and hummingbird plant, offering both ease of care and drought tolerance. Removal of dead flowers is not needed to keep it blooming for a full three months. Rates a blue ribbon* because it gives a lot for just a little bit of your time.

Agastache 'Tutti Frutti' with caladiums and purple fountain grass

New varieties of agastache are definitely worthy of space in your perennial garden. 'Blue Fortune' is but one of several new hybrids making its way into nurseries. Huntsville Botanical Garden has been quite happy with the performance of the 'Blue Fortune,' as well as the 'Tutti Fruti' and 'Acapulco' series.

Regional Differences: Agastache is outstanding in a dry garden. In very humid, rainy areas of the coastal south, grow it in a raised bed to improve drainage and air circulation.

Color Period: Blooms from late spring to late fall, blooming constantly.

Buying Tips: Lots of new agastaches are constantly appearing. Some have the reputation for getting a bit rangy. We have only tried the three pictured (left) and have been happy with all of them.

**Blue ribbon plants are defined on page 12. For blue ribbon performance, follow the planting and maintenance guidelines on pages 28 to 46.*

Companions: Agastache likes plenty of sun and rather dry conditions, so it is best teamed up with other dry garden standouts, such as black-eyed Susans or ornamental grasses. 'Blue Fortune' looks great with mound-forming, yellow flowers, such as coreopsis, or you can pair it with drought-tolerant annuals, like cuphea, gomphrena, or 'Profusion' zinnias.

'Blue Fortune' grows three feet tall when it's in full bloom, so it has no trouble rising up behind a foreground planting of coreopsis. Because of its upright form and bottlebrush-shaped flower spikes, agastache is ideal for mixing with mounding plants with daisy-shaped blossoms.

Since 'Blue Fortune' has such a long bloom period, pair it with some other southern superstars for a bed that blooms all season long, as shown below.

Agastache 'Blue Fortune' and some companions for easy color layers

Black-Eyed Susans (above, left) are one of the best perennials to use with 'Blue Fortune' because they both bloom for most of the summer, like full sun, and have different shaped flowers. The blue and yellow colors contrast well, too. Since black-eyed Susans grow to about 18 inches tall, plant them in front of the 'Blue Fortune.'

'Knock Out' Roses (above, right) bloom spring, summer, and fall, so they will keep the bed in color for the entire growing season. These tough roses crave sun, like both the black-eyed Susans and agastaches. They grow taller than the 'Blue Fortune,' so plant them as the tallest plant in the bed.

GROWING CONDITIONS

Light: Full sun, at least 6 hours per day.

Water: Low after establishment. Likes water every week or two during the growing season, depending on its environment.

Soil: For the garden, plant in any fertile, well-drained soil that has been enriched with organic matter. Use only good-quality potting mix for containers.

Hardiness: Zones 6 to 9

Propagation: Division in spring. Better yet, root 4 inch stem tip cuttings taken in early summer. Hybrid plants do not breed true from seed.

Pest Problems: Rare

PLANTING & MAINTENANCE

When to Plant: Agastache from containers can be planted anytime. Fall is best because they establish easier in cooler weather. Expect a modest bloom the first year, with a much more robust clump and heavier set of flowers in subsequent seasons.

Trimming: Agastaches don't need much trimming when they are blooming. Removing dead flowers is not necessary, but the plants might need some neatening up at some point in the summer. Cut back the dead foliage (to the ground) after it freezes in late fall or early winter.

Fertilization: Medium. Fertilize at planting time and each spring with a timed-release product (page 47). Less fertilizer is needed with the application of more organics.

Division: Divide in spring or fall, but fall is best. Division is not necessary to keep the plant healthy, so do it every 3 to 5 years only if you want more plants.

1ST Amsonia, Blue Star

CHARACTERISTICS

Plant Type: Deciduous perennial (dies back in winter).

Average Size: About 3 feet tall by 3 feet wide.

Growth Rate: Slow for the first year, moderate in subsequent seasons.

Leaf: Narrow, olive green, thread-like leaves.

Flower: Clusters of star-shaped flowers.

Origin: Native to South and Midwest US.

Spacing: 18 inches on center (measure from the center of each plant). Plants look good in groups of 3 to 5.

Cautions: Sap or juice can irritate skin. Somewhat resistant to deer.

Flower Colors: Blue

Amsonia tabernaemontana is another similar plant that does equally as well as this blue star. The main difference is the shape and size of the leaves.

Award-winning perennial that offers almost year-round color from both flowers and leaves. Fast show of intense, blue flowers in spring. Attractive, feathery foliage glows gold in the fall. Great companion for other spring-blooming shrubs and perennials. It rates a blue ribbon* because of its high performance and ease of care.

Native to the stream banks of Arkansas, this trouble-free perennial made the Georgia Perennial Plant Association's list of the top ten perennials for sun. It was also named an Arkansas Select plant in 2001, and many gardeners name it as their favorite foliage plant for fall. The slate-blue flowers that come in spring have earned amsonia many common names, including blue jean flower. After the flowers fade, amsonia enriches the garden with its airy texture. In fall, the foliage turns bright banana yellow and holds its color for more than a month. Deer usually leave blue star alone, so it's a great plant for gardens plagued with hungry deer.

Regional Differences: Blue star is easy to grow throughout the south. In zones seven and eight, it performs best with some break from the summer sun.

Color Period: Blooms around Mid-April to mid-May for about six weeks. Foliage color is banana yellow around October.

Buying Tips: If you can't find this plant at your local garden center, shop for it online. There is another blue star with thicker leaves (pictured at left) that performs as well as this one.

**Blue ribbon plants are defined on page 12. For blue ribbon performance, follow the planting and maintenance guidelines on pages 28 to 46.*

Companions: Envision blue star as an ornamental grass. It makes a great bed partner for purple coneflower, black-eyed Susan, or any type of coreopsis. And, like ornamental grasses, blue star mixes well with daffodils and other spring-flowering bulbs planted on the edge of the root zone. Plan ahead for blue star's fall color by allowing space nearby for pink or purple chrysanthemums or asters (they can be planted on top of dormant daffodils). Large drifts of five amsonia plants form a dramatic sea of fine-textured foliage.

Amsonia looks at its best mixed with other spring-blooming flowers. Try layering it with azaleas and kerria, as shown below. Plant them in an area of morning sun and afternoon shade.

Amsonia with some companions that form easy color layers

Azaleas (above, left) bloom at about the same time as amsonia, and both do well in morning sun and afternoon shade. Maintain the azaleas at about four feet tall, and plant the shorter (three feet tall) amsonias in front.

Kerria (above, right) usually blooms at the same time as both the azaleas and the amsonia. Let them grow to their full height of six feet and plant them behind the azaleas, as the tallest plants in this grouping.

This combination will give you many years of color with very little care.

GROWING CONDITIONS

Light: Full sun to partial shade. Foliage color is best if they get at least a half day of sun.

Water: Medium after establishment. Likes water once or twice a week during the growing season, depending on its environment.

Soil: For the garden, plant in any fertile, well-drained soil that has been enriched with organic matter.

Hardiness: Zones 5 to 9

Propagation: Seeds, rooted cuttings, division. Clumps rarely need division, so the best way to increase your supply of plants is to take stem tip cuttings in late spring, dip the ends in rooting powder, and set them to root for 4 to 6 weeks before planting them in the garden.

Pest Problems: This plant is remarkably pest free.

PLANTING & MAINTENANCE

When to Plant: Amsonia from containers can be planted anytime. Fall is best because they establish easier in cooler weather. Be patient, as amsonia needs a season to establish itself in the garden.

Trimming: In early summer after flowering, you can cut off the dead flowers if you don't like the way they look, but it's not necessary. In winter, the foliage will turn yellow-tan, which some people like, and others don't. If it bothers you, cut it off. If not, leave the old foliage on the plants all the way through winter, and trim it back to the ground first thing in the spring.

Fertilization: Medium. Fertilize at planting time and each spring with a timed-release product (page 47). Less fertilizer is needed with the application of more organics.

Division: Divide in spring every 3 to 5 years when you notice a hole in the middle of the clump.

1ST Aster, New England

CHARACTERISTICS

Plant Type: Deciduous perennial (dies back in winter).

Average Size: Plants remain small (about 18 inches tall) until they bloom; then they grow to about 2.5 to 3 feet tall.

Growth Rate: Medium

Leaf: Narrow, gray-green leaves

Flower: Flat, 1 inch wide daisy-like flowers.

Origin: Native to Eastern US

Spacing: About 18 inches on center (measure from the center of each plant).

Cautions: Sap or juice can irritate skin. Somewhat resistant to deer.

Flower Colors: Purple, blue, pink

Late-blooming asters end the color season with a bang as fall's last big blast of color. Easy to grow if you choose the New England aster, which is native not only to that region but also to the south. Easily rates a blue ribbon* because of its color impact with very little care.

'Purple Dome' aster

Asters snooze through much of the season and then bloom so heavily in fall that the foliage is hidden beneath thousands of starry flowers (aster is Latin for star). You can grow tall ones against a picket fence or stud the garden with more compact varieties, such as the two foot 'Purple Dome' or 'English Countryside,' a lighter, purplish blue. In addition to their beauty, asters serve as nectar plants for several species of butterflies, and monarchs often stop to sip aster nectar as they migrate southward in fall.

Regional Differences: Perennial asters are easy to grow throughout the south. Do not confuse them with annual asters, which are often troubled by disease.

Color Period: The species described here, commonly called New England aster, blooms very late, in October and November for about three weeks.

Buying Tips: Some asters are difficult to grow in the south. Look for the name 'New England Aster' or 'Aster novae-angliae' on the label for the best ones.

**Blue ribbon plants are defined on page 12. For blue ribbon performance, follow the planting and maintenance guidelines on pages 28 to 46.*

Companions: Asters are natural bed partners for yellow chrysanthemums, though the asters usually continue to bloom after the mums are finished. If you clean up your garden in October, when asters are on the brink of bloom, consider plugging in a few pale yellow pansies, which work like footlights for asters grown as specimen plants.

Firespike is a wonderful companion for asters not only for its similar bloom time but also its different flower shape. Try the two of them together with violas, as shown below.

'Purple Dome' aster and some companions

Firespike (above, top right) is one of the best perennials to use as a backdrop for asters. It blooms from about August until the first frost. Since it grows quite tall (to four feet), plant it behind the shorter asters. Stick to sun (or morning sun and afternoon shade) for best blooming from both of them. We have tried firespike in temperatures down to fifteen degrees, but don't know if it would survive colder temperatures.

Yellow Violas (above, bottom) are annuals that work well as a border for both firespike and asters. They grow to about six inches tall and bloom happily in light shade to full sun. Violas bloom from October until the following spring.

GROWING CONDITIONS

Light: Full sun to partial afternoon shade.

Water: Medium to low. Plants grow best when they receive water twice weekly through the first half of summer. They tolerate late summer drought extremely well.

Soil: For the garden, plant in any fertile, well-drained soil that has been enriched with organic matter. Use only good-quality potting mix for containers.

Hardiness: Zones 5 to 8

Propagation: In spring, use a hand trowel to dig up the small-rooted stems that emerge from the base of the old plant. You also can root stem-tip cuttings taken in spring.

Pest Problems: Several species of butterfly larvae (caterpillars) eat aster leaves, but the flowers hide the damage from view.

PLANTING & MAINTENANCE

When to Plant: Asters from containers can be planted anytime. Fall is best because they establish easier in cooler weather. Divisions taken from established clumps can be dug and moved until the first of June.

Trimming: Some tall asters require quite a bit of pinching to maintain their compact form. 'Purple Dome' and some of the other compact varieties do not need pinching. After the first hard frost, trim it to the ground.

Fertilization: Medium. Fertilize at planting time and each spring with a timed-release product (page 47). Less fertilizer is needed with the application of more organics.

Division: Dig and divide established clumps every 2 to 3 years, in spring. The outer growth usually has the most healthy plants. Discard the center if it looks bad.

2ND Baptisia, False Indigo

CHARACTERISTICS

Plant Type: Deciduous perennial (dies back in winter).

Average Size: 3 to 4 feet tall by 3 feet wide.

Growth Rate: Slow during first two years, then moderate.

Leaf: Pea-like green leaflets on purplish or charcoal stems.

Flower: Pea-like blossoms on long spikes that open from the bottom upward

Origin: Southeast and Midwest US.

Spacing: About 2 feet on center (measure from the center of each plant). They spread to form a dense clump.

Cautions: Toxic to some. Do not eat this plant. Almost never damaged by deer.

Flower Colors: Blue, purple, white

UNIVERSITY AWARDS

1996: Georgia Gold Medal Winner

Different species of baptisia feature different colored flowers.

Graceful white or blue spikes for a month in late spring. So easy you can plant it and almost forget about it! This native plant brings drama to the back of a perennial bed in spring. Easily rates a red ribbon* for high performance with little care - provided you give it good drainage.

Baptisia australis

Southern gardeners often have trouble growing lupines and sweet peas, but we can grow baptisias, which make fine substitutes. These upright, native plants put on a lovely spring show of blue flowers, followed by black seedpods that are attractive as well. White-blooming selections, such as *Baptisia alba*, grow to four feet tall, and their white flowers on purplish stems continue for up to six weeks in spring. A hybrid between the white species and blue baptisia called 'Purple Smoke' grows three feet tall. 'Purple Smoke' has a tight growing habit and soft blue flower color that looks lovely in combination with its charcoal gray stems. It has done quite well in many trial gardens.

This plant seldom blooms until its second year in the garden.

Regional Differences: Baptisias do well throughout the south.

Color Period: Blooms in late March in zone eight, April in zone seven, and May in zone six. Both the blue and white ones bloom for one to five weeks, averaging three weeks each year. The seed pods that follow after flowering are interesting and often used as rattles by children.

Buying Tips: Baptisias are slow to get started, so the ones you see in the garden center could be quite small. Don't hesitate to buy these small ones because they fill out well after you plant them.

**Red ribbon plants are defined on page 12. For blue ribbon performance, follow the planting and maintenance guidelines on pages 28 to 46.*

Companions: Baptisia's white or blue flowers go with everything and look especially beautiful behind sun-loving flowers that appear at the same time, like iris. The blue-green foliage persists through summer, and its sprightly texture contrasts well with that of coarser coneflowers or black-eyed Susan. Baptisia is also a good perennial to grow along the edge of a yard near a rustic fence or low stone wall.

Baptisias work well as a specimen plants surrounded by your favorite irises, as shown below.

Blue baptisia with some companion iris

Dutch Iris 'Oriental Beauty' (above, top left) is a late blooming iris that often flowers at the same time as baptisia. Its soft, yellow color looks lovely with the soft blue of the baptisia, and it thrives in the sun as well. Plant a clump of this two-foot tall iris around the base of the baptisia.

White Bearded Iris (above, bottom left) also combine well with blue flowers of the false indigo. Plant clumps around the base of your baptisia, with the yellow and blue iris.

GROWING CONDITIONS

Light: Full sun, at least 6 hours per day for best performance of the blue baptisia. The white-flowered species takes more shade.

Water: Medium after establishment. Likes water once or twice a week during the growing season, depending on its environment.

Soil: For the garden, plant in any fertile, well-drained soil that has been enriched with organic matter. This plant requires good drainage.

Hardiness: Zones 4 to 8

Propagation: Seed germination is slow and erratic, so it's best to start with nursery-grown plants.

Pest Problems: Rare

PLANTING & MAINTENANCE

When to Plant: Baptisias from containers can be planted anytime. Take care not to injure the deep, fragile tap root. Early fall or late winter is the best time to plant. Plants often do not begin to bloom well until their second year in the garden.

Trimming: If you trim it shortly after it blooms in spring, the form of the shrub will be better in summer, as it has a tendency to fall over. However, you lose the interesting seed pods if you trim then. In midsummer, when the black seedpods shrivel, you may cut them off to improve the appearance of the plants. Otherwise this plant requires little care until winter. Cut back the dead foliage (to the ground) after it freezes in late fall or early winter.

Fertilization: Medium. Fertilize at planting time and each spring with a timed-release product (page 47). Less fertilizer is needed with the application of more organics.

Division: Do not disturb established clumps of baptisia.

Black-Eyed Susans

CHARACTERISTICS

Plant Type: Deciduous perennial (dies back in winter).

Average Size: About 2 feet tall by 2 to 3 wide for the 'Goldstrum' variety.

Growth Rate: Moderate first year, fast after that.

Leaf: Somewhat coarse green leaves, slightly hairy.

Flower: 3 to 6 inches across, usually with dark centers.

Origin: Native to Central and Eastern US.

Spacing: About 18 inches on center (measure from the center of each plant). They will grow together into clumps.

Cautions: Toxic both to skin and your digestive system, so don't eat this plant. Occasionally damaged by deer.

Colors: Flowers are yellow-orange petals, sometimes with mahogany markings, surrounding rounded eyes that may be brown, black, or green.

UNIVERSITY AWARDS

1999: Mississippi Medallion Award for 'Indian Summer' black-eyed Susan.

Annual black-eyed Susans, which only last about six months. Be sure to check the plant tag on the black-eyed Susans you see at your garden center. They could be annuals rather than the 'Goldstrum' perennials described on these two pages.

One of the easiest and longest-blooming perennials for the south. Bold golds all summer and into fall. Beyond providing vibrant summer color, black-eyed Susans attract butterflies and make superb cut flowers. Looks better when deadheaded (dead flowers removed) so it just misses a ribbon.

Black-eyed Susans are present in most perennial gardens in the south, and for good reason. Easy to grow and tolerant of heat and drought, vigorous varieties such as 'Goldstrum,' often bloom for three months. 'Goldstrum' was named Perennial Plant of the Year in 1999, and is on the roster of Louisiana Select plants, too. 'Goldstrum' grows to about two feet tall by two to three feet wide, a useful size for southern gardens.

So many other new cultivars of black-eyed Susans come on the market each year that it is hard to keep up with all of them! We don't know if you can make a bad choice because all we have tried have done well, although the 'Goldstrum' is our favorite.

Regional Differences: Black-eyed Susans are easy to grow throughout the south.

Color Period: Bloom from June through July, if you don't remove the dead flowers. June through September, if you do.

Buying Tips: Our favorite is the 'Goldstrum,' which is usually well labeled at the garden center. Also, black-eyed Susans come in an annual form (*Rudbeckia hirta*) that only live for about six months.

Companions: Black-eyed Susans are one of the most valuable plants for summer gardens because of their color intensity and long bloom period. 'Knock Out' roses share the long bloom period and look good behind black-eyed Susans. Scabiosa also has a long bloom period and works well as a border for black-eyed Susans.

For intense color and a long bloom period, combine black-eyed Susans with the plants shown below.

Black-eyed Susans with some companions for easy color layers

Dwarf Crapemyrtles (above, left) bloom for up to 90 days if you remove the dead flowers. Their bloom period coincides with black-eyed Susans, and both plants thrive in full sun. Since dwarf crapemyrtles grow from three to five feet tall, use them behind the shorter (two to three foot) black-eyed Susans.

'Homestead Purple' Verbena (above, right) blooms for the entire warm season, from spring until fall. And, like the black-eyed Susan, it loves sun. Use this low-growing (about a foot tall) verbena as a front border for the crapemyrtle and the black-eyed Susans. This hot combo will stop traffic in your neighborhood!

GROWING CONDITIONS

Light: Full sun to partial afternoon shade.

Water: Medium after establishment. Likes water once or twice a week during the growing season, depending on its environment. See pages 34 to 37 for more information.

Soil: For the garden, plant in any fertile, well-drained soil that has been enriched with organic matter.

Hardiness: Zones 4 to 8

Propagation: Division, rooted cuttings, seed.

Pest Problems: Powdery mildew sometimes causes white patches to form on leaves. It weakens plants but does not kill them.

PLANTING & MAINTENANCE

When to Plant: Black-eyed Susans from containers can be planted anytime. Fall is best because they establish easier in cooler weather, but you are more likely to find them at your garden center in spring or summer, when they are blooming. Plant new divisions in spring.

Trimming: Deadhead (remove dead flowers) black-eyed Susans every two weeks to help prolong the blooming period. If the planting appears ragged in August, trim the plants back by half their size to coax a heavy rebloom in early fall. Cut back the dead foliage (to the ground) after it freezes in late fall or early winter.

Fertilization: Medium. Fertilize at planting time and each spring with a timed-release product (page 47). Less fertilizer is needed with the application of more organics.

Division: Black-eyed Susans stay healthy without being divided. So, divide them in spring only to get more plants or control the size of the clump.

Canna

CHARACTERISTICS

Plant Type: Perennial rhizome; deciduous (dies back in winter).

Average Size: About 2 to 6 feet tall and 1 to 2 feet wide, depending on variety.

Growth Rate: Fast

Leaf: Large, paddle-shaped leaves may be green, red or variegated. The foliage of some cannas is even more colorful than the flowers.

Flower: Clusters of large, open-faced tubular blossoms atop upright stems.

Origin: Central and South America

Spacing: About 24 inches on center (measure from the center of each plant). Closer in containers.

Cautions: None known

Colors: Flowers come in yellow, orange, pink, peach, or red. Leaves are green, green and yellow, or multi-colored.

1. Yellow canna flower
2. Red canna flower
3. Yellow-striped canna leaf
4. Tropicana canna leaf

Strong textural plants set a tropical mood for months. With big, bright flowers and flashy foliage, modern cannas set the summer garden on fire.

Red cannas with loropetalum planted behind them. Yellow daylilies peak out on the right side and purple heart is planted in front.

We shied away from cannas in our trial gardens for many years because of their reputation for requiring a lot of care. But, their flowers are so spectacular that we gave into temptation one year and purchased some rhizomes from a catalog. We were pleasantly surprised by their performance. The biggest problem was holes in the leaves from caterpillars and Japanese beetles. We sprayed a few times, but gave up on it. Surprisingly, we still liked the cannas, bugs and all. However, the bugs don't stay all season. All in all, we groomed the plants about once a month, which is more care than we give most other plants. But, we loved the flowers and found the effort well worth it.

Regional Differences: Cannas grow well throughout the south. They die back in the winter in areas that freeze. Conservatively, they return in zones eight through ten. They have returned in our north Georgia trial gardens (zone seven) for a few years now.

Color Period: Bloom almost constantly from late spring to late fall. Cannas with colored leaves add leaf color as well as flower color.

Buying Tips: Large, blooming canna plants are common in garden centers in summer. Be sure to check out online suppliers to see the incredible variety of cannas that are easily available.

Companions: Consider both flower and foliage colors when partnering cannas with other plants. For cannas with dark leaves, consider lime green companions, like margarite sweet potato vines, as shown in this container (below, left).

To maximize the color punch of cannas that feature yellow-striped foliage, contrast them with bright flowers, like the red dragon wing begonias shown in the green container (below, right).

Or, mix cannas with different colored leaves in the same garden, as shown in the bottom photo.

GROWING CONDITIONS

Light: Most cannas need full sun, at least 6 hours per day.

Water: Medium. Once or twice a week works well. More water is required for cannas in containers.

Soil: For the garden, plant in any fertile, well-drained soil that has been enriched with organic matter. Use only good-quality potting mix for containers.

Hardiness: Zones 7 to 10. In zones 7 to 9, leave the plant in the ground and mulch on top of it to get it to return next spring.

Propagation: Division or rhizomes

Pest Problems: Canna leaf roller, Japanese beetles. Fungus, shown by brown spots on the leaves.

PLANTING & MAINTENANCE

When to Plant: Plant cannas in containers when they are available in spring or summer. Plant rhizomes in spring, after the soil has warmed. Cut the rhizomes so they contain only 2 or 3 eyes. Plant 18 to 24 inches apart and cover with 4 to 6 inches of soil.

Trimming: Clip off old flowers to keep the plants looking neat. Should plants become damaged by insects or storms, cut them off at the ground, and new shoots will soon appear. Remove dead foliage in winter after the leaves have been killed by frost. Cut them down, leaving about 6 inches of leaves above the ground.

Fertilization: Medium. Fertilize at planting time and each spring with a timed-release product (page 47). Less fertilizer is needed with the application of more organics. See pages for more instructions.

Division: If the center of the clump dies, or the clump simply looks too crowded, spring is the best time to dig plants from the edges of established clumps to transplant to other parts of the garden.

Coneflower

CHARACTERISTICS

Plant Type: Deciduous perennial (dies back in winter).

Average Size: Most coneflowers average 2 to 3 feet tall by 18 inches wide. A few cultivars top out at over 3 feet tall.

Growth Rate: Medium

Leaf: Oval, green leaves with pointed tips, 3 inches long and 2 inches wide.

Flower: Broad daisy-like flowers, 2 to 7 inches across, with centers comprised of a bristly cone.

Origin: The prairies and eastern US.

Spacing: About 18 to 24 inches on center (measure from the center of each plant). Place smaller varieties closer together than larger ones.

Cautions: Attracts bees, but seldom damaged by deer. This flower has well known medicinal uses, but sometimes causes allergic reactions if ingested.

Flower Colors: Mauve, white, orange, yellow, purple, bright pink.

1. *Traditional coneflower color*
2. *'Big Sky Sunrise' coneflower*
3. *'Big Sky Twilight' coneflower*
4. *'Big Sky After Midnight' coneflower.*

One of the most dependable bloomers in the south. Long-blooming perennial attracts clouds of butterflies to the garden. Favorite of most perennial gardeners. Just misses a ribbon because it looks better when deadheaded (dead flowers removed).

Visitors to Huntsville Botanical Garden have seen as many as three to six butterflies on a single coneflower plant!

Coneflowers are one of the stars of our southern perennials. While many perennials, like shasta daisy, require frequent grooming to look good, coneflowers can make it with only one cutback in fall. They look neater with a few groomings (nipping off dried flower spikes) each summer, but look reasonably attractive without it. Since they bloom all summer with so little attention, most gardeners want them, but the number of new cultivars is daunting. You may see a dozen different kinds at one garden center. The good news is we have never found a bad one - it looks like you can't make a bad choice! Most of the new hybrids are improvements over the originals - more compact, more intense colors, more different colors, and more flowers on each plant.

Regional Differences: Coneflowers grow well throughout the south.

Color Period: Strongest bloom comes in early summer. Very vigorous varieties continue to produce flowers through late summer and fall.

Buying Tips: Be sure to read the tag at the garden center to see how large your selection grows. They vary from two to over three feet tall, which can make difference as to where you place it in your garden. If you don't see any you like, most of the new, exciting varieties are available online.

Companions: Use coneflowers in perennial beds filled with other easy perennials that bloom in summer. Salvia and agastache look good with coneflower because their spiky flowers contrast with the coneflower's round one. Or, combine different-colored coneflowers together, as shown right.

For easy color layers, butterfly bush and 'Miss Huff' lantana make great partners for coneflower and attract droves of butterflies. Check out this combo below.

'Big Sky Twilight,' 'Sunrise,' and 'Sundown' coneflowers.

Coneflower 'Primadonna Deep Rose' with some companion plants.

'Miss Huff' Lantana (above, top right) is one of the few perennial lantanas that dependably comes back each spring in the south, blooming from about July until November. It reaches about three feet tall and is a perfect backdrop for shorter, two to three foot coneflowers.

'Purple Emperor' Butterfly Bush (above, bottom right) is one of the newer, more compact butterfly bushes that grows to about four feet tall and, like coneflower, blooms for most of the summer. Plant it behind the shorter lantana, with the coneflowers in front as a border. All three plants thrive in full sun.

GROWING CONDITIONS

Light: Light shade to full sun

Water: Medium. Although established plantings tolerate drought, the plants grow and bloom much better when they get water once or twice weekly in summer.

Soil: For the garden, plant in any fertile, well-drained soil that has been enriched with organic matter. Use only good-quality potting mix for containers.

Hardiness: Zones 3 to 9

Propagation: Seeds or division

Pest Problems: Pest problems are rarely serious, though Japanese beetles sometimes eat both flowers and leaves.

PLANTING & MAINTENANCE

When to Plant: Coneflowers from containers can be planted anytime. Fall is best because they establish easier in cooler weather, but you are more likely to find them at your garden center in spring or summer, when they are blooming.

Trimming: Remove old flowers when the petals become tattered. Plants that are deadheaded (dead flowers removed) regularly, bloom longer and stronger and do not shed unwanted seeds. Cut back the dead foliage (to the ground) after it freezes in late fall or early winter.

Fertilization: Medium. Fertilize at planting time and each spring with a timed-release product (page 47). Less fertilizer is needed with the application of more organics. Be careful not to overfeed coneflowers, which can make them produce more leaves than flowers.

Division: When flower production declines in plantings more than 4 years old, dig, divide, and replant. Fall is the best time, but you can also divide them in spring.

1ST Coreopsis, Threadleaf

CHARACTERISTICS

Plant Type: Deciduous perennial (dies back in winter).

Average Size: 18 inches tall by 12 to 18 inches wide.

Growth Rate: Medium

Leaf: Tiny, thread-like green leaves

Flower: Flat daisy-like blossoms with a tuft of yellow stamens in the centers.

Origin: Southeastern US

Spacing: About 18 inches on center (measure from the center of each plant). Closer in containers.

Cautions: Attracts bees, but seldom damaged by deer.

Flower Colors: Yellow

These easy, sun-loving flowers rebloom repeatedly all summer. The 'Moonbeam' cultivar won the Perennial Plant Association's 'Plant of the Year' award. Soft texture for the perennial garden. Blooms for months with very little care.

Coreopsis 'Moonbeam'

Coreopsis is one of the ten best-selling perennials. There are many different types, but most of our experience has been with threadleaf coreopsis, which differs from the rest because of its tiny, needle-like leaves. Threadleaf coreopsis has the reputation for being one of the toughest of all of them and blooms for quite a while with no attention at all other than weekly watering. Many of the other kinds of coreopsis require frequent deadheading (removal of dead flowers) to keep blooming. Two of the best performers are pictured here: 'Moonbeam' (above), which is the best-known, and 'Zagreeb' (opposite) which is sure to please. 'Moonbeam' won the Perennial Plant of the Year award in 1992.

Regional Differences: Perfectly adapted to the inland south, coreopsis may lack vigor in the coastal south in unusually rainy years.

Color Period: May or June through July, with a final flush of flowers in the fall. The best varieties bloom for three months or more.

Buying Tips: Threadleaf coreopsis doesn't look great in a nursery pot, as it is a bit thin and floppy when in a container. It does beautifully after it has been planted for just a short time.

**Blue ribbon plants are defined on page 12. For blue ribbon performance, follow the planting and maintenance guidelines on pages 28 to 46.*

Companions: Grow coreopsis with other perennials that take baking sun, such as agastache and scabiosa. Since coreopsis is so fine-textured, the larger agastache and scabiosa flowers show up well with it.

The combination below shows coreopsis with 'Big Sky Twilight' coneflower and 'Homestead Purple' verbena. The three fit together well as three layers of different heights. And, with internet shopping, you can now find all these plants, even if you can't locate them at your local garden center.

'Zagreb' coreopsis with some companions that form easy color layers

'Big Sky Twilight' Coneflower (above, left) is an excellent choice as a background for threadleaf coreopsis. The textures of the plants are quite different, they both like sun, and they share the same bloom period. This coneflower grows to about 30 inches tall. Place the 18 inch coreopsis in front of it.

'Homestead Purple' Verbena (above, right) blooms for the entire warm season, from spring until fall. And, like the coreopsis, it loves sun. Use this low-growing (about a foot tall) verbena as a front border for the coneflowers and the coreopsis. This hot combo will stop traffic in your neighborhood!

GROWING CONDITIONS

Light: Full sun, at least 6 hours per day.

Water: Low after establishment. Likes water every week or two during the growing season, depending on its environment. Blooms are reduced with too much water, but takes water up to twice a week well.

Soil: Very well-drained soil that has been enriched with organic matter. Coreopsis does very well in heavy clay soil provided it is not compacted.

Hardiness: Zones 3 to 9

Propagation: The best coreopsis are propagated from rooted cuttings taken in spring or by digging and dividing large clumps.

Pest Problems: Rare, but can develop fungus problems if overwatered.

PLANTING & MAINTENANCE

When to Plant: Coreopsis from containers can be planted anytime. Fall is best because they establish easier in cooler weather, but you are more likely to find them at your garden center in spring or summer, when they are blooming.

Trimming: If the plants become unsightly in late summer, cut them back to 8 to 10 inches to encourage a rebound of healthy, new growth. Cut back the dead foliage (to the ground) after it freezes in late fall or early winter.

Fertilization: Medium. Fertilize at planting time and each spring with a timed-release product (page 47). Less fertilizer is needed with the application of more organics.

Division: Divide every 2 to 5 years in fall or spring to maintain the vigor of the plants. The plants divided from the edges will be the healthiest. Discard the center if it appears weak.

Crocosmia

1ST

CHARACTERISTICS

Plant Type: Deciduous perennial (dies back in winter).

Average Size: About 2 to 4 feet tall by 1 to 2 feet wide.

Growth Rate: Grows quickly vertically but spreads slowly like an iris.

Leaf: Swordlike, bright green, 2 to 4 feet long.

Flower: Tall spikes topped with showy groups of flowers.

Origin: South Africa

Spacing: About 12 inches on center (measure from the center of each plant) when planting nursery-grown plants. 6 to 8 inches apart for corms.

Cautions: None known

Flowers Colors: Red, yellow, or orange. 'Lucifer' is the brightest-red type.

Crocosmia 'Walburton Yellow'

A gorgeous, garden, focal point in mid-summer that thrives in hot weather. Blue ribbon plant* because it blooms well with very little care.. However, it blooms longer if you also deadhead (remove dead flowers). Attracts butterflies and hummingbirds.

Crocosmia's fantastic, bright red flowers dominate the landscape from June to August. Although it comes in yellow and orange as well, it's the intensity of the red 'Lucifer' cultivar that steals the show. The sword-like foliage is similar to iris. However, the rich, green color of crocosmia foliage is more attractive than the dull, green of the iris leaves.

Regional Differences: No differences throughout the south.

Color Period: June through August. Blooms for eight weeks without removal of dead flowers. You'll get about four more weeks of blooms if you perform this chore.

Buying Tips: All the crocosmias you see will perform well. The main difference between the cultivars is the color of the flowers. If you can't find this one at your local garden center, try online suppliers. Since it grows from a corm (large root), it is quite easy to ship.

**Blue ribbon plants are defined on page 12. For blue ribbon performance, follow the planting and maintenance guidelines on pages 28 to 46.*

Attracts Butterflies

Attracts Hummingbirds

Avg. Weeks of Color

Botanical Name: *Crocosmia x spp.*
Family: Iridacea

Companions: Crocosmia adds not only bright color but also texture to the perennial garden. Use it with other colors and textures to best show it off, as shown here. The orange flowers are surrounded by grey grass, coneflowers, and cleomes in a wild mix that just looks wonderful!

GROWING CONDITIONS

Light: Full sun. Flowering is reduced in light shade.

Water: Low after establishment. Likes water every week or two during the growing season, depending on its environment. See pages 34 to 37 for more information.

Soil: For the garden, plant in any fertile, well-drained soil that has been enriched with organic matter.

Hardiness: Zones 5 to 9

Propagation: Divisions or corm (large roots) offsets.

Pest Problems: Rare. Spider mites damage leaves occasionally.

PLANTING & MAINTENANCE

When to Plant: Plant container-grown plants anytime, although they are easiest to establish when planted in fall. Plant corms (bulbs) in spring or fall, 2 to 3 inches deep and 6 to 8 inches apart.

Trimming: Removing dead flowers extends the bloom period. Cut back the dead foliage (to the ground) after it freezes in late fall or early winter.

Fertilization: Medium. Fertilize at planting time and each spring with a timed-release product (page 47). Less fertilizer is needed with the application of more organics. See pages 46 to 49 for more instructions.

Division: Benefits from division every 5 years or whenever you see it dying out in the center, as shown below. Divide in fall.

Daffodil

1ST

CHARACTERISTICS

Plant Type: Perennial bulb that is bare of leaves in summer.

Average Size: 6 to 16 inches tall, depending on variety. Individual plants are less than 4 inches wide yet often grow into foot-wide clumps.

Growth Rate: Medium

Leaf: Narrow, strap-shaped, green leaves.

Flower: Flared petals around a central cup, with great variety of types and sizes. Some are fragrant.

Origin: Mediterranean region

Spacing: For a full display, plant 4 to 5 large daffodils or 7 to 11 miniature daffodils per square foot.

Cautions: Minor toxicity for some. Do not eat this plant. Mice, deer, and other wildlife do not eat these bulbs.

Colors: Yellow, white, orange, and apricot-pink.

1. *'Pink Charm' daffodil*
2. *'Rijnveld's Early Sensation' daffodil*
3. *'Fortissimo' daffodil*
4. *'Barrett Browning' daffodil*

Daffodils are one of the easiest flowers to grow in the south. They live without irrigation, resist deer, grow in clay soil (the small-flowered varieties), and go for years requiring no care except occasional fertilization. Although each variety only blooms for about a month, you can buy bulb mixes that include different varieties for months of blooms each spring. Blue ribbon plant.*

'Ice Follies' daffodils, one of the strongest ever

For low-maintenance gardeners, daffodils only require care once every decade or so (separating the clumps). Trimming off the dead leaves annually makes the plants look better, but it is not necessary for their health. Daffodils bloom from winter to spring, each variety blooming about a month. Dainty yellow 'Rijnveld's Early Sensation' blooms in December or January, even when tortured by ice and snow. Of showier varieties that bloom later, 'Jetfire' (a yellow daffodil with a fragrant orange cup) has a strong reputation for standing up to the warm, wet soils of the south. The same goes for tall 'Ice Follies' (above), which blooms year after year with little care.

Regional Differences: Daffodils are persistent and long-lived in zones six through eight.

Color Period: Mid winter to spring, depending on variety. Many mixes are sold by bulb nurseries with staggered blooms so the bed stays in bloom for months. Blooms for about two to three weeks, a bit shorter if temperatures are unusually warm.

Buying Tips: Daffodils are available from local nurseries, catalogs, and online. The varieties are endless! Check with each supplier to see if the daffodils they sell have done well in the south.

**Blue ribbon plants are defined on page 12. For blue ribbon performance, follow the planting and maintenance guidelines on pages 28 to 46.*

Botanical Name: *Narcissus* species and hybrids
Family: Amaryllidaceae

Companions: Plant pansies over spots where daffodils rest in the fall; the bulbs will push up through the foliage. You also can grow daffodils in groundcovers, such as ivy or perennial vinca. In beds, grow daffodils, daylilies, and hybrid Asiatic lilies together. The summer blooming lilies will hide the fading foliage of the daffodils.

If you would like to plant daffodils with other flowering plants that bloom at the same time, be sure to check the bloom dates of the specific daffodils you have. For daffodils that bloom in February, try planting them in areas that also feature the plants shown below.

Yellow daffodils and some companions

Cherry Trees (above, left) are not featured in two-page plant profiles in this book because they are short-lived and sometimes hard to establish. However, they are widely planted in some parts of the south and bloom the same time as daffodils. Placing the two plants in the same area creates a spectacular sight when they both come into bloom at the same time.

Many Camellias (above, right) bloom in February or early March as well. Be sure to keep the evergreen camellias from blocking all the sun the daffodils need to bloom.

**Lives on rainwater alone in all but the most extreme situations.*

GROWING CONDITIONS

Light: Full winter sun, which may become filtered shade in late spring when trees leaf out. Morning sun is fine when the trees have leaves but do give shade from hot afternoon sun.

Water: Very low after establishment. Lives on rainwater alone, without supplemental water, in all but the most extreme conditions.

Soil: Any well-drained soil that has been enriched with organic matter. Miniature daffodils can adapt to unimproved soil, provided they are fed properly, but large-flowered varieties need good garden-quality soil.

Hardiness: Zones 3 to 8

Propagation: Division

Pest Problems: Rare

PLANTING & MAINTENANCE

When to Plant: Any time, when planting mature plants from containers. Plant bulbs from October to December in zone 6 and November through December in zones 7 and 8. Store bulbs in the refrigerator prior to planting.

Planting Depth: Cover with soil to twice the height of the bulb.

Trimming: It is important to allow the foliage of daffodils to remain intact until it turns yellow in early summer (at least 6 weeks after blooming), at which time it can be clipped off.

Fertilization: Medium. Fertilize at planting time and each spring with a timed-release product (p. 47). Less fertilizer is needed with the application of more organics.

Division: Dig and divide to increase your supply or to relieve overcrowding. When adequately fed, daffodils should not need dividing more often than once a decade. If they stop blooming, they need either division or fertilization.

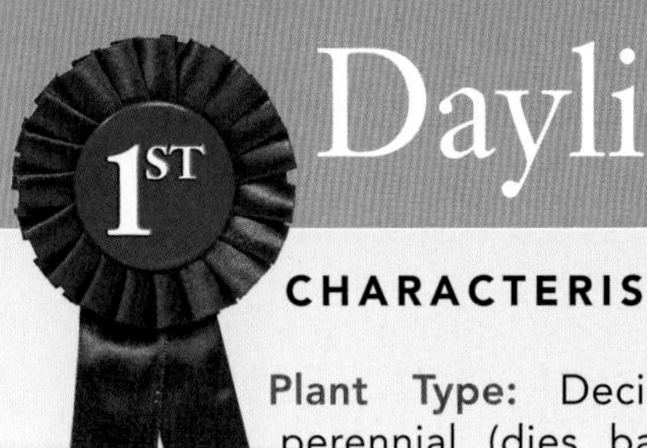

Daylily

CHARACTERISTICS

Plant Type: Deciduous perennial (dies back in winter) in colder areas. Some are evergreen in zones 8 and 9.

Average Size: 18 inches to 4 feet tall, depending on variety. The best everblooming daylilies grow less than 2 feet tall and equally as wide.

Growth Rate: Fast

Leaf: Long, strap-like leaves

Flower: Large, showy flowers 4 to 6 inches across.

Origin: China

Spacing: About 12 inches on center (measure from the center of each plant) when planting nursery-grown plants. 6 to 8 inches apart for corms.

Cautions: Some types produce edible blossoms. Frequently eaten by deer, except for the Stella de Oro.

Flower Colors: Orange, yellow, red, pink, lilac, maroon, in endless variations.

One of the easiest plants for southern gardens. Reblooming selections provide colorful blossoms from early summer to fall. Easily rates a blue ribbon.*

Daylilies at the home of Mrs. Bill Taylor, Jr. of Louisville, Mississippi.

Daylilies have been one of the most popular plants in southern gardens for generations. They hybridize easily, which explains why there are more than 20,000 cultivars from which to choose.The cultivars vary greatly in length of bloom time. Most bloom once for about a month. But, for the gardener who wants longer-lasting color, the daylilies to plant are reblooming hybrids, which bloom heavily in early summer and then intermittently until fall. Three of the best rebloomers for the south are 'Happy Returns', 'Hyperion', and 'Stella de Oro.' Many other daylilies have shorter bloom times, but they remain valuable for their exciting colors and forms.

Gardeners spend different amounts of time maintaining their daylilies. Some leave them alone most of the time; for these people, daylilies are an easy, blue ribbon plant. Others deadhead (remove dead flowers) daily, greatly increasing the maintenance as well as the floral display.

Regional Differences: Daylilies are easy to grow throughout the south. In zones eight and nine, many are evergreen.

Color Period: Early summer to fall. The best reblooming types bloom from June to fall with deadheading (removal of dead flowers) but not as much without it. They bloom for an average of three to four months. Daylilies that bloom only once do so in late spring or early summer for three to four weeks.

Buying Tips: Widely available both in garden centers and online.

**Blue ribbon plants are defined on page 12. For blue ribbon performance, follow the planting and maintenance guidelines on pages 28 to 46.*

Companions: Daylilies are outstanding for mass plantings along driveways, or you can use them to soften fences. They do a great job of camouflaging the failing foliage of daffodils or other spring-flowering bulbs.

Daylily collectors often plant huge beds of just daylilies, putting lots of different kinds together.

Daylilies also work very well with other southern, flowering shrubs and colorful groundcovers. The companions shown below offer months of color with very little care. The color period will be extended if you have time to remove the dead flowers from the daylilies and the crapemyrtle.

Yellow reblooming daylily and some companions for easy color layers.

Red Dwarf Crapemyrtles (above, left) bloom for up to ninety days if you remove the dead flowers. Their bloom period coincides with reblooming yellow daylilies (like 'Stella de Oro'), and both plants thrive in full sun. Since dwarf crapemyrtles grow from three to five feet tall, use them behind the shorter (two to three foot) daylilies.

Purple Heart (above, right) is a perennial ground cover that grows to about one foot tall, fitting nicely as a border in front of the daylilies and dwarf crapemyrtle. purple heart gives you constant color from May until the first frost of fall.

**Reblooming daylilies bloom for up to 18 weeks.*

GROWING CONDITIONS

Light: Full sun to partial shade. In shady spots, flowering stems often stretch toward the sun, which is not unattractive, provided they do not turn away from the direction from which they are most often viewed.

Water: Low after establishment. Likes water every week or two during the growing season, depending on its environment. See pages 34 to 37 for more information.

Soil: Fertile, well-drained soil that has been amended with organic matter.

Hardiness: Zones 3 to 9

Propagation: Division is most common. Dig crowns from the outside of established clumps, and transplant them.

Pest Problems: Few. Aphids sometimes. Daylily rust, a fungal disease, occasionally.

PLANTING & MAINTENANCE

When to Plant: You can plant daylilies any time, but the best times are early fall and late winter. Daylilies planted in early fall bloom beautifully the following summer.

Trimming: Clip off old flower stems, which make otherwise handsome plants appear bedraggled. However, millions of daylilies bloom all over the south without being trimmed. Cut back the dead foliage (to the ground) after it freezes in late fall or early winter.

Fertilization: Medium. Fertilize at planting time and each spring with a timed-release product (p. 47). Less fertilizer is needed with the application of more organics.

Division: Daylilies produce fewer flowers after about 5 years. Divide them after they have bloomed. For instructions, go to http://www.daytonnursery.com/tips/Daylilies.htm

1ST Elephant Ears

CHARACTERISTICS

Plant Type: Deciduous perennial (dies back in winter) or annual (lives for one season), depending on species and zone.

Average Size: Varies greatly by species. From about 18 inches tall by equally as wide to 8 feet tall and 6 feet wide.

Growth Rate: Fast

Leaf: Large, reaching up to 3 feet long and 2 feet wide in the tropics.

Flower: Insignificant

Origin: Tropical and subtropical areas throughout the world.

Spacing: Depends on size. From 2 to 6 feet on center (measure from the center of each plant).

Cautions: Toxic both to skin and your digestive system, so don't eat this plant. Seldom damaged by deer.

Flower Colors: Flowers are insignificant. Plant this one for its leaves, which range from black to green.

Elephant ear planted as the centerpiece of a container. Dragon wing begonias and creeping Jenny are planted around the edge.

Great landscape or container plant for summer use. Commonly used as focal points of annual plantings in public places. In the warmer areas of the south, dies back in winter and reappears the next spring . Rates a blue ribbon* because it is so easy to grow.

Colocasia 'Illustris' elephant ear

Elephant ears are thought of as tropical plants but do quite well in major portions of the south. Their large leaves add drama to the landscape. These plants are great for adding instant impact to otherwise mundane, boring beds. They are also one of the best centerpieces for container gardens - a sure-fire way of getting a good outcome. Just plant one in the middle and surround it with smaller plants, and it looks great every time.

Regional Differences: Elephant ears die back with the first frost of fall. In zones eight and nine (along with protected areas of zone seven), they come back the next spring. In zone six and unprotected areas in zone seven, remove and store the corms (roots) in fall for replanting the next spring (see instructions on opposite page).

Color Period: Flowers are insignificant. Use this one for the leaves, which are present from about April until November.

Buying Tips: Good elephant ears are easy to find. We have never bought one that did poorly. However, it helps if the plant tag tells you how tall it gets. We purchased the one in the container, shown left, thinking it was a dwarf that would only get two feet tall. It grew to over five feet in height!

**Blue ribbon plants are defined on page 12. For blue ribbon performance, follow the planting and maintenance guidelines on pages 28 to 46.*

Companions: Use elephant ears with plants that contrast both with the size and color of the leaves. Lime green elephant ears look great in the middle of dark colored flowers and leaves. Conversely, dark elephant ears look good with light leaves, as shown in the container below. *Colocasia 'Illustris'* is planted as the centerpiece of this black and lime green container. Lime and black sweet potato vines are alternated with lime sedum 'Angelina.'

GROWING CONDITIONS

Light: Most prefer shade, but we have grown them in our Georgia trial gardens in full sun. Check the tag on any purchased plants for the light needs.

Water: Medium. Watering twice weekly is ideal in sun, once a week in shade, after the establishment period, and more in containers. These plants take wet areas and are a good choice for spots that don't drain well.

Soil: For the garden, plant in any fertile, well-drained soil that has been enriched with organic matter. Use only good-quality potting mix for containers.

Hardiness: In zones 8 and higher, leave them in the ground. In protected areas of zone 7, they may or may not come back the next year.

Propagation: Corms (large roots)

Pest Problems: Rare

PLANTING & MAINTENANCE

When to Plant: Spring or summer. When planting corms (large roots), the pointed end goes up and the blunt end goes down. Plant deep enough to just cover the tip.

Trimming: Cut back the dead foliage (to the ground) after it freezes in late fall or early winter.

Fertilization: Medium. Fertilize at planting time and each spring with a timed-release product (p. 47). Less fertilizer is needed with the application of more organics.

To Store Corms: Dig up the corms in fall and let them dry outside for about a week. Store them in a cool (but not freezing), dry place over the winter. Be sure they neither rot nor dry out. Plant them in spring after the last frost.

Division: In spring, dig up the plant and pull the roots apart into 3 sections. Replant. They may wilt for a while. About 75% live.

Ferns

1ST

CHARACTERISTICS

Plant Type: Perennials, some evergreen and some deciduous. Autumn fern is the only one that is evergreen throughout the south. See individual descriptions on opposite pages for additional information.

Average Size: Japanese painted fern, 12 to 18 inches tall by equally as wide; holly fern, 2 feet tall by equally as wide. Cinnamon fern, 4 to 5 feet tall by 2 feet wide. Autumn fern, 2 1/2 feet tall by 3 feet wide.

Growth Rate: Medium for Japanese painted fern. Fast for holly fern, cinnamon fern, and autumn fern.

Origin: Japanese painted fern, Japan; holly fern and autumn fern, China; cinnamon fern, eastern US.

Spacing: About 12 to 18 inches on center for Japanese painted fern. 2 to 3 feet on center for holly fern and cinnamon fern. 3 to 3 1/2 feet on center for the autumn fern.

Cautions: Almost never eaten by deer.

UNIVERSITY AWARDS

2001: Georgia Gold Medal Winner. Autumn fern.

Japanese painted ferns

Ferns are one of the easiest and most dependable plants for shade. Easily rate a blue ribbon.* Extremely deer-resistant. Here are some that have other outstanding qualities as well.

Japanese painted fern

Ferns are one of the best choices for shade in the south. Their appearance evokes a pleasant woodland, and they are incredibly easy to care for if you provide them good drainage. Autumn fern is probably the most popular because it is one of the few that is evergreen throughout the south. Cinnamon fern is the tallest, reaching four to five feet tall. Holly fern is the coarsest, with foliage that resembles that of holly trees. And Japanese painted fern is both the smallest and the prettiest, with its fascinating colorations. The Japanese painted fern 'Pictum' (shown in these photos) won the 2004 Perennial Plant of the Year award.

Regional Differences: These four ferns all live throughout the south. However, only autumn fern is completely evergreen throughout the area. Both Japanese painted fern and holly fern die back in winter north of zone eight. Cinnamon fern dies back in winter in all of the south.

Color Period: Japanese painted ferns offer the most color, from about April until November. Autumn ferns have rust accents from about August until March.

Buying Tips: Ferns are easy to find at your garden centers.

**Blue ribbon plants are defined on page 12. For blue ribbon performance, follow the planting and maintenance guidelines on pages 28 to 46.*

Autumn Fern (***Dryopteris erythrosora***) is the southern star of ferns, not only because it is evergreen in all the south, but also because it tolerates more sun than most ferns. Autumn fern is also distinctive for the pinkish-copper color on its new growth in spring, and its golden bronze color in fall.

Cinnamon Fern (***Osmunda cinnamonea***) is different from many other ferns both for its large size (four to five feet tall) and its erect stature (only two feet wide). Its brown stalks resemble cinnamon sticks. In fall, the fronds turn an attractive yellow followed by orange. However, the fern is deciduous (dies back in winter) throughout the south.

Holly Fern (***Cyrtomium falcatum)*** is an evergreen fern as far north as zone eight. However, it only shows cold damage at about seven degrees, so it stays green in zone seven winters. Holly fern offers coarse texture that resembles a holly shrub. It offers the darkest green color of any of these ferns. We have tried four cultivars, and they worked equally as well.

Japanese Painted Fern (***Athyrium niponicum)*** is the most attractive and smallest of these ferns. Its striking color pattern really stands out and brightens a dull spot. Japanese painted fern is deciduous (dies back in winter) in zones north of zone eight.

GROWING CONDITIONS

Light: Holly fern and Japanese painted fern takes the least light, from medium to dense shade. Cinnamon and autumn fern need more light, from light to medium shade. Morning sun is okay for all 4 of these ferns.

Water: Medium. after establishment. Likes water once or twice a week during the growing season, depending on its environment. See pages 34 to 37 for more information.

Soil: For the garden, plant in any fertile, well-drained soil that has been enriched with organic matter. Use only good-quality potting mix for containers. See page 30 for specific instructions on soil preparation.

Hardiness: Japanese painted ferns, zones 4 to 9; holly fern, zones 7 to 10; autumn fern and cinnamon fern, zones 5 to 9.

Propagation: Division

Pest Problems: Rare

PLANTING & MAINTENANCE

When to Plant: Ferns from containers can be planted at any time. Fall is best because they establish easier in cooler weather.

Trimming: For evergreen ferns, each year in spring remove older fronds that are laying on the ground. For deciduous ferns, cut back the dead foliage (to the ground) after it freezes in late fall or early winter.

Fertilization: Medium. Fertilize at planting time and each spring with a timed-release product (p. 47). Less fertilizer is needed with the application of more organics.

Division: Every 3 to 5 years, divide clumps with a sharp spade in late fall or just before new growth starts in spring.

* *Only cinnamon fern is a southern native.*

Firespike

1ST

CHARACTERISTICS

Plant Type: Deciduous perennial (dies back in winter) in zones 8 and 9. Treat as an annual in zones 6 and 7.

Average Size: 4 feet tall by 3 feet wide.

Growth Rate: Fast

Leaf: Dark green and pointed; 3 to 6 inches long.

Flower: Red spikes ranging from 4 to 8 inches long. Dramatic and showy.

Origin: Central America

Spacing: 3 to 5 feet on center (measure from the center of each plant).

Cautions: None known

Flower Colors: Red

UNIVERSITY AWARDS

2007: Georgia Gold Medal Winner

Hummingbirds flock to firespike.

Dramatic red flower spikes that attract butterflies and are the favorite food of hummingbirds. New plant for the south that did very well in our trial gardens. Great late summer and fall color that is easy to grow and lasts up to three months.

Firespike is fairly well-known in south Florida but not in the deep south. We tried it as a summer annual in Mississippi (zone eight), and were extremely surprised to see it return the next season, blooming in the fall. It bloomed dependably every fall for the next five years and, as far as we know, is still blooming in the same garden. Other southerners have also had good results with this plant. It was awarded the Gold Medal by University of Georgia in 2007, but as an annual rather than a perennial. Firespike blooms for up to three months and doesn't require deadheading (removal of dead flowers). This combination of a long bloom period with so little care is quite difficult to find in the south.

We have observed hummingbirds around many different kinds of plants, and none have attracted as many as firespike. If everyone who is reading this book plants a firespike, just think what will happen to the hummingbird population of the south!

Regional Differences: Firespike grows year-round in zone 10. It dies back in the winter in zones eight and nine.

Color Period: From late summer through the first frost of fall, blooming constantly.

Buying Tips: Firespike is hard to find in southern garden centers because it is so new to the area. It is easier to find online. Be sure to buy the red one, because the purple one didn't bloom for us in the south.

**Blue ribbon plants are defined on page 12. For blue ribbon performance, follow the planting and maintenance guidelines on pages 28 to 46.*

Companions: Use firespike with other plants that bloom at the same time. Asters, mums, and many perennial salvias are good bets. *Salvia leucantha* blooms dependably in fall, like the firespike. Combine the two and accent the bed with some yellow annuals, like pansies or violas, as shown below.

Firespike and some companions

Salvia leucantha (top left) is another spectacular, fall-blooming perennial that looks fantastic with firespike. Both plants grow to about the same height, about four feet tall, so plant them side by side. For best flowering, plant them in light shade to full sun. Both plants bloom from late summer until the first frost.

Yellow Violas (bottom left) are annuals that work well as a border for both firespike and salvia leucantha. They grow to about six inches tall and bloom happily in light shade to full sun. Violas (and their close relative, pansies) bloom from October until the following spring. Melampodiums are a great summer annual to replace the violas when they are finished.

GROWING CONDITIONS

Light: Medium shade to full sun. Blooms the same in either situation. Not for dense shade.

Water: Medium after establishment. Likes water once or twice a week during the growing season, depending on its environment. See pages 34 to 37 for more information.

Soil: For the garden, plant in any fertile, well-drained soil that has been enriched with organic matter. Use only good-quality potting mix for containers. See pages 30 to 31 for specific instructions on soil preparation.

Hardiness: Zones 8 to 11

Propagation: Cuttings. Very easy to root in spring.

Pest Problems: Snails occasionally, although we had no pests at all on our firespikes.

PLANTING & MAINTENANCE

When to Plant: Spring or summer

Trimming: Firespike needs almost no trimming when it is in bloom. If you see a branch fall to the ground, cut it back to the base. Cut back the dead foliage (to the ground) after it freezes in late fall or early winter.

Fertilization: Medium. Fertilize at planting time and each spring with a timed-release product (p. 47). Less fertilizer is needed with the application of more organics. See pages 30 to 31 for more instructions.

Division: We have never divided this plant. It roots quite easily from cuttings.

1ST Grasses, Small (Under 2 Feet Tall)

CHARACTERISTICS

Plant Type: Varies by type.

Average Size: 2 to 24 inches tall.

Growth Rate: Varies by type

Leaf: Long, grass-like leaves

Flower: Tall upright spikes

Origin: Varies by type

Spacing: Mondo grass, 6 inches on center; Carex 'Toffee Twist,' 24 inches on center; Liriope, 12 to 18 inches on center; Dwarf Sweet Flag, 8 inches on center (measure from the center of each plant). Closer in containers.

Cautions: Skin irritant

Flower Colors: Lavender-blue for liriope. The rest have insignificant flowers.

Juncus grass forms the centerpiece of this container, surrounded by impatiens and creeping Jenny. This grass is good for summer containers but turns brown in winter. Cut back this warm-season grass, in fall or spring, to the ground (you can leave a few inches). Divide anytime spring through mid-summer. Sun or partial shade. Zones 4 to 10.

We use small grasses both in the landscape and in containers. Here are five of our favorites. All of them are incredibly easy to use, and rate blue ribbons.*

'Toffee Twist' carex grass has worked quite well in our container gardens. It is shown here surrounded by coleus in a side-planted basket from www.kinsmangarden.com.

Carex 'Toffee Twist' is an award-winning grass that we have used extensively as a centerpiece in containers. It grows 18 to 24 inches, smaller than the similar purple fountain grass shown on page 139. We like the fact that the grass stays evergreen down to five degrees. Cut 'Toffee Twist' back in very early spring (see 'Trimming,' far right). Divide it in early spring. It grows well in zones four to nine, but dies back in winter in zones four to seven. Use this grass in full sun to light shade.

Regional Differences: Varies by type

Color Period: Most grasses bloom in summer and fall.

Buying Tips: Garden centers are loaded with many different grasses in spring or summer. Luckily, most are labeled clearly with their names. Unfortunately, the labels won't include bad tendencies of the grasses, such as the aggressive growth that some have. Take this book with you so you can check them out.

**Blue ribbon plants are defined on page 12. For blue ribbon performance, follow the planting and maintenance guidelines on pages 28 to 46.*

Dwarf White Striped Sweet Flag (*Acorus gramineus*). We have used this grass in containers and loved it because of its small size: only six to fifteen inches tall. It is quite useful as a small filler in containers or massed as a groundcover in the garden.

It grows as a perennial in zones five to eleven and takes light shade to full sun. This is an evergreen, grass-like plant that can only be divided in spring and prefers normal to wet soils. Native to Japan and eastern Asia.

Mondo Grass (*Ophiopogon japonicus*) Small (two to six inches tall) grass used as a border and groundcover in dense to light shade. It takes morning sun, but protect it from afternoon sun. Its leaves are narrower than the similar liriope (shown below). Mondo grass requires almost no maintenance but grows so slowly that it can take quite a while to cover a large area. It looks attractive enough in winter, but gets a bit raggedy if temperatures drop to under ten degrees. Cut back the bad leaves in spring. Zones seven to ten. Native to Korea and Japan.

Liriope (*Liriope muscari*) is a useful, 18 to 24 inch grass used for borders or massed as a groundcover. It blooms in July and August with a small white or purple flower.

Green liriope does well in full sun to dense shade, while the variegated forms may bleach out some in full sun. It needs no irrigation once it's established (in normal conditions), and lives in zones six to ten. Native to Taiwan, China, and Japan.

**Liriope lives on rainwater alone in all but the most extreme situations. Both mondo grass and acorus grass need more water.*

GROWING CONDITIONS

Light: For full sun to light shade, use dwarf sweet flag, *Carex* 'Toffee Twist', *Juncus* grass, or liriope. For medium to dense shade, use liriope or mondo grass. Mondo takes light shade as well.

Water: Liriope can live without irrigation after establishment. Water the rest of these small grasses every week or two.

Soil: For the garden, plant in any fertile, well-drained soil that has been enriched with organic matter. Use only good-quality potting mix for containers. See pages 30 to 31 for specific instructions on soil preparation.

Hardiness: Varies by type

Propagation: Division

Pest Problems: Rare

PLANTING & MAINTENANCE

When to Plant: Anytime from containers. Spring is best when planted from divisions.

Trimming: Cut it back to the ground just before new growth begins: February in zone 8, March in zone 7, and April in zone 6. Your goal is to trim off the old growth from the previous year. Don't wait too long because if you cut back new growth that appears in spring, the tips will be blunt and discolored.

Fertilization: Medium. Fertilize at planting time and each spring with a timed-release product (page 47). Less fertilizer is needed with the application of more organics.

Division: We don't divide these small grasses often because they don't spread too quickly. However, if they spread too much, or you simply want more plants, dig the whole root ball out of the ground, divide it into 4 pieces, and replant them in spring.

1ST Grasses, Medium (2 to 3 Feet Tall)

CHARACTERISTICS

Plant Type: Many grasses are deciduous (lose their leaves in winter). All of the grasses shown here are evergreen except red fountain grass, which is an annual in most of the south.

Average Size: From 6 to 36 inches tall.

Growth Rate: Varies by type

Leaf: Long, grass-like leaves

Flower: Tall upright spikes

Origin: 'Hameln' fountain grass is native to Japan and eastern Asia. Purple fountain grass is native to Africa. Purple muhly grass is native to much of the eastern US as well as Texas north to Oklahoma.

Spacing: Varies by type

Cautions: Skin irritant

Colors: Muhly grass flowers are pink or purple. White for 'Hameln' fountain grass and acorus grass. Rust for red fountain grass.

Purple fountain grass is often used in the landscape with other annuals. Here it is planted with pentas and celosia.

Grasses are the rage throughout the south, and the photo below shows why. They are gorgeous! But choosing the right ones can be tricky. Some last only one season, and some last for years. Some only require maintenance once a year, and others will take over your garden in no time. Here are some we have really liked in our trials. All rate blue ribbons.*

'Hameln' (Pennisetum alopecuroides 'Hameln'), dwarf form of green fountain grass

We have tried many grasses both in our Georgia trial gardens as well as at Huntsville Botanical Garden. The 'Hameln' fountain grass (shown above) has been quite impressive as well as useful with its small, two-to-two-and-a-half foot height. It blooms from June until September and looks quite attractive in winter as well. And, although the purple fountain grass lasts only for one season, this 'Hameln' fountain grass has been thriving at Huntsville Botanical Garden for ten years! It easily wins a blue ribbon because it requires only one chore per year: trimming. And this plant does well in the south with no irrigation after it is established. Use 'Hameln' in zones five to nine.

Regional Differences: No regional differences

Color Period: Fountain grasses bloom from June until September, but the 'Hameln' remains attractive in winter as well. Purple muhly grass flowers from August until the first frost.

Buying Tips: Garden centers are loaded with many different grasses in spring or summer. Luckily, most are labeled clearly with their names. Unfortunately, the labels won't include bad tendencies of the grasses, such as the aggressive growth that some have. Take this book with you so you can check them out.

**Blue ribbon plants are defined on page 12. For blue ribbon performance, follow the planting and maintenance guidelines on pages 28 to 46.*

Purple Fountain Grass (*Pennisetum setaceum 'Rubrum'*) This fountain grass, unlike any other of the grasses on pages 136 to 141, is an annual (only living for one season) in any zone colder than zone nine. It is worth using not only because of its low cost but also because it shows up so well surrounded by other annual plantings.

The purple grass grows to about three feet tall and prefers full sun. It is commonly sold in garden centers in summer and is known for its lovely, long-lasting flowers.

We use it quite a bit as a centerpiece plant in containers, as shown left. It is surrounded by coleus. The container is the Octagon Planter, 20 inches in diameter, in creme from www.potteryalliance.com.

Purple Muhly Grass (*Muhlenbergia capillaris.*) This native grass is rapidly becoming many a southerner's favorite. Its best features are its gorgeous purple or pink flowers that bloom from August until the first frost. They hover like a big, colorful, smoke-like cloud above the plant.

Its leaves are narrow and needle-like as opposed to the flat blade shape common to most grasses. The plant grows three feet tall and equally as wide. Plant it in full sun for best flowering.

This gorgeous grass has been thriving at Huntsville Botanical Garden for five years, and shows no signs of slowing down yet!

Protect the plant from cold in zone six. It does better in zones seven to nine.

**Fountain grass lives on rainwater alone in all but the most extreme situations. Purple muhly grass probably needs more water, and is the only grass on this page that is native to the south.*

GROWING CONDITIONS

Light: All of these grasses grow in light shade to full sun. They flower more in full sun, at least six hours per day.

Water: Fountain grasses can live on rainwater (no irrigation) after they are established. Purple muhly grass is fairly drought-tolerant, but we have never tried it with no supplemental water at all.

Soil: For the garden, plant in any fertile, well-drained soil that has been enriched with organic matter. See pages 30 to 31 for specific instructions on soil preparation.

Hardiness: Varies by type

Propagation: Seeds or division, but many don't come true from seed.

Pest Problems: Rare

PLANTING & MAINTENANCE

When to Plant: Anytime from containers. Spring is best when planted from divisions.

Trimming: Cut it back to the ground just before new growth begins: February in zone 8, March in zone 7, and April in zone 6. Your goal is to trim off the old growth from the previous year. Don't wait too long because, if you cut back new growth that appears in spring, the tips will be blunt and discolored.

Fertilization: Low. Fertilize at planting time with a timed-release product (p. 47). Less fertilizer is needed with the application of more organics. In the years after planting, fertilization needs vary based on the nutrients in your soil.

Division: We don't divide these small grasses often because they don't spread too quickly. However, if they spread too much or you simply want more plants, dig the whole root ball out, divide it into 4 pieces and replant them in spring.

1ST Grasses, Large (Over 3' Tall)

CHARACTERISTICS

Plant Type: Semi-evergreen, perennial grass.

Average Size: Feather reed grass grows to about 3 feet tall with 6 foot flower spikes. The clump eventually grows to about 3 feet wide. *Panicum* 'North Wind' is about 4 to 5 feet tall with another foot added by the flower. It is 2 feet wide. *Panicum* 'Cloud Nine' grows to about 6 to 8 feet tall with another foot added when in flower. It grows to about 6 feet wide.

Growth Rate: Medium to fast

Leaf: Feather reed grass leaves are 3 feet long by 1/2" wide, dark green. Switch grass leaves measure 1 1/2 to 2 inches wide and as long as it is tall. Metallic blue and hairy.

Flower: Feather reed grass flowers are 8 to 12 inches long, delicate, feathery spikes about 2 inches wide. Switch grass flowers are Light and airy plumes. The flowers of *Panicum* 'Cloud Nine' rest above the foliage.

Origin: Feather reed grass is native to Europe and Asia, while switch grass originated from central America to southern Canada.

Spacing: Feather reed grass, 4 feet on center; 'Cloud Nine' switch grass, 6 feet on center. 'North Wind' switch grass, about 3 to 4 feet on center.

Cautions: Skin irritant

Colors: Feather reed grasses' flowers start out pink and change to golden as the seed pods mature. Switch grass flowers are light reddish gold when seen close up and a smokey color from a distance.

Here are three, taller grasses (three to six feet tall) that offer high, blue-ribbon* performance. Very easy to grow, only requires one annual pruning. These grasses won't take over the garden like so many other grasses do.

'Karl Foerster' feather reed grass

While many grasses are so aggressive they attempt to take over the garden, feather reed grass grows compactly. The first grass to bloom in summer, this grass produces a tall, erect flower that is showy enough to have won the coveted Perennial Plant of the Year award for 2001. Switch grass, which is getting a lot of attention as a bio-fuel, also offers some varieties that are quite attractive in the landscape. They are taller than most other easy grasses and add bold, dramatic stature to the garden. Two of our favorites are 'Cloud Nine' and 'North Wind.' 'Cloud Nine' is light and airy, resembling smoke, when the flowers bloom. 'North Wind' is smaller and more columnar, making it a better choice for smaller spaces.

Regional Differences: See individual descriptions, opposite page.

Color Period: See individual descriptions, opposite page.

Buying Tips: 'Karl Foerster' is the feather reed grass you are most likely to find at your garden center, and it's a good one. 'Overdam' is a variegated form that doesn't show up too well because the leaves are so narrow that the variegation appears blurred. At least 20 different varieties of switch grass are on the market. Most, like 'Heavy Metal' and 'Shenandoah,' do fairly well but have a problem with heat, which is the norm for southern summers. Stick to 'Cloud Nine' and 'North Wind' for the best performance of switch grasses in hot, humid weather.

**Blue ribbon plants are defined on page 12. For blue ribbon performance, follow the planting and maintenance guidelines on pages 28 to 46.*

Lives on Rain Water *

Southern Native *

Avg. Weeks of Color

Botanical Name: Varies by type
Family: Poaceae

'Karl Foerster' feather reed grass (*Calamagrostis x acutiflora* 'Karl Foerster') is the smallest of the three, growing to about three feet tall with six-foot flower spikes. It eventually forms a clump about three feet wide. Feather reed grass does best in zones six, seven, and the upper part of zone eight. It's performance declines farther south. It is the first grass to flower, beginning in June and continuing until winter. The flower dries and remains until you cut the plant back in spring. Winner of the Perennial Plant of the Year award in 2001.

Switch or Panicum grass 'North Wind' *(Panicum virgatum* 'Northwind') grows to about four to five feet tall and is quite narrow, only two feet wide.

It does equally well throughout the south. 'North Wind' blooms from July until August or September. Seed plumes remain well into winter.

Switch or Panicum grass 'Cloud Nine *(Panicum virgatum* 'Cloud Nine') grows to about six to eight feet tall by about six feet wide.

It does equally well throughout the south. 'Cloud Nine' blooms from July until August or September. Seed plumes remain well into winter.

GROWING CONDITIONS

Light: All three grasses take full sun to light shade. Switch grass falls over in too much shade.

Water: These grasses can live without irrigation after establishment in all but the most severe situations.

Soil: Any fertile, well-drained soil that has been enriched with organic matter.

Hardiness: Feather reed grass, zones 4 to 8A. Switch grass grows in zones 5 to 9.

Propagation: With feather reed grass, propagate by division because seeds are sterile, eliminating unwanted seedlings. Switch grass grows from seeds or division.

Pest Problems: Rare

PLANTING & MAINTENANCE

When to Plant: Anytime from containers. Spring is best when planting from division.

Trimming: Cut it back to the ground just before new growth begins: February in zone 8, March in zone 7, and April in zone 6. Your goal is to trim off the old growth from the previous year. Don't wait too long because, if you cut back new growth that appears in spring, the tips will be blunt and discolored.

Fertilization: Fertilize only after planting, particularly for switch grass. Too much fertilizer can cause it to go into hypergrowth and fall over.

Division: Plants do best if divided about every 3 years in spring, especially if they have gotten so thick that the clump is falling over. Divide them right after you have cut back the tops. Dig the entire clump out of the ground and split the roots into 4 parts with a sharp shovel. Plant the new grasses promptly.

**Lives on rainwater alone in all but the most extreme situations. Switch grass is a southern native while feather reed grass in not.*

Heuchera, Coral Bells

1ST

CHARACTERISTICS

Plant Type: Semi-evergreen perennial.

Average Size: 8 to 18 inches tall by 12 to 24 inches wide, depending on variety.

Growth Rate: Fast

Leaf: 3 to 4-inch wide rounded, begonia-like leaves, often variegated.

Flower: Small, airy flowers sway atop stiff, upright stem.

Origin: The original, native species (*Heuchera americana*) is native to the southeastern US. The heucheras shown here are hybrids.

Spacing: 14 to 18 inches on center (measure from the center of each plant).

Cautions: None known. Seldom damaged by deer.

Colors: Flowers may be coral, pink, or white, depending on variety. Leaves show unique combinations of green, purple, red and silver.

1. *Heuchera 'Creme Brulee'*
2. *Heuchera 'Key Lime Pie'*
3. *Heuchera 'Licorice'*
4. *Heuchera 'Creme de Menthe'*

Spectacular foliage and dainty flowers make heuchera do double-duty as shade garden plants. Evergreen and easy to grow, rating a blue ribbon.* Seldom damaged by deer.

Heucheras do equally as well planted in containers or in the ground. Left to right: Heuchera 'Dolce Key Lime Pie,' 'Black Currant,' and 'Peach Melba.'

Hostas and ferns have long needed some colorful company, and now there are dozens of heucheras to fill this need. What began as a native plant in the southern mountains is now a colorful shade garden standout, and many new varieties are showing up in your garden centers. Too many new ones, in fact, for us to have tried anywhere near all of them. 'Palace Purple' stands out, however, since it won the Perennial Plant of the Year award in 1991.

Huntsville Botanical Garden has planted heucheras in many locations and found that most of the them have done pretty well. Heucheras with darker leaves seem a little easier, not only growing larger, but also taking more sun. The lime green heucheras have not done quite as well. The staff at the garden have learned to be sure they place the newer heuchera varieties in enough shade. Morning sun and afternoon shade works well in summer. Heucheras take more sun in winter.

Regional Differences: No regional differences

Color Period: Early summer, sometimes reblooming for up to three months. Heuchera foliage is most attractive in cool weather, but gives color from spring until the first frost.

Buying Tips: You will find many varieties of heuchera in your garden center in spring. We have only tried a fraction of them. Luckily, most have done pretty well.

**Blue ribbon plants are defined on page 12. For blue ribbon performance, follow the planting and maintenance guidelines on pages 28 to 46.*

Companions: Heucheras grow well beneath deciduous trees, where they can avail themselves of winter sun and then rest in summer shade. They partner well with hostas, ferns, azaleas, and woodland phlox make great border plants for spring-flowering bulbs. Among annuals, winter pansies and summer begonias make great neighbors for heucheras.

Heuchera foliage is so striking that it is best displayed in the front of a bed, so the mound becomes part of an edging. Combining heucheras with autumn ferns creates a beautiful, evergreen, shade garden.

Mix different colors of heucheras together for a nice contrast that is very hard to find in southern evergreen shade plants.

For dramatic color, plant variegated hostas with dark heucheras and red wax begonias, as shown below.

Heuchera 'Licorice' and some companions

Hosta 'Great Expectations' (above, left) grows to about two feet tall and its variegated leaves contrast well with the dark leaves of 'Licorice' heuchera. Both plants do well in morning sun and afternoon shade. The hosta loses its leaves in the winter, so having a heuchera nearby takes up some of the slack, since it is evergreen.

Red Wax Begonias (above, right) spice up the mix in summer. The begonias grow slightly smaller (about 10 to 12 inches) than the 14 inch heuchera, so they work well as a border. Begonias thrive in the same, shady light conditions as hostas and heucheras.

GROWING CONDITIONS

Light: Filtered sun year round, or winter sun and summer shade. In summer, morning sun and afternoon shade works well.

Water: High to medium. Dry soil conditions will cause poorly rooted heucheras to collapse. Once established, the plants grow well with watering once or twice a week.

Soil: For the garden, plant in any fertile, well-drained soil that has been enriched with organic matter. Use only good-quality potting mix for containers. See pages 30 to 31 for specific instructions on soil preparation.

Hardiness: Zones 4 to 9

Propagation: Many nursery-grown plants are propagated by tissue culture. In the garden, dig and divide plants every three years to increase your supply.

Pest Problems: Roots may rot in overly wet soil, and leaves may burn if exposed to excessive sun.

PLANTING & MAINTENANCE

When to Plant: Heucheras from containers can be planted anytime. Fall is best because they establish easier in cooler weather.

Trimming: Clip off old flower stalks to encourage plants to rebloom. Trimming off withered leaves periodically also helps heucheras look well groomed.

Fertilization: Medium. Fertilize at planting time and each spring with a timed-release product (page 47). Less fertilizer is needed with the application of more organics. See pages for more instructions.

Division: We have never divided our heucheras. They don't make huge clumps. However, you can divide them after they have been in the ground for 3 years if you want more plants.

Hibiscus, Perennial or Hardy

CHARACTERISTICS

Plant Type: Deciduous perennial (dies back in winter).

Average Size: 2 to 6 feet tall by 2 to 4 feet wide, depending on variety.

Growth Rate: Slow in cool spring weather, becoming rapid after soil warms to above 70 degrees.

Leaf: Broad-lobed, green leaves, sometimes showing red veins.

Flower: Huge open flowers with prominent stamens to 12 inches across.

Origin: Some hibiscus (like swamp hibiscus) are native to Louisiana and other parts of the south. The ones shown here are hybrids.

Spacing: 3 to 4 feet on center (measure from the center of each plant).

Cautions: None known, except it is often damaged by deer.

Flower Colors: Pink, red, white, lavender, and many bicolors.

1. *Hibiscus 'Luna Red'*
2. *Hibiscus 'Luna Pink Swirl'*
3. *Hibiscus 'Luna Rose'*

Big splashes of bold color from summer to frost. Hibiscus produce the largest, showiest flowers in the summer garden. Requires a bit more trimming and fertilizer than most other plants in this book, so they don't rate a ribbon, but they are well-worth the effort for the huge, beautiful flowers.

Hibiscus 'Luna White'

Several types of native hibiscus have been grown in southern gardens for generations, but new, patented varieties of hardy hibiscus have set new standards for performance. Propagated from rooted stem cuttings rather than seeds, these varieties feature fuller plants and more robust flowers in clear colors. They also come in manageable sizes, such as two-foot tall dwarfs suitable for containers, and four-foot tall bushes ideal for the rear of sunny garden beds. And, unlike tropical hibiscus, hardy hibiscus needs no winter protection. In true perennial form, hardy hibiscus dies back to the roots in winter and regrow after the soil warms in spring.

Regional Differences: Easily grown throughout the south

Color Period: Starts blooming in early June in zone eight, mid-June in zone seven, and late June in zone six. Continues blooming for six to eight weeks. Some rebloom again in October for about another month.

Buying Tips: Pay attention to the size on the plant tag at the garden center. Since different varieties of hibiscus vary from two to six feet tall, be sure the one you choose fits your space.

**Blue ribbon plants are defined on page 12. For blue ribbon performance, follow the planting and maintenance guidelines on pages 28 to 46.*

Attracts Butterflies Attracts Hummingbirds Avg. Weeks of Color Southern Native

Botanical Name: *Hibiscus moscheutos*
Family: Malvaceae

Companions: The height of tall cultivars make them useful for the back of sunny beds, while mid-sized and dwarf cultivars fit better up close, where they can serve as specimen plants. The crepe-paper texture of hibiscus blossoms beckons up-close viewing, so it is nice to locate plants where the blossoms can be touched. The coarse texture of big hibiscus flowers and leaves are best offset by heat-tolerant flowers with a finer texture, such as angelonia, lantana, or 'Profusion' zinnias.

Try the flowers shown below for some textural as well as color contrast. All three bloom during the hottest part of summer.

Hibiscus 'Luna White' and some companion plants

'Purple Emperor' Butterfly Bush (above, left) is one of the newer, more compact butterfly bushes that grows to about four feet tall and, blooms at the same time as the 'Luna' hibiscus. Plant it behind the shorter hibiscus (two to three feet tall).

Coreopsis (above, right) also blooms at the same time as 'Luna' hibiscus. The fine texture of the coreopsis contrasts well with the coarser textured hibiscus. Use the shorter coreopsis (about 18 inches tall) as a border for the butterfly bush and the hibiscus. All three plants do well in full sun.

GROWING CONDITIONS

Light: Full sun to slight afternoon shade.

Water: Medium after establishment. Likes water once or twice a week during the growing season, depending on its environment. See pages 34 to 37 for more information.

Soil: For the garden, plant in any fertile, well-drained soil that has been enriched with organic matter. Use only good-quality potting mix for containers.

Hardiness: Most varieties are adapted in Zones 5 to 10. Tropical hibiscus have similar flowers but won't take freezes.

Propagation: The 'Belle' series can be grown from seed, but most superior varieties are grown from rooted stem cuttings, which are easy to do.

Pest Problems: Japanese beetles can be a serious problem.

PLANTING & MAINTENANCE

When to Plant: Hibiscus from containers can be planted anytime. Fall is best because they establish easier in cooler weather.

Trimming: To help plants grow bushy, pinch back growing tips at least twice in late spring and early summer. Even when pinched, plants often need staking when stems become heavy with buds. After cold weather kills back the plants, lop off the tops, leaving a 6 inch stub, before mulching over the plants' root zones.

Fertilization: Medium. Fertilize at planting time and annually with a top-quality, timed release product that includes minor elements. See pages 46 to 47 for more specifics.

Division: Hibiscus doesn't require division, and are easier to propagate from stem cuttings. However, it can be divided every 5 years in spring.

Hostas

1ST

CHARACTERISTICS

Plant Type: Deciduous perennial (dies back in winter).

Average Size: 1 to 3 feet high and equally as wide, depending on variety.

Growth Rate: Fast

Leaf: Size varies greatly by variety, from only a few inches to 20 inches long. Leaves stay smaller in the south than in cooler areas.

Flower: Tubular light pink, lilac, or white flowers on upright stalks.

Origin: Eastern Asia

Spacing: From 8 inches to 3 feet on center (measure from the center of each plant), depending on variety.

Cautions: None known, except it is one of deer's favorite foods.

Colors: Leaf color and texture varies, ranging from blue-green to chartreuse, some varieties with glossy surfaces, others puckered and quilted, and many with white or cream variegation; flowers range from pale lavender to white.

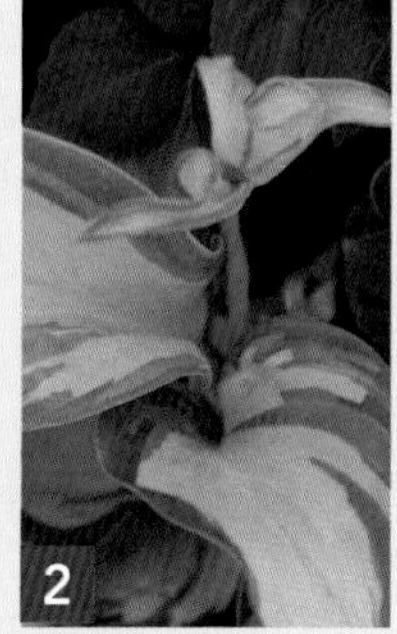

1. White hosta flower
2. Hosta 'Great Expectations'

A shade garden's best friend, hostas provide striking foliage where few other plants grow. Take care if you have deer in your neighborhood, however, because hostas are one of their favorite foods. Easy to grow and maintain if you provide good drainage. Rots in winter with poor drainage.

Tough, dependable and easy to please, hostas are a mainstay in shady sites. There are hundreds of varieties from which to choose, which vary in size, color, and texture. Dark green hostas with crisp white edges have a tailored look that combines well with white or pale pastel flowers. Very large hostas are always a dramatic presence, but they need a deep, fertile root run in order to prosper. Medium-sized cultivars are more forgiving of less than perfect soil conditions. Hostas have traditionally been valued for their leaves. Recently, breeders have been stressing flowers, fragrance, and red stems.

Regional Differences: Hostas require substantial shade in the coastal south, but they can tolerate a half day of morning sun in the upper south.

Color Period: Use hostas primarily for leaf color, which lasts about six months, from spring until the first hard frost. Hostas bloom from early to midsummer. Some gardeners remove the flower spikes to preserve the appearance of the leaves.

Buying Tips: Choosing hostas can be daunting because there are so many for sale. Some varieties that have done quite well at Huntsville Botanical Garden include the following: 'Sum and Substance,' a lime green hosta with very large leaves; H. sieboldiana 'Elegans,' an extra large, bluish-green variety; 'Guacomole,' which features light green leaves with a dark green edge and has a better sun tolerance than most hostas; and 'Albo Marginata,' has variegated leaves - solid green center with white margins. If you can't find these hostas at your local garden center, they are usually available online.

**Blue ribbon plants are defined on page 12. For blue ribbon performance, follow the planting and maintenance guidelines on pages 28 to 46.*

Botanical Name: *Hosta* species and hybrids
Family: Liliaceae

Companions: Pair hostas with other plants that do not need much sun, such as ferns, caladiums, shade-tolerant coleus, heucheras, begonias, and mondo grass. Hostas also do a wonderful job of keeping spring-blooming azalea beds interesting through summer. Hostas can be interplanted with small daffodils, which adapt well to spots that get winter sun followed by summer shade. Lenten roses share hostas' site preferences and make good bed partners as well.

You can use small hostas to mask the bases of trees, provided you can find suitable planting pockets between tree roots. Hostas also work well when planted in drifts between clumps of azaleas in open woodland gardens. Small hostas make a good edging plant because their broad leaves naturally shade out weeds.

For bright color in shade, mix hostas with annuals, as shown below.

Hosta 'Patriot Fire' with some companions

Persian Shield (above, left) an annual that looks great with hostas. Since it grows to about two feet tall place it in front of a taller hosta or behind a shorter one. Persian shield lasts for the entire growing season and thrives in shade with the hostas.

Red Wax Begonias (above, right) are another annual that shares the hostas comfort in shade. Since the begonias are the shortest (about 10 to 12 inches tall) of the three, use them as a border for the Persian sheild and hostas.

GROWING CONDITIONS

Light: Light to medium shade

Water: Above average. Hostas will collapse if the soil becomes dry.

Soil: For the garden, plant in any fertile, well-drained soil that has been enriched with organic matter. Use only good-quality potting mix for containers.

Hardiness: Zones 3 to 8

Propagation: Division

Pest Problems: Slugs, snails, voles and deer can damage hostas. Be prepared to trap or bait slugs in damp areas where this pest is well established.

PLANTING & MAINTENANCE

When to Plant: Hostas from containers can be planted anytime. Fall is best because they establish easier in cooler weather.

Trimming: Trimming off leaves that turn yellow or become disfigured by pests does not seriously weaken the plants. Some people trim off flower spikes as soon as they appear, or enjoy the flowers and then lop off the spikes. Cut back the dead foliage (to the ground) after it freezes in late fall or early winter.

Fertilization: Medium. Fertilize at planting time and each spring with a timed-release product (page 47). Less fertilizer is needed with the application of more organics. See pages for more instructions.

Division: Hostas seldom need division and grow well without it. However, if you want more plants divide established clumps in early spring or early fall every 3 to 5 years by cutting straight down between new crowns with a sharp spade. Replant immediately, but expect a year to pass before the divided plants show good vigor. Divided plants can be held in pots for up to a year.

2ND Ice Plant

CHARACTERISTICS

Plant Type: Deciduous perennial (dies back in winter).

Average Size: 3 to 6 inches tall, spreading 18 to 24 inches wide.

Growth Rate: Fast

Leaf: Plump, gray-green, succulent leaves, needle-shaped, ¼ inch wide and 2 inches long.

Flower: Starry, daisy-shaped flowers about 2 inches across.

Origin: South Africa

Spacing: About 16 to 24 inches on center (measure from the center of each plant).

Cautions: Often damaged by deer

Colors: Flowers are lavender-blue, pink, coral, or yellow.

An excellent blooming groundcover for hot, dry places, such as atop retaining walls or along walkways. Needs little maintenance, so it rates a red ribbon.* Blooms most of the summer in zone six, a bit less further south. Best attribute is its low water needs. Lives on just rainwater after it is established.

Virtually unknown in gardens only ten years ago, ice plant has steadily gained ground in Southern gardens thanks to its tremendous tolerance of hot sun and dry conditions. The plants hoard moisture in their succulent leaves and can go without water even in times of summer drought. Their spreading habit makes them especially valuable when planted so they cascade over walls, or use them to dress the edges of hot, concrete walkways. This plant's only weakness is a low tolerance for soggy winter conditions, so be sure to locate it where rainwater is quick to drain away (see pages 28 to 29). A light mulch that helps keep the foliage dry in summer is beneficial, too.

Regional Differences: As long as the site is sunny and well drained, ice plants grow easily throughout the south but bloom more in cooler parts, like zone six.

Color Period: Plants cover themselves with blossoms in late spring and then bloom sporadically through summer and into fall. More flowers in zone six.

Buying Tips: We have only been growing this plant for about three years, so we don't have extensive experience with different cultivars. If you can't find any ice plants at your garden center, try online suppliers.

1. *'Sequins' ice plant*
2. *'Red Mountain' ice plant*

**Red ribbon plants are defined on page 13. For blue ribbon performance, follow the planting and maintenance guidelines on pages 28 to 49.*

Companions: You can get nice blooms in shades of pink by planting creeping phlox, and deep pink ice plant atop a retaining wall, or among stones on a rocky bank. In beds, ice plant makes a great groundcover to grow between widely-spaced roses, or you can use it as a low-growing companion plant for other drought-tolerant sun lovers such as agastache, coreopsis, gomphrena, or tall ornamental grasses.

For drought-tolerant layers, use sedum 'Autumn Joy' as the tallest layer, yellow lantana for the middle layer, and ice plant for the border. Both ice plant and sedum are succulents and live on only rainwater. Lantana, however, looks better when watered every week or so.

'Sequins' ice plant with some companions for drought-tolerant, color layers.

Yellow Lantana (above, left) is an annual that blooms for the entire spring, summer, and fall season. It grows to about one foot tall, so plant it behind the shorter ice plant. Since the yellow lantana spreads quite a bit, keep the center of the lantana a full three feet away from the center of the ice plant. That way, they won't crush each other. Both prefer full sun.

'Autumn Joy' Sedum (above, right) blooms in fall and grows 18 to 24 inches tall. Plant it as the tallest layer of this grouping, with the lantana as the middle layer and the ice plant as the border. The sedum's flowers stay lime green for about a month before turning pink. The lime color contrasts well with the purple ice plants.

**Lives on rainwater alone in all but the most extreme situations.*

GROWING CONDITIONS

Light: Full sun. Tolerates some afternoon shade.

Water: Very low after establishment. Lives on rainwater alone, without supplemental water, in all but the most extreme conditions.

Soil: Any fertile, well-drained soil that has been enriched with organic matter. Requires good drainage. See pages 28 to 31 for instructions.

Hardiness: Zones 6 to 9

Propagation: Plants grown from seed bloom in about 4 months. 'Mesa Verde' is patented and is grown from rooted stem cuttings. Large masses can be dug and divided in early spring. Root 4-inch-long stem tip cuttings whenever the plants are not in bloom. All varieties occasionally self-sow in areas where they are happy.

Pest Problems: Rare. Very wet winter conditions can cause plants to rot.

PLANTING & MAINTENANCE

When to Plant: Ice plants from containers can be planted at any time. Fall is best because they establish easier in cooler weather.

Trimming: Ice plant needs only casual deadheading (removal of dead flowers) through early summer. If plants appear ragged in mid summer, shearing them back by one-third their size will encourage the development of new bud-bearing stems.

Fertilization: Low. Fertilize at planting time with a timed-release product (page 46). Less fertilizer is needed with the application of more organics. In the years after planting, fertilization needs vary based on the nutrients in your soil.

Division: Divide every 3 to 5 years if you want more plants.

Iris

1ST

CHARACTERISTICS

Plant Type: Most irises are evergreen perennials that grow from bulbs; some are deciduous (lose their leaves in winter).

Average Size: Sizes range from tiny (4 inches tall) to tall (5 feet tall). Most are from 18 to 24 inches tall.

Growth Rate: Medium

Leaf: Flat, sword-shaped green to greenish-blue leaves.

Flower: Exotic, open blossoms with some petals outcurved and others clasping toward the flower's center.

Origin: Various species native to America, Europe, and Asia.

Spacing: Varies with type. Set rhizomes of bearded iris at least 8 inches apart. Closer spacing is better with other types of iris, which grow into dense clumps when set 3 to 8 inches apart.

Cautions: Poisonous; often damaged by deer.

Colors: Flowers are blue, white, yellow, pink, purple, and many blends and bicolors.

Bearded irises have a fuzzy spot on their petals.

Glamorous plants that are easy to grow in the south, if you choose the right one. Thousands of different choices. Great plants to collect. Rate blue ribbon* because of ease of care.

Dutch iris 'Oriental Beauty'

Irises are one of the most glamorous plants for southern gardens. Although they only bloom for a short time, the visual impact of the blooms, coupled with their ease of care, make them definitely worth while. The hardest part is choosing the right one for your garden because there are thousands available. The five described on the opposite page do well in the south as a whole.

Regional Differences: Most types of iris grow quite well in zones six through eight. Louisiana iris grows well as far south as zone ten, provided it has a very moist site.

Color Period: Most bloom early to late spring (for about two weeks) depending on variety. A few rebloom in the fall. Iris often do not bloom in the first season after they have been dug and divided.

Buying Tips: Not only are there thousands of irises on the market, hundreds more appear each year. Local garden centers are often good sources of information about which irises do best in your area. Online suppliers are endless! For more information, see www.irises.org.

**Blue ribbon plants are defined on page 12. For blue ribbon performance, follow the planting and maintenance guidelines on pages 28 to 49.*

Bearded Iris 'Sarah Taylor'

Bearded Iris (*Iris germanica*, left): Eight to twenty four inches tall. Hugely popular, often bloom for years with little care beyond regular feeding. Do not overwater because this one likes to be on the dry side. More susceptible to iris borer than the other varieties. Divide in August.

Dwarf Crested Iris (*Iris cristata*, right): Four to six inches tall. Tiny groundcover iris native to many southern woodlands. Foliage disappears in winter. Best in light shade, but tolerates medium shade. Needs more water in full sun. Large masses produce wonderful color.

Dwarf Crested Iris

Japanese Iris 'Goldbound'

Japanese Iris (*Iris ensata*, left): Ten to twelve inches tall. Very easy to grow. Softer leaves than other iris, bending instead of standing straight up. Do not overwater because this one likes to be on the dry side. Grows into nice-sized clumps in just two or three years. Divide in fall.

Louisiana Iris *(Iris spathula hexagonae*, right): Three to five feet tall. Marshland plants that thrive when given ample moisture and acid soil, so they are a top choice for growing near (or even in) water or in low places. Evergreen in most of the south. Divide in late summer.

Louisiana Iris 'James Dickenson'

Siberian Iris 'Butter and Sugar'

Siberian Iris (*Iris sibirica*, left): Varies from one to three feet tall. The largest flowers of the genus. Takes wet or dry situations. Leaves get fewer pests than the other varieties. Blooms best when allowed to grow into thick clumps and can be divided right after bloom or while they are dormant from fall to early spring.

**Only the dwarf crested and Louisiana iris are native to the south.*

GROWING CONDITIONS

Light: Light shade to full sun

Water: Medium for most, but Louisiana iris needs more moisture and can even be grown in shallow water. Avoid overwatering other iris, however, because rot can result.

Soil: Fertile, well-drained soil that has been enriched with organic matter suits most irises. Louisiana iris requires acid soil.

Hardiness: Varies. Many iris are hardy to zone 3. Some Louisiana iris grow as far south as zone 10.

Propagation: Although some grow from seed, all grow from division.

Pest Problems: Iris borer can seriously damage bearded iris rhizomes. Affected plants are weak, bloom poorly, and have holes in their roots. Treat with the least toxic pesticide available. Another problem is rot caused by overwatering, mulch, or burying the rhizomes too deep.

PLANTING & MAINTENANCE

When to Plant: Iris from containers can be planted at any time. Fall is best because they establish easier in cooler weather. Plant rhizomes or bulbs in early spring or in late summer. Arrange the bulb or rhizome so the new or leaf end is pointing up.

Planting Depth: Plant bearded iris rhizomes right on top of the soil so they get sun. Plant the rest about one inch deep.

Trimming: If desired, use scissors to cut away leaves or flower stems that turn brown. Cut back to near the ground the iris foliage that dies back in the winter.

Fertilization: Fertilize in early spring, soon after new growth appears (page 46). If plants are set out (or divided) in late summer, fertilize them again.

1ST Joe Pye Weed 'Gateway'

CHARACTERISTICS

Plant Type: Deciduous perennial (dies back in winter).

Average Size: 4 to 6 feet tall by 4 feet wide. Other Joe Pye weeds grow considerably larger.

Growth Rate: Fast

Leaf: Green and oblong, about 2 inches wide by 4 inches long. Stems are purple.

Flower: Large, dome-shaped flower clusters that grow as large as a small soccer ball. Flat, dome-shaped top.

Origin: Eastern and northern United States.

Spacing: 4 feet on center (measure from the center of each plant).

Cautions: Seldom damaged by deer.

Flower Colors: Flowers are pink or purplish mauve.

'Gateway' flower. Notice the attractive, purple stem.

Lovely, native perennial for spectacular blooms in August and September. Huge masses of pink blooms attract butterflies. Flowers the size of a small soccer ball. Very easy to grow, rating a blue ribbon.* Only requires one trimming per year.

Joe Pye weed is new in gardens in the US, after years of popularity in England. Since it is native to the US, it makes sense that we use more of this gorgeous perennial, which is one of the showiest fall bloomers. The 'Gateway' cultivar is more compact than most other Joe Pye weeds, making it more useful in most residential gardens. Huntsville Botanical Garden has been growing them for 20 years with great success.

Regional Differences: Grows equally well throughout the south

Color Period: August and September for four to six weeks

Buying Tips: This plant is difficult to find in many garden centers but easily available online.

**Blue ribbon plants are defined on page 12. For blue ribbon performance, follow the planting and maintenance guidelines on pages 28 to 49.*

Attracts Butterflies

Avg. Weeks of Color

Southern Native

Botanical Name: *Eupatorium maculatum 'Gateway'*

Family: Asteraceae/Compositae

Companions: Since Joe Pye weed blooms at both the end of the summer and the beginning of fall, it combines well with both late summer and fall bloomers. Some late summer bloomers that combine well with Joe Pye weed include butterfly bush, spider lilies, agastache, canna lilies, scabiosa, coneflowers, black-eyed Susans, crocosomias, daylilies, hibiscus, and yarrow. Fall bloomers to combine with Joe-pye include *Sedum* 'Autumn Joy,' *Salvia leucantha,* and firespike.

For a bed of easy color layers that will have at least one plant in bloom for at least five months, try the flowers shown below.

Joe Pye weed with some companion plants that form easy color layers

'Miss Huff' Lantana (above, left) is a perennial lantana that blooms from July until November. Its flowers feature three colors: orange, yellow, and pink. The pink tones blend well with the flowers of the Joe Pye weed. Place the three-foot tall lantana in front of the four-foot-tall Joe Pye weed.

Coreopsis 'Moonbeam' (above, right) is a wonderful companion for both because its light texture is so different from the coarser-textured lantana and Joe Pye weed. It blooms from June until September and grows about 18 inches tall, so place it as a front border. All three plants thrive in full sun.

GROWING CONDITIONS

Light: Light shade to full sun

Water: Low after establishment. Likes water every week or two during the growing season, depending on its environment. See pages 34 to 37 for more information. Tolerates wet spots well.

Soil: Any fertile, well-drained soil that has been enriched with organic matter. See pages 30 to 31 for instructions.

Hardiness: Zones 5 to 9

Propagation: Division

Pest Problems: Rare. Root rot can develop if plants are kept too wet.

PLANTING & MAINTENANCE

When to Plant: Joe Pye weeds in containers can be planted at any time. Fall is best because they establish easier in cooler weather, but you are more likely to find them at your garden center in summer, when they are blooming.

Trimming: Cut back the dead foliage (to the ground) after it freezes in late fall or early winter.

Fertilization: Low. Fertilize at planting time with a timed-release product. Less fertilizer is needed with the application of more organics. In the years after planting, fertilization needs vary based on the nutrients in your soil. See pages 46 to 47 for more instructions.

Division: Divide every 3 to 5 years in fall or spring to maintain the vigor of the plants. The plants divided from the edges will be the healthiest. Discard the center if it appears weak.

Lantana 'Miss Huff'

1ST

CHARACTERISTICS

Plant Type: Deciduous perennial (dies back in winter).

Average Size: About 3 to 4 feet tall by 3 feet wide.

Growth Rate: Fast, once the new growth emerges in spring. This is one of the last perennials to come out of the ground, often as late as mid May.

Leaf: Medium green, serrated and pointed. About 1 inch long by 1/2 inch wide.

Flower: Clusters of tiny flowers forming larger flowers of about 1 inch across.

Origin: Tropical America

Spacing: About 3 feet on center (measure from the center of each plant). Closer in containers.

Cautions: Poisonous to humans, dogs, and livestock. Can cause serious illness or death. Almost never damaged by deer.

Colors: Flowers are orange, yellow, and pink, all on the same plant. These three colors are the key to telling 'Miss Huff' lantana apart from the others you will see at your garden center.

UNIVERSITY AWARDS

2003: Georgia Gold Medal Winner

The only lantana we have found (after testing tons of them!) that dependably comes back each spring in all of the south except for zone six. Doesn't bloom as long as annual lantana (five months compared with seven months), but you don't have to replace it, either! Attracts butterflies and hummingbirds, resists deer, and lives on little water! Blue ribbon plant.*

'Miss Huff' lantana is one of the easiest and longest blooming perennials for the south. It starts blooming two months later than annual lantana and doesn't bloom as profusely. But it is one of the few perennials that blooms for a full four to five months with only one trimming a year! That's it - not even extra water in all but the most extreme situations! And both hummingbirds and butterflies love it, while deer leave it alone! If everyone reading this book plants one 'Miss Huff' lantana, the butterfly population of the south will all say, "Thanks!"

The only negative to this lantana is that it really likes it dry and can have problems in years that are unusually wet.

Regional Differences: Temperatures below zero degrees can kill this lantana.

Color Period: July to late fall, blooming constantly

Buying Tips: This plant is tricky to find because there are so many lantanas that look alike. Take this book with you to your garden center and look for lantana flowers that are bright pink, yellow, and orange - all on the same plant.

**Blue ribbon plants are defined on page 12. For blue ribbon performance, follow the planting and maintenance guidelines on pages 28 to 49.*

Botanical Name: *Lantana camara*
Family: Verbenaceae

Companions: 'Miss Huff' lantana should be a staple in southern perennial gardens. Plant it among others that bloom in summer and fall. Agastache 'Blue Fortune,' canna lilies, purple heart, scabiosa, coneflowers, coreopsis, and 'Homestead Purple' verbena all offer long bloom periods that coincide with the bloom period of this lantana.

For easy color layers that not only bloom for a long time but also attract lots of butterflies, try the combination shown below.

'Miss Huff' lantana and some companions that form easy layers.

'Black and Blue' Salvia (above, top left) is another long-blooming perennial, flowering from about June until October. The salvia's blue, spiky flowers contrast well with the lantana's round clusters. It grows about the same size as the lantana (three to four feet) so plant them side by side. Be sure to give the Salvia about five feet in which to spread, or it will fall over on its neighbors. Both plants bloom best in full sun.

'Pink Profusion' Zinnias (above, bottom left) grow to about one foot tall and make a great border for both the lantana and the Salvia. Be sure to plant the zinnias at least three to four feet from the center of the larger plants so they don't get crushed. The round, daisy-like zinnia flower contrasts well with the spiky Salvia and the lantana cluster. All three of these plants bloom best in full sun - at least six hours per day.

**Lives on rainwater alone in all but the most extreme situations.*

GROWING CONDITIONS

Light: Full sun, at least 6 hours per day.

Water: Very low after establishment. Lives on rainwater alone, without supplemental water, in all but the most extreme conditions.

Soil: Any fertile, well-drained soil that has been enriched with organic matter. This plant really needs good drainage and won't perform well without it (pages 28 to 31).

Hardiness: Zones 7 to 9

Propagation: Cuttings

Pest Problems: If brown spots appear on the leaves, it is a fungus. If possible, cut back on water. Spray only if the problem becomes quite severe.

PLANTING & MAINTENANCE

When to Plant: Lantana from containers can be planted at any time. Spring is best (and fall is worst) because this plant needs summer heat for root establishment

Trimming: Annually, with some choices:

This lantana is best protected from winter cold if you leave the dead foliage on it after it freezes. But, it looks awful that way! You can also cut the dead foliage to the ground and cover it with pine straw. Don't use pine bark because it can rot lantana.

Another alternative is to reduce its size by half in fall and then cut it to the ground in late March or early April.

Fertilization: Medium. Fertilize at planting time and each spring with a timed-release product (page 46). Less fertilizer is needed with the application of more organics. See pages 46 to 49 for more instructions.

Division: 'Miss Huff' lantana grows best from cuttings or seeds. It doesn't divide well.

Lenten Rose

1ST

CHARACTERISTICS

Plant Type: Evergreen perennial.

Average Size: About 12 to 16 inches tall and equally as wide.

Growth Rate: Medium. Plants need 2 to 3 years to attain mature size. They need 5 years to flower from seed.

Leaf: Glossy green leaflets to 4 inches long, usually with serrated edges.

Flower: 1 to 2 inch wide, rose-like bracts with centers comprised of pincushion clusters of stamens.

Origin: Greece and Asia Minor

Spacing: About 14 inches on center (measure from the center of each plant). Closer in containers.

Cautions: All plant parts are poisonous. Almost never damaged by deer.

Colors: Flowers come in shades of pink, purple, burgundy, green, white, yellow, red, and bicolors.

UNIVERSITY AWARDS

1999: Georgia Gold Medal Winner

Lenten rose 'Royal Heritage Strain'

One of the few evergreen perennials that is almost never damaged by deer! Lenten roses perform so well they earn a blue ribbon.* Their delightful, nodding blossoms in late winter are framed by glossy foliage. Before winter ends, lenten roses bring the woodland garden to life with up to two months of lovely flowers.

Any garden that gets winter sun followed by summer shade is a good home for lenten roses, which have the unusual talent of blooming in late winter, with flowers that survive ice and snow. Lenten roses need little help to form long-lived colonies beneath the shelter of large oaks or other shade trees. Because the blossoms face downward, you will enjoy this plant most if you grow it in raised beds, along steps, or atop a retaining wall. Lenten rose blossoms make good cut flowers if you sear the stem ends to hold in the sap. The blossoms look particularly nice when floating in a bowl.

Regional Differences: Make sure the plants get excellent drainage in the coastal south, where wet weather may cause them to rot in summer.

Color Period: Late January to February in zone eight, February to March in zone seven, and March to April in zone six. Plants often bloom for two to three months.

Buying Tips: Since lenten roses take five years from the time a seed is planted until the plant grows large enough to flower, buy the largest plants you can find and afford!

**Blue ribbon plants are defined on page 12. For blue ribbon performance, follow the planting and maintenance guidelines on pages 28 to 49.*

Companions: Shade garden plants, such as azaleas, hostas, and heucheras, make good partners for lenten roses, or you can grow them with daffodils or other spring-flowering bulbs. Edge lenten rose beds with liriope, and set annual begonias among the plants in early summer, when lenten rose foliage becomes thin. Also, try planting lenten roses beneath Japanese maples or ornamental cherries.

Gardeners who often feel impatient for the arrival of spring love to grow lenten roses in big window boxes, situated so the blooms can be enjoyed from indoors while cold winds still blow. Plant such a box in late spring, and keep it in a shady spot outdoors until mid-winter.

For easy color layers, try camellias and azaleas with lenten rose, as shown below.

Lenten roses and some companion plants for easy color layers

Camellias (above, left) bloom at the same time as lenten roses, if you plant the right one. Ask your local garden center for a cultivar that shares the same bloom time. Both plants appreciate light shade.

Azaleas (above, right) also bloom at the same time as lenten roses. Plant the Camellia as the tallest layer, with the azaleas as the mid-layer. Border the grouping with lenten roses.

GROWING CONDITIONS

Light: Partial shade, or winter sun and summer shade.

Water: Low after establishment. Likes water every week or two during the growing season, depending on its environment. See pages 34 to 37 for more information.

Soil: Any fertile, well-drained soil that has been enriched with organic matter. Requires good drainage. See pages 28 to 31 for instructions.

Hardiness: Zones 4 to 9

Propagation: Seeds or division. Plants with remarkably colorful flowers are propagated by division, but it can be fun to simply allow a planting to reseed on its own, which often leads to novel shades of pink, purple, and cream. The flowers from seedlings are not necessarily the same color as their parents' flowers.

Pest Problems: None severe

PLANTING & MAINTENANCE

When to Plant: Lenten roses from containers can be planted at any time. Fall is best because they establish easier in cooler weather. Lenten roses reseed, and young plants can be dug and moved to new locations in late summer, after the bloom season ends.

Trimming: Allow lenten rose foliage to grow freely until it yellows and dies back, which varies from early to late summer, depending on site and climate. Use scissors to cut back faded foliage at the soil line.

Fertilization: Medium. Fertilize at planting time and each spring with a timed-release product (page 46). See pages for more instructions.

Division: Lenten rose clumps can be left alone for up to 20 years. They recover from division very slowly. Use its prolific seedlings if you want more plants.

1ST Lilies, Asiatic and Oriental

CHARACTERISTICS

Plant Type: Deciduous perennial (loses its leaves in winter).

Average Size: 24 to 48 inches tall by 12 to 24 inches wide, depending on variety.

Growth Rate: Fast

Leaf: Narrow, dark green leaves

Flower: Large flared trumpets, often with contrasting throats or speckles. Some are fragrant.

Origin: Asia

Spacing: Set bulbs 6 to 12 inches apart.

Cautions: Frequently damaged by deer.

Colors: Flowers are white, red, pink, yellow, orange, and many blends and bicolors.

1. *'Stargazer' Oriental lily*
2. *'Rosella's Dream' Asiatic lily*

Magnificent blossoms appear from late spring to mid summer. Always impressive, elegant lilies are among a gardener's finest pleasures. The blooms are so gorgeous that it is hard to believe they are actually quite easy to grow, which earns them a blue ribbon.*

Oriental lily 'Casa Blanca'

There are dozens of types of lilies, but Asiatic and Oriental hybrids stand out in terms of dependability and overall substance. The Asiatics typically grow to about 30 inches tall and produce five or more six inch wide blossoms at the end of each stem in late spring. Excellent varieties include yellow 'Nova Centro,' pink 'Vivaldi,' and pink and white 'Lollipop.' Oriental hybrids grow taller, to 40 inches or more, and produce four to eight huge, fragrant blossoms in early summer. They benefit from staking to keep them upright. White 'Casa Blanca' and red and white 'Stargazer' can be credited with causing many cases of lily fever among gardeners. When well pleased, these lilies form colonies that get bigger and better every year.

Regional Differences: In wet areas of the south, excellent drainage is needed to keep lily bulbs from rotting.

Color Period: Late spring to early summer for Asiatic hybrids; mid to late summer for Oriental hybrids. Both bloom for about seven to ten days.

Buying Tips: Good lilies are easy to find. Blooming plants are common in garden centers in spring and summer. Bulbs are easily available from catalogs or online.

**Blue ribbon plants are defined on page 12. For blue ribbon performance, follow the planting and maintenance guidelines on pages 28 to 49.*

Companions: Have fun with lilies! Frequent garden centers in spring and early summer and splurge on whatever blooming lilies make you smile. Plant them as punctuation points in your garden - wherever you need to draw the eye. In a few years, your garden will look like a show-place!

Tiger lilies, which grow three to four feet tall, are one of the most common lilies in the south. They stand out with flowers of different sizes and shapes, like the other summer bloomers shown below.

Tiger lilies and some companions for easy color layers

Black-Eyed Susans (above, top right) light up a bed that includes the tiger lilies. Both the flower colors and textures contrast well. Black-eyed Susans grow to about two feet tall and bloom for most of the summer. Since tiger lilies bloom in mid summer, the black-eyed Susans are dependable companions. Both plants appreciate the same light conditions: full sun to light shade. Use the four foot tall tiger lilies as the tallest plants in the bed and plant the smaller, black-eyed Susans in front of them.

'Homestead Purple' Verbena (above, bottom right) is one of the longest-blooming perennial groundcovers for the south. It starts blooming with a burst in spring and slows down somewhat in summer. Since it is one of the few groundcovers that blooms this long, it is definitely worth planting. This verbena grows to about one foot tall. It makes the ideal border for the tiger lilies and black-eyed susans.

GROWING CONDITIONS

Light: Full sun to partial shade

Water: Medium after establishment. Likes water once or twice a week during the growing season, depending on its environment.

Soil: Any fertile, well-drained soil that has been enriched with organic matter.

Hardiness: Zones 4 to 9

Propagation: Division

Pest Problems: Root rot in wet soil. Aphids sometimes spread viral diseases, which will cause stunted growth and mottled leaves. Dig up and dispose of infected plants.

PLANTING & MAINTENANCE

When to Plant: Lilies grown in containers can be planted any time. Plant bulbs in late winter to early spring. Plant deeply enough so that the tops of the bulbs are covered with 4 to 6 inches of soil.

Trimming: Wait until the foliage naturally begins to turn yellow to trim it back to a height that is mostly hidden by the foliage of other plants. After the first freeze, cut off remaining foliage at ground level.

Fertilization: Medium. Fertilize at planting time and each spring with a timed-release product (page 46). Less fertilizer is needed with the application of more organics.

Division: Divide only every 4 to 6 years in early spring. Dig carefully from beneath and immediately separate and replant bulbs.

Staking: Flowers sometimes become so heavy they need staking or they fall over. It is best to place the stake next to the bulb at planting or during the dormant season, so the stake does not damage the bulb.

Lilies, Naked Ladies

1ST

CHARACTERISTICS

Plant Type: Hardy bulb; tall foliage dies back in late spring, like daffodils. This is the reverse of most plants. The plant flowers in summer with no leaves.

Average Size: About 18 to 24 inches tall in bloom; 14 inches wide during foliar growth phase.

Growth Rate: Fast

Leaf: Medium green, strap-shaped fleshy leaves; 16 inches long and 1 to 2 inches wide. Foliage emerges in the fall (in zones 8 and 9) or early spring (in zones 6 and 7) and persists until spring.

Flower: Clusters of 4 or more florets atop bare stems; blossoms are flared trumpets, more typical of lilies.

Origin: China and Japan

Spacing: About 8 inches on center (measure from the center of each plant) and 6 inches deep.

Cautions: Bulbs are mildly toxic if eaten. Somewhat resistant to deer.

Colors: Flowers are pink or mauve.

Incredibly easy plant that gives spectacular impact with very little care. Blooms in late summer or early fall, when many other summer bloomers are done. Easily rates a blue ribbon.*

Naked ladies with black eyed susans

After baking in hot soil through the summer dry season, naked ladies send up bare stems, topped by dramatic flower clusters, overnight after a deep, drenching rain. The plants are called naked ladies because they bloom when they are bare of leaves. The flowers are supported by bare stems. which produce long, green leaves in spring that die back in early summer. Although the bloom time is short, lasting less than three weeks, these bulbs endear themselves by persisting for decades with no care and providing lovely color when little else is in bloom.

Naked ladies multiply quickly.

Regional Differences: All naked ladies grow well throughout the south.

Color Period: Begins as early as June and may continue to early fall. Blooms last about three weeks.

Buying Tips: If you can't find these plants at your local garden center, they are readily available online or from catalog companies.

**Blue ribbon plants are defined on page 12. For blue ribbon performance, follow the planting and maintenance guidelines on pages 28 to 49.*

Companions: Naked ladies steal the show when they are in bloom, so they are definitely a focal point flower. Plant them near a water feature, birdbath, mailbox, or close to your deck or patio where they can't be missed. Light pink naked ladies look great before a background of evergreen shrubs or when allowed to peek out from dark ivy groundcovers. They also work well interspersed between clumps of daylilies, which hide the failing foliage from view in early summer. These bulbs need a period of summer dryness, so avoid combining them with plants that need abundant water. They are easy to naturalize beneath deciduous trees alongside daffodils and other spring-blooming bulbs.

Naked ladies flower in summer, when a number of our best perennials and shrubs are in flower as well. Try layering it with the high performers shown below for a dazzling summer show.

Naked ladies with companion plants that form easy color layers

'Endless Summer' Hydrangea (above, left) grows three to four feet tall and blooms for most of the summer, coordinating with the naked ladies' flower time. The large, hydrangea flowers contrast well with the smaller, naked lady flowers. Use this hydrangea as the tallest layer of this grouping.

Luna Hibiscus (above, right) grows two to three feet tall and blooms at the same time as the hydrangea and naked ladies. Use it as the mid-layer, and border the grouping with the smaller, naked ladies.

GROWING CONDITIONS

Light: Partial shade to sun in winter; partial shade in summer.

Water: Very low after establishment. Lives on rainwater alone, without supplemental water, in all but the most extreme conditions. See pages 34 to 37 for more information.

Soil: Any well-drained soil. Drainage is essential, so be sure to loosen clay under the bulb if you are planting in clay. See pages 28 to 31 for more information.

Hardiness: Zones 5 to 9

Propagation: Division

Pest Problems: Rare

PLANTING & MAINTENANCE

When to Plant: Naked ladies from containers can be planted at any time. Fall is best because they establish easier in cooler weather. Plant bulbs at any time except spring. Regardless of planting time, they may not bloom their first year. Dig, divide and replant bulbs in early summer, just as the foliage fades away or right after they flower.

Planting Depth: Twice as deep as the diameter of the bulb.

Division: Dig, divide, and replant in early summer to increase your supply, but no more often than every 4 or 5 years.

Trimming: When the leaves turn brown in early summer, trim them off with a sharp knife or pruning shears if you find them unsightly.

Fertilization: Medium. Fertilize at planting time and each spring with a timed-release product. Less fertilizer is needed with the application of more organics. See pages 46 to 47 for more instructions.

1ST Lilies, Spider or Hurricane

CHARACTERISTICS

Plant Type: Hardy bulb; tall winter foliage dies back in summer, which is the reverse of most plants. The plant flowers with no leaves. The flowers wilt before new leaves form.

Average Size: About 14 to 20 inches tall in bloom; 14 inches wide during foliar growth phase.

Growth Rate: Fast

Leaf: Dark green leaves with a gray stripe down the center. Leaves are narrow, like grass. Foliage emerges in the fall and persists until spring.

Flower: Clusters of 4 or more florets atop bare stems; spider lilies have long stamens, with florets resembling those of azaleas.

Origin: China and Japan

Spacing: About 7 to 9 inches on center (measure from the center of each plant).

Cautions: Bulbs are mildly toxic if eaten. Somewhat resistant to deer.

Colors: Flowers are red.

ALTERNATE SELECTIONS

If you have a partially shaded white garden, seek out the white flowering spider lily (*Lycoris. x albiflora*), the perfect companion for 'Monroe White' liriope. Yellow-flowered species *(Lycoris aurea)* are available, but they are often not as dependable as red spider lilies.

Sudden bursts of color in late summer or early fall that provide strong and dramatic accents. Short bloom period but incredibly easy to grow. Survive both droughts and floods. Easily rates a blue ribbon.*

Like their cousins the bare naked ladies, spider lilies spend most of the summer hibernating until late August or early September. At that time, their bare stems pop out of the ground with clusters of predominately red flowers. In the fall, they develop thin grass-like leaves. They are often called hurricane lilies because their blooms often follow on the heels of tropical storms. They develop thin, grass-like leaves in fall that persist until spring. Although the bloom time is short, lasting less than three weeks, these bulbs endear themselves by persisting for decades with no care,, and providing lovely color when little else is in bloom. These bulbs multiply rapidly.

Regional Differences: Spider lilies grow well in most of the south, except the coldest parts of zone six.

Color Period: Late August to early October, depending on rainfall. Blooms last about three weeks. Spider lilies frequently don't bloom until their second year in the ground.

Buying Tips: If you can't find these plants at your local garden center, they are readily available online or from catalog companies.

**Blue ribbon plants are defined on page 12. For blue ribbon performance, follow the planting and maintenance guidelines on pages 28 to 49.*

Companions: Spider lilies steal the show when they are in bloom, so they are definitely a focal point flower. They work well interspersed between clumps of daylilies, which hide the failing foliage from view in early summer. These bulbs need a period of summer dryness, so avoid combining them with plants that need abundant water.

For major color impact, combine spider lilies with flowers of contrasting colors, like blue and yellow. Try layering this lily with blue perennial salvia and golden shrimp plants for a high-impact accent area, as shown below.

Spider lilies with companion plants that form easy layers of color

Black and Blue Salvia (top left) grows to about four feet tall and dependably blooms at the same time as spider lilies. This salvia also grows well in light shade, an ideal light condition for spider lilies. Use this salvia as the tallest layer in this grouping.

Golden Shrimp Plants (bottom left) is an annual that is always blooming in the late summer/early fall period when the spider lily flowers. Use it as the mid-layer in this grouping, with the spider lilies as the border.

GROWING CONDITIONS

Light: Sun in winter; partial shade in summer.

Water: Low after establishment. Likes water every week or two during the growing season, depending on its environment. See pages 34 to 37 for more information.

Soil: Any fertile, well-drained soil that stays dry in the summer. See pages 28 to 29 for drainage tips.

Hardiness: Zones 7 to 10; survives in zone 6, if planted in a protected location.

Propagation: Division

Pest Problems: Rare

PLANTING & MAINTENANCE

When to Plant: Spider lilies from containers can be planted at any time. Fall is best because they establish easier in cooler weather. Plant bulbs at any time except spring. Regardless of planting time, they may not bloom their first year.

Planting Depth: 4 to 6 inches

Trimming: When the leaves turn brown in early summer, trim them off with a sharp knife or pruning shears if you find them unsightly.

Fertilization: Medium. Fertilize at planting time and each spring with a timed-release product. Less fertilizer is needed with the application of more organics. See pages 46 to 47 for more instructions.

Division: Dig, divide, and replant in early summer to increase your supply but no more often than every four or five years. Newly planted bulbs often take two years to bloom.

1ST Phlox, Woodland or Wild Sweet William

Lovely native groundcover that blooms in spring. One of the few blooming, creeping groundcovers that take shade. Also, one of the few evergreen perennials. Don't confuse this phlox with annual phlox (only lasts one season) that is also sold in garden centers in spring. Be sure the tag says *Phlox divaricata,* woodland phlox, or wild sweet William. Easily wins a blue ribbon* because of ease of care.

CHARACTERISTICS

Plant Type: Semi evergreen perennial (loses some leaves in winter).

Average Size: About 12 to 15 inches tall by 12 inches wide.

Growth Rate: Medium

Leaf: Dark green, linear, and willow-like. About 1 inch long by 1/2 inch wide.

Flower: Star-shaped flowers with flat tops. About 1 to 2 inches across.

Origin: Central United States north to Quebec.

Spacing: About 18 inches on center (measure from the center of each plant). Closer in containers.

Cautions: Often damaged by deer

Colors: Flowers are bluish purple, reddish purple, or white.

A scene from Huntsville Botanical Garden. Phlox are the low, reddish-purple plants under the tree. White tulips are planted in the foreground, with purple pansies in the back.

'Sherwood Blue' woodland phlox with white foam flower

Woodland phlox are completely covered with blue flowers in spring. The effect is beautiful, like a blooming carpet. This native, woodland plant likes moist stream banks in the wild. Woodland phlox is not a fast grower but eventually forms large colonies.

Be sure to provide this plant with good drainage (pages 28 to 29) because it does not do well without it.

Regional Differences: Woodland phlox does well in zones six through eight in the south. It doesn't grow well in zone nine.

Color Period: Late March until April for three to four weeks

Buying Tips: All the woodland phlox (*Phlox divaricata*) we have tried have done well. Look for them in your garden centers when they bloom in spring. If you can't find them locally, order from online suppliers. *Phlox subulata* grows in sandy soil (it is quite picky about that) and doesn't bloom quite as long.

**Blue ribbon plants are defined on page 12. For blue ribbon performance, follow the planting and maintenance guidelines on pages 28 to 49.*

Attracts Butterflies Avg. Weeks of Color Southern Native

Botanical Name: *Phlox divaricata*
Family: Polemoniaceae

Companions: Pair woodland phlox with other spring-blooming perennials, bulbs and shrubs - including azalea, camellia, amsonia, baptisia, iris, and lenten rose. The phlox also make an attractive groundcover under spring-blooming trees, including Carolina silverbell, dogwood, and redbud trees. Usually, the trees bloom at the same time as the phlox, and the color underneath greatly intensifies the overall color impact of the group.

Native azaleas and kerria are wonderful companions for woodland phlox, as shown below.

Woodland phlox and some companions

Native Azaleas (above, left) not only bloom at the same time as woodland phlox but also do quite well planted directly above them. Since these azaleas reach six to twelve feet, they look like small trees compared with the small, 12 inch tall phlox. Both plants are comfortable in winter sun and summer shade. Since the azaleas lose their leaves in winter, this suits the phlox just fine.

Kerria (above, right) usually blooms at the same time as both the azaleas and the woodland phlox. Let them grow to their full height of six feet, and plant them beside of the azaleas, with the phlox as a low groundcover or border. These three plants do well in light shade.

GROWING CONDITIONS

Light: Light to medium shade. Takes morning sun but no afternoon sun.

Water: Low after establishment. Likes water every week or two during the growing season, depending on its environment. See pages 34 to 37 for more information. We have seen this plant grown successfully without irrigation, but don't know if it would do so in most situations.

Soil: Any fertile, well-drained soil that has been enriched with organic matter. Requires good drainage. See pages 28 to 31 for instructions.

Hardiness: Zones 3 to 8

Propagation: Division, seeds, cuttings.

Pest Problems: Powdery mildew, rabbits, and spider mites. Cut back after blooming to avoid powdery mildew, which is the most serious pest.

PLANTING & MAINTENANCE

When to Plant: Phlox from containers can be planted at any time. Fall is best because they establish easier in cooler weather, but you are more likely to find them at your garden center in early spring, when they are blooming.

Trimming: Trim back after flowering to diminish the chance of powdery mildew.

Fertilization: Medium. Fertilize at planting time and each spring with a timed-release product. Less fertilizer is needed with the application of more organics. See pages 46 to 47 for more instructions.

Division: This phlox is seldom divided because it grows so slowly.

Phlox 'David'

CHARACTERISTICS

Plant Type: Deciduous perennial (dies back in winter).

Average Size: 3 to 5 feet tall by 3 feet wide. Some smaller, dwarfs are new to the market, which we haven't tried yet.

Growth Rate: Medium

Leaf: 4 to 5 inches long by 1/2 to 1 inch wide, dark green.

Flower: 4 to 6 inches tall by 3 inches wide, dome-shaped.

Origin: Eastern US

Spacing: About 2 to 3 feet on center (measure from the center of each plant). Keep the plants well-spaced because they do better with some air circulation.

Cautions: Often damaged by deer

Colors: Flowers are white.

One of the south's showier perennials, blooming for about one to three months in mid summer and early fall. The 'David' phlox is the only cultivar that resists powdery mildew that plagues much of this species. Misses a ribbon because it looks better with deadheading (removal of dead flowers).

This lovely native perennial was once present in every garden, and it has been making a well-deserved comeback in recent years. Because of its height, summer phlox makes a beautiful backdrop plant, and it attracts butterflies, too. White flowered varieties, such as fragrant 'David,' 2002 Perennial Plant of the Year, are especially useful because they resist the mildew common with most phlox.

Phlox 'David' makes an outstanding cut flower, but the flowers are so large that the plant sometimes requires staking. Thunderstorms can cause the clumps to fall over.

Regional Differences: Easy to grow throughout the region. In zones eight and nine, be sure to locate plants in partial shade, as bright sun causes the blossoms to bleach and fall quickly.

Color Period: Blooms for about four weeks in June or July with no deadheading (removal of dead flowers). Blooms for another month or two if you have time to do this chore.

Buying Tips: Be sure to look for the words Phlox 'David' on the label. Many other phlox look similar but are plagued with mildew.

Attracts Butterflies

Avg. Weeks of Color

Botanical Name: *Phlox paniculata* 'David'
Family: Polemoniaceae

Companions: Plant phlox with other mid summer bloomers, like agastache, black-eyed Susans, cannas, and coneflowers.

Since Phlox 'David' blooms for quite a while if you remove the dead flowers, try it with other long-bloomers for a prolonged summer show, as shown below.

Phlox 'David' with some companions

'Knock Out' Roses (above, left) bloom spring, summer, and fall, so they keep the bed in color for the entire growing season. They grow taller than the phlox, so plant them as the tallest plant in the bed. The 'Knock Out' roses come in bright pink (as shown above) or a paler pink that would also look wonderful with the white phlox.

'Homestead Purple' Verbena (above, right) blooms for most of the warm season, from spring until fall. Use this low-growing (about a foot tall) verbena as a front border for the roses and the phlox.

GROWING CONDITIONS

Light: Light shade to full sun

Water: Medium after establishment. Likes water once or twice a week during the growing season, depending on its environment. See pages 34 to 47 for more information.

Soil: Any fertile, well-drained soil that has been enriched with organic matter. Requires good drainage.

Hardiness: Zones 3 to 8

Propagation: Division or cuttings; division is easier.

Pest Problems: Powdery mildew weakens the plants, but it does not kill them. Severity varies greatly from year to year; the variety named here is resistant. Spider mites can be a problem in hot, dry weather.

PLANTING & MAINTENANCE

When to Plant: Phlox from containers can be planted at any time. Fall is best because they establish easier in cooler weather.

Trimming: Cut back the dead foliage (to the ground) after it freezes in late fall or early winter. When the first shoots emerge from the soil in spring, trim 10 or 12 crowded ones down by half. The remaining 4 to 6 stems strengthen, so you might not need to stake them. Phlox 'David' appreciates deadheading (removing dead flowers) but keeps blooming without it.

Fertilization: Medium. Fertilize at planting time and each spring with a timed-release product. See pages 46 to 47 for more instructions.

Division: Dig, divide, and replant about every five years, or whenever you notice a loss of vigor or the bed seems too crowded. Fall or spring is fine. Divide clumps into smaller clumps with at least three crowns.

Purple Heart or Purple Queen

1ST

CHARACTERISTICS

Plant Type: Deciduous perennial (dies back in winter).

Average Size: 10 to 14 inches tall by 16 inches wide.

Growth Rate: Fast

Leaf: Deep purple, 3-inch long leaves on brittle, angular stems.

Flower: Small, triangular flowers to 1/2 inch across.

Origin: Eastern Mexico

Spacing: About 10 inches on center (measure from the center of each plant). Closer in containers.

Cautions: Sap is an irritant. Seldom bothered by deer.

Colors: Leaves are deep purple in sun, slightly greenish in shade; orchid-pink flowers.

BUDGET GARDENING TIP

Covering a lot of ground with purchased plants can be expensive. However, one purple heart plant can spread quite a bit, even in its first season, due to its fast growth and ease of propagation. Throughout summer, stem cuttings will root readily in moist soil or in a jar of water.

Purple heart's flowers are rather insignificant. Its best feature is the purple leaf color.

One of the few, low-growing perennials that offers five to six months of color with almost no care! Bold purple foliage with coarse texture is a high contrast player in the summer garden. Easily rates a blue ribbon.*

Purple heart planted with pink vinca

Purple heart is a champion summer groundcover that tolerates heat, drought, salt spray, and even comes back when mowed. Long billed as an annual under the name of *Setcreasea*, this sprawling spreader is surprisingly hardy, capable of surviving winter temperatures to zero degrees. It's a great plant to use in areas bordered by turf, or for remote spots that are difficult to water. A potent source of both dark purple color and coarse texture, purple heart is ideal for framing plantings when your goal is to maximize contrast.

Regional Differences: In zone six, mow down the foliage and mulch over the roots in mid-autumn to enhance winter hardiness.

Color Period: Late summer to fall. Flowers open in the morning and close at night. The flowers are rather insignificant, however. The main feature of this plant is the purple leaves.

Buying Tips: Purple heart is available at quite a few garden centers in spring. If you just buy a few, you can easily root cuttings from them to make quite a few more plants.

**Blue ribbon plants are defined on page 12. For blue ribbon performance, follow the planting and maintenance guidelines on pages 28 to 49.*

Companions: Purple heart is quite versatile in the spring, summer, and fall garden. It works well in a number of different color schemes. Lime green is a wonderful companion color, in the form of coleus, sweet potato vine, hostas, or heucheras. Pale pink is a softer choice, from the flowers of vinca, petunias, or pentas. Or, try it with yellow melampodium and red dragon wing begonias for a traffic-stopping combination.

For very easy color, try purple heart with the great performers shown below. This combination gives you drought tolerance as well.

Purple heart with some companion plants

Dwarf Crapemyrtles (above, left) bloom for up to 90 days if you remove the dead flowers. Their bloom period coincides with the purple heart's summer color period. Since dwarf crapemyrtles grow from three to five feet tall, use them behind the shorter purple heart and yellow lantana.

'New Gold' Lantana (above, right) is an annual that blooms for the entire spring, summer, and fall season. It grows to about one foot tall. Alternate clumps of lantana with the similar-sized purple heart. Since the yellow lantana spreads quite a bit, keep the center of the lantana a full two and a half to three feet away from the center of the purple heart. That way, the lantana won't take over the purple heart. Both prefer full sun.

GROWING CONDITIONS

Light: Light shade to full sun. Loses color in too much shade.

Water: Low. Once established, purple heart's semi-succulent leaves and stems help it tolerate drought. Ours have always been watered weekly, so we haven't tried it without any irrigation.

Soil: Any fertile, well-drained soil that has been enriched with organic matter. Requires good drainage.

Hardiness: Zones 7 to 10. In very cold winter areas, cuttings can be rooted, potted up, and kept through winter as indoor houseplants, then planted outdoors in spring.

Propagation: Throughout summer, stem cuttings will root readily in moist soil or in a jar of water

Pest Problems: We never had a pest on our purple heart in the 15 years we've grown it.

PLANTING & MAINTENANCE

When to Plant: Purple heart from containers can be planted at any time. Fall is best because they establish easier in cooler weather, but you are more likely to find them at your garden center in spring or summer.

Trimming: Purple heart doesn't need trimming in most situations during the growing season. However, if it gets too wild-looking for you, cut it back to half its size. Cut back the dead foliage (to the ground) after it freezes in late fall or early winter.

Fertilization: Medium. Fertilize at planting time and each spring with a timed-release product. See pages 46 to 47 for more instructions.

Division: Seldom need division. Rooted cuttings will yield more plants.

2ND Red Hot Poker Plant

CHARACTERISTICS

Plant Type: Deciduous perennial (dies back in winter).

Average Size: About 3 to 4 feet tall by 1 1/2 feet wide. Flower spikes sometimes reach 4 feet tall.

Growth Rate: Fast

Leaf: Long, narrow, grass-like leaves about 2 feet long by 1/2 foot wide. Skinnier than daylilies.

Flower: Unique, spiky flower shaped like a poker.

Origin: South Africa

Spacing: About 2 to 3 feet on center (measure from the center of each plant). Closer in containers.

Cautions: Almost never damaged by deer.

Colors: Flowers are orange, yellow, and red. Red flowers are often lime or yellow on the bottom of the bloom as they age.

Red hot poker plants with gaillardia.

Great color impact from a plant that loves heat and drought. Great, hot colors. Very easy to grow if you give it good drainage. Rates a red ribbon.*

Red hot poker plants have been thriving at Huntsville Botanical Garden for over fifteen years.

The best features of red hot poker plants are the unique, flower shape and hot colors. Their bloom period is not the longest, but the color impact makes them worth planting. Use a few clumps of these flowers in your summer gardens for lots of oohs and aahs!

Regional Differences: Red hot poker plants require winter protection in zone six. Mulch does quite well.

Color Period: Blooms for four to six weeks from June to August

Buying Tips: We have tried only a few different kinds, and all have done well.

**Red ribbon plants are defined on page 13. For blue ribbon performance, follow the planting and maintenance guidelines on pages 28 to 49.*

Attracts Butterflies

Attracts Hummingbirds

Resists Deer

Avg. Weeks of Color

Botanical Name: *Kniphofia uvaria*
Family: Liliaceae

Companions: Use red hot poker plants in clumps to accent summer flower beds. They look best with flowers of different colors and shapes, including agastache, black-eyed Susan, lantana, coneflowers, coreopsis, verbena, and yarrow.

Red hot poker plants look good alternated with clumps of daylilies and bordered by purple heart, as shown below.

Red hot poker plants with some companions

'Stella de Oro' Daylily (top left) is one of the longest blooming perennial daylilies, blooming for up to three months each summer. Its 18 to 24 inch height fits well in front of the 36 inch poker plants. Plant both in full sun for most blooms.

Purple Heart (bottom left) is an excellent perennial that gives your garden strong color from spring to the first frost of fall or early winter. Plant it in front of your daylilies and poker plants as a border.

GROWING CONDITIONS

Light: Full sun, at least 6 hours per day.

Water: Medium after establishment. Likes water once or twice a week during the growing season, depending on its environment. See pages 34 to 37 for more information.

Soil: Any fertile, well-drained soil that has been enriched with organic matter. Requires good drainage. See pages 28 to 31 for instructions.

Hardiness: Zones 5 to 9, if you protect them with mulch in winter in zones 5 and 6.

Propagation: Division

Pest Problems: We have never had a pest on this plant, but root rot is a major problem in wet soils.

PLANTING & MAINTENANCE

When to Plant: Red hot poker plants from containers can be planted at any time. Fall is best because they establish easier in cooler weather, but you are more likely to find them at your garden center in spring or summer.

Trimming: For best appearance, cut off the dead flower spikes as they begin drying, if they bother you. Cut back the dead foliage (to the ground) after it freezes in late fall or early winter.

Fertilization: Medium. Fertilize at planting time and each spring with a timed-release product. Less fertilizer is needed with the application of more organics. See pages 46 to 47 for more instructions.

Division: Red hot poker plants become rather crowded about every 5 years. Remove the clump from the ground in spring or fall. Separate the clumping root system and replant promptly. New plants take 2 to 3 years to bloom.

Salvia, Argentine Skies and Black & Blue

CHARACTERISTICS

Plant Type: Deciduous perennial (dies back in winter).

Average Size: About 3 to 4 feet tall by equally as wide.

Growth Rate: Fast

Leaf: Bright green leaves shaped like elongated hearts 3 to 4 inches wide by 2 to 4 inches long.

Flower: Tubular flowers on spikes attract hummingbirds and butterflies.

Origin: Argentina, Brazil, and Paraguay.

Spacing: About 4 feet on center (measure from the center of each plant).

Cautions: Almost never damaged by deer.

Colors: Flowers are cobalt blue, light blue, and blue with dark navy calyxes.

BUDGET GARDENING TIP

Look for this plant in one-gallon containers, which should cost about $8. Since these salvias spread so wide, one plant can cover 16 square feet, or 50 cents per foot. Many other perennials in that price range only cover 2 to 4 square feet, or $2 to $4 per foot.

1. Salvia 'Argentine Skies'
2. Salvia 'Black and Blue'

One of the few perennials that blooms from early summer to frost, although not as heavily as annuals. Rare source of true blue for the summer garden on a large, bushy plant that sometimes falls over. Attracts both butterflies and hummingbirds. Misses a ribbon because it looks best with several trimmings each year.

'Black and Blue' Salvia has been happily living at Huntsville Botanical Garden for over ten years, taking temperatures down to three degrees.

Many color schemes call for blue, which can be hard to come by after the weather turns hot. This big, almost shrub-like perennial can deliver the goods, and it is easy to grow in any well-drained site that gets at least a half day of sun. 'Argentine Skies' and 'Black and Blue' are among the few salvias we have tried that have dependably lived through our zone seven winters. Both are quite informal plants with a tendency to sprawl.

Regional Differences: We haven't had experience with this plant in the colder parts of zone 7 or in zone 6, so we can't say if it will live through the winters there. If you live in these areas, mulch this heavily in winter and delay hard pruning until spring to enhance winter hardiness.

Color Period: Mid summer to fall. In the perennial garden at the University of Georgia, this plant typically blooms for 30 weeks.

Buying Tips: We have tested many salvias that we thought were perennials but didn't live through southern winters. Check the plant label to be sure it says 'Black and Blue' or 'Argentine Skies' if you want a perennial that blooms all season and will return next spring.

Attracts Butterflies Attracts Hummingbirds Resists Deer 30 Avg. Weeks of Color

Botanical Name: *Salvia guaranitica.*
Family: Lamiaceae

Companions: This is an excellent background plant for beds planted with assorted daylilies, or you can use it as an anchor plant in a pink and blue garden planted with scaevola, begonias, petunias, or pentas. Be sure to give this plant quite a bit of space, or it will crush its neighbors.

To create a hummingbird heaven, plant this salvia with firespike, pentas, and lantana.

For high-contrast color, plant this salvia with the perennials shown below.

'Black and Blue' Salvia and some companions

Yarrow (above, right) is an easy perennial companion for this salvia. Yellow yarrow lights up a garden for about two to three months in summer and contrasts wonderfully with the spiky flowered salvia. Yarrow grows to about three feet tall, so place it in front of the taller salvia.

'Big Sky Twilight' Coneflower (above, left) is an excellent choice for a companion for 'Black and Blue' salvia and yarrow. The textures of the plants are quite different and all prefer sun. This coneflower grows to about 30 inches tall, so alternate it with the yarrow, with the larger salvia as a background plant.

GROWING CONDITIONS

Light: Full sun, at least 6 hours per day. Falls over in too much shade.

Water: Medium after establishment. Likes water once or twice a week during the growing season, depending on its environment. See pages 34 to 37 for more information.

Soil: Any fertile, well-drained soil that has been enriched with organic matter. Requires good drainage. See pages 28 to 31 for instructions.

Hardiness: Zones 7 to 10

Propagation: Take divisions from the outside of established clumps in spring, or root stem tip cuttings taken in early summer.

Pest Problems: White flies occasionally.

PLANTING & MAINTENANCE

When to Plant: Salvia from containers can be planted at any time. Fall is best because they establish easier in cooler weather, but you are more likely to find them at your garden center in spring or summer.

Trimming: When plants are about 12 inches tall in spring, pinch them back to encourage strong, bushy growth. After the leaves die back in winter, trim plants to about 20 inches, and then prune again in early spring, just as new growth begins. These salvias can get floppy, especially after thunderstorms. Stake them if they fall over.

Fertilization: Medium. Fertilize at planting time and each spring with a timed-release product. Less fertilizer is needed with the application of more organics. See pages 46 to 47 for more instructions.

Division: Older plants grow into thick clumps. Dig out extra plants from the outside of the clump in spring or fall, and transplant them to new areas of the garden.

2ND Salvia leucantha, Mexican Sage

CHARACTERISTICS

Plant Type: Deciduous perennial (dies back in winter).

Average Size: 2 to 5 feet tall by 3 to 5 feet wide, depending on cultivar.

Growth Rate: Fast

Leaf: Arching spikes densely packed with small, tubular flowers.

Flower: Hundreds of small, open-centered blossoms.

Origin: Mexico and Central America.

Spacing: About 3 to 5 feet on center (measure from the center of each plant), depending on cultivar. Closer in containers.

Cautions: Almost never damaged by deer.

Colors: Flowers are purple, often with white florets.

Some Mexican sages have solid purple flowers, as shown above. Others have purple and white flowers, as shown opposite.

One of our most spectacular fall bloomers. Attracts butterflies, hummingbirds, and human admirers! Deer almost never eat this plant. Easy to grow but cold sensitive in many parts of the south. Earns a red ribbon* because it looks best with two trimmings each year.

Mexican sage with yellow lantana

Mexican sage is so showy it almost stops traffic when it blooms. Plants of this species typically grow four to five feet tall and equally as wide, which gives them a strong presence in the garden. A compact dwarf form, two-foot tall 'Santa Barbara,' makes a lovely statement as a rounded mound. In any size, Mexican sage covers itself with richly-textured, purple flowers as soon as days become short in late summer. Mexican sages come with either purple and white flowers (above) or solid purple flowers (left).

Regional Differences: Mexican sage is often not winter hardy in zone six, and is sometimes killed in winter in zone seven. In zones eight and nine, plants may grow so vigorously that they need periodic pruning to control their size.

Color Period: Late August to the first freeze

Buying Tips: Look for this salvia at your garden center when it blooms in late summer to early fall. If you can't find it, this plant is definitely worth shopping for online.

**Red ribbon plants are defined on page 13. For blue ribbon performance, follow the planting and maintenance guidelines on pages 28 to 49.*

Attracts Butterflies

Attracts Hummingbirds

Resists Deer

Avg. Weeks of Color

Botanical Name: *Salvia leucantha*
Family: Lamiaceae

Companions: Mexican sage shows best with other fall bloomers, like firespike, chrysanthemums, and asters.

This showy sage also combines well with summer bloomers whose flowers still thrive in fall. Try it with lantana and zinnias, as shown below.

Mexican sage with some companions

'Miss Huff' Lantana (above, left) is a perennial lantana that blooms from July until November. Like the Mexican sage, it attracts both hummingbirds and butterflies, so your creatures will be quite happy if you plant both of them together! This lantana grows to about three feet tall, so place it behind your Mexican sage (if it is a dwarf) or in front of it (if it is the more common type, which grows four to five feet tall.).

'Profusion' Zinnias (above, right) grow to about one foot tall and make a great border for both the lantana and the sage. These zinnias will also please your butterflies. The round, daisy-like zinnia flower contrasts well with the spiky sage and the lantana cluster. All three of these plants bloom best in full sun - at least six hours per day.

GROWING CONDITIONS

Light: Light shade to full sun

Water: Low after establishment. Needs less water than most other salvias. We haven't tried it on less than weekly water during the growing season. See pages 34 to 37 for more information.

Soil: Any fertile, well-drained soil that has been enriched with organic matter. Requires good drainage.

Hardiness: Zones 8 to 10 without protection. Zone 7 with protection.

Propagation: Rooted suckers, rooted stem cuttings taken in early summer. In early summer, propagate plants by digging and cutting away rooted stems that appear near the outside of the clump, and transplanting them to containers. These can be kept in a cool, unheated garage through winter and planted out the following spring to replace plants lost to winter's cold.

Pest Problems: None severe

PLANTING & MAINTENANCE

When to Plant: Salvia from containers can be planted at any time. Fall is best because they establish easier in cooler weather.

Trimming: Leaving the old growth intact through winter helps shelter the base of the plants from cold winds and ice. In early spring, trim the plants down to about a foot tall. Then, either cut back again by half in mid summer, or stake the plant when it starts blooming (to keep it from falling over).

Fertilization: Low. Fertilize at planting time and each spring with a timed-release product. Less fertilizer is needed with the application of more organics. See pages 46 to 47 for more instructions.

Division: Divide this salvia to keep it in bounds or to get more plants every 3 to 5 years.

Scabiosa, Pincushion Flower

CHARACTERISTICS

Plant Type: Deciduous perennial (dies back in winter).

Average Size: About 12 to 18 inches tall (including the flowers) by 12 to 15 inches wide.

Growth Rate: Fast

Leaf: Grayish green, fine-textured, little linear teeth less than an inch long.

Flower: About 2 inches wide; resembles pincushions.

Origin: Europe and Asia

Spacing: About 12 inches on center (measure from the center of each plant). Closer in containers.

Cautions: Occasionally damaged by deer.

Colors: Flowers are lavender-blue.

Scabiosa offers a long bloom period without too much care. Needs deadheading (removal of dead flowers) but returns the favor by attracting lots of butterflies. Misses a ribbon because of this chore but is quite easy to grow.

Scabiosa 'Butterfly Blue' is one of the butterfly's favorite foods when it first comes into bloom in spring. Huntsville Botanical Garden has been growing this plant successfully for fifteen years.

If you love butterflies, treat them to some scabiosa. When it first opens up in spring, they flock to the newest delicacy on the block. It blooms most at first, slowing down as the season progresses. But it delivers an acceptable percentage of color for four to five months if you deadhead (remove the dead flowers). This high performance earned Scabiosa 'Butterfly Blue' the Perennial Plant of the Year award in 2000.

The flowers are borne on top of the foliage, making them easy for the butterflies to land on.

Regional Differences: Scabiosa does equally well throughout the south.

Color Period: If you deadhead (remove dead flowers), scabiosa blooms from May until September, nonstop. Without deadheading, it blooms from May until July or early August. It blooms most at first, slowing down as the season progresses.

Buying Tips: Scabiosa is quite fine-textured and looks somewhat scrawny in the containers in your garden center. However, if fills out nicely once you have it in the ground.

Scabiosa 'Harlequin Blue'

Companions: Scabiosa's low stature (twelve to eighteen inches tall) makes it an ideal border plant for many taller perennials and flowering shrubs. Try it with 'Knock-Out' roses and coneflowers, as shown below.

Scabiosa 'Butterfly Blue' and some companions

'Knock Out' Roses (above, left) are shrubs that bloom spring, summer, and fall, so they will keep the bed in color for the entire growing season. Since scabiosa blooms heaviest in May, the roses will be at their showiest at the same time. These roses grow four to six feet tall, so plant them as the tallest plant in the bed. The 'Knock Out' roses come in bright pink (as shown above) or a paler pink that would also look wonderful with the scabiosa.

'Big Sky Twilight' Coneflower (above, right) is an excellent perennial choice for a companion for the roses and scabiosa. This yellow coneflower blooms from about May until August, which coincides with the flowering period the other two plants. The textures of the plants are quite different, and all prefer sun. This coneflower grows to about three feet tall, so plant it as the middle layer, in between the roses and the scabiosa.

GROWING CONDITIONS

Light: Full sun, at least 6 hours per day.

Water: Medium after establishment. Likes water once or twice a week during the growing season, depending on its environment. See pages 34 to 37 for more information. Scabiosa doesn't tolerate wet soils.

Soil: Any fertile, well-drained soil that has been enriched with organic matter. Requires good drainage. See pages 28 to 31 for instructions. Scabiosa doesn't tolerate wet soils.

Hardiness: Zones 5 to 9

Propagation: Seeds or division

Pest Problems: Rare

PLANTING & MAINTENANCE

When to Plant: Scabiosa from containers can be planted at any time. Fall is best because they establish easier in cooler weather, but you are more likely to find them at garden centers when they are blooming in summer.

Trimming: Deadhead (remove dead flowers) throughout the blooming season to increase bloom time. Cut back the dead foliage (to the ground) after it freezes in late fall or early winter.

Fertilization: Medium. Fertilize at planting time and each spring with a timed-release product. Less fertilizer is needed with the application of more organics. See pages 46 to 47 for more instructions.

Division: Divide in fall if you want more plants. The clumps do well for years without division.

Sedum 'Autumn Joy'

2ND

CHARACTERISTICS

Plant Type: Deciduous perennial (dies back in winter).

Average Size: About 18 to 24 inches tall and equally as wide.

Growth Rate: Fast

Leaf: Light to medium green, fleshy, rounded; 2 to 3 inches across.

Flower: The flowers start out small and keep growing into large, dome-shaped clusters. About 6 inches across, like a softball.

Origin: China, Korea

Spacing: About 12 to 18 inches on center (measure from the center of each plant). Closer in containers.

Cautions: Seldom damaged by deer.

Colors: Flowers are red or pink. They start out lime green and progress to pink or red.

1. *'Autumn Joy' sedum flowers start out lime green in July.*
2. *Flowers turn bright, rosy, pink by late fall.*

'Autumn Joy' sedum is one of our showiest fall bloomers, with flowers the size of a softball for up to three months. Sedum is a succulent, which needs less water than most other plants. No deadheading (removal of dead flowers) required, which makes sedum easier than most other perennials. Requires two trimmings each year, so it rates a red ribbon.*

With hundreds of sedums on the market, 'Autumn Joy' outsells them all. While most plants that grow well in the south store water primarily in the roots, sedums are succulents that also store water in their leaves, making them more tolerant of drought. And while many succulents can't adapt to the south's rainy periods, 'Autumn Joy' handles them well, provided it has good drainage (see pages 28 to 29).

This sedum is one of the easiest perennials in this book because it requires no deadheading (removal of dead flowers).

Regional Differences: Grows equally well throughout the south

Color Period: From August or September until frost, continuously

Buying Tips: Look for the label 'Autumn Joy' in your garden center to be sure you are buying this one. However, many new cultivars are coming out each spring which show a lot of promise.

**Red ribbon plants are defined on page 13. For blue ribbon performance, follow the planting and maintenance guidelines on pages 28 to 49.*

6

Attracts Butterflies | Lives on Rain Water * | Avg. Weeks of Color

Botanical Name: *Sedum spectabile* 'Autumn Joy'

Family: Crassulaceae

Companions: Plant sedums with other fall bloomers, like Mexican sage, chrysanthemums, asters, pansies, and firespike.

Try the combination shown below for easy color layers that will, once again, stop traffic on your street.

'Autumn Joy' sedum with some companions

Mexican Sage (above, left) works wonderfully with sedum because they bloom at the same time and offer lots of color. The taller varieties grow to five feet tall, so plant the shorter sedum in front as a border. Mexican sage lives without winter protection as far north as zone eight.

'Purple Dome' Asters (above, right) also peak in fall, and grow about three feet tall. Plant them in between the tall sage and the shorter sedum. All three plants like sun but will bloom with some shade.

**Lives on rainwater alone in all but the most extreme situations.*

GROWING CONDITIONS

Light: Light shade to full sun

Water: Very low. Grows without irrigation (in all but the most extreme conditions) after the establishment period. However, it looks better with some extra water, especially during drought times in the heat of summer. See page 34 to 37 for more information.

Soil: Any fertile, well-drained soil that has been enriched with organic matter. Requires good drainage. See pages 28 to 31 for instructions.

Hardiness: Zones 3 to 9

Propagation: Division or cuttings

Pest Problems: Rare. Root rot can develop if plants are kept too wet.

PLANTING & MAINTENANCE

When to Plant: Sedum from containers can be planted at any time. Spring is best because they establish easier in cooler weather. However, you are more likely to find them in your garden centers in fall, when they are blooming.

Trimming: In spring or early summer, cut them back to about half when they are 8 inches tall. This cutback will make them fuller for their fall season. Deadheading (removal of dead flowers) is not needed. Cut back the dead foliage (to the ground) after it freezes in late fall or early winter.

Fertilization: Medium. Fertilize at planting time and each spring with a timed-release product. Less fertilizer is needed with the application of more organics. See pages 46 to 47 for more instructions.

Division: Divide every 3 to 5 years in spring when the middle of the plant goes into a decline.

1ST Spanish Bluebells

CHARACTERISTICS

Plant Type: Deciduous perennial (loses its leaves in winter).

Average Size: About 18 inches tall and 12 inches wide.

Growth Rate: Fast

Leaf: Dark green, strap-shaped leaves to 12 inches long.

Flower: Bell-shaped blossoms on upright spikes.

Origin: Spain and Portugal

Spacing: Set bulbs 4 to 6 inches apart; they will fill in to form a clump.

Cautions: None known. Somewhat resistant to deer.

Colors: Flowers are blue, pink, white.

This old-fashioned, spring-flowering bulb is ideal for southern shade gardens. Extremely easy, requiring almost no care, so it rates a blue ribbon.* Unique color that complements many other traditional, spring-flowering plants of the south.

Spanish bluebells bloom just as the last daffodils are fading.

If your spring color scheme calls for soft pastels beneath the open shade of deciduous trees, Spanish bluebells should be a garden essential. In mid to late spring, spikes emerge that are studded with dozens of bell-shaped blossoms. Blue is the strongest color, but there also are varieties that bloom pink ('Queen of Pinks') or white ('White City'). This is the perfect bulb to grow at the base of trees or near pink or white azaleas. Once planted, Spanish bluebells persist for years with little attention. The bulbs actually benefit from a dry period in summer and then begin growing roots when the soil cools in the fall. Some varieties are fragrant, and all make excellent cut flowers.

Regional Differences: Easily grown throughout the south

Color Period: Bloom for about two weeks in mid to late spring, just as the last daffodils are fading.

Buying Tips: Available from internet suppliers if you can't find them at your local garden center.

**Blue ribbon plants are defined on page 12. For blue ribbon performance, follow the planting and maintenance guidelines on pages 28 to 49.*

Companions: Spanish bluebells mix well with all of the spring-blooming shade garden plants - azaleas, dogwoods, lenten roses, hostas, and liriope. Plant them near the base of a dogwood or other tree, or place them behind big hostas, which leaf out at the perfect time hiding the fading bluebell foliage from view. After the weather warms and bluebells become dormant, you can set caladiums or begonias over the resting bulbs.

The blue color of the bluebells looked wonderful with pink native azaleas and yellow forsythia, as shown below.

Spanish bluebells and some companion plants

Native Azaleas (above, top) not only bloom at the same time as Spanish bluebells but also do quite well planted directly above them. Since these azaleas reach six to twelve feet tall, they look like small trees compared with the 18 inch tall bluebells. Both plants are comfortable in winter sun and summer shade. Since the azaleas lose their leaves in winter, this suits the bluebells just fine.

Forsythia (above, bottom) is a shrub that blooms at the same time as both the azalea and the bluebells and grows to about six feet tall. Forsythia takes light shade, but too much shade will prevent it from blooming. Use it next to the azaleas, with the bluebells bordering both taller plants.

GROWING CONDITIONS

Light: Partial shade (winter sun, summer shade).

Water: Low after establishment. Likes water every week or two during the growing season, depending on its environment. See pages 34 to 37 for more information.

Soil: Any fertile, well-drained soil that has been enriched with organic matter. See pages 30 to 31 for instructions.

Hardiness: Zones 4 to 8

Propagation: Division. Bulbs vary in size, but those that are more than 2 inches in diameter are the strongest bloomers. Seedlings or small bulblets will grow to blooming size in about three years.

Pest Problems: Rare. Bulbs may rot in extremely wet soil.

PLANTING & MAINTENANCE

When to Plant: Any time when planting mature plants from containers. Set out dormant bulbs in the fall. Every 5 to 6 years, dig, divide and replant crowded clumps in summer or fall after the foliage fades.

Planting Depth: Plant 5 inches deep, to the base of the bulb.

Division: Every 5 to 6 years, dig, divide and replant crowded clumps in summer or fall.

Trimming: Spanish bluebells often reseed if ripe flower spikes are left on the plants until they die back naturally. If you don't want the plants to spread, clip off the spikes as soon as the flowers fade.

Fertilization: Medium. Fertilize at planting time and each spring with a timed-release product. Less fertilizer is needed with the application of more organics. See pages 46 to 47 for more instructions.

Stokesia, Stokes' Aster

CHARACTERISTICS

Plant Type: Deciduous perennial (dies back in winter) in zones 6 and 7. Evergreen in zones 8 and 9.

Average Size: 12 to 18 inches tall by 12 inches wide.

Growth Rate: Fast

Leaf: Oblong to pointed, lance-shaped, green leaves, 2 to 4 inches long.

Flower: Open, daisy-shaped blossoms with fringed edges, 2 to 4 inches across.

Origin: Pine forests of the southeastern US.

Spacing: About 12 inches on center (measure from the center of each plant). Plants grow into colonies. Closer in containers.

Cautions: Often damaged by deer

Colors: Flowers are lavender-blue, white, pink, or yellow.

1. *'Peachy' stokesia*
2. *'Purple Pixie' stokesia*
3. *'Color Wheel' stokesia*

Native perennial that is extremely dependable and easy to grow. Its best qualities are its blue color and fairly long bloom period. However, you have to trim it to keep it blooming, so it doesn't rate a ribbon. Great butterfly plant.

Blue flowers always have a cooling influence in the garden, which is exactly the special effect you can expect with Stokes' aster. This low-growing perennial is trouble-free in the garden and makes an excellent cut flower for the home. Although Stokes' aster doesn't bloom as long as the similar scabiosa, it is extremely easy to grow. This plant requires deadheading (removal of dead flowers) to keep it looking tidy and to increase the bloom period.

Regional Differences: Stokesia persists as a green rosette of foliage through winter in zone eight. In colder places, it often dies back to the roots in winter and emerges first thing in spring.

Color Period: Heaviest bloom period is early summer, but blooming often will continue for many weeks if old flowers are removed. Blooming starts in early May in zone eight, mid to late May in zone seven, and June in zone six. Blooms continue for six weeks without deadheading (removal of dead flowers) and six more weeks with deadheading. Most varieties will produce a second flush of flowers in the fall after enjoying a mid summer break from blooming.

Buying Tips: Look for 'Blue Danube' and 'Klaus Jelitto', which have done well for us. We haven't tried the other cultivars.

Companions: In low-maintenance borders, stokesias are perfect for planting in front of tall daylilies. But because gentle stokesias go with almost everything, why not put them to work as camouflage plants? For example, use stokesia as foreground plants for late-blooming chrysanthemums. By the time the mums need elbow room, the stokesia can be cut back for a mid summer break. Grow stokesias alongside daffodils. In late spring, the stokesia foliage will hide the withering daffodil leaves from view.

Stokesia also shows well when layered with other plants that have peak bloom periods in early summer.

Stokes' aster with some companions for easy color layers

'Sunny Knock Out' Rose (top left) has a more compact growth habit than the original 'Knock Out,' growing to about four feet tall. The flowers start out yellow and fade to cream. Both colors compliment the Stokes' aster. This rose blooms on and off from spring until fall, so it should be in bloom with the aster. Use the rose as the tallest plant of this grouping.

Yarrow (bottom left) also starts blooming in early summer and continues until late summer. Use it as the mid layer, in between the roses and the Stokes' aster. Plant them in full sun.

GROWING CONDITIONS

Light: Light shade to full sun, preferring full sun.

Water: Low to medium. Stokesias are quite drought-tolerant once established. However, we have always watered ours weekly during the growing season, so we don't know how it does with no irrigation.

Soil: Any fertile, well-drained soil that has been enriched with organic matter. Requires good drainage. See pages 28 to 31 for instructions.

Hardiness: Zones 5 to 9

Propagation: Seed, cuttings, division (preferred). Plants divided and replanted in fall bloom reliably the following summer.

Pest Problems: Very rare. Stokes' asters are remarkably resistant to insects and diseases.

PLANTING & MAINTENANCE

When to Plant: Stokes' asters from containers can be planted at any time. Fall is best because they establish easier in cooler weather.

Trimming: Cut back flowers and remove spent stems after they fade to keep the plants from producing seeds and to prolong the bloom time of the plants. Cut back the dead foliage (to the ground) after it freezes in late fall or early winter.

Fertilization: Medium. Fertilize at planting time and each spring with a timed-release product. Less fertilizer is needed with the application of more organics. See pages 46 to 47 for more instructions.

Division: Dig, divide, and replant established clumps every 3 years in early spring or late summer. If necessary, plants dug in fall can be held in containers until the following spring.

Verbena 'Homestead Purple'

1ST

CHARACTERISTICS

Plant Type: Deciduous perennial (dies back in winter).

Average Size: About 8 to 12 inches tall by 30 to 36 inches wide.

Growth Rate: Fast

Leaf: Dark green, leathery leaves on rambling stems.

Flower: Clusters of small, tubular flowers; attractive to butterflies.

Origin: Eastern US, Virginia to Florida.

Spacing: About 3 feet on center (measure from the center of each plant). Closer in containers.

Cautions: Skin irritant. Often damaged by deer.

Colors: Flowers are purple.

UNIVERSITY AWARDS

1994: Georgia Gold Medal Winner

'Homestead Purple' verbena alternated with yellow celosia and pink wave petunias in our Georgia trial gardens.

One of the best blooming groundcovers for the south. Lots of blooms in spring and fall with some blooms almost all season long. No deadheading (removal of dead flowers) necessary. Easily earns a blue ribbon* for outstanding performance with very little care. Great for butterflies.

'Homestead Purple' verbena has been thriving at Huntsville Botanical Garden for 15 years.

'Homestead Purple' verbena blooms longer than any other low-growing plant we tried. It flowers for about six months, taking short breaks, but almost always has some blooms. This verbena spreads well, too, so be sure to give it space.

Regional Differences: Some cultivars may not be reliably winter hardy in the coldest sections of the zone six. In the zone nine, these verbenas are often evergreen.

Color Period: It starts blooming with a bang in early spring and is covered with flowers, as shown above. Although the blooms taper off during summer, it is almost never without flowers. And, in fall, it undergoes another big bang, blooming until the first hard frost.

Buying Tips: There are many purple verbenas in your garden centers that resemble this one, but they are annuals (only last one season). Check the plant tag and be sure it says 'Homestead Purple' verbena if you want the perennial form. The annual verbenas are much more common in southern garden centers in spring and summer than the perennial form.

**Blue ribbon plants are defined on page 12. For blue ribbon performance, follow the planting and maintenance guidelines on pages 28 to 49.*

Attracts Butterflies

Attracts Hummingbirds

Avg. Weeks of Color

Southern Native

Botanical Name: *Verbena canadensis* 'Homestead Purple'
Family: Verbenaceae

Companions: This verbena is quite useful in the flower garden because it is one of the lowest-growing perennials. Its small stature makes it ideal for borders, and the deep purple color complements most colors well. Use it with other long-blooming perennials, like agastache, lantana, phlox, salvia, and black-eyed Susans. It also looks great with daylilies and flowering shrubs, like butterfly bush and 'Knock-Out' roses.

For easy color layers that bloom a long time, try the combination shown below.

'Homestead Purple' verbena and some companions

Canna Lilies (above, left) are perennials in most of the south (zones seven to nine) and bloom for much of the summer. Their height varies from three to six feet, so use them as the tallest plant in this grouping.

Coreopsis 'Moonbeam' (above, right) is a wonderful companion for both because its light-textured leaves are not only different from the coarser-textured canna but also quite a bit smaller than the verbena. It blooms from June until September and grows about 18 inches tall, so place in between the taller canna and shorter verbena. All do well in full sun.

GROWING CONDITIONS

Light: Light shade to full sun

Water: Low after establishment. Likes water every week or two during the growing season, depending on its environment. See pages for 34 to 37 more information. Since this plant is native to fields in the south, it stands to reason that it should live without irrigation, but we are yet to decide.

Soil: Any fertile, well-drained soil that has been enriched with organic matter. Requires good drainage, especially in winter. See pages 28 to 31 for instructions.

Hardiness: Zones 6 to 9

Propagation: Cutting or division. Plants eagerly develop roots where stems touch the ground.

Pest Problems: Rare; powdery mildew occasionally.

PLANTING & MAINTENANCE

When to Plant: Verbenas from containers can be planted at any time. Fall is best because they establish easier in cooler weather.

Trimming: Cut back the dead foliage (to the ground) after it freezes in late fall or early winter.

Fertilization: Medium. Fertilize at planting time and each spring with a timed-release product (page 46). Less fertilizer is needed with the application of more organics.

BUDGET GARDENING TIP

One plant can cover a lot of ground, even in its first season. When you plant it, understand that a single plant spreads a full three feet across. Look underneath the spreading stems, and you'll see roots. Cut off small pieces with roots, and plant them elsewhere. Since one plant can cover 9 square feet, you could have a lot of purple by the end of the summer!

Yarrow, Achillea

CHARACTERISTICS

Plant Type: Perennial

Average Size: 18 to 30 inches tall, spreads into patches from 18 to 24 inches wide.

Growth Rate: Fast

Leaf: Finely-cut, feathery green leaves, slightly aromatic.

Flower: Flat-topped clusters of tiny flowers; clusters 2 to 4 inches wide.

Origin: Europe

Spacing: About 24 inches on center (measure from the center of each plant). Closer in containers.

Cautions: Yarrow was historically used as a medicinal herb to stop bleeding of wounds. Almost never eaten by deer.

Colors: Flowers are white, pink, red, yellow, orange, or lilac.

ALTERNATE SELECTIONS

Cultivars of fern-leaf yarrow (*Achillea filipendulina*) grow taller and produce large clusters of yellow flowers over a period of two months, from late spring through early summer. This species often performs well in zone 6 and in very well-drained beds in zone 7 gardens. However, high rainfall and warm humidity of the coastal south gives it trouble.

Feathery foliage all year; flowers in early summer. A truly low-care perennial for sunny spots, yarrow provides soft texture even when it is not in bloom. However, it looks better with several trimmings, so it misses a ribbon.

Yarrow's ferny foliage spread quickly to form a thick mass, so this perennial doubles as a flowering ground cover for sunny spots. Available in a rainbow of shades, you can grow a single color or choose from mixtures that are keyed to certain color schemes. For example, 'Summer Pastels' includes soft shades of pink, yellow and lilac, while 'Debutante' features hotter shades of orange and red. 'Debutante' also reblooms more willingly than older varieties.

Yarrow is a must-have if you enjoy fresh-cut flowers. The blossoms keep their colors well when dried, too. To dry them, pick the flowers as they get their full color and hang upside down in a cool dry shady place with low humidity (such as in a basement or storage room).

Regional Differences: Yarrow grows well throughout the south. In the humid conditions of the coastal south, excellent drainage and good air circulation are critical.

Color Period: Late May through the end of July without deadheading (removal of dead flowers). Blooms a month or so longer with deadheading. Foliage often persists year round.

Buying Tips: 'Coronation Gold,' 'Moonshine,' 'Cerise Queen,' and 'Rosea Paprika' have all done well at Huntsville Botanical Gardens.

Attracts Butterflies

Resists Deer

Avg. Weeks of Color

Botanical Name: *Achillea millefolium*
Family: Compositae

Companions: Yarrow works best with other plants that bloom at the same time, including most of our summer perennials. Try it with the companions shown below for both color and butterfly attraction.

This log cabin is part of Garry and Ramona Hughes's garden in Louisville, Mississippi. It features yellow yarrow in a wild flower garden. Yarrow transitions well from the wild garden to the manicured garden, looking good in more formal, suburban gardens as well.

Yarrow and some companions

'Purple Emperor' Butterfly Bush (above, left) is one of the newer, more compact butterfly bushes that grows to about four feet tall and blooms at the same time as the yarrow. Plant it behind the shorter yarrow (18 to 30 inches tall).

Scabiosa (above, right) is a low-growing perennial (12 to 18 inches tall) that blooms for most of the growing season, from May until October. Plant it as the front border for the butterfly bush and yarrow. All three do well in full sun.

GROWING CONDITIONS

Light: Full sun, at least 6 hours per day.

Water: Low to medium. Yarrow is quite drought-tolerant once established. However, we have always watered ours weekly during the growing season, so we don't know how it does with no irrigation.

Soil: Any fertile, well-drained soil that has been enriched with organic matter. Requires good drainage. See pages 28 to 31 for instructions.

Hardiness: Zones 3 to 8

Propagation: Seed, division. The best times to dig and divide established plantings are spring and fall.

Pest Problems: Root rot if the soil is too wet or not well drained.

PLANTING & MAINTENANCE

When to Plant: Yarrow from containers can be planted at any time. Fall is best because they establish easier in cooler weather. Start seeds indoors in late winter and set out the seedlings in early spring. Purchased plants can be set out in spring or fall.

Trimming: Deadhead (remove dead flowers) to help prolong bloom time. Also, trim off any foliage that turns brown to keep the patch looking neat, which can be done in late July. You can even trim it down to the ground at this time if it is dead-looking. Cut back the dead foliage (to the ground) after it freezes in late fall or early winter.

Fertilization: Medium. Fertilize at planting time and annually with a timed-release product (page 46). Less fertilizer is needed with the application of more organics.

Division: The best times to dig and divide established plantings are spring and fall every 3 to 5 years or whenever the center dies out.

Other Perennials that Deserve Mention

Agapanthus
Agapanthus spp.

Excellent blue color for zones 8 and 9. Blooms in spring or early summer for about 6 weeks. 18 to 30 inches tall. Light shade to full sun. Medium water. Grows from a rhizome.

Ajuga
Ajuga reptans

Groundcover with beautiful green or purple-bronze foliage with blue flowers on 6 inch spikes. Ajuga provides a mat of dark-colored foliage that spreads by runners. Must have great drainage to prevent crown rot, which occurs frequently in the south. 3 to 6 inches tall. Medium shade to morning sun. Medium water.

Amaryllis
Amaryllis belladonna

Another of the 'naked ladies' bulbs that sends up foliage in the spring and flowers in late summer on leafless stalks. Beautiful, fragrant, trumpet shaped pink flowers on 2 to 3 foot stems for 2 to 3 weeks. Not reliably hardy below 20 F. Full sun to light shade. Low water. Zones 8 to 10.

Amemone, Japanese
Anemone japonica

Nice, fall-blooming perennial for all of the south. May be slow to establish but grows rapidly, filling in a large area. Blooms September-October for 3 to 5 weeks. 2 to 3 feet tall. Morning sun to light shade. Medium water. Zones 4 to 8.

Angel's Trumpet
Brugmansia spp.

Spectacular flowers on a plant that is highly poisonous (even dangerous to smell the flowers!), so be careful with this one. Blooms in summer for about 3 months. Many different types available. Medium shade to full sun. Medium water. Zones 7 to 11.

Artemisia
Artemisia 'Powis Castle'

The best perennial plant for silvery blue foliage. This selection holds up well during the summer heat, forming a dense mound of delicate, lacy foliage. Stays neat in the garden, not invasive. 3 feet tall and wide. Full sun to light shade. Low water. Zones 6 to 9.

Bulbine
Bulbine frutescens

An excellent perennial for low water gardens in zones 9 to 11 (we are hearing people from zone 8 saying they grow it as well). 12 inches tall. Full sun. Flowers for about 8 months a year in zone 10. Great textural accent for the garden.

Cactus
Varies with genus & specie

Cactus does well in dry areas; doesn't thrive in the south's wet times. Best used as an indoor plants, or summer accent in the garden. Good for containers. Be careful with spines. Zones 6 to 10, depending on variety. Very low water. Sun.

Candytuft
Iberis sempervirens

Evergreen perennial with willow-like, dark green foliage. White flowers in spring cover the low-growing mounds for about 3 weeks. Prefers cooler temperatures. 6 to 8 inches tall. Full sun. Medium water. Zones 3 to 8.

Cape Honeysuckle
Tecomaria capensis

Great plant for fall color. Hummingbirds love it! Orange flowers for a few months each fall. Showy, but very informal plant. Not appropriate for formal gardens. Evergreen in areas that don't freeze. About 4 feet tall. Full sun. Zones 8 to 11.

Cast Iron Plant
Aspidistra elatior

Tough plant that likes light to dense shade. Grows about 2 feet tall. Green and variegated forms. Zones 7b to 11. We have seen problems with brown spotting on the leaves in zone 7a.

Chrysanthemum
Chrysanthemum spp.

Garden mums are a long-time, southern favorite. New names and selections are everywhere. 'Clara Curtis' is an excellent, old-fashioned garden mum with beautiful pink flowers blooming in fall for about 2 weeks. 2 to 3 feet tall. Full sun. Medium water. Zones 5 to 9.

**Blue ribbon plants are defined on page 12. For blue ribbon performance, follow the planting and maintenance guidelines on pages 33 to 46.*

Confederate Rose
Hibiscus mutablis

Tender perennial in zones 6 to 7, Confederate rose astounds gardeners with its changing flower colors from white to pink to red as the sun moves from east to west. Blooms for 2 to 6 weeks. Single and double flower forms. 6 to 8 feet tall. Full sun. Medium water. Zones 7 to 9.

Creeping Jenny
Lysimachia nummularia

We have only used this plant in containers, so don't know how it does long term as a landscape plant. Outstanding container plant. About 3 inches tall. Trails over the edge of containers. Medium shade to full sun. Zones 3 to 9. Medium water.

Crinum Lily
Crinum spp.

Dramatic, tropical looking plant with large flowers. Poisonous. Many sizes available. Some varieties are very susceptible to pests. Grows from a bulb. Zones 8 to 11. Full sun.

Crocus
Crocus spp.

Easy, small, flowering bulb suitable for naturalizing in zones 6 to 7; struggles in the deep south. Early to bloom (often in areas with snow on the ground) for about two weeks. Rich colors of yellow, purple, white and shades in between. 3 to 6 inches tall. Full sun. Low water. Zones 3 to 8.

Dahlia
Dahlia spp.

Tender perennial from large tuberous roots producing magnificent flowers for 6 to 8 weeks with deadheading. Numerous flower types available. Flowers are gorgeous but need attention to perform well in the south. 1 1/2 to 6 feet tall. Full sun. Medium water. Zones 8 to 10.

Daisies, Shasta
Leucanthum x superbum

Excellent perennial, but requires frequent dead heading to keep it looking good - more than most perennials in this book. White, daisy-like flowers with golden eyes. Flowers open in May and last several weeks. 2 feet tall. Full sun to light shade. Medium water. Zones 4 to 9.

Dianthus, Cottage Pinks
Dianthus gratianopolitanus

Wonderful, small perennials that flower in spring for 2 to 3 weeks heavily, and sporadically for the rest of summer. 'Bath's Pink' and 'Tiny Rubies' have been recognized as superior selections. 8 to 12 inches tall. Full sun to light shade. Low water. Zones 3 to 9.

Dwarf Chenille
Acalypha pendula

Flowering groundcover that did quite well as far north as zone 8 in our trials. Blooms all summer and fall. Great trailer for containers. 3 to 4 inches tall. Takes heat very well. Zones 8 to 11. Dies back in areas that freeze and returns the following spring. Dense shade to full sun. Low water.

Foxglove
Digitalis purpurea

A short-lived perennial for most of the south, but the flower show in spring is worth the effort. Spikes to 4' tall bearing numerous flowers in rich colors open in spring for 2 to 3 weeks. Poisonous. 2 to 3 feet tall (foliage). Full sun to light shade. Medium water. Zones 4 to 9.

Gaillardia, Blanket Flower
Gaillardia pulchella

Excellent, Drought-tolerant, native perennial that attracts butterflies. Hot colors of red, yellow, and orange in single or double forms bloom most of the summer. Heat and humidity tolerant. 1 to 2 feet tall. Full sun. Low water. Zones 4 to 9.

Gaura
Gaura lindheimeri

Drought-tolerant perennial native to the southwest that does very well in the south. 2 to 3 foot plants send up numerous, airy spikes of flowers in white, pink or red for much of the summer. May need to be deadheaded to keep neat appearance. Full sun. Low water Blooms 12 to 16 weeks. Zones 5 to 9.

Ginger Lily
Hedychium coronarium

Tender perennial for zones 6 to 7, this wonderful plant knocks you over with its sweet fragrance from late summer to the first frost. White flowers open atop stems of strap-shaped leaves. 4 to 6 feet tall. Full sun to light shade. Medium water (can take wet feet). Zones 7 to 9.

Other Perennials that Deserve Mention

Ginger, Variegated
Alpinia zerumbet

Tender perennial prized for its beautiful, variegated foliage and not necessarily its flowers. Strap-shaped leaves 2 feet long by 6 inches wide of deep green and bands of gold makes a striking accent plants in the landscape. 2 to 3 feet tall. Light shade to morning sun. Medium water. Zones 8 to 10.

Gladiolus
Gladiolus spp.

Bulbs with sword-shaped leaves and trumpet like flowers. Excellent cut flower. Best for back of border to hide bottom of plant. Blooms for 3 to 4 weeks. May need staking. Tender in zone 6. 2 to 3 feet tall. Full sun. Medium water. Zones 5 to 9.

Goldenrod
Solidago rugosa

Wonderful perennial that has gotten a bad rap. Goldenrod does not cause allergies - ragweed does. This Drought-tolerant, native perennial is easy to grow and provides beautiful yellow flowers in fall for 4 to 6 weeks. 'Fireworks' is a shorter growing selection. 4 to 6 feet tall. Full sun. Low water. Zones 3 to 9.

Grass, Miscanthus
Miscanthus sinensis

Widely planted, ornamental grass hardy in all the south. Erect growth habit that does not flop. Flower plumes emerge in late August depending on cultivar. Concern over invasive potential may curb enthusiasm for this ornamental. 4 to 8 feet tall. Full sun. Low water. Zones 4 to 9.

Grass, Pampas
Cortaderia selloana

Widely planted, ornamental grass for zones 7 to 9. Prized for the magnificent, floral plumes opening in August. Coarse-textured foliage (will cut you if not careful) is semi-evergreen. Cut back in late winter to 6 to 12 inches tall. 6 to 8 feet tall. Full sun. Low water. Zones 7 to 9.

Hyacinth, Grape
Muscari americanum

Blooms for 2 to 3 weeks in early spring. Foliage is grass-like, and flower spikes are small, often getting lost in the garden. Easy to grow; multiplies rapidly; must be seen up close to appreciate. 3 to 6 inches tall. Full sun to light shade. Low water. Zones 3 to 8.

Iris, African
Dietes vegetata

Seldom bloomed in our Florida trials, but the spiky texture of the leaves is very useful in containers. Flower is lovely during its brief appearances. Zones 8 to 11. Sun to light shade.

Iris, Apostles
Neomarica gracilis

Forms large clumps with 3 foot leaves. Gorgeous flowers open for only one day, take a rest, and open again several days later in spring. Usually grown as an annual in the south because this bulb is subtropical. Light shade. Medium water.

Lamb's Ear
Stachys byzantina

Prized for the coarse-textured, hairy, almost quilted foliage in silvery-blue, lamb's ear is a great foil in the mixed perennial border among hot-color combinations. The soft, hairy leaves beg to be touched and children love them. Good drainage a must. 1 to 2 feet tall. Full sun to light shade. Low water. Zones 4 to 8.

Lamium
Lamium maculatum

We have only tried this plant in containers for the summer, and it did quite well. Don't know how it does long term. Light to medium shade. Hardy to zone 3. Medium water.

Monarda, Bee Balm
Monarda didyma

Old garden favorite that attracts butterflies and can be made into a tea. Rosy red flowers open in May and will flower all summer with deadheading. Heat tolerant but is prone to powdery mildew. 2 to 3 feet tall. Full sun. Medium water. Zones 4 to 8.

Obedient Plant
Physostegia virginiana

A definite misnomer - this native perennial spreads aggressively in the garden, so give it plenty of room. Spiky flowers look like snapdragons and open in mid-summer for 3 to 4 weeks in shades of pink and white. 3 to 4 feet tall. Full sun to light shade. Medium water. Zones 3 to 9.

**Blue ribbon plants are defined on page 12. For blue ribbon performance, follow the planting and maintenance guidelines on pages 33 to 46.*

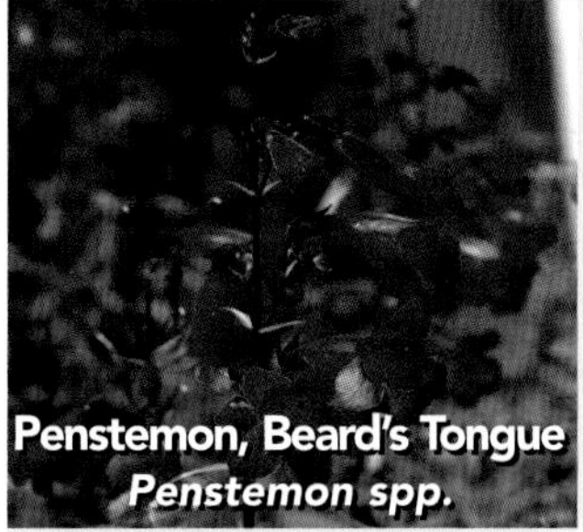

Penstemon, Beard's Tongue
Penstemon spp.

Numerous selections available - most not suitable for the heat and humidity of the south. Blooms for 4 to 6 weeks. P. smallii is a pink-flowering, native wildflower to the southeast. 1 to 3 feet tall. Light shade - morning sun. Low water. Zones 3 to 8.

Phormium, Flax
Phormium spp.

Phormium or flax is an excellent, blue ribbon plant. Extremely easy. Likes temperatures from 40 to over 100. Over winter it inside with bright light, unless you live in zone 9 south. Light shade to full sun outdoors. 2 feet tall. Low water.

Ruellia
Ruellia brittoniana

Prolific bloomer with a wild form. Cut it back for more controlled growth. Grows well in zone 8, but limited use in zone 7, so we don't know its exact cold tolerance. Becoming invasive in some areas. 2 feet tall. Low water. Light shade to full sun.

Sage, Autumn
Salvia greggi

Autumn sage is another salvia worth growing in your garden. Native to the southwest, they are Drought-tolerant, can take the heat but must have good drainage. Red flowers in late summer for 9 to 12 weeks. 2 to 3 feet tall. Full sun to light shade. Low water. Zones 7 to 9.

Snowflakes
Leucojum aestivum

Excellent, naturalizing bulb for the south, with beautiful bell-shaped white flowers with tiny green dots. Easy to grow, often shared from one generation to another. Needs little winter chill, so it grows well in zone 8. 12 to 18 inches tall. Full sun. Low water. Zones 4 to 8.

Trillium
Trillium spp.

Wonderful woodland plant native to much of the southeast. Particular about its environment - rich organic soil under the shade of deciduous trees. This native wildflower opens in early spring and blooms for 2 to 3 weeks per species. 3 to 6 inches tall. Medium shade. Medium water. Zones 3 to 9.

Tulip
Tulipa x

Most popular bulb sold in the US. Often give southerners fits. Heat and heavy rains spoil most tulip displays before their time, but we have found the peony-style selections, like 'Angelique,' will hold up to our weather conditions and bloom for about 2 to 3 weeks. Best to replant every year; they do not come back reliably. Full sun. Low water.

Veronica
Veronica spp.

We have only used this plant once and were quite surprised to find it bloomed for 4 months straight! Many different types available. The one we tried grew 18 inches tall. Light shade to full sun. Medium water.

Chapter 4

Shrubs & Vines

The shrubs and vines in this chapter represent some of the best the south has to offer. And new cultivars make gardening with color easier than ever.

✿ Flowering shrubs are generally less work to maintain than perennials. Many shrubs in this chapter only require a chore or two per year and give you months of color in return.

✿ Since shrubs develop larger root systems than perennials, most need less water than perennials.

✿ Shrubs with short bloom periods, like hydrangeas and azaleas, are now available in reblooming forms. These new shrubs bloom about twice as much as the older ones.

✿ Many flowering shrubs - like butterfly bush, loropetalum, and althea - grow too large for most residences. Plant breeders have introduced many new, more compact forms that are much more useful in residential settings.

Above: The white-flowered hydrangeas are called 'Annabelle.' The blue ones are 'Penny Mac,' one of the new, reblooming hydrangeas.

Left: The dark-leaved shrub is loropetalum, with a bridalwreath spiraea blooming in the background. Loropetalums have grown huge in the past, but the new, dwarf varieties fit better in many residences.

1ST Abelia

CHARACTERISTICS

Plant Type: Evergreen shrub.

Average Size: Both large and small abelias are available, ranging from 3 to 5 feet tall to 6 to 10 feet tall. ('Regional Differences,' right).

Growth Rate: Fast

Leaf: Most common types emerge bronze, change to dark green in summer, and turn purplish in fall; some newer, cultivars are variegated or multicolored. 1 1/2 inches long.

Flower: Tubular shaped, fragrant

Origin: China

Spacing: From 3 to 6 feet on center (measure from the center of each plant), depending on mature size of abelia you are planting.

Cautions: Seldom damaged by deer.

Colors: See 'Buying Tips'

UNIVERSITY AWARDS

2003: Mississippi Medallion Winner, 'Edward Goucher' abelia.

2005: Georgia Gold Medal Winner for both 'Rose Creek' and 'Canyon Creek' abelia.

Abelia chinensis

One of the easiest flowering plants in this book. Lives without irrigation in all but the most extreme situations. Butterfly and hummingbird attractor that is seldom damaged by deer. Blooms for most of the summer. New, small varieties give new flexibility to this old, southern plant. Easily rates a blue ribbon.*

Award-winning 'Rose Creek' abelia

Abelia has been used for generations in the south. But, the original varieties (shown, left) grow quite tall, from six to ten feet, which limits their use in residential gardens. New, dwarf varieties (shown above) not only stay smaller but also bloom more. This smaller stature (three to five feet tall) has greatly increased the use of abelia, particularly as foundation planting for homes.

Regional Differences: The larger abelias grow quite a bit taller in warmer areas of the south. In zone eight, they grow ten feet tall, whereas they only grow six feet tall in zone six. Expect some winter die-back in zone six, but this won't affect the next season's flowering period.

Color Period: From May until the first hard frost. Actually, the white flower falls off, but the calix below is pink, and it persists even in winter.

Buying Tips: Be sure the abelia you are buying fits your space. 'Canyon Creek' and 'Rose Creek' abelia grow three to five feet tall and bloom more than older, larger varieties. Also, *Abelia x grandiflora* has a darker green leaf, coppery color on the stem, more pink flowers, and blooms longer. *Abelia chinensis* has more bronze than purple leaves with a tan stem and more solid white flowers.

**Blue ribbon plants are defined on page 12. For blue ribbon performance, follow the planting and maintenance guidelines on 28 to 49.*

Botanical: *Abelia x grandiflora* (Glossy Abelia)
Abelia chinensis (Chinese Abelia)
Family: Caprifoliaceae

Companions: Abelia is frequently used with green shrubs, like juniper and boxwood.

For easy color layers with green-leafed abelia, try the large abelia with the flowering plants below.

'Kaleidoscope' abelia (shown right) looks best with pink or peach flowers.

Abelia x grandiflora, glossy abelia, with some companions

'Cherry Dazzle' Dwarf Crapemyrtle (above, left) blooms from July until September if you deadhead (remove the dead flowers). Its bloom period coincides with the abelia's summer color. Since dwarf crapemyrtles grow from three to five feet tall, use them in front of the taller, glossy abelia.

'Homestead Purple' Verbena (above, bottom right) is one of the longest-blooming perennial groundcovers for the south. It starts blooming with a burst in spring and slows down somewhat in summer. Since it is one of the few groundcovers that blooms this long, it is definitely worth planting. This verbena grows to about one foot tall and works well as a border for the other two plants.

**Lives on rainwater alone in all but the most extreme situations.*

GROWING CONDITIONS

Light: Light shade to full sun

Water: Very low after establishment. Lives on rainwater alone, without supplemental water, in all but the most extreme conditions. See pages 34 to 37 for more information.

Soil: For the garden, plant in any fertile, well-drained soil that has been enriched with organic matter. Good drainage is essential for abelia. See pages 28 to 29 for instructions.

Hardiness: Zones 4 to 9

Propagation: Hardwood cuttings work well.

Pest Problems: Rare

PLANTING & MAINTENANCE

When to Plant: Abelia from containers can be planted at any time. Fall is best because they establish easier in cooler weather.

Trimming: This shrub doesn't need much trimming as it has a nice, natural form. A frequent mistake is to cut the top out which really hurts the form of the shrub for years. Thinning every 2 or 3 years is a better choice.

Large abelia: Every few years, cut 2 or 3 of the oldest, longest stems to the ground.

Small abelia: Trim off any wayward shoots that come out of the top. Cut them at the ground.

Fertilization: Low. Fertilize at planting time with a timed-release product. Less fertilizer is needed with the application of more organics. In the years after planting, fertilization needs vary, based on the nutrients in your soil. See pages 46 to 49 for more instructions.

1ST Althea, Rose of Sharon

CHARACTERISTICS

Plant Type Deciduous shrub (loses its leaves in winter).

Average Size: Most altheas grow quite tall, 10 to 12 feet. They spread 6 to 8 feet wide. New dwarfs grow only about 3 feet tall.

Growth Rate: Fast

Leaf: Green, 3-lobed leaves, about 3 inches long.

Flower: Vase-shaped blossoms to 4 inches across with prominent stamens.

Origin: China and India

Spacing: About 6 feet on center (measure from the center of each plant). Closer for the dwarfs.

Cautions: Seedlings from the older varieties are a pain in the neck. Occasionally damaged by deer.

Colors: Flowers are white, purple, violet, pink, blue, including many bicolors.

1. *'Blue Chiffon' althea*
2. *'Little Kim' althea*
3. *'Rose Satin' althea*

Exotic, tropical-looking flowers from early summer to fall. Heat tolerant and easy to grow. Old ones seed enough to be a nuisance, but new ones don't. Easily rates blue ribbon* because of high performance with very little care.

'White Chiffon' althea

Thomas Jefferson planted seeds of this shrub at Monticello in 1794, and it went on to win a place in most southern gardens. Yet, old varieties tend to shed too many seeds and become weedy, and their flowers are often small and not very showy. Newer altheas have much more to offer, including larger flowers and a longer period of bloom, and several varieties produce very few seeds. If you are looking for low maintenance, be sure you choose a sterile one!

Regional Differences: Easily grown throughout the south

Color Period: Older varieties bloom in midsummer, with some flowering continuing until fall. Newer varieties begin blooming in June and continue to set buds until September.

Buying Tips: We have done well with the Goddess series, as well as 'Chiffon,' and 'Satin.' 'Little Kim' is a tiny dwarf we have tried for only one season with great success.

**Blue ribbon plants are defined on page 12. For blue ribbon performance, follow the planting and maintenance guidelines on 28 to 49.*

Companions: Altheas go well with many summer-blooming perennials and shrubs that like sun, including agastache and black-eyed Susans.

For a long-blooming shrub garden, combine althea with 'Knock Out' roses and shrub crapemyrtle, as shown below.

Althea and some companions

'Sunny Knock Out' Rose (above, top) has a more compact growth habit than the original 'Knock Out,' growing to about four feet tall. The flowers start out yellow and fade to cream. Both colors complement the althea. This rose blooms on and off from spring until fall, so it should bloom with the althea. Use the althea as the tallest plant of this grouping, with the rose in front of it.

'Cherry Dazzle' Dwarf Crapemyrtle (above, bottom) blooms from July until September, if you deadhead (remove the dead flowers). Its bloom period coincides with althea's summer color period. Since dwarf crapemyrtles grow from three to five feet tall, plant them beside the roses. All three of these plants prefer sun.

GROWING CONDITIONS

Light: Full sun, at least 6 hours per day.

Water: Low after establishment. Likes water every week or two during the growing season, depending on its environment. See pages 34 to 37 for more information.

Soil: For the garden, plant in any fertile, well-drained soil that has been enriched with organic matter. Use only good-quality potting mix for containers. See page 30 to 31 for specific instructions on soil preparation.

Hardiness: Zones 4 to 9

Propagation: Seeds or cuttings

Pest Problems: Rare. White flies, aphids, and Japanese beetles occasionally.

PLANTING & MAINTENANCE

When to Plant: Althea from containers can be planted at any time. Fall is best because they establish easier in cooler weather.

Trimming: Doesn't need annual pruning unless you are trying to maintain it at a smaller-than-mature size. Any pruning should be done in early spring, before new growth starts.

Fertilization: Low. Fertilize at planting time with a timed-release product. Less fertilizer is needed with the application of more organics. In the years after planting, fertilization needs vary, based on the nutrients in your soil. See pages 46 to 49 for more instructions.

ALTERNATE SELECTIONS

See hibiscus on page 144 if you want the showy flowers of althea on a smaller plant that dies back to the ground in winter.

1ST Aucuba

CHARACTERISTICS

Plant Type: Evergreen shrub.

Average Size: Easily maintained at sizes between 4 to 8 feet tall and 3 to 4 feet wide.

Growth Rate: Slow to medium

Leaf: 3 to 4 inches wide by 6 to 8 inches long. Oval, with a pointed tip.

Flower: Insignificant

Origin: Japan

Spacing: 4 to 5 feet on center (measure from the center of each plant). Closer in containers.

Cautions: Frequently damaged by deer.

Colors: Leaves are solid green or variegated (yellow and green).

Aucuba japonica 'Crotonifolia'

Great plant for shade, brightening up an otherwise dark spot. Adds interest in an area that doesn't have enough light for most flowering plants. Keep it out of any sun. Very easy to grow - one of the easiest plants in this book, easily rating a blue ribbon.*

Aucuba japonica 'Golden King'

While many evergreens stretch and grow lanky in shade, aucuba loves it! Take care with its placement, however, because it doesn't like any sun at all, even winter sun. (If you need tips on judging the year-round shade potential of a spot, see pages 26 to 27).

Aucuba does well when planted under large trees, which many plants don't like. It also does quite well in containers.

Regional Differences: Might die back a little in zone six in winter. No other differences throughout the south.

Color Period: Flowers are insignificant. However, green forms of aucuba have bright, red berries in fall. They hang under the foliage, so they are not easy to see. Female plants don't produce fruit unless a male plant is in the neighborhood.

Buying Tips: All the aucubas we have tried have done equally well.

**Blue ribbon plants are defined on page 12. For blue ribbon performance, follow the planting and maintenance guidelines on 28 to 49.*

Companions: Plant aucuba with other shade-loving plants, like ferns, hostas, mondo grass, and heucheras.

For a woodland look, layer aucuba with the two plants shown below.

Aucuba japonica 'Picturata' and some companions

Autumn Fern (above, left) is an evergreen fern that grows three feet tall, so plant it in front of the taller aucuba. The coarse-textured aucuba contrasts well with the light-textured fern. Both do well in shade.

'Great Expectations' Hosta (above, right) is a deciduous (loses its leaves in winter) perennial that grows two feet tall and fits well in front of the aucuba and fern. It also likes shade.

The three plants vary in texture and color, providing an attractive, woodland look.

GROWING CONDITIONS

Light: Medium to dense shade. Burns in any sun at all, even in winter.

Water: Low after establishment. Likes water every week or two during the growing season, depending on its environment. See pages 34 to 37 for more information.

Soil: For the garden, plant in any fertile, well-drained soil that has been enriched with organic matter. Good drainage is essential. See pages 28 to 31 for specific instructions on soil preparation and drainage.

Hardiness: Zones 6 to 9, but expect a little die-back in winter zone 6.

Propagation: Cuttings

Pest Problems: Root rot with poor drainage.

PLANTING & MAINTENANCE

When to Plant: Aucuba from containers can be planted at any time. Fall is best because they establish easier in cooler weather.

Trimming: Aucuba grows fairly slowly, so it requires little trimming - just a touch up every 2 to 3 years in fall or early spring. Be sure to remove any dead branches when you trim it.

Fertilization: Medium. Fertilize at planting time and each spring with a timed-release product. Less fertilizer is needed with the application of more organics. See pages 46 to 49 for more instructions.

1ST Azalea, Evergreen

CHARACTERISTICS

Plant Type: Evergreen shrub

Average Size: 2 to 12 feet tall and wide, depending on cultivar.

Growth Rate: Medium

Leaf: Small green to bronze, slightly hairy leaves with pointed tips.

Flower: Honeysuckle-like blossoms as large as 3 inches across with prominent stamens.

Origin: Japan and Taiwan

Spacing: About 2 to 8 feet on center (measure from the center of each plant), depending on cultivar.

Cautions: Toxic to some people, so don't eat this plant. Frequently damaged by deer.

Colors: Flowers are white, pink, lavender, red, salmon, yellow, orange.

1. *'Autumn Cheer' Encore azalea*
2. *'Autumn Chiffon' Encore azalea*
3. *'Autumn Royalty' Encore azalea*
4. *'Autumn Twist' Encore azalea*

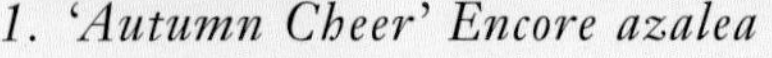

Evergreen azaleas, long-lived and dependable, are one of the most popular flowering plants for partial shade in the south. Classic flowers in spring, fall, or both. Qualifies for a blue ribbon,* but likes more water than most plants in this book.

'Encore' azaleas and ferns

There are 10,000 to 15,000 different kinds of azaleas. They range in size from small dwarfs to large shrubs. Many bloom only in spring, with the flowers so dense they cover the shrub entirely, as shown, right. Others, like the reblooming 'Encore' azaleas shown above, bloom several times during the growing season but don't have quite the intensity of color. The 'Encores' have become wildly popular but require more fertilizer than the older azaleas.

Regional Differences: Repeat-blooming azaleas grow well throughout the south but can show some damage with hard, spring freezes. Of the Encore azaleas, 'Autumn Amethyst' have shown the best cold tolerance at Huntsville Botanical Garden.

Color Period: Most older varieties bloom only in spring, with different cultivars starting at different times - from March through May. Each plant blooms for about three weeks. Repeat bloomers produce flowers in spring and in fall and, sometimes, during the summer as well.

Buying Tips: Most azaleas sold in garden centers do well but check the zone hardiness on the label to be sure they work in your area. Many azaleas are grown in coastal areas that are quite warm. Good nurseries sell varieties that are known to grow well in local areas.

**Blue ribbon plants are defined on page 12. For blue ribbon performance, follow the planting and maintenance guidelines on 28 to 49.*

Companions: Plant azaleas with other plants that bloom in spring, including trees, like dogwoods. Shrubs, such as some camellias, and forsythia also make good companions for azaleas.

For an easy, spring color accent, try azalea with amsonia and kerria, as shown below.

Azaleas and some companions

Amsonia (above, left) is a perennial that grows three feet tall and blooms in April and May, usually coinciding with the azalea blooms. Plant them in front of the taller azaleas in light shade.

Kerria (above, right) usually blooms at the same time as both the azaleas and the amsonia. Let them grow to their full height of six feet, and plant them along side of the azaleas, with the amsonia as a border. These three plants do well in light shade.

GROWING CONDITIONS

Light: Light shade with no afternoon sun. Morning sun is fine.

Water: High the first season after planting, when azaleas should not be allowed to dry out. Medium after establishment. Likes water once or twice a week during the growing season, depending on its environment.

Soil: For the garden, plant in any fertile, well-drained soil that has been enriched with organic matter. Azaleas are picky about pH (5.5 to 6 is ideal), so take some soil to your county extension for testing prior to planting.

Hardiness: Zones 6 to 9

Propagation: Rooted stem cuttings, taken in late spring.

Pest Problems: Root rot is the leading cause of death. Good drainage is essential. Aphids or lacebugs can usually be controlled with insecticidal soap.

PLANTING & MAINTENANCE

When to Plant: Azaleas from containers can be planted at any time. Fall is best because they establish easier in cooler weather, but you are more likely to find them at your garden center in early spring, when they are blooming.

Trimming: Azaleas need very little trimming and should be pruned only if they become extremely overgrown or have damaged branches that need to be removed. Trim only in early summer because azaleas bloom on old wood. Thinning is much better than trimming them into little meatballs.

Fertilization: Medium. Fertilize at planting time and each spring with a timed-release product. Less fertilizer is needed with the application of more organics. 'Encore' azaleas need more fertilizer than the others.

Azalea, Deciduous

1ST

CHARACTERISTICS

Plant Type: Deciduous shrub (loses its leaves in winter).

Average Size: Easily maintained at sizes between 6 to 12 feet tall and 4 to 6 feet wide.

Growth Rate: Medium

Leaf: Medium green with a linear form. 3 to 4 inches long by 1 inch wide.

Flower: Looks like a honeysuckle, with cluster of funnel-like shapes.

Origin: Southeastern US or cultivars.

Spacing: About 6 feet on center (measure from the center of each plant). Looks nice planted in clusters of 3.

Cautions: Toxic to some people. Do not eat this plant. Frequently damaged by deer.

Colors: Flowers are yellow, orange, pink, white, red, and bicolors.

UNIVERSITY AWARDS

2007: Georgia Gold Medal Winner for 'Admiral Semmes' azalea.

Unusual azalea that only accounts for about ten percent of azaleas planted in the south. Unlike most azaleas, this one loses its leaves in winter. Some species of this azalea are native to the south. Gorgeous when blooming and relatively easy to grow. Qualifies for a blue ribbon,* but likes more water than most plants in this book.

There are twelve different species of deciduous azaleas, some of which are native to the south. These azaleas bloom on bare stems, becoming a breathtaking vision in late spring, especially when planted in an open woodland garden. Their form is quite different from evergreen azaleas. Deciduous azaleas are long and lanky, not neat and compact. With space, they fill out nicely but never compactly.

Regional Differences: None

Color Period: Different species bloom from March until July, each one lasting about two to three weeks.

Buying Tips: The most popular deciduous azaleas are the pink *Rhododendron candescens* (the Piedmont azalea) and the yellow or orange *Rhododendron austrinum* (the Florida azalea). A hybrid series called the 'Confederate' series features larger flowers than most and better heat tolerance. The 'Aromi' series offers a good combination of larger flowers and heat tolerance, also.

**Blue ribbon plants are defined on page 12. For blue ribbon performance, follow the planting and maintenance guidelines on 28 to 49.*

Companions: Plant azaleas with other plants that bloom in spring, including camellias, forsythia, amsonia, and kerria. And, they always look good with other azaleas, as shown right.

For an easy, spring color accent, try azalea with dogwood trees and Spanish bluebells, as shown below.

Azaleas and some companions

Dogwood Trees (above, left) not only bloom the same time as many of these azaleas but is also native to the same forests in the south. Plant the azaleas either under or in the same area as the dogwoods, so you can see both blooming at the same time.

Spanish Bluebells (above, right) look wonderful planted in front of native azaleas. At eighteen inches tall, they are a good size for a border. They bloom at the same time and like the same light shade as azaleas.

GROWING CONDITIONS

Light: Light shade with no afternoon sun.

Water: Low after establishment. Likes water every week or two during the growing season, depending on its environment. See pages 34 to 37 for more information.

Soil: Any fertile, well-drained soil that has been enriched with organic matter. Requires good drainage. See pages 28 to 31 for instructions.

Hardiness: Zones 6 to 9

Propagation: Seeds or cuttings

Pest Problems: Rare. Root rot can develop if plants are kept too wet.

PLANTING & MAINTENANCE

When to Plant: Azaleas from containers can be planted at any time. Fall is best because they establish easier in cooler weather, but you are more likely to find them at your garden center in early spring, when they are blooming.

Trimming: Trim to shape, not to attempt to keep it tight and compact. Once every few years, trim the older canes to the ground after the shrub has finished blooming.

Fertilization: Medium. Fertilize at planting time and each spring with a timed-release product. Less fertilizer is needed with the application of more organics. See pages 46 to 49 for more instructions.

1ST Boxwood

CHARACTERISTICS

Plant Type: Evergreen shrub.

Average Size: Easily maintained at sizes between 1 to 6 feet tall and 1 to 3 feet wide.

Growth Rate: Slow

Leaf: Tiny, green leaves

Flower: Inconspicuous

Origin: Europe, Asia, Africa, Madagascar, south and central America, and the Caribbean.

Spacing: About 1 to 4 feet on center (measure from the center of each plant).

Cautions: Juice or sap can cause skin problems. Seldom damaged by deer.

Colors: Leaves are green; flowers are insignificant.

1. *'Wintergreen' Korean boxwood*
2. *Buxus sempervirens*

One of the most popular shrubs in the south. Historically thought of as a plant of the aristocracy. Evergreen, so it looks the same all year. Gives structure to the garden. Rates a blue ribbon.*

There are 70 different species of boxwoods, which vary primarily in their cold tolerance and growth rate. Although all make good hedges and foundation plants, choose the one that fits your climate as well as the ultimate size desired for your space.

Boxwoods are considered the premier hedge material for the south.

Regional Differences: English, Korean, and American boxwood do well in zones six and seven. Japanese and 'Little Leaf' boxwoods do well in zones eight and nine.

Color Period: Insignificant

Buying Tips: Be sure to purchase boxwoods that take your climate well.

**Blue ribbon plants are defined on page 12. For blue ribbon performance, follow the planting and maintenance guidelines on 28 to 49.*

English Boxwood, (*Buxus sempervirens 'Suffruticosa,'* right), only grows 18 to 36 inches tall so used only for small hedges and edging. Does well in zones five to seven but is not happy in zones eight or nine. Only grows about two inches per year, so it seldom needs trimming.

Korean Boxwood, (*Buxus microphylla var. koreniana,* right), is quite cold tolerant, growing from zone four to seven, but not in zones eight and nine. Grows as tall as four feet tall and equally as wide. 'Winter Gem' and 'Winter Green' hold their color better in winter.

American or Common Boxwood, (*Buxus sempervirens,* left), is used primarily for rounded foundation plantings of four to six feet tall and equally as wide. Does well in zones six and seven. Struggles with the heat in zones eight and nine.

Japanese Boxwood, (*Buxus microphylla var. japonica,* left), grows faster than the rest, to about four to six feet tall and equally as wide. Grows in zones six to nine, but better in the heat of zones eight and nine than the American or English boxwood.

Little Leaf Boxwood, (*Buxus microphylla,* left). Dwarf boxwoods (like 'Kingswood Dwarf,' 'Morris Midget,' or 'Justin Bauer') only grow one foot tall by one foot wide. They are not widely available. Do well in zones eight or nine.

GROWING CONDITIONS

Light: Light shade to full sun

Water: Medium after establishment. Likes water once or twice a week during the growing season, depending on its environment. See pages 34 to 37 for more information.

Soil: Any fertile, well-drained soil that has been enriched with organic matter. Requires good drainage. See pages 28 to 31 for instructions.

Hardiness: Zones 4 to 9, depending on type.

Propagation: Cuttings

Pest Problems: Rare. Root rot can develop if plants are kept too wet.

PLANTING & MAINTENANCE

When to Plant: Boxwood from containers can be planted at any time. Fall is best because they establish easier in cooler weather, but you are more likely to find them at your garden center in early spring, when they are blooming.

Trimming: Most boxwoods are pruned annually. They can be sheared. However, it is best to thin the American boxwood rather than shear it. The American boxwoods (shown, left top) have been at Huntsville Botanical Garden for 15 years without any shearing, just a bit of thinning every few years. This plant has an excellent, natural growth habit for low maintenance gardening!

Fertilization: Medium. Fertilize at planting time and each spring with a timed-release product. Less fertilizer is needed with the application of more organics. See pages 46 to 49 for more instructions.

Butterfly Bush

CHARACTERISTICS

Plant Type: Semi-evergreen shrub

Average Size: 4 to 8 feet tall and wide, depending on variety.

Growth Rate: Fast

Leaf: Gray-green to blue-green, narrow leaves to 4 inches long, with lighter undersides.

Flower: 6 to 12-inch long panicles studded with hundreds of tiny florets.

Origin: China

Spacing: Set plants 8 feet apart, or grow them as single specimen.

Cautions: Almost never damaged by deer.

Colors: Flowers are lilac, purple, pink, magenta-red, blue, and white.

This photo of the Buddleia davidii mix shows many of the different colors of butterfly bushes.

Through the hottest part of summer, butterflies flock to the flowers that may grow 12 inches long. This is a very easy shrub to grow and invaluable for its ability to bloom through the hottest part of summer. Deer leave it alone, too. Needs dead-heading (removal of dead flowers) to look good, so it misses a ribbon.

'Peacock' butterfly bush is one of the newer, more compact varieties. It did quite well in our trials.

Butterfly bushes are one of the best plants for attracting butterflies. The older varieties are quite tall and have a tendency to look straggly. Some newer varieties are quite a bit more compact and are a great improvement over previous cultivars. They grow about four feet tall by four feet wide, and look great all season. All butterfly bushes look quite a bit better with dead-heading (removal of dead flowers).

Regional Differences: In zone six, cold weather may cause plants to shed their leaves in winter, and some stems may be killed back, too. The plants will regrow from the roots in spring.

Color Period: Mid May to fall, provided old flower spikes are removed every few weeks.

Buying Tips: For compactness, look for the 'English Butterfly' series, which includes the 'Adonis,' 'Peacock,' and 'Purple Emperor.' If you can't find them at your local garden center, try online suppliers. 'Black Knight' is a great large species (eight foot) because the dark purple color really shows up well.

Companions: Use butterfly bush to anchor an island bed filled with other butterfly magnets, such as lantana, pentas, verbena, and single-flowered zinnias. Because the plants need regular trimming during their flowering season, be sure to allow space for easy access.

Combine butterfly bush with coneflower and coreopsis for easy color layers, as shown below.

'Purple Emperor' butterfly bush and some companions

'Big Sky Twilight' Coneflower (above, left) is an excellent choice as a companion for butterfly bush. The textures of the flowers are quite different, they both like sun, and they share the same bloom period. This coneflower grows about 30 inches tall. Place it in front of the taller butterfly bush.

Threadleaf Coreopsis (above, right) also blooms at the same time as both the butterfly bush and the coneflower. The fine texture of the coreopsis contrasts well with the coarser-textured flowers. Use the shorter coreopsis (about 18 inches tall) as a border for the butterfly bush and the coneflower. All three plants do well in full sun.

GROWING CONDITIONS

Light: Full sun, at least 6 hours per day.

Water: Medium after establishment. Likes water once or twice a week during the growing season, depending on its environment. Plants are drought-tolerant after establishment, but they don't bloom as much without water.

Soil: For the garden, plant in any fertile, well-drained soil that has been enriched with organic matter. Use only good-quality potting mix for containers. See pages 28 to 31 for specific instructions on soil preparation.

Hardiness: Most varieties are adapted in zones 5 to 9; plants usually shed their leaves in winter in zones 5 and 6.

Propagation: Cuttings

Pest Problems: Rare; aphids and spider mites occasionally.

PLANTING & MAINTENANCE

When to Plant: Butterfly bushes from containers can be planted at any time. Fall is best because they establish easier in cooler weather.

Trimming: In late winter, use pruning loppers to cut plants back to at least 2 feet tall. If desired, they may be pruned back to the ground. In early summer, use pruning shears to shape plants if needed. This pruning delays flowering but improves the overall bushiness of the plants. Throughout summer, clip off old flowers as they turn brown. As new growth emerges, every stem tip will bear blooms.

Fertilization: Low. Fertilize at planting time with a timed-release product. Less fertilizer is needed with the application of more organics. In the years after planting, fertilization needs vary based on the nutrients in your soil.

1ST Camellia

CHARACTERISTICS

Plant Type: Evergreen shrub.

Average Size: 4 to 15 feet tall, depending on cultivar, and 4 feet to 8 feet wide.

Growth Rate: Slow. Once established, camellias grow slowly for decades.

Leaf: Glossy green, oval leaves with pointed tips 2 to 4 inches long.

Flower: Single or double blossoms to 5 inches across, often with prominent stamens; numerous novel flower forms.

Origin: China and Japan

Spacing: Usually grown as specimen shrubs in foundation or boundary planting, but can be planted 6 feet apart to form an evergreen hedge.

Cautions: Occasionally damaged by deer. Some varieties bear the leaves used to make green tea.

Colors: Flowers are pink, white, red, a few yellows, and bicolors.

UNIVERSITY AWARDS

2002: Mississippi Medallion Winner, 'Shishigashira' camellia.

Evergreen shrubs with gorgeous flowers in winter and spring. State flower of Alabama. Wonderful for cut flowers to bring inside and float in a bowl of water. Rates a blue ribbon.*

For decades, beautiful camellias were grown only in the warmest parts of the south, but in recent years, cold-hardy hybrids have extended this shrub's range northward into zone six. Many revered, old, winter-blooming varieties are still best grown in zone eight and nine, but hardy fall or spring-blooming varieties can be grown throughout the region. For fall bloom, look for *Camellia sassanqua* hybrids that have 'Autumn' in their name. If you also want spring-blooming plants, choose *C. japonica* hybrids with 'April' in their cultivar name. The hardiest camellias are *C. oleifera* hybrids, and although many have 'Winter' in their name, they usually bloom in the fall. Buy plants locally or from nurseries nearby and ask them if their camellias are cold tolerant for your area. Some years are better than others with camellias, with the best blooming when February and March are mild. Camellias are not as dependable as azaleas.

Regional Differences: All camellias will grow in zones eight and nine, most will grow in zone seven, but gardeners in zone six are restricted to only the most cold hardy.

Color Period: October to December for fall bloomers. November to February for winter bloomers, and March to April for spring-blooming varieties. Each type blooms for about two to three weeks.

Buying Tips: Huntsville Botanical Garden has had good luck with 'Debutante,' 'Pink Perfection,' 'Lady Claire,' 'Professor Sargent,' 'Herme,' 'Snowflurry' and 'Bernice Boddy.'

**Blue ribbon plants are defined on page 12. For blue ribbon performance, follow the planting and maintenance guidelines on 28 to 49.*

Companions: Camellias are ideal evergreen shrubs to work into foundation plantings on the east side of your house, where they will get morning sun and afternoon shade. Camellias are also an excellent choice for a blooming, evergreen hedge that rarely needs pruning.

Combine camellias with azaleas and Spanish bluebells, as shown below, for easy color layers.

Camellia (photo by Carlos Gi) and some companions

White Azaleas (above, left) bloom in early spring, usually in April. Since camellia's bloom periods vary by species, check to see when yours blooms before pairing it with the azalea, if you want both to bloom at the same time. Plant the shorter azalea in front of the camellia.

Spanish Bluebells (above, right) look wonderful planted in front of azaleas. They bloom at the same time and like the same light, light shade. Spanish bluebells grow 18 inches tall, which is an ideal size for bordering camellias and azaleas.

GROWING CONDITIONS

Light: Light shade. Morning sun and afternoon shade is ideal.

Water: Low after establishment. Likes water every week or two during the growing season, depending on its environment. See pages 34 to 37 for more information.

Soil: For the garden, plant in any fertile, well-drained soil that has been enriched with organic matter. Camellias like acidic soil similar to azaleas. See pages 28 to 31 for specifics instructions on soil preparation.

Hardiness: Zones 6 to 9

Propagation: Seeds or grafts. Named cultivars are usually grafted onto seedling rootstock.

Pest Problems: Scale insects occasionally. Squirrels often harvest buds for breakfast. Sudden cold snaps can ruin otherwise perfect camellia blossoms. Cover blossom-bearing shrubs overnight with blankets to avoid this occurrence.

PLANTING & MAINTENANCE

When to Plant: Camellias from containers can be planted at any time. Fall is best because they establish easier in cooler weather.

Trimming: These slow-growing, woody shrubs need very little pruning. Tip back branches that grow awkwardly long, but generally allow the plants to find their own natural shape.

Fertilization: Low. Fertilize at planting time with a timed-release product. Less fertilizer is needed with the application of more organics. In the years after planting, fertilization needs vary, based on the nutrients in your soil. See pages 46 to 49 for more instructions.

1ST Carolina Jessamine

CHARACTERISTICS

Plant Type: Evergreen vine

Average Size: 10 to 20 feet tall, needs support; will climb most anything.

Growth Rate: Fast

Leaf: Bright green, lance-shaped leaves 2 inches long by 1/2 inch wide.

Flower: Bright yellow trumpet or funnel-shaped flowers, 2 inches long by 1 inch wide.

Origin: Virginia to Florida, west to Texas.

Spacing: Plant one at each post of a pergola or arbor or about 6 feet on center (measure from the center of each plant). One vine will cover a mailbox.

Cautions: All parts are poisonous and sap or juice can cause skin irritation. Seldom damaged by deer.

Colors: Flowers are yellow.

UNIVERSITY AWARDS

2008: Georgia Gold Medal Winner for 'Pride of Augusta' Carolina jessamine.

'Margarita' Carolina jessamine

Prolific, native vine dotting our woodlands with a profuse flowering in early spring. Fast growing, blue ribbon* evergreen vine. Excellent selection for covering arbors, pergolas, and fences. Has been planted throughout the south since colonial times.

The state flower of South Carolina, this vigorous evergreen vine is easy to grow, provided you begin with young plants and do not spoil them with too much water or fertilizer. Carolina jessamine is happier to simply grow as the wild thing that it is and will reward you with thousands of fragrant, yellow flowers each spring. In mild winters, it often produces a few surprise blossoms well ahead of its customary bloom time, which is early spring.

Regional Differences: Winter bloom is most common in zone nine and occasionally in zone eight. In severe winters in zone six, plants may shed some of their leaves and regrow a fresh crop in spring.

Color Period: Blooms for about three weeks in late winter in zone nine, early spring in zone eight, mid-April in zone seven, and a little later in zone six. May rebloom sporadically throughout summer.

Buying Tips: Several cultivars are available, but 'Staright' is an excellent choice. 'Pride of Augusta,' a double-flowering form, received the 2008 Georgia Gold Medal for vines.

**Blue ribbon plants are defined on page 12. For blue ribbon performance, follow the planting and maintenance guidelines on 28 to 49.*

Attracts Butterflies

Attracts Hummingbirds

Southern Native

Avg. Weeks of Color

Botanical Name: *Gelsemium sempervirens*
Family: Loganiaceae

Companions: Space companion plantings at least four to six feet away from this vine, so they don't get tangled up with each other.

Plant this jessamine with other plants that bloom at the same time. Here is an idea for plants that look good in front of Carolina jessamine that is supported by a wall or fence:

Carolina jessamine and some companions

'Pink Knock Out' Rose (above, left) blooms on and off from spring until fall. Spring, when the Carolina jessamine usually blooms, is one of the peak bloom times for this rose. It grows about four feet tall, so plant it in front of the jessamine that is supported on a wall or fence. Plant the rose at least six feet out from the vine.

Amsonia (above, right) is a perennial that grows three feet tall and blooms in April and May, usually coinciding with the bloom period of the jessamine and the rose. Plant the amsonia in front as a border to the larger plants. All plants do well in full sun.

GROWING CONDITIONS

Light: Full sun to light shade

Water: Low after establishment. Likes water every week or two during the growing season, depending on its environment. See pages 34 to 37 for more information.

Soil: Any fertile, well-drained soil that has been enriched with organic matter. Prefers good drainage. See pages 28 to 31 for instructions.

Hardiness: Zones 6 to 9, but sometimes shows cold damage in zone 6.

Propagation: Improved varieties are propagated by rooting stem tip cuttings taken in late spring. You also can dig out sprouts growing near the base and transplant them to where you want them to grow.

Pest Problems: None serious. Most frequent problem with this vine is lack of flowers due to overfertilization.

PLANTING & MAINTENANCE

When to Plant: Carolina jessamine from containers can be planted at any time. Fall is best because they establish easier in cooler weather, but you are more likely to find them at your garden center in early spring, when they are blooming.

Trimming: Trim it shortly after flowering. This vine doesn't require much trimming, only to train it or remove some of the older branches if the vine is old. Remove any dead branches Don't prune it in winter or early spring or it might not bloom that season.

Fertilization: Low. Fertilize at planting time with a timed-release product. Less fertilizer is needed with the application of more organics. In the years after planting, fertilization needs vary, based on the nutrients in your soil.

Cleyera

1ST

CHARACTERISTICS

Plant Type: Evergreen shrub.

Average Size: 'Big Foot' grows 10 to 12 feet tall by 6 feet wide. 'Bronze Beauty' and 'Leann' grow 8 to 10 feet tall by 8 feet wide. Either can be maintained as low as 6 feet tall by pruning.

Growth Rate: Medium

Leaf: 3 to 4 inches long by 1 inch wide; elliptical; new growth is copper-colored.

Flower: Flowers are insignificant, but fruit that follows is good bird food.

Origin: Japan

Spacing: About 6 to 8 feet on center (measure from the center of each plant). Closer in containers.

Cautions: None known

Colors: Flowers are white, but insignificant.

Cleyera 'Big Foot' planted as a hedge.

Nice, evergreen shrub that deserves more use throughout the south. Great substitute for red tip photinia, which is plagued with disease. Excellent, low-maintenance, hedge material that easily rates a blue ribbon.*

Cleyera 'Leann'

Cleyera is a good evergreen shrub for foundation plantings or a hedge. Huntsville Botanical Garden has a hedge (used for screening) that is twenty feet long and ten feet tall. It has been there for twenty years and only requires trimming every three or four years. The plant keeps its full shape nicely, without requiring a lot of trimming.

Regional Differences: Cleyera is marginal in zone six because it shows cold damage at temperatures under zero degrees. Does very well in zones seven to nine.

Color Period: Insignificant flowers in late spring

Buying Tips: 'Bronze Beauty,' 'Leann,' and 'Big Foot' are three new cultivars that show promise.

**Blue ribbon plants are defined on page 12. For blue ribbon performance, follow the planting and maintenance guidelines on 28 to 49.*

Companions: Cleyera comes in many shades of green, including the solid, dark green 'Big Foot' shown right. For contrast, mix it with bright-colored flowers, like crapemyrtle. Or, combine any of the different, green cleyeras with plants that have contrasting textures, like the Japanese yew and juniper shown below.

Cleyera 'Bronze Beauty' and some companions

'Yewtopia' Japanese Yew (above, left) makes a good companion for cleyera because of the strong textural difference. Since the yew grows two to three feet tall, plant it in front of the cleyera.

Parson's Juniper (above, right) adds another texture to this group. Since it is quite short, use it to border the cleyera and Japanese yew. Plant this grouping in full sun. Although the cleyera takes shade, the other two plants prefer sun.

GROWING CONDITIONS

Light: Full sun to medium shade. Stretches a bit in shade.

Water: Low after establishment. Likes water every week or two during the growing season, depending on its environment. See pages 34 to 37 for more information.

Soil: Any fertile, well-drained soil that has been enriched with organic matter. Requires good drainage. See pages 28 to 31 for instructions.

Hardiness: Zones 7 to 9. Shows damage at 0 degrees.

Propagation: Seeds or cuttings

Pest Problems: Rare

PLANTING & MAINTENANCE

When to Plant: Cleyera from containers can be planted at any time. Fall is best because they establish easier in cooler weather.

Trimming: Cleyera doesn't need much trimming, at most once a year. Late winter or early spring is the best time.

Fertilization: Low. Fertilize at planting time with a timed-release product. Less fertilizer is needed with the application of more organics. In the years after planting, fertilization needs vary, based on the nutrients in your soil. See pages 46 to 49 for more instructions.

1ST Crapemyrtle, Dwarf

CHARACTERISTICS

Plant Type: Deciduous shrub (loses its leaves in winter).

Average Size: Easily maintained at sizes between 3 to 5 feet tall and 3 to 4 feet wide.

Growth Rate: Fast

Leaf: Deep green with shades of red, 2 inches long by 1 inch wide. Nice fall color, turning yellow to bright red, depending on cultivar.

Flower: Frilly, crepe-paper like

Origin: China

Spacing: About 3 to 4 feet on center (measure from the center of each plant). Closer in containers.

Cautions: Almost never damaged by deer.

Colors: Flowers are red, pink, white, or lavender.

1. *'Dazzle Me Pink'*
2. *'Raspberry Dazzle'*
3. *'Snow Dazzle'*
4. *Fall color on leaves of 'RaspberryDazzle.'*

One of the top flowering shrubs for the south. Blooms for 90 to 120 days during the heat of summer. Great color impact with almost no maintenance. Lives without irrigation. Easily rates a blue ribbon.*

'Victor' crapemyrtle hedge at Huntsville Botanical Garden, where it has been growing for 16 years.

Most southerners are familiar with crapemyrtle trees, which are one of the best flowering trees for the south. New, dwarf crapemyrtles grow smaller and into shrubs instead of trees. They are incredibly easy to grow and offer a long bloom period. Crapemyrtles are also quite dependable - blooming through both wet and dry years.

Regional Differences: No differences in zones seven to nine in the south. In zone six, die-back occurs at minus 10 degrees.

Color Period: Varies some from year to year. They start blooming in July, when they have the highest intensity of color. In August, they continue blooming, but the seed pods are forming, so they don't have quite as much color. If you trim the seed pods, they should continue blooming through September.

Buying Tips: We have had the longest period of experience with the 'Victor' crapemyrtle, shown above. It has done very well for 16 years. Another, called 'Pokomoke,' also does well. New, more compact varieties promise even more flowering. We have just started testing 'Cherry Dazzle,' which did beautifully its first year.

**Blue ribbon plants are defined on page 12. For blue ribbon performance, follow the planting and maintenance guidelines on 28 to 49.*

Botanical Name: *Lagerstroemia indica*

Family: Lythraceae

Companions: Since crapemyrtles bloom for so long (July until September), there are many other shrubs and perennials that flower at the same time. Altheas are a particularly nice background plant for crapemyrtle. 'Miss Huff' lantana fits well in front of the crapemyrtle and blooms for even longer (June until October).

For easy color layers, plant re-blooming daylilies and scabiosa in front of crapemyrtle, as shown below.

'Cherry Dazzle' crapemyrtle and some companions.

'Stella de Oro' Daylily (top left) is one of the longest blooming perennial daylilies, blooming for up to three months each summer. Its 18 to 24 inch height fits well in front of the taller crapemyrtles. Plant both in full sun for most blooms.

Scabiosa (above, right) is another one of the longest-blooming perennials for the south, flowering from May until September if you deadhead (remove dead flowers). It grows 12 to 18 inches tall, so use it as a front border for the taller crapemyrtle and daylilies.

**Lives on rainwater alone in all but the most extreme situations.*

GROWING CONDITIONS

Light: Full sun, at least 6 hours per day. The number one reason crapemyrtles don't flower is too much shade.

Water: Very low after establishment. Likes water every week or two during the growing season, depending on its environment, but lives without irrigation after it is eastablished. See pages 34 to 37 for more information.

Soil: Any fertile, well-drained soil that has been enriched with organic matter. Requires good drainage. See pages 28 to 31 for instructions.

Hardiness: Zones 6 to 10, but occasionally damaged in zone 6 if the temperatures fall below -10 degrees.

Propagation: Seeds or cuttings

Pest Problems: Rare. Root rot can develop if plants are kept too wet.

PLANTING & MAINTENANCE

When to Plant: Crapemyrtles from containers can be planted at any time. Fall is best because they establish easier in cooler weather, but you are more likely to find them at your garden center in summer, when they are blooming.

Trimming: Two choices:

1. Cut the whole shrub back to the ground in late winter. It will only grow about 2 to 3 feet tall the next season.

2. Cut it back to the ground every few years if you want it to grow taller.

Fertilization: Low. Fertilize at planting time with a timed-release product (page 47). Less fertilizer is needed with the application of more organics. In the years after planting, fertilization needs vary, based on the nutrients in your soil.

Forsythia

1ST

CHARACTERISTICS

Plant Type: Deciduous shrub (loses its leaves in winter).

Average Size: 6 feet high and wide.

Growth Rate: Fast

Leaf: 3 to 5-inch long, narrow, green leaves turn yellow or bronze in late fall.

Flower: Abundant, bright-yellow, four-petaled flowers cover the bare stems in early spring.

Origin: Hybrid of *F. suspensa* and *F. viridissima*, which are native to China.

Spacing: About 6 to 8 feet on center (measure from the center of each plant).

Cautions: Occasionally damaged by deer.

Colors: Flowers are golden yellow.

Forsythia and pansies are great companions.

Sudden explosion of gold announces the coming of spring. Blooms in March, long before the last freeze. Continues blooming for about a month. Spectacular color with very little care. Easily earns a blue ribbon.*

In addition to opening the color season with a bang, forsythias are among the easiest shrubs to grow. They adapt to sun or partial shade, good soil or bad, and they are at their most beautiful when left unpruned. The natural fountain shape of a mature forsythia is breathtaking, but patience is required. Young plants often appear a bit stiff, but after three years or so, the branches lengthen into an artful arch.

In late winter's bare landscape, forsythias are easily seen from afar, so they are ideal for the distant corners of your yard. They are also good for accenting fences or other boundaries, and they mix easily with other flowering and evergreen shrubs.

Regional Differences: This shrub blooms heavily and dependably in zones six through eight. Due to limited winter chilling, it is less spectacular in zone nine, where winter warm spells may coax it to bloom sporadically rather than all at once.

Color Period: Late winter or very early spring, usually in mid-March. It keeps blooming for two to four weeks.

Buying Tips: There are quite a few different varieties for sale. We have not found too much difference between them.

**Blue ribbon plants are defined on page 12. For blue ribbon performance, follow the planting and maintenance guidelines on 28 to 49.*

Companions: Forsythia looks great planted near cherry trees, which bloom at the same time. Pansies and violas make a great border for forsythia.

Or, try them with irises, as shown below.

Dutch Iris 'Oriental Beauty'
Plant Profile: Page 152

White Bearded Iris
Plant Profile: Page 152

Dutch Iris 'Oriental Beauty' (above, left) blooms in mid-spring, like the forsythia. They grow in clumps that reach about two feet tall. This 'Oriental Beauty' cultivar really looks nice with the yellow forsythia flowers.

White Bearded Iris (above, right) is another plant that usually blooms at the same time as forsythia. It, too, grows into clumps about two feet tall. Both iris and forsythia prefer full sun. Plant clumps of each iris near the base of the forsythia.

GROWING CONDITIONS

Light: Full sun to partial shade. Flowers are not quite as thick on forsythias that grow in shade.

Water: Low after establishment. Likes water every week or two during the growing season, depending on its environment. See pages 34 to 37 for more information.

Soil: For the garden, plant in any fertile, well-drained soil that has been enriched with organic matter. See pages 28 to 31 for specific instructions on soil preparation.

Hardiness: Zones 5 to 9

Propagation: Rooted cuttings. Or follow this procedure for layering. In late spring, bend a long branch down and pin it to the ground with a stone or brick (after removing the leaves from the section of stem that will be in contact with the ground). By the following spring, the layered stem will be rooted and ready to transplant.

Pest Problems: None serious

PLANTING & MAINTENANCE

When to Plant: Forsythia from containers can be planted at any time. Fall is best because they establish easier in cooler weather.

Trimming: Every three to four years, just after the flowers fade, use sturdy pruning loppers to cut the oldest branches close to the ground, removing no more than one-quarter of the total branches. Do not attempt to shear this one into a mushroom, or it will look ridiculous.

Fertilization: Low. Fertilize at planting time with a timed-release product. Less fertilizer is needed with the application of more organics. In the years after planting, fertilization needs vary, based on the nutrients in your soil. See pages 46 to 49 for instructions.

Groundcovers, Small Vining

1ST

CHARACTERISTICS

Plant Type: Evergreen groundcover.

Average Size: Varies

Growth Rate: Medium

Leaf: Varies by type

Flower: Both ivy and pachysandra have inconspicuous flowers. Vinca has small flowers that resemble periwinkles.

Origin: Vinca and ivy are native to Europe. Japanese pachysandra is from Japan. Allegheny spurge is native from Virginia to Florida, west to Texas.

Spacing: Varies by type

Cautions: Ivy is frequently damaged by deer. Both vinca and pachysandra are seldom damaged by deer.

Colors: Vinca vine has blue or white flowers.

Variegated ivy is alternated with coleus and red wax begonias in the sides and along the edges of this 36-inch side-planted window box from www.kinsmangarden.com. The trellis is hung separately and is available from the same source. We like ivy better in containers than in the ground because it is easier to control.

Three vining groundcovers for shady areas. Grow in areas that are too shady for grass. They use less water and care than grass and easily win a blue ribbon.*

Small, vining groundcovers can be used to cover fences or walls, as shown above. Take great care with ivy because it can go wild in natural areas, killing whole forests that stand in its way. Photo by Joy Brown.

These three shade groundcovers thrive in areas that are too shady for grass. Take care with ivy, however, because it is considered invasive, damaging our native forests by smothering the trees and other native vegetation.

Regional Differences: See individual descriptions, opposite.

Color Period: Vinca vine is the only one that has significant flowers. It blooms for about three weeks, starting sometime in April.

Buying Tips: These groundcovers are available at many garden centers. Or, check out online suppliers.

**Blue ribbon plants are defined on page 12. For blue ribbon performance, follow the planting and maintenance guidelines on 28 to 49.*

Lives on Rain Water *

Botanical Name: Varies by type
Family: Varies by type

Pachysandra (Japanese Pachysandra *P. terminalis* and Allegheny spurge, *P. procumbens*) are two related groundcovers that are better suited for zones five to seven than farther south. They take light to dense shade in zones six and seven but only medium to dense shade in zones eight and nine. Japanese pachysandra grows faster than Allegheny spurge, but neither is as fast as ivy. Japanese pachysandra is bright green, while Allegheny spurge is bluish green with some variegation.

Ivy, (*Hedira helix,* left), Ivy is the number one groundcover sold in the south. It covers the ground quickly in areas that are so dark that not too many other plants grow. However, it grows up as well as out, covering everything in its way. Ivy has covered whole forests and can kill the trees that get in its way. It climbs up houses, damaging the wood behind it. So, be very careful with this one. Space ivy plantings one to two feet on center, depending on the size of the plants. It takes morning sun to dense shade.

Vinca Vine, (*Vinca minor,* left*),* is an attractive groundcover with dark, green leaves and blue flowers that bloom in spring for about three weeks (usually in mid-April). It covers the ground fairly quickly. Avoid its relative, *Vinca major*, because it is quite difficult to control. Vinca with dark green leaves do better as landscape plants than those with variegated leaves. It takes full sun to light shade in zone six and less sun further south. Stick to medium to light shade in zones eight or nine. Vinca vine grows about six inches tall. Space new plants one to two feet on center.

GROWING CONDITIONS

Light: All of these groundcovers prefer varying degrees of shade. See individual descriptions for more specifics.

Water: Ivy has very low water needs and lives without supplemental irrigation after establishment. Pachysandra has low water needs after establishment. Likes water every week or two during the growing season, depending on its environment. Vinca has medium water needs after establishment. Likes water once or twice a week during the growing season, depending on its environment. See pages 34 to 37 for more information.

Soil: Any fertile, well-drained soil that has been enriched with organic matter. Requires good drainage. See pages 28 to 31 for instructions.

Hardiness: Vinca vine is hardy from zones 4 to 8. Ivy's cold tolerance depends on the cultivar. Pachysandra grows in zones 5 to 9.

Propagation: Division or cuttings

Pest Problems: Rare

PLANTING & MAINTENANCE

When to Plant: Groundcovers from containers can be planted at any time. Fall is best because they establish easier in cooler weather.

Trimming: Vinca vine and pachysandra only need occasional trimming to keep them within bounds. Ivy needs hard trimming every few years. Set the blade of a mower on high and mow it, or cut it with a weed eater.

Fertilization: Medium. Fertilize at planting time and each spring with a timed-release product. Less fertilizer is needed with the application of more organics. See pages 46 to 49 for more instructions.

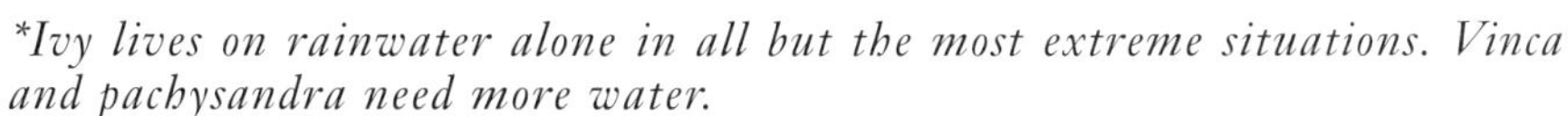

**Ivy lives on rainwater alone in all but the most extreme situations. Vinca and pachysandra need more water.*

Hollies, Smaller

1ST

CHARACTERISTICS

Plant Type: Evergreen shrub.

Average Size: Easily maintained at sizes between 2 to 10 feet tall and 2 to 6 feet wide, depending on type.

Growth Rate: Most are fast, but dwarf forms are slower.

Leaf: Rounded, glossy green or bronze leaves, 1 to 2 inches long and wide.

Flower: Hundreds of small, open-centered blossoms.

Origin: Several species are native to the southeastern US; the rest are from the far east.

Spacing: About 4 feet on center (measure from the center of each plant). Closer in containers.

Cautions: Some of the leaves have spines. Berries of some hollies are poisonous. Seldom to occasional damage by deer. Lots of bees when blooming.

Colors: Holly flowers are insignificant, but some have attractive berries in both red and dark blue to black.

1. *Ilex helleri*
2. *Ilex cornuta*

One of the most popular evergreen shrubs in the south. Most landscapes include at least one holly. Less expensive than boxwood. Very easy to grow, rating a blue ribbon.*

Inkberry holly

Hollies are quite well adapted to the southern climate. There are many different kinds, that vary mostly in leaf shape and the size of the plant. Some hollies have smooth leaf edges, and others have spines, like the ones associated with Christmas. The two photos, left, show how different the leaves can be.

Regional Differences: Dwarf yaupon holly and inkberry grow equally well throughout the south. Chinese and Japanese holly are not cold tolerant in zone six.

Color Period: Blooms are insignificant. Berries appear on some species in fall and winter.

Buying Tips: The most important consideration is size and light. All of these smaller hollies do well in light shade to full sun. In medium shade, choose another shrub, like aucuba. Also, know the mature size you need. A frequent mistake is to plant hollies that outgrow their spaces.

**Blue ribbon plants are defined on page 12. For blue ribbon performance, follow the planting and maintenance guidelines on 28 to 49.*

Attracts Birds

Lives on Rain Water *

Southern Native *

Botanical Name: *Ilex* spp.

Family: Aquifoliaceae

Chinese Holly, (*Ilex cornuta,* left), is the standard for foundation planting. This popular holly features spines on the leaves and red berries. There are many different cultivars ranging from three to 30 feet tall, so be sure you get the right one! Zones seven to nine.

Japanese Holly, (*Ilex crenata,* right), also known as the 'poor man's boxwood.' Resembles boxwood from a distance, but not quite as refined, although it has the smallest leaves of any of the hollies. Often trimmed like little green meatballs and looks better thinned than sheared. Averages three to four feet tall by three feet wide, so space them two to three feet apart. Zones seven to nine.

Inkberry, (*Ilex glabra,* left), grows four to six feet tall and wide, so space them four feet apart. Native, and one of the few hollies that can take wet soils. 'Nordic' and 'Shamrock' are two of the most popular cultivars. Blue/black berries in late fall to winter. Grows to mature size quickly. Better thinned than sheared. Zones four to nine.

Dwarf Yaupon holly, (*Ilex vomitoria 'Nana,'* right), is one of the twenty most popular landscape plants. Good substitute for boxwood and suitable for shearing. Easy to maintain at two to three feet tall by equally as wide, so space them at two to three feet apart. Grows five feet without trimming. 'Shillings' is the best cultivar for hedges. Very drought tolerant, surviving without irrigation in interstate plantings. Zones six to ten.

**Yaupon holly lives on rainwater alone in all but the most extreme situations. Both yaupon and inkberry are southern natives.*

GROWING CONDITIONS

Light: Light shade to full sun

Water: Varies by type. Yaupon holly has very low water needs after establishment. Lives on rainwater alone, without supplemental water, in all but the most extreme conditions. Chinese holly, Japanese holly and inkberry have low water needs after establishment. Like water every week or two during the growing season, depending on the environment. Inkberry is native to wet areas, and is one of the few hollies that takes wet soils. See pages 34 to 37 for more information.

Soil: Any fertile, well-drained soil that has been enriched with organic matter. Requires good drainage. See pages 28 to 31 for instructions.

Hardiness: Varies by species from zones 4 to 10.

Propagation: Cuttings; seeds are difficult.

Pest Problems: Rare. Root rot can develop if plants are kept too wet. Aphids and scales occasionally.

PLANTING & MAINTENANCE

When to Plant: Holly from containers can be planted at any time. Fall is best because they establish easier in cooler weather.

Trimming: Most hollies look good with one annual pruning in late winter to early spring. Some require a few more shapings throughout the growing season.

Fertilization: Medium. Fertilize at planting time and each spring with a timed-release product. Less fertilizer is needed with the application of more organics.

BUDGET GARDENING TIP

Holly is less expensive than boxwood. Keep this in mind if you are buying quite a few for a hedge.

Hollies, Larger

1ST

CHARACTERISTICS

Plant Type: Evergreen shrub.

Average Size: Can be maintained at sizes between 8 to 10 feet tall and 4 to 6 feet wide.

Growth Rate: Depends on type

Leaf: Rounded, glossy green or bronze leaves, 1 to 2 inches long and wide.

Flower: Hundreds of small, open-centered blossoms.

Origin: Several species are native to the southeastern US; the rest are from the Far East.

Spacing: About 6 to 12 feet on center (measure from the center of each plant) depending on cultivar.

Cautions: Some of the leaves have spines; berries of some hollies are poisonous; hollies attract lots of bees when blooming but seldom attract any deer.

Colors: Holly flowers are insignificant, but some have attractive berries in both red and dark blue to black.

1. Ilex 'Nellie Stevens'
2. Ilex opaca, American holly
3. Ilex verticillata, Winterberry

One of the most popular evergreen shrubs in the south. Most landscapes include at least one holly. Less expensive than boxwood. Very easy to grow, rating a blue ribbon.*

Some hollies are quite tall, like this 'Nellie Stevens' (the tallest plant in the photo); while others are small, like these small, round, Japanese hollies the smallest plants in this photo).

Hollies are quite well adapted to the southern climate. There are many different kinds that vary mostly in leaf shape and the size of the plant. Some hollies have smooth leaf edges, and others have spines, like the ones associated with Christmas. Hollies vary quite a bit in size, as shown in the photo, above. Plant any of these large hollies at least eight feet away from your house. A common landscape mistake is to plant them too close to a building.

Regional Differences: 'Nellie Stevens,' American holly, and winterberry grow equally well throughout the south. Foster's holly can show some cold damage in zone six.

Color Period: Blooms are insignificant. Berries appear on some species in fall and winter.

Buying Tips: The most important consideration is size and light. All of these hollies do well in light shade to full sun. In medium shade, choose another shrub, like aucuba. Also, know the mature size you need. A frequent mistake is to plant hollies that outgrow their spaces.

**Blue ribbon plants are defined on page 12. For blue ribbon performance, follow the planting and maintenance guidelines on 28 to 49.*

Foster's Holly, (*Ilex x attenuata,* right) is 20 feet tall by six to eight feet wide. Can maintain it as low as 15 feet tall. Space them eight feet apart. Standard, Christmas tree form. Lighter in texture than 'Nellie Stevens.' Lots of berries in winter. Shape it at least once a year in winter. Zones seven through nine.

Winterberry, (*Ilex verticillata,* right), is six to ten feet tall by four to six feet wide. Space them six feet apart. This holly has a looser form, more like a crapemyrtle tree, and is deciduous. Used primarily for its beautiful, winter display of berries from September until February. Need a male pollinator in the area to have fruiting. Slower growing than evergreen hollies. Very tolerant of low or high water situations. Most cold tolerant, growing from zones three to nine.

American Holly, (*Ilex opaca,* left), Largest of the hollies on this page, growing to 30 feet tall by 15 feet wide. Can be maintained at 12 feet tall. Pyramidal growth habit and red berries. Similar to 'Nellie Stevens.' Plant this native if you want fast height. Space them ten feet apart for specimen or six feet apart for screening. Very drought tolerant, surviving without irrigation. Zones five to nine.

Nellie Stevens Holly, (*Ilex Nellie R. Stevens,* left) is 15 to 20 feet tall but can be maintained in the 10 to 12 foot range. Space 8 to 10 feet apart. More of these have been sold than any other pyramidal holly. Leaves have spines. Can be sheared, but better grown naturally into its neat, pyramidal form. Zones six to nine.

GROWING CONDITIONS

Light: Light shade to full sun

Water: American holly has very low water needs after establishment. Lives on rainwater alone, without supplemental water, in all but the most extreme conditions. Nellie Stevens, winterberry and Foster's holly have low water needs after establishment. Like water every week or two during the growing season, depending on the environment. Winterberry takes wet soils as well. See pages 34 to 37 for more information.

Soil: Any fertile, well-drained soil that has been enriched with organic matter. Requires good drainage. See pages 28 to 31 for instructions.

Hardiness: Varies by species from 3 to 10.

Propagation: Cuttings; seeds are difficult.

Pest Problems: Rare. Root rot can develop if plants are kept too wet. Aphids and scales occasionally.

PLANTING & MAINTENANCE

When to Plant: Holly from containers can be planted at any time. Fall is best because they establish easier in cooler weather.

Trimming: Most hollies look good with one annual pruning in late winter to early spring. Some require a few more shapings throughout the growing season.

Fertilization: Medium. Fertilize at planting time and each spring with a timed-release product. Less fertilizer is needed with the application of more organics. See pages 46 to 49 for more instructions.

**Only American holly lives on rainwater alone in all but the most extreme situations. American holly and winterberry are southern natives.*

Honeysuckle, Trumpet or Coral

1ST

CHARACTERISTICS

Plant Type: Deciduous vine (loses its leaves in winter).

Average Size: 10 to 20 feet tall, needs support.

Growth Rate: Fast

Leaf: Small, rounded leaves emerging in early spring with tinges of red or purple changing to a blue-green in summer.

Flower: Abundant tubular flowers of red or red-orange on the outside with yellow to yellow-orange on the inside; 4 inches long.

Origin: New England to Florida, west to Texas.

Spacing: Plant one at each post of a pergola or arbor, or 6 feet on center (measure from the center of each plant).

Cautions: Occasionally damaged by deer. Poisonous to some, so don't eat this plant.

Colors: Red, orange, yellow, pink

1. *'Mardi Gras' honeysuckle*
2. *'Harlequin' honeysuckle*
3. *'John Clayton Bailey' honeysuckle*

Spectacular, colorful, spring flowers on a fast-growing, twining vine. Native to the south, and easy to grow, rating a blue ribbon.*

Honeysuckle is an outstanding native vine for showy spring flowers. It is a great hummingbird attractor, with butterflies enjoying it as well. This large vine grows to 20 feet with support or stays in a large clump if allowed to grow on its own. This is a good selection for southern gardens - not as aggressive as the Japanese honeysuckle, which is an invasive species.

Regional Differences: None

Color Period: Early to mid spring for about two months. Starts in early April in zone eight, mid-April in zone seven, and early May in zone six. May re-bloom sporadically throughout summer.

Buying Tips: Cultivars are available based on color of flowers. 'Magnifica' and 'Alabama Crimson' both have red flowers. 'Sulphurea' or 'Flava' are pure yellow and 'Cedar Lane' is a selection from Madison, Georgia, that blooms over a longer period of time.

**Blue ribbon plants are defined on page 12. For blue ribbon performance, follow the planting and maintenance guidelines on 28 to 49.*

Companions: Space companion plantings at least four to six feet away from this vine, so they don't get tangled up.

Plant this vine with other plants that bloom at the same time. Here is an idea for plants that look good in front of honeysuckle that is supported by a wall or fence:

Honeysuckle and some companions

'Sunny Knock Out' Rose (above, left) has a more compact growth habit than the original 'Knock Out,' growing about four feet tall. The flowers start out yellow and fade to cream. Both colors complement the honeysuckle. This rose blooms on and off from spring until fall, so it should bloom with the honeysuckle. Use the honeysuckle as the tallest plant of this grouping, with the rose in front of it.

Amsonia (above, left) is a perennial that grows three feet tall and blooms in April and May, usually coinciding with the honeysuckle and the rose. Plant them in front as a border to the larger plants. All three plants do well in full sun.

GROWING CONDITIONS

Light: Light shade to full sun

Water: Very low after establishment. Lives on rainwater alone, without supplemental water, in all but the most extreme conditions, although it drops its leaves in severe droughts. See pages 34 to 37 for more information.

Soil: Any fertile, well-drained soil that has been enriched with organic matter. Requires good drainage. See pages 28 to 31 for instructions.

Hardiness: Zones 4 to 9

Propagation: Seeds or cuttings

Pest Problems: None serious. Leaf spots may persist in wet weather.

PLANTING & MAINTENANCE

When to Plant: Honeysuckle from containers can be planted at any time. Fall is best because they establish easier in cooler weather, but you are more likely to find them at your garden center in early spring, when they are blooming.

Trimming: Trim it shortly after flowering. This vine doesn't require much trimming, only to train it or remove some of the older branches if the vine is old. Remove any dead branches.

Fertilization: Medium. Fertilize at planting time and each spring with a timed-release product. Less fertilizer is needed with the application of more organics. See pages 46 to 49 for more instructions.

**Lives on rainwater alone in all but the most extreme situations.*

1ST Hydrangea, Annabelle

Lovely, huge, white flowers that grow up to one foot across. Unlike mophead hydrangeas, this one blooms with white flowers even if the winter has been quite cold. Largest flowers of any of the hydrangeas. Qualifies for a blue ribbon,* but likes more water than most plants in this book.

CHARACTERISTICS

Plant Type: Deciduous shrub (loses its leaves in winter).

Average Size: 3 to 5 feet tall by 4 to 6 feet wide.

Growth Rate: Medium

Leaf: Dark green leaves, 3 to 8 inches long.

Flower: Huge, white balls from 8 to 12 inches across.

Origin: Eastern US

Spacing: About 3 to 4 feet on center (measure from the center of each plant).

Cautions: Poisonous to some people, so don't eat this plant. Juice or sap is a skin irritant. Occasionally damaged by deer.

Colors: Flowers are white.

UNIVERSITY AWARDS

1995: Georgia Gold Medal Winner

Annabelle is one of the most dependable hydrangeas. It blooms each spring, regardless how cold it gets the previous months.

The blooms are so large, however, that they tend to fall over, particularly after rain. To reduce the chance of this problem, plant at least three plants together so they support one another. Pruning stems to the ground in late winter helps to strengthen them. Or, put a short wire fence around each plant.

Regional Differences: None

Color Period: Starts blooming in mid May in zones eight and nine, late May in zone seven, and early June in zone six. Blooms for about a month with white flowers and another month with lime green flowers. The flowers stay brown throughout the winter.

Buying Tips: It is best to buy this plant when it is blooming. Other white hydrangeas with much smaller, flatter flowers are often confused with this one until they bloom.

The flowers bloom white for about a month and then turn lime green for another month.

**Blue ribbon plants are defined on page 12. For blue ribbon performance, follow the planting and maintenance guidelines on 28 to 49.*

Companions: 'Annabelle' hydrangea looks wonderful mixed with pink and blue mophead hydrangeas that bloom at the same time.

Or, plant a pretty annual border in front of your hydrangea, as shown below.

Annabelle hydrangea and some companions

Blue Salvia (above, left) is an annual that looks good with this hydrangea because its spiky, blue flower contrasts well with the hydrangea's large, round ball. This salvia grows well in the partial shade that the hydrangea likes, but be sure to give it morning sun.

Dragon Wing Begonias (above, right) are another annual that is a nice companion for 'Annabelle' hydrangeas because the two together have more color impact than either one alone. Alternate clumps (three plants each) of the begonias and salvia in front of the hydrangea.

GROWING CONDITIONS

Light: Light shade, or morning sun and afternoon shade.

Water: Medium after establishment. Likes water once or twice a week during the growing season, depending on its environment. Quite intolerant of drought. See pages 34 to 37 for more information.

Soil: Any fertile, well-drained soil that has been enriched with organic matter. Requires good drainage. See pages 28 to 31 for instructions.

Hardiness: Zones 5 to 9

Propagation: Cuttings

Pest Problems: None serious. This hydrangea has excellent resistance to many pests that plague other types of hydrangeas.

PLANTING & MAINTENANCE

When to Plant: Hydrangeas from containers can be planted at any time. Fall is best because they establish easier in cooler weather, but you are more likely to find them at your garden center in early spring, when they are blooming.

Trimming: Prune annually in late winter (February or March). Cut it to the ground each year.

Fertilization: Medium. Fertilize at planting time and each spring with a timed-release product. Less fertilizer is needed with the application of more organics. See pages 46 to 49 for more instructions.

Hydrangea, Mophead and Lacecap

CHARACTERISTICS

Plant Type: Deciduous shrub.

Average Size: Vary by type from 3 to 6 feet tall and equally as wide.

Growth Rate: Fast

Leaf: Rounded, green leaves, 4 to 6 inches long and wide.

Flower: Large, pom-pom or delicate, lacecap blooms.

Origin: Japan

Spacing: About 4 to 6 feet on center (measure from the center of each plant), depending on the mature size of the hydrangea.

Cautions: Poisonous to some people, so don't eat this plant. Juice or sap is a skin irritant. Occasionally damaged by deer.

Colors: Flowers are pink or blue. Color depends on pH of the soil and availability of aluminum. See http://www.hydrangeashydrangeas.com/colorchange.html for instructions.

1. *'Endless Summer'*
2. *'Endless Summer Blushing Bride'*
3. *'Endless Summer Pink'*
4. *'Midnight Dutchess' lacecap*

One of the most common hydrangeas planted in the south. New, reblooming types are more dependable than older cultivars, particularly in areas that might have a severe spring freeze. The most cold-sensitive hydrangea. Qualifies for a blue ribbon,* but likes more water than most plants in this book.

'Mini Penny' blue reblooming hydrangea

'Why doesn't my mophead hydrangea bloom?' This is the most common question asked of the horticultural staff at Huntsville Botanical Garden. Nine times out of ten, it's because of a late spring freeze, which is a frequent occurrence in zones six and seven. Older mopheads and lacecap hydrangeas will have no flowers for an entire year after a late freeze. However, the new reblooming mopheads will bloom later on if it freezes in spring. In years without late freezes, the rebloomers flower twice, once in spring and again in fall. This doubles the normal bloom time of this type of hydrangea.

Regional Differences: Mophead and lacecap hydrangeas often show cold damage in zones six and seven. This cold damage can keep them from blooming that season.

Color Period: Without a late freeze, they bloom for about a month in May or June. Rebloomers bloom again later in the summer or in early fall.

Buying Tips: It makes sense to buy reblooming hydrangeas. They are now available in both mophead and lacecap forms. We have had good luck with 'Endless Summer,' 'Blushing Bride,' 'Penney Mac,' and 'Let's Dance.' Reblooming hydrangeas are commonly available in most garden centers in spring.

**Blue ribbon plants are defined on page 12. For blue ribbon performance, follow the planting and maintenance guidelines on 28 to 49.*

Companions: Mophead and lacecap hydrangeas look good planted with white 'Annabelle' hydrangeas (pictured together on page 193; information about 'Annabelle' hydrangea on pages 226 and 227).

Using an annual border around your hydrangeas will keep the bed in color for the entire growing season, as shown below.

Hydrangea with some companions

White Begonias are one of the best annuals to use for borders of reblooming hydrangeas. They like the same, light shade and keep blooming for the entire season.

Trailing Torenia makes a great border for hydrangeas. It is frequently sold in hanging baskets but also thrives when planted in the ground. The blue color is a perfect contrast to the pink hydrangea. Plant this combination in light shade.

GROWING CONDITIONS

Light: Light shade, or morning sun and afternoon shade.

Water: Medium after establishment. Likes water once or twice a week during the growing season, depending on its environment. Quite intolerant of drought. See pages 34 to 37 for more information.

Soil: Any fertile, well-drained soil that has been enriched with organic matter. Requires good drainage and likes the same, acid soil as azaleas. See pages 28 to 31 for instructions.

Hardiness: Zones 6 to 9. Often shows cold damage in zones six and seven. This cold damage can keep them from blooming that season.

Propagation: Cuttings or layering

Pest Problems: Root rot is the worst. Leaf spot sometimes from overhead irrigation.

PLANTING & MAINTENANCE

When to Plant: Hydrangea from containers can be planted at any time. Fall is best because they establish easier in cooler weather, but you are more likely to find them at your garden center in spring, when they are blooming.

Trimming: Prune shortly after it flowers. Take the older canes (with the parchment bark), and cut them to the ground. This takes about 5 minutes. Do not cut them any later, or they won't bloom the next season.

Fertilization: Medium. Fertilize at planting time and each spring with a timed-release product. Less fertilizer is needed with the application of more organics. See pages 46 to 49 for more instructions.

1ST Hydrangea, Oakleaf

CHARACTERISTICS

Plant Type: Deciduous shrub.

Average Size: 6 to 12 feet tall and wide, depending on cultivar.

Growth Rate: Medium

Leaf: Leathery-lobed green leaves to 8 inches long; turn red in the fall.

Flower: Elongated clusters 6 to 18 inches long, 6 inches in diameter.

Origin: Southeastern US (Alabama, Georgia, Mississippi, and north Florida).

Spacing: Set plants 5 to 8 feet apart. Allow plenty of room for lateral growth when planting this shrub near walls or buildings.

Cautions: Poisonous to some people, so don't eat this plant. Juice or sap is a skin irritant. Occasionally damaged by deer.

Colors: All oakleaf hydrangea flowers start out white and then change color. But, there is a lot of variability in the species. Most age to pink, cream, and red.

UNIVERSITY AWARDS

2000: Georgia Gold Medal Winner for 'Alice' hydrangea.

2000: Mississippi Medallion Award for 'Snowflake' hydrangea.

A four season performer with different looks from the same plant. Clusters of white flowers open in early summer and persist until fall, changing colors along the way. Very easy to grow. Qualifies for a blue ribbon,* but likes more water than most plants in this book.

Honored as an Arkansas Select plant and a Mississippi Medallion winner, oakleaf hydrangea has something for every season. In winter, the exfoliating coppery-tan bark is interesting. In spring, the large leaves emerge, giving a coarse, tropical texture to the garden, more so than any of the other hydrangeas. The flowers are huge, white clusters that change colors as they age, as shown opposite. Be sure to choose a variety that fits the space you have for it. 'Alice' and 'Alison' will eventually grow to 12 feet wide, while 'Pee Wee' is much smaller at 6 to 8 feet wide.

Regional Differences: Easily grown throughout the south, provided the soil is acidic rather than alkaline.

Color Period: Early May to June, with flowers remaining white for about a month. As the flowers dry, they often blush pink and persist as light brown clusters until fall.

Buying Tips: The best-selling cultivar is 'Snowflake,' which grows eight feet tall and has huge, 18-inch-long flower clusters. They are so heavy they weep, and are the best ones for dried flowers. 'Amythest' has wine-red flowers and outstanding fall color.

**Blue ribbon plants are defined on page 12. For blue ribbon performance, follow the planting and maintenance guidelines on 28 to 49*

GROWING CONDITIONS

Light: Light shade, or morning sun and afternoon shade.

Water: Medium after establishment. Likes water once or twice a week during the growing season, depending on its environment. Quite intolerant of drought. See pages 34 to 37 for more information.

Soil: Any fertile, well-drained soil that has been enriched with organic matter. Requires good drainage and likes the same, acid soil as azaleas. See pages 28 to 31 for instructions.

Hardiness: Zones 5 to 9

Propagation: Cuttings or layering

Pest Problems: Root rot is the worst. Leaf spot sometimes from overhead irrigation.

PLANTING & MAINTENANCE

When to Plant: Hydrangeas from containers can be planted at any time. Fall is best because they establish easier in cooler weather, but you are more likely to find them at your garden center in spring or early summer, when they are blooming.

Trimming: After they finish with the white flowers, cut one or two of the tallest old canes to the ground. This plant does not branch too well, so this thinning encourages more branching. Also, remove any branches that are killed by accidents or violent winter weather. If you find the withered flower clusters unsightly in winter, simply snip them off.

Fertilization: Medium. Fertilize at planting time and each spring with a timed-release product. Less fertilizer is needed with the application of more organics. See pages 46 to 49 for more instructions.

1ST Hydrangea, Panicle

CHARACTERISTICS

Plant Type: Deciduous shrub (loses its leaves in winter).

Average Size: New, dwarf varieties are about 3 to 4 feet tall and equally as wide. Largest varieties are 6 to 8 feet tall by equally as wide.

Growth Rate: Fast

Leaf: 6 inches long by 3 inches wide; pointed, medium green. Leaves are not as attractive as the oakleaf or mophead hydrangeas.

Flower: Cone-shaped panicle at least 8 inches long.

Origin: Japan

Spacing: About 6 to 8 feet on center (measure from the center of each plant) for the larger ones, and 3 to 4 feet for smaller ones.

Cautions: Poisonous to some people, so don't eat this plant. Juice or sap is a skin irritant. Occasionally damaged by deer.

Colors: Blooms in pure white and changes color as it ages to tan, pink, red, or chartreuse.

The last hydrangea to bloom. Takes more sun and cold than the other hydrangeas. Most cultivars are larger than mopheads (eight to ten feet tall). Choose this hydrangea for a long bloom period of white flowers. Qualifies for a blue ribbon,* but likes more water than most plants in this book.

Hybridizers have gone crazy with this plant. New ones are springing up constantly. The good news is that we have liked all the ones we have tried. And many of the new ones are quite a bit smaller (about four feet tall) than their large predessesors (up to ten feet tall). This hydrangea takes cold better than the mopheads, blooming even if you have a hard, spring freeze.

Regional Differences: None

Color Period: Begins in mid June in zone eight, beginning of July in zone seven, and mid July in zone six. Blooms stay white for about a month and start to fade. They stay on the shrub until the first hard freeze.

Buying Tips: Huntsville Botanical Garden has tried many of the new, panicle hydrangea cultivars and liked all of them. 'Chantilly Lace' (shown, left) is a favorite because its three to four foot size fits well in so many home landscapes.

**Blue ribbon plants are defined on page 12. For blue ribbon performance, follow the planting and maintenance guidelines on 28 to 49.*

Companions: Since panicle hydrangea grows in more sun than the other hydrangeas, it works with more flowering plants. The 'Limelight' hydrangea, shown below, grows six to eight feet tall, so it works well as a background plant. Try it with the perennials shown below for easy color layers.

'Limelight' hydrangea and some companions

'Blue Fortune' Agastache (above, left) is one of the longest blooming southern perennials and looks great with this hydrangea. The blue, spiky flowers contrast well with the conical, hydrangea flowers. And the blue color works as the hydrangea flowers change colors from white to pink to lime green. Since the agastache reaches three feet tall, plant it in front of the hydrangea.

Threadleaf Coreopsis (above, right) also blooms at the same time as both the hydrangea and the agastache. The fine texture of the coreopsis contrasts well with the coarser textured flowers. Use the shorter coreopsis (about 18 inches tall) as a border for the agastache and hydrangea in full sun. The hydrangea works in partial shade as well.

GROWING CONDITIONS

Light: Light shade to full sun. This hydrangea takes more sun than the others.

Water: Medium after establishment. Likes water once or twice a week during the growing season, depending on its environment. See pages 34 to 37 for more information.

Soil: Any fertile, well-drained soil that has been enriched with organic matter. Requires good drainage. See pages 28 to 31 for instructions.

Hardiness: Zones 3 to 9. This is the most cold hardy of all the hydrangeas.

Propagation: Cuttings

Pest Problems: Rare. Root rot can develop if plants are kept too wet.

PLANTING & MAINTENANCE

When to Plant: Hydrangeas from containers can be planted at any time. Fall is best because they establish easier in cooler weather, but you are more likely to find them at your garden center in summer, when they are blooming.

Trimming: Trim in late winter before new growth starts. Can be cut back heavily to control its size.

Fertilization: Medium. Fertilize at planting time and each spring with a timed-release product. Less fertilizer is needed with the application of more organics. See pages 46 to 49 for more instructions.

1ST Indian Hawthorn

CHARACTERISTICS

Plant Type: Evergreen shrub.

Average Size: Easily maintained at sizes between 3 to 6 feet tall and 3 to 6 feet wide.

Growth Rate: Medium

Leaf: Oval, evergreen with serrated margins. Leaves are 2 to 3 inches long by 1 inch wide; dark green with bluish cast. Very coarse-textured, leathery appearance.

Flower: Small, white 5 petaled flowers born in clusters in late spring (April-May). Flowers literally cover the mounded shrubs making quite a show for 2 to 3 weeks.

Origin: Japan, Korea

Spacing: About 3 to 4 feet on center (measure from the center of each plant).

Cautions: None known

Colors: Flowers are white, pink, rose-red with lots of variations in color intensity.

'Calisto' Indian hawthorn

Very popular evergreen shrub with fantastic floral display in spring. Clusters of white or pink flowers cover the mounded shrubs for two to three weeks in March and April. Newer selections have more disease resistance and improved cold hardiness. Low water. Easily rates a blue ribbon because of high performance and low care.

Indian hawthorn has quickly become a leading shrub in the south. It's compact growth habit means very little trimming required. Similar to smaller hollies in form, Indian hawthorn has the added benefit of flowers in the spring. Good salt tolerance has led to popularity in coastal areas. The only problem is the fact that it is becoming more popular in zone seven, where severe cold could kill it.

Regional Differences: May be tender in zone seven in severe winters. Many were killed in 1980's but have been widely planted in the last 10 years with no ill effects. However, it makes sense to be cautious in zone six and the colder parts of zone seven.

Color Period: First of April in zone eight, after April 15 in zones 6 and seven.

Buying Tips: Several cultivars are available in garden centers with improved disease resistance and cold tolerance. 'Springtime,' 'Eskimo,' and 'Ballerina' are good selections. 'Spring Sonata' is part of the Southern Living collection. 'Callisto' and 'Rosalinda' are two new, promising cultivars.

**Blue ribbon plants are defined on page 12. For blue ribbon performance, follow the planting and maintenance guidelines on pages 30 to 49.*

Companions: Indian hawthorn is frequently used as a landscape shrub with other evergreen plants, like boxwoods and hollies. It looks good with green plants that have different textures as well, like juniper and Japanese yew.

For spring color, pair it with azaleas and phlox, as shown below. This grouping will give you up to three weeks of color.

Photo by Cathy K. Bishop

Indian hawthorn and some companions

Azalea (above, left) blooms in early spring, usually at the same time as the Indian hawthorn. Keep the Indian hawthorn maintained at about three feet tall and plant it in front of the taller azalea (four to five feet tall). Both will grow in partial shade.

Woodland Phlox (above, right) is another shade plant that blooms in early spring. Since the phlox stays low (about 12 to 16 inches tall), use it as a border for the other two, taller plants. All three plants do well in light shade.

GROWING CONDITIONS

Light: Light shade to full sun

Water: Low after establishment. Likes water every week or two during the growing season, depending on its environment. See pages 34 to 37 for more information.

Soil: Any fertile, well-drained soil that has been enriched with organic matter. Requires good drainage. See pages 34 to 37 for instructions.

Hardiness: Zones 7b to10

Propagation: Seeds or cuttings

Pest Problems: Rare. Root rot can develop if plants are kept too wet.

PLANTING & MAINTENANCE

When to Plant: Indian hawthorns from containers can be planted at any time. Fall is best because they establish easier in cooler weather, but you are more likely to find them at your garden center in early spring, when they are blooming.

Trimming: Trim once a year in shortly after spring flowering to shape. It is best to prune by thinning rather than shearing.

Fertilization: Medium. Fertilize at planting time and annually with a timed-release product. Less fertilizer is needed with the application of more organics. See pages 46 to 49 for more instructions.

1ST Japanese Plum Yew

CHARACTERISTICS

Plant Type: Evergreen shrub.

Average Size: 2 to 3 feet tall and equally as wide.

Growth Rate: Slow to medium

Leaf: Needle-like, 1 to 1 1/2 inches long by 1/4 inch wide; arranged spirally around the stem.

Flower: Insignificant

Origin: Japan

Spacing: About 3 feet on center (measure from the center of each plant).

Cautions: Almost never damaged by deer.

Colors: Leaves are dark green. Flowers are insignificant.

UNIVERSITY AWARDS

1994: Georgia Gold Medal Winner.

BUDGET GARDENING TIP

Japanese yews, like most plants that grow slowly, are expensive. They are most commonly sold in 3 gallon containers. Ask the nursery if they can get them in smaller, 1 gallon containers. You'll need to wait about a year to make up for the size difference, but you'll save about 70 per cent.

Fine-textured, evergreen shrub that stays small enough to be considered a groundcover. One of the easiest plants in this book! Takes southern heat beautifully. Easily rates a blue ribbon.*

Japanese yew is a valuable landscape plant for the south. It is evergreen, takes sun or light shade, and requires almost no care at all. And deer leave it alone! Japanese yew resembles the yews that are commonly-grown in the northern states, but won't take southern heat. This yew takes heat beautifully, and adds an interesting texture to the southern, evergreen garden.

This plant looks better its second and third year in the ground. The first year, it looks a bit asymmetrical. Expect some branches to yellow and die shortly after planting. Simply trim them off.

Regional Differences: None

Color Period: Insignificant

Buying Tips: We are familiar with three different cultivars: 'Prostrata,' 'Nana,' and 'Duke Gardens.' All three do well, along with 'Yewtopia.'

**Blue ribbon plants are defined on page 12. For blue ribbon performance, follow the planting and maintenance guidelines on pages 30 to 49.*

Companions: The best feature of Japanese yew is its coarse texture. This texture is best shown off by using different textures around it.

Layer it with 'Bronze Beauty' cleyera and 'Blue Rug' juniper to accentuate the interesting textures of all three plants, as shown below.

'Yewtopia' plum yew and some companions

'Bronze Beauty' Cleyera (above, left) is a shrub that grows up to eight feet tall, making a nice backdrop for the shorter, Japanese yew. The textures of both plants are quite different, which makes each plant show up better.

'Blue Rug' Juniper (above, right) is a low-growing shrub that is so low it resembles carpet. Juniper's texture is quite different from both other plants. Since it only grows six inches tall, use it as the lowest plant in this grouping.

GROWING CONDITIONS

Light: Light shade to full sun

Water: Low after establishment. Likes water every week or two during the growing season, depending on its environment. See pages 34 to 37 for more information.

Soil: Any fertile, well-drained soil that has been enriched with organic matter. Requires good drainage. See pages 28 to 31 for more information.

Hardiness: Zones 6 to 9

Propagation: Seeds or cuttings. Seeds can take up to 2 years to germinate.

Pest Problems: Rare

PLANTING & MAINTENANCE

When to Plant: Japanese plum yew from containers can be planted at any time. Fall is best because they establish easier in cooler weather.

Trimming: Very little trimming needed. Prune out dead branches whenever you notice them.

Fertilization: Medium. Fertilize at planting time and annually with a timed-release product. Less fertilizer is needed with the application of more organics. See pages 46 to 49 for more instructions.

1ST Juniper

CHARACTERISTICS

Plant Type: Evergreen shrub.

Average Size: Shrub junipers grow from 6 inches to over 5 feet tall. See individual descriptions on the opposite page. Tree juniper is covered on pages 282 to 283.

Growth Rate: Slow to medium

Leaf: Parson's juniper has scale-like, grey-green needles on a long spray of branches. 'Nick's Compact' and 'Blue Rug' leaves are more like needles than scales, and it is darker green.

Flower: Insignificant

Origin: Parson's juniper is from Asia, Siberia, and Japan. 'Nick's Compact' is from China. 'Blue Rug' is from North America. 'Mint Julep' is from Asia and southeast Russia. 'Grey Owl' is native to east and central North America. 'Pfitzer' juniper is from China and Japan.

Spacing: About 4 feet on center (measure from the center of each plant), if you want them to grow together quickly. 5 or 6 feet on center otherwise.

Cautions: None known. Seldom damaged by deer.

Colors: Flower is insignificant. Berries are blue-black.

Parson's juniper with berries

Juniper is one of the most popular shrubs in the south. It is also one of the easiest. Deer leave it alone, and it lives without irrigation in all but the most severe situations. Just give it good drainage, and you may never need to touch it again! Easily rates a blue ribbon.*

Parson's juniper

Juniper is one of the most popular shrubs in the south. They are commonly planted in difficult environments, like along interstate highways. Juniper is also quite useful for stabilizing slopes. The nice, green foliage is attractive, and contrasts well with other shrubs.

There are many different sizes and shapes of junipers, from low, creeping groundcovers to large, conical trees.

The two most common mistakes made with junipers are to plant them too close together or in wet soil. They need good air circulation to prevent diseases.

Regional Differences: Be sure the juniper you buy is cold-tolerant for your zone.

Color Period: Flowers are insignificant. Blue berries appear in September and October on some varieties.

Buying Tips: Easy to find at most garden centers.

**Blue ribbon plants are defined on page 12. For blue ribbon performance, follow the planting and maintenance guidelines on pages 30 to 49.*

Resists Deer

Lives on Rain Water *

Southern Native *

Botanical Name: *Juniperus spp.*
Family: Cupressaceae

Parson's Juniper (*Juniperus davurica parsonii,* right) grows to about two feet tall by six feet wide. Well-suited for slopes, but the branches are too stiff to cascade well over the sides of planters. Showy, blue fruit.

'Mint Julep' juniper (*Juniperus chinensis* 'Mint Julep,' right) grows four to six feet tall by equally as wide. Frequently used for bonsai.

'Pfitzer' juniper (*Juniperus chinensis 'Pfitzeriana',* right) grows about five feet tall by eight feet wide. Foliage has a lacy appearance.

Blue Rug Juniper (*Juniperus horizontalis 'Wiltoni,'* left) is the most popular of the so-called 'carpet' junipers, which resemble rugs. It is only about six or eight inches tall and spreads six to eight feet wide. This juniper is especially common on hillsides because it helps to stabilize the slope.

'Nick's Compact' juniper (*Juniperus chinensis* 'Nick's Compact,' left) is a medium-sized, flat-topped juniper growing two and a half feet tall and six feet wide. Most of the juniper you see planted along interstate highways is this one.

'Grey Owl' juniper (*Juniperus virginiana 'Grey Owl,'* left) grows three to three and a half feet tall by five to six feet wide. Scale-like, silvery green foliage. Female forms produce berries.

**Lives on rainwater alone in all but the most extreme situations. Only 'Grey Owl' juniper is a southern native.*

GROWING CONDITIONS

Light: Full sun for all junipers. Plants receiving less that 4 hours of sun thin out.

Water: Very low after establishment. Lives on rainwater alone, without supplemental water, in all but the most extreme conditions. See pages 34 to 37 for more information.

Soil: Any fertile, well-drained soil that has been enriched with organic matter. Requires good drainage. See pages 28 to 31 for instructions.

Hardiness: Zones 6 to 9 for Parson's juniper and 'Mint Julep'; 4 to 9 for 'Blue Rug' juniper, 'Nick's Compact,' 'Grey Owl,' and 'Pfitzer' zones 3 to 9.

Propagation: Cuttings

Pest Problems: Root rot can develop if plants are kept too wet. Watch out for blackening of stems. Spider mites and phomopsis blight occasionally.

PLANTING & MAINTENANCE

When to Plant: Juniper from containers can be planted at any time. Fall is best because they establish easier in cooler weather.

Trimming: Trim junipers if they outgrow their space or to remove dead branches. Other than that, they don't need trimming.

Fertilization: Medium. Fertilize at planting time and annually with a timed-release product. Less fertilizer is needed with the application of more organics. See pages 46 to 49 for more instructions.

BUDGET GARDENING TIP

Junipers in 1 gallon containers will save you about 70 per cent over the same plant in a 3 gallon container. Since they grow fairly quickly, they will make up the difference in no time!

1ST Kerria, Japanese

CHARACTERISTICS

Plant Type: Deciduous shrub (loses its leaves in winter).

Average Size: 4 to 6 feet wide and equally as wide.

Growth Rate: Medium to fast

Leaf: Long, pointed, deeply serrated, with prominent veins. Up to 4 inches long. Nice, green color.

Flower: Bright yellow and frilly; about 2 inches wide.

Origin: China

Spacing: About 4 feet on center (measure from the center of each plant). This plant tends to sucker, so it forms a large mass over time.

Cautions: Seldom damaged by deer.

Colors: Yellow flowers in spring. Nice, yellow leaves in fall. Light green stems in winter.

Double flower of 'Pleniflora' kerria

Free-flowering shrub that grows in shade. Old-fashioned, carefree, and tough. Seen on old, southern homesteads with no care for years. Has been grown in the south since the 1800's. Easily rates a blue ribbon.*

This is a great choice for spring color in shade. Also called the 'Yellow Rose of Texas,' it is not actually a rose but in the rose family. Nice, open, arching growth habit with green leaves and stems that feature pretty flowers to brighten up a shady spot.

Japanese kerria offers interest in each season. One of the first shrubs to leaf out in spring, its best feature are its yellow flowers that quickly follow. The leaves feature a nice, yellow color in fall. The light green stems show up well in winter.

Regional Differences: None

Color Time: Starts blooming in late March to April and lasts about two weeks. Sometimes, it has intermittent blooms in summer.

Buying Tips: There are three cultivars: 'Floriplena,' 'Pleniflora,' and 'Shannon.' They all do well. 'Pleniflora' has double flowers.

**Blue ribbon plants are defined on page 12. For blue ribbon performance, follow the planting and maintenance guidelines on pages 30 to 49.*

Companions: Use kerria with other plants that share the same bloom period. Amsonia and azaleas work well with kerria, as shown on pages 111. Other companions are listed in the color calendar on pages 52 to 53.

Or, try these yellow flowers with lenten rose and phlox, as shown below.

Photo by Copit

Kerria with some companions

Lenten Rose (above, left) blooms in early spring in shade, as does kerria.

Woodland Phlox (above, right) is another shade plant that blooms in early spring. Since the phlox and the lenten rose both stay low (about 12 to 16 inches tall), alternate clumps of them in front of the taller kerria.

GROWING CONDITIONS

Light: Light to medium shade. Morning sun is fine, but protect it from afternoon sun.

Water: Very low after establishment. Lives on rainwater alone, without supplemental water, in all but the most extreme conditions. See pages 34 to 37 for more information.

Soil: Kerria will grow in clay, but it prefers better soil. See pages 28 to 31 for instructions.

Hardiness: Zones 4 to 9

Propagation: Division or cuttings

Pest Problems: Rare. Root rot can develop if plants are kept too wet.

PLANTING & MAINTENANCE

When to Plant: Kerria from containers can be planted at any time. Fall is best because they establish easier in cooler weather, but you are more likely to find them at your garden center in early spring, when they are blooming.

Trimming: Prune in May or June, after it flowers. Thin out the older branches when their stems turn light brown.

Fertilization: Low. Fertilize at planting time with a timed-release product. Less fertilizer is needed with the application of more organics. In the years after planting, fertilization needs vary, based on the nutrients in your soil. See pages 46 to 49 for more instructions.

**Lives on rainwater alone in all but the most extreme situations.*

1ST Loropetalum, Fringe Flower

CHARACTERISTICS

Plant Type: Evergreen to semi evergreen shrub.

Average Size: Easily maintained at sizes between 6 to 15 feet tall by 4 to 8 feet wide. There are also compact varieties that have been on the market for less than 2 years which we have not tested thoroughly. 'Purple Pixie' grows only 2 feet tall by 3 to 4 feet wide and 'Purple Diamond,' 5 feet tall by 5 feet wide.

Growth Rate: Fast

Leaf: Burgundy or light green, 2 inches long by 1 inch wide, oval shaped.

Flower: Fringe like, 1 inch long by 1/4 inch wide, four petals.

Origin: China and Japan

Spacing: About 4 to 5 feet on center.

Cautions: This plant grows quickly and gets much larger than most people expect. Since many different sizes are available, be sure the size you buy fits your space. Deer seldom damage this plant.

Colors: Flowers are pink, red, white, lavender, and fuchsia. Leaves are burgundy or green.

UNIVERSITY AWARDS

1997: Georgia Gold Medal Winner

2001: Mississippi Medallion Winner.

1. 'Ever Red' loropetalum
2. 'Little Rose Dawn' loropetalum

One of the few shrubs that gives year-round color - even in winter - with very little care. Burgundy, evergreen leaves form a wonderful contrast in the landscape. Easily rates a blue ribbon.*

Loropetalum with daylilies, red cannas, purple heart, and periwinkles at the home of Mrs. Melba Pearson in Louisville, Mississippi.

With the advent of the new burgundy leaf forms of this shrub, garden centers can't keep this plant in stock. It is a wonderful, evergreen shrub that retains color year-round and is easy to grow. As an added bonus it blooms most in the spring and continues sporadically throughout the spring to fall growing season. However, the blooms are not always dependable, so buy this plant for its leaf color. And, many loropetalum varieties grow bigger than most people realize. Since there are many sizes available, be sure you buy one that fits your space. Large loropetalums make great screens or hedges and can also be grown as small trees, with a maximum height of 15 feet when mature.

Regional Differences: Reliable in zones seven to nine. Marginal in zone six because it will not tolerate zero degree weather. The 'Bill Wallace' variety did not do well in zone six and was marginal in zone seven, evidenced by winter kill.

Color Period: Biggest bloom in late spring, with more flowers appearing sporadically through summer.

Buying Tips: Garden centers have a variety of the burgundy leaf shrub. So far all the ones we have tried have done well except for the 'Bill Wallace' variety, which did not tolerate the cold in zone seven. You will need to ask if you are getting a compact or dwarf variety if your space for planting is limited.

**Blue ribbon plants are defined on page 12. For blue ribbon performance, follow the planting and maintenance guidelines on pages 30 to 49.*

Companions: Loropetalum is one of the most useful shrubs in the south because it gives year-round color in sun to partial shade. Its leaf color lasts all year, so use if primarily for that feature. The dark leaves show up quite well against lime green, like 'Gold Mound' spiraea.

Or, combine loropetalum with plants that have a long bloom period, like the 'Knock Out' roses and scabiosa shown below.

Loropetalum is spectacular when it blooms, but the color from the flowers doesn't last as long as the leaf color.

Loropetalum with some companions

'Knock Out' Roses (above, left) bloom spring, summer, and fall, so they keep the bed in color for the entire growing season. Since 'Knock Outs' grow about five feet tall, place them in front of taller loropetalums or behind shorter loropetalums (since loropetalums come in so many sizes). The 'Knock Out' roses come in bright pink (as shown above) or a paler pink that would also look wonderful with the burgundy loropetalum.

Scabiosa (above, right) is another one of the longest-blooming perennials for the south, flowering from May until September, if you deadhead (remove dead flowers). It grows 12 to 18 inches tall, so use it as a front border for the taller roses and loropetalum.

GROWING CONDITIONS

Light: Full sun to partial shade. Blooms best and has most attractive leaf color in full sun. Very heat tolerant.

Water: Very low after establishment. Lives on rainwater alone, without supplemental water, in all but the most extreme conditions. See pages 34 to 37 for more information.

Soil: For the garden, plant in any fertile, well-drained soil that has been enriched with organic matter. Use only good-quality potting mix for containers. See page 28 to 31 for specific instructions on soil preparation.

Hardiness: Zones 7 to 9

Propagation: Rooted cuttings taken in early summer.

Pest Problems: Rare. Aphids may occasionally feed on tender, new growth but seldom require control.

PLANTING & MAINTENANCE

When to Plant: Loropetalum from containers can be planted at any time. Fall is best because they establish easier in cooler weather.

Trimming: Use pruning loppers to trim back very long branches in early summer, after the biggest show of blooms has ended. When planted in a site it likes, loropetalum can grow very large and may need to be cut back rather aggressively in late winter. Do not be timid about trimming this shrub, but do follow its natural shape and never attempt to prune it into a ball.

Fertilization: Medium. Fertilize at planting time and each spring with a timed-release product. Less fertilizer is needed with the application of more organics. See pages 46 to 49 for more instructions.

**Lives on rainwater alone in all but the most extreme situations.*

2ND Rose, 'Knock Out'

CHARACTERISTICS

Plant Type: Evergreen shrub in Zones 7 to 9. Deciduous shrub in Zones 5 and 6 (loses its leaves in winter).

Average Size: Easily maintained at sizes between 4 feet tall by 4 feet wide and 8 feet tall by 8 feet wide.

Growth Rate: Fast

Leaf: Deep green to bronzy purple on new growth. 3 inches long by 2 inches wide.

Flower: Singles have 5 to 7 overlapping petals. Doubles have 20 to 30 petals. All have yellow stamens. Flower is 3 to 3 1/2 inches wide.

Origin: Roses are originally native to China. This one was hybridized in the U.S.

Spacing: About 4 to 6 feet on center (measure from the center of each plant).

Cautions: Frequently damaged by deer. Be careful of thorns.

Colors: See opposite page for flower colors.

'Double Knock Out' rose

This shrub blooms the longest with the least amount of care of any shrub in this book. Good color from spring til hard frost. The 'Knock Outs' take the maintenance out of roses. Rates a red ribbon* because of Japanese beetle attacks, but the shrub recovers quickly from the damage.

If you have ever been surprised by a plant - this is it! In the past, many have thought that roses were just too much work. The 'Knock Out' roses changed all the rules. They are low maintenance, carefree shrubs that require no deadheading and little spraying, fertilizing, or trimming. And, they bloom continuously from spring until the first heavy frost. They have taken the blue ribbon prize at the Huntsville Botanical Garden as a spectacular show stopper, blooming for the last five to six years in front of an 80 foot wood fence. The only limitation is that they do not produce a long stemmed rose suitable for cutting. Another negative about this rose is its susceptibility to Japanese beetles. If you live in an area that the beetles frequent, expect to see holes in the leaves and half-eaten flowers in early to mid summer unless you plan to spray. However, the shrub is such a vigorous grower that new growth hides the holes shortly after the beetles leave in mid summer.

Regional Differences: Hardy through zone five. Evergreen in zones seven through nine. Deciduous in zones five and six.

Color Period: Continuous from April until hard frost. Tolerates light freezes.

Buying Tips: Garden centers are carrying several of the cultivars that are clearly tagged. They are also available on-line.

**Red ribbon plants are defined on page 13. For blue ribbon performance, follow the planting and maintenance guidelines on pages 30 to 49.*

1. 'Knock Out' rose
2. 'Double Knock Out' rose
3. 'Pink Knock Out' rose
4. 'Pink Double Knock Out' rose
5. 'Rainbow Knock Out' rose
6. 'Blushing Knock Out' rose
7. 'Sunny Knock Out' rose

At Huntsville Botanical Garden the single red variety (simply called 'Knock Out' rose) is the most vigorous bloomer, with 'Rainbow' the least prolific.

GROWING CONDITIONS

Light: Full sun to light shade

Water: Medium after establishment. Likes water once or twice a week during the growing season, depending on its environment. See pages 34 to 37 for more information. Has been known to grow without irrigation, depending on rainfall amounts and it's individual environment.

Soil: For the garden, plant in any fertile, well-drained soil that has been enriched with organic matter. Use only good-quality potting mix for containers. See pages 28 to 31 for specific instructions on soil preparation.

Hardiness: Zones 5 to 9

Propagation: Prohibited; plants are currently patented.

Pest Problems: Japanese beetles may be a problem for about 3 to 4 weeks. They eat the leaves and flowers. The plants are so vigorous that they quickly replace the damaged flowers and leaves as soon as the beetles leave in mid summer. Black spot and powdery mildew are almost non existent. Plant will tolerate downy mildew, which is seldom seen in the south.

PLANTING & MAINTENANCE

When to Plant: Roses from containers can be planted at any time. Fall is best because they establish easier in cooler weather, but you are more likely to find them at your garden center in early spring and summer.

Trimming: Once a year in late winter to early spring. Reduce the plant size by one half.

Fertilization: Medium. Fertilize at planting time and each spring with a timed-release product. Less fertilizer is needed with the application of more organics. See pages 46 to 49 for more instructions.

Roses, Other Easy Ones

2ND

CHARACTERISTICS

Plant Type: Evergreen or deciduous shrub, depending on variety.

Average Size: Varies with variety. Most shrub roses grow 3 to 5 feet tall and 3 feet wide.

Growth Rate: Medium. Roses need a year to become established and reach mature size after 3 to 4 seasons.

Leaf: Glossy, green, oval leaves with serrated edges, often turning reddish in cold weather.

Flower: Huge range in flower size and form. Most disease-resistant shrub roses bear double flowers to 3 inches across, with prominent stamens in the centers.

Origin: Man-made hybrids, most involving parent species from China.

Spacing: To allow ample space for air to circulate through the foliage, add 2 feet to the mature width of plants when using roses in groups or as hedge plants. Set plants that grow to 3 feet wide 5 feet apart.

Cautions: Beware of thorns, and do not plant roses with thorns in high traffic areas. 'Lady Banks' roses are thornless. Rose berries, or hips, make a nutritious tea, provided the plants are grown without using systemic pesticides. Roses are frequently damaged by deer.

Colors: Flowers are pink, white, red, yellow, and many bicolors and blends.

Velvet-petaled blossoms in flushes from late spring to autumn. Advances in disease resistance are bringing sentimental, softly-scented roses back into southern gardens. Rates a red ribbon.*

'Lady Banks' roses

Roses bring a romantic presence to the garden, so they are on every color gardener's wish list. The unfortunate reality is that the most beautiful roses are temperamental and prone to disease. Yet, there are a handful of modern hybrids capable of reblooming from late spring to fall that do not require constant spraying to keep them alive. Often called shrub or landscape roses, these varieties bear smallish blossoms with only a little fragrance, but they are pretty! Use these shrubs for the overall color impact rather than the intricate beauty of the flowers.

Regional Differences: Roses vary widely in how well they grow in different places. Local rose growers, called rosarians, can often recommend the best adapted varieties. In the coastal south, roses grafted onto nematode-resistant 'Florida' rootstock are preferred.

Color Period: Biggest bloom period is in late spring and early summer. Reblooming varieties continue to set buds sporadically through summer, and often bloom heavily in the fall. Length of bloom varies by type (see next page).

Buying Tips: Good roses are abundant in local garden centers, or you can easily order them online. Three great online suppliers are www.antiqueroseemporium.com, www.chambleeroses.com and www.JacksonandPerkins.com.

**Red ribbon plants are defined on page 13. For blue ribbon performance, follow the planting and maintenance guidelines on pages 30 to 49.*

Butterfly or Mutalibis Rose (right) opens yellow, changing through orange to a rich pink and finally crimson. Blooms off and on all summer, for an average of 10 weeks, often with multiple colors of flowers. Grows four to ten feet tall by six feet wide. Zones five to ten. Deciduous.

'Home Run' (right) is three to four feet tall and wide. One of the few shrubs that blooms a solid five to six months straight with almost no care at all! Susceptible to Japanese beetles. Evergreen to semi-evergreen. Zones five to nine.

'New Dawn' (right) is the #1 climber of all time, blooming heavily in the spring and then sporadically throughout its growing season. It climbs to about twelve feet tall by six feet wide and is maintained by cutting back the side canes to the main trunk after spring blooming. Zones five to nine.

'Carefree Beauty' (left) has a double pink, four to five inch blossom and is easily maintained at four to five feet tall by four feet wide. This rose flowers for most of the summer and is deciduous. It is disease resistant and hardy in zones six through nine.

'Fairy' (left) is a small rose, growing about two feet tall by three to four feet wide. It blooms profusely several times each season. Semi-evergreen. Zones four to nine.

'Lady Banks' (left) grows to twenty feet and is often seen at historical landmarks in the south. It blooms with yellow clusters for two to three weeks each spring. It is evergreen in zone eight and deciduous farther north. Hardy in zones seven to nine.

GROWING CONDITIONS

Light: Full sun to partial afternoon shade. Full morning sun is mandatory.

Water: Medium after establishment. Likes water once or twice a week during the growing season, depending on its environment. See pages 34 to 37 for more information.

Soil: For the garden, plant in any fertile, well-drained soil that has been enriched with organic matter. Use only good-quality potting mix for containers. See pages 28 to 31 for specific instructions on soil preparation.

Hardiness: Zones 3 to 9; varies with variety.

Propagation: Rooted cuttings or grafts.

Pest Problems: Japanese beetles may be a problem for about 3 to 4 weeks. They eat the leaves and flowers. The plants are so vigorous that they quickly replace the damaged flowers and leaves as soon as the beetles leave in mid summer. Black spot and powdery mildew are almost non existent.

PLANTING & MAINTENANCE

When to Plant: Roses from containers can be planted at any time. Fall is best because they establish easier in cooler weather.

Trimming: Once a year in late winter to early spring. Reduce the plant size by one half.

Fertilization: Medium. Fertilize at planting time and each spring with a timed-release product. Less fertilizer is needed with the application of more organics. See pages 46 to 49 for more instructions.

Spiraea, Bridalwreath

1ST

CHARACTERISTICS

Plant Type: Deciduous shrub (loses its leaves in winter).

Average Size: Easily maintained at 6 to 8 feet tall by 5 to 6 feet wide with annual pruning after it blooms.

Growth Rate: Fast

Leaf: Bright green, 2 inches long by 1/2 inch wide, finely toothed.

Flower: Double-rose cluster that runs up and down the stem. 1/4 inch long by 1/2 inch wide.

Origin: China and Japan

Spacing: 4 to 6 feet on center (measure from the center of each plant).

Cautions: Seldom damaged by deer.

Color: Flowers are white.

Loropetalum with spiraea

The pure white blossoms tell us spring is right around the corner. Great beauty and impact in exchange for an annual pruning that takes less than ten minutes! Easily rates a blue ribbon.*

This shrub is a favorite because of its graceful, arching form that is covered with tiny, rose-like blossoms in early spring. The blooms, which occur on old wood, appear before the leaves bud out, so the effect is spectacular. Tough as nails, bridalwreath spiraea is easily maintained with annual pruning. But be aware that, without this regular pruning, the shrub becomes unwieldy.

To lengthen spring bloom time of spiraeas, you might want to consider adding Vanhoutte spiraea (*Spiraea x vanhouttei*) to your landscape. While this shrub is similar to the bridalwreath, the bloom time is two to three weeks later, giving you over a month of early spring blossoms. Although this shrub flowers after the leaves appear, the flower is twice the size of bridalwreath and clearly visible. The dark green leaves make a beautiful contrasting background to the pure white blossoms.

Regional Differences: No difference in zones six to eight. Marginal in zone nine.

Color Period: Early spring (March or early April), for two to three weeks.

Buying Tips: If you can't find this one at your local garden center, it is available from online suppliers.

**Blue ribbon plants are defined on page 12. For blue ribbon performance, follow the planting and maintenance guidelines on pages 30 to 49.*

Botanical Name: *Spiraea prunifolia*
Family: Rosaceae

Companions: Plant bridalwreath spiraea with other plants that bloom in early spring, as shown below.

Azalea
Plant Profile: Page 200

Woodland Phlox
Plant Profile: Page 1164

Bridalwreath spiraea and some companions

Azalea (above, left) blooms in early spring, usually at the same time as the spiraea. Since the azalea is smaller (four to five feet tall), plant it in front of the spiraea. Both will grow in partial shade.

Woodland Phlox (above, right) is another plant that blooms in early spring. Since the phlox stays low (about 12 to 16 inches tall), use it as a border for the spiraea and azalea. All three plants do well in light shade.

GROWING CONDITIONS

Light: Full sun to light shade

Water: Very low after establishment. Lives on rainwater alone, without supplemental water, in all but the most extreme conditions. Maximum of once a week watering during very dry conditions. See pages 34 to 37 for more information.

Soil: For the garden, plant in any fertile, well-drained soil that has been enriched with organic matter. Use only good-quality potting mix for containers. See pages 28 to 31 for specific instructions on soil preparation.

Hardiness: Zones 4 to 9

Propagation: Cuttings

Pest Problems: Rare

PLANTING & MAINTENANCE

When to Plant: Spiraea from containers can be planted at any time. Fall is best because they establish easier in cooler weather, but you are more likely to find them at your garden center in early spring, when they are blooming.

Trimming: Prune 1/3 of the old canes right down to the ground after blooming, which only means (on the average) 4 to 5 pruning cuts. This quick pruning will give you a beautiful, well groomed, flowering shrub year after year.

Fertilization: Medium. Fertilize at planting time and each spring with a timed-release product. Less fertilizer is needed with the application of more organics. See pages 46 to 49 for more instructions.

**Lives on rainwater alone in all but the most extreme situations.*

1ST

Spiraea, 'Gold Mound'

CHARACTERISTICS

Plant Type: Deciduous shrub (loses its leaves in winter).

Average Size: A compact form, it is easily maintained at 2 to 3 feet tall by 2 to 3 feet wide.

Growth Rate: Slow

Leaf: Yellow-green leaf measuring 1 to 2 inches long by 1/2 inch wide; tiny serrations along the edge.

Flower: Small, pink flowers measuring 1 inch across. They bloom in clusters of 3 to 5 flowers.

Origin: Japan

Spacing: About 2 to 3 feet on center (measure from the center of each plant).

Cautions: Seldom damaged by deer.

Colors: Flowers are pink. Leaves are lime green, turning orange in fall.

1. *'Anthony Waterer' spiraea*
2. *Fall color on spiraea*

One of the best dwarf shrubs for foundation planting, with summer blossoms and yellow-green foliage to brighten your landscape from spring to fall. Minimum maintenance means a blue ribbon* for this colorful shrub.

'Gold Mound' spiraea

This new, 'Gold Mound' dwarf spiraea is a real plus for foundation planting. The bright, yellow-green foliage is an added bonus as it is in sharp contrast to the evergreens that are traditionally used in the foundation beds. This variety holds its leaf color better that other gold varieties and offers a colorful surprise, turning orangy red, before the leaves drop with a hard frost. Butterflies are attracted to its pink blossoms.

There are four other summer-blooming dwarf spiraea varieties that are both easy to grow and easy to find in local garden centers: 'Lime Mound,' which has pink flowers; 'Anthony Waterer' (largest of the dwarfs at four feet by four feet) blooms red; 'Dart's Red' has a deep red flower; and 'Shirobana' is quite interesting as it blooms with white, pink, and red flowers.

Regional Differences: In zone eight, very hot summer sun requires planting in an area that gets morning sun and afternoon shade.

Color Period: Blooms heavily for two weeks in May or June and sporadically thereafter. Use in the landscape for the color contrast the yellow-green leaf provides.

Buying Tips: Readily available in garden centers

**Blue ribbon plants are defined on page 12. For blue ribbon performance, follow the planting and maintenance guidelines on pages 30 to 49.*

Companions: Use this spiraea both for its flower color as well as its leaf color. For flowering companions, see the color calendar on pages 52 and 53. The leaf color lasts quite a bit longer than the flowers. The yellow-green leaves contrast well with dark leaves, like those of loropetalum and purple queen, shown below. Plant the spiraea in between the two, dark-leaved plants to break up the dark colors.

'Parasol' is another kind of spiraea.

'Gold Mound' spiraea with some companions

Loropetalum (top, right) is an evergreen shrub that has dark leaves that contrast well with the yellow-green leaves of the spiraea. Plant the taller loropetalum behind the shorter spiraea.

Purple Heart (bottom, right) is a low-growing, perennial groundcover that also contrasts well with the yellow-green spiraea. Plant it in front of the taller spiraea. All do well in light shade to full sun.

GROWING CONDITIONS

Light: Full sun to light shade. In zone 8, the plant performs better with morning sun only, otherwise very hot summer sun may scorch leaves.

Water: Low after establishment. Likes water every week or two during the growing season, depending on its environment. See pages 34 to 37 for more information.

Soil: For the garden, plant in any fertile, well-drained soil that has been enriched with organic matter. Use only good-quality potting mix for containers. See page 28 to 31 for specific instructions on soil preparation.

Hardiness: Zones 4 to 8

Propagation: Cuttings

Pest Problems: Rare

PLANTING & MAINTENANCE

When to Plant: Spiraea from containers can be planted at any time. Fall is best because they establish easier in cooler weather, but you are more likely to find them at your garden center in spring, when they are blooming.

Trimming: Prune annually by thinning out the old canes. Flowers can be deadheaded if you wish to increase blossoming.

Fertilization: Medium. Fertilize at planting time and each spring with a timed-release product. Less fertilizer is needed with the application of more organics. See pages 46 to 49 for more instructions.

1ST Viburnum, Chinese Snowball

CHARACTERISTICS

Plant Type: Deciduous shrub (loses its leaves in winter).

Average Size: Easily maintained at sizes between 8 to 12 feet tall by 6 to 8 feet wide.

Growth Rate: Fast

Leaf: Deep green, whitish on underside, oval shaped; 4 inches long by 2 inches wide.

Flower: A round ball, 6 to 8 inches across, composed of florets less than 1 inch across.

Origin: China

Spacing: About 8 feet on center (measure from the center of each plant).

Cautions: Blossoms do not hold up when dried for arrangements. Occasionally damaged by deer.

Colors: As the flower unfolds, it is a Granny Smith apple color (green), eventually turning white.

UNIVERSITY AWARDS

2005: Mississippi Medallion Winner.

2006: Georgia Gold Medal Winner

'Kern's Pink' viburnum has blossoms tinged with pink. Its blooms are smaller than the Chinese snowball.

This plants puts on a breathtaking show when it comes in to bloom in early spring. A tough shrub and easily maintained, it definitely rates a blue ribbon.*

Chinese snowball viburnum and purple pansies at Huntsville Botanical Garden.

The giant snowballs that cover this shrub causes a "jaw dropping" experience for all those who see it blossom in early spring. At the Huntsville Botanical Garden, there are three Chinese snowball viburnums planted on a triangle. When they bloom, they stop traffic! This plant needs a lot of space, so be sure to keep that in mind when placing it in your landscape.

Regional Differences: No regional difference in zones six through eight. Late spring freezes can burn the blossoms.

Color Period: For two to three weeks in early spring, starting about March 15 in zone eight; the beginning of April in zone seven; and mid April in zone six.

Buying Tips: There is more than one plant called a snowball bush. For the very large, baseball-sized blossoms shown here, be sure you have *Viburnum macrocephalum* (which means big head). Other smaller blossoming shrubs that are available include the Japanese snowballs, whose blooms are half the size; 'Kern's Pink' viburnum (pictured, left), whose blossoms are shades of pink; and 'Popcorn', which also has a white blossom.

**Blue ribbon plants are defined on page 12. For blue ribbon performance, follow the planting and maintenance guidelines on pages 30 to 49.*

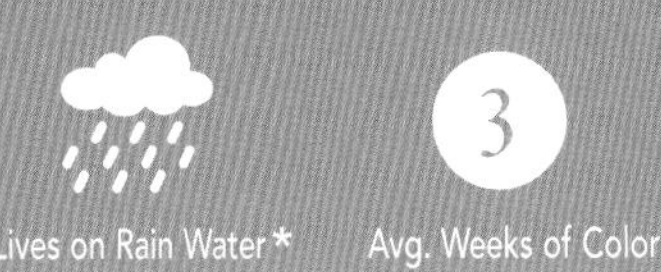

Companions: You will love the effect of early blooming flowers, like amsonia and baptisia, planted in front of this viburnum. And when it finishes blooming it is a great back drop for tall perennials and annuals.

Try this viburnum with azaleas and amsonia, as shown below.

Chinese snowball viburnum with some companions

Azalea (above, left) blooms in early spring, usually at the same time as the viburnum. Since the azalea is smaller (four to five feet tall), plant it in front of the viburnum. Both will grow in light shade.

Amsonia (above, right) is a perennial that grows three feet tall and blooms in April and May, usually coinciding with the azalea and viburnum blooms. Plant them in front of the taller azaleas in light shade.

Be sure to place the viburnum where it gets at least half a day of sun. Ideal light for this group of plants would be on the east side of your house or in an area that gets morning sun and afternoon shade. The viburnum and amsonia can take full sun, but the azalea will burn up with that much light.

**Lives on rainwater alone in all but the most extreme situations, although we had one report of it dying in a severe drought.*

GROWING CONDITIONS

Light: Full sun to partial shade. Blooms best and has most attractive leaf color in full sun. Very heat tolerant.

Water: Very low after establishment. Lives on rainwater alone, without supplemental water, in all but the most extreme conditions.* We have seen it growing on old, southern homesteads without irrigation for generations, but had one report of a death without irrigation in Canton, Georgia.

Soil: For the garden, plant in any fertile, well-drained soil that has been enriched with organic matter. Use only good-quality potting mix for containers.

Hardiness: Zones 6 to 9

Propagation: Cuttings

Pest Problems: Rare

PLANTING & MAINTENANCE

When to Plant: Viburnum from containers can be planted at any time. Fall is best because they establish easier in cooler weather, but you are more likely to find them at your garden center in early spring, when they are blooming.

Trimming: Annual pruning right after bloom time in late April to early May.

Fertilization: Medium. Fertilize at planting time and each spring with a timed-release product. Less fertilizer is needed with the application of more organics. See pages 46 to 49 for more instructions.

BUDGET GARDENING TIP

Since this plant grows quickly, you can buy small, inexpensive ones that will fill out in no time! And since this plant stops traffic, it is a high-impact plant for a low price.

1ST Viburnum, Doublefile

CHARACTERISTICS

Plant Type: Deciduous shrub (loses its leaves in winter).

Average Size: Easily maintained at 8 to 12 feet tall by 6 to 8 feet wide with annual pruning.

Growth Rate: Fast

Leaf: Deep green leaf, 4 to 5 inches long by 2 to 3 inches wide. Leaves grow opposite of one another, with prominent veins. Leaves are rough to the touch.

Flower: White lace caps that are 2 inches across, in pairs, on a 2 foot long branch.

Origin: China and Japan

Spacing: About 6 feet on center (measure from the center of each plant).

Cautions: May get a little leaf scorch on hot, summer days. Occasional damage from deer.

Colors: Flowers are white.

This viburnum has red berries in summer.

A beautiful floral display in late spring after the dogwoods have stopped blooming. Blue ribbon plant* that requires very little care.

This shrub gives a magnificent floral display in late spring. Its horizontal branching (shown, left) is quite distinctive. The lace cap blossoms come in pairs, opposite each other along the stem, and are presented for viewing against beautiful, dark green foliage. Butterflies love the flowers, and in summer, for a short period, this plant produces red berries that are a treat for the birds.

Regional Differences: None

Color Period: Late spring, for about two weeks

Buying Tips: Available at your local garden center and also from online suppliers. Other cultivars to look for that were introduced by the National Arboretum's breeding project are: 'Shasta' (its flowers are three to four inches across and will completely cover the bush) and 'Shoshoni' (a more compact shrub that grows to six feet tall by six feet wide). You also may want to try 'Mariesii,' which is a vigorous floral performer.

**Blue ribbon plants are defined on page 12. For blue ribbon performance, follow the planting and maintenance guidelines on pages 30 to 49.*

Attracts Butterflies

Attracts Birds

Avg. Weeks of Color

Botanical Name: *Viburnum plicatum var. tomentosum*

Family: Caprifoliaceae

Companions: This shrub has a shallow root system that is best left undisturbed, so it is wise to provide long-lived companion plants stationed nearby, but not right atop its root zone.

Plant it near hydrangeas and woodland phlox, as shown below.

Doublefile viburnum with some companions

'Mini Penny' Hydrangea (above, left) is a reblooming shrub that blooms for the first time in late spring, usually at the same time as the viburnum in zones seven to nine (provided there is no late freeze). Since the hydrangea is smaller (three to four feet tall), plant it in front of the viburnum. Both will grow in light shade.

Woodland Phlox (above, right) is another plant that blooms in spring. Since the phlox stays low (about 12 to 16 inches tall), use it as a border for the hydrangea and the viburnum. This group of plants does best in light shade.

GROWING CONDITIONS

Light: Light shade to full sun. Takes more shade than the snowball viburnum.

Water: Low after establishment. Likes water every week or two during the growing season, depending on its environment. See pages 34 to 37 for more information.

Soil: For the garden, plant in any fertile, well-drained soil that has been enriched with organic matter. Use only good-quality potting mix for containers. See pages 28 to 31 for specific instructions on soil preparation.

Hardiness: Zones 5 to 8

Propagation: Cuttings

Pest Problems: None serious, except for a fungal disease imported from California in 2003, which the nursery industry has taken aggressive steps to control. New plants set out in that year should be carefully watched for unusual problems and reported to your local extension agent.

PLANTING & MAINTENANCE

When to Plant: Viburnum from containers can be planted at any time. Fall is best because they establish easier in cooler weather, but you are more likely to find them at your garden center in late spring, when they are blooming.

Trimming: Thin once a year after the heavy bloom period. Prune a few older canes to the ground or back to the main trunk.

Fertilization: Medium. Fertilize at planting time and each spring with a timed-release product. Less fertilizer is needed with the application of more organics. See pages 46 to 49 for more instructions.

1ST Wax Myrtle

CHARACTERISTICS

Plant Type: Evergreen shrub.

Average Size: The largest type grows 10 feet tall as far north as zone 7, and 20 feet tall further south. If you need a smaller one, try 'Don's Dwarf,' which grows 4 feet tall by 3 to 4 feet wide.

Growth Rate: Fast

Leaf: Willow shaped, long and elliptical; 1/2 inch long by 3 inches long.

Flower: Very tiny (inconspicuous) flowers that cluster at the base of the leaves.

Origin: Southeastern US

Spacing: About 6 feet on center (measure from the center of each plant).

Cautions: Almost never damaged by deer.

Colors: Flowers are yellow.

A fantastic, native evergreen that is particularly useful for shady areas, although it takes full sun as well. Extremely easy to grow, rating a blue ribbon.* Attracts birds, and lives without irrigation.

Wax myrtle at Huntsville Botanical Garden

Since many evergreens are coarse textured, like most hollies, wax myrtle adds another texture to the mix. The leaves are light-textured, like a willow. The shrub has beautiful, blue fruit in fall that attract birds.

Wax myrtles are native to many different types of environments from zone seven to ten. Plants that can live in so many different temperature zones and adapt to wet and dry regions tend to be quite easy to grow.

Regional Differences: Sensitive to cold in zone six if the temperatures drop below zero degrees. Grows well in zones seven to ten.

Color Period: Flowers are insignificant in late winter to mid spring. Blue fruit that follows is attractive.

Buying Tips: Wax myrtles are available in different sizes. The largest grows ten feet tall as far north as zone seven and twenty feet tall further south. If you need a smaller one, try 'Don's Dwarf,' (shown, left) which grows four feet tall by three to four feet wide.

'Don's Dwarf' wax myrtle

**Blue ribbon plants are defined on page 12. For blue ribbon performance, follow the planting and maintenance guidelines on pages 30 to 49.*

Botanical Name: *Myrica cerifera*
Family: Myricaceae

Companions: For an evergreen grouping featuring different textures, try wax myrtle with Japanese yew and blue rug juniper, as shown below.

Japanese Yew
Plant Profile: Page 235

Blue Rug Juniper
Plant Profile: Page 238

Wax myrtle with some companions

Japanese Yew (above, left) adds a different texture to the group. Plant the yew, which grows two to three feet tall, in front of the wax myrtle.

'Blue Rug' Juniper (above, right) is a low-growing shrub that is so low it resembles carpet. Juniper's texture is quite different from both other plants. Since it only grows six inches tall, use it as the lowest plant in this grouping.

GROWING CONDITIONS

Light: Medium shade to full sun. Grows looser in shade.

Water: Very low after establishment. Lives on rainwater alone, without supplemental water, in all but the most extreme conditions. See pages 34 to 37 for more information.

Soil: Wax myrtles prefer good soil but will make it in clay. For best results, plant them in any fertile, well-drained soil that has been enriched with organic matter. Requires good drainage. See pages 28 to 31 for instructions.

Hardiness: Zones 7 to 10

Propagation: Seeds or cuttings

Pest Problems: Rare. Root rot can develop if plants are kept too wet.

PLANTING & MAINTENANCE

When to Plant: Wax myrtles from containers can be planted at any time. Fall is best because they establish easier in cooler weather, but you are more likely to find them at your garden center in early spring, when they are blooming.

Trimming: Trim once a year or as needed. Thinning is better than shearing, but the dwarfs take shearing well. Wax myrtles are more attractive with a natural growth habit than sheared into a meatball.

Fertilization: Medium. Fertilize at planting time and annually with a timed-release product. Less fertilizer is needed with the application of more organics. See pages 46 to 49 for more instructions.

**Lives on rainwater alone in all but the most extreme situations.*

Witch Hazel

1ST

CHARACTERISTICS

Plant Type: Deciduous shrub (loses its leaves in winter).

Average Size: Easily maintained at sizes between 8 to 12 feet tall and 6 to 8 feet wide.

Growth Rate: Slow to medium

Leaf: 6 inches long by 3 inches wide; dark green veins and wavy margins.

Flower: Fringe-like flowers, similar to loropetalum in shape; blooms appear on bare stems.

Origin: Southeast and midwest US

Spacing: About 8 to 10 feet on center (measure from the center of each plant). Often used as a specimen.

Cautions: Occasional damage by deer.

Colors: Native flower is yellow. Hybrids are yellow, orange, or red.

Great native shrub that gives fantastic fall color from its foliage and attractive flowers in winter. Slightly fragrant as well. A blue ribbon plant* because it is easy to grow.

The main benefit of witch hazel is that it blooms in winter, when few other plants flower. The only negative is that the leaves stay on the trees after they turn brown, which is unattractive.

Witch hazel is an old plant, with frequent references made in history books. Its branches have been used for divining rods, and its bark used by Indians as a medicine. Many other parts of this plant have been used for herbal and medicinal purposes as well.

Regional Differences: None

Color Period: The original, native witch hazel blooms in October and November. Many hybrids have been developed that bloom from January until March. If you plant an assortment of different witch hazels, you will have flowers from October until March. Each shrub blooms for about three weeks.

Buying Tips: 'Arnold's Promise' is the best-selling cultivar.

**Blue ribbon plants are defined on page 12. For blue ribbon performance, follow the planting and maintenance guidelines on pages 30 to 49.*

Southern Native Avg. Weeks of Color

Botanical Name: *Hamamelis virginiana*
Family: Hamamelidaceae

Companions: Use witch hazel with other plants that bloom at the same time. Since the different kinds of witch hazels bloom from October until March, be sure to check the bloom period of the one you buy. See the color calender on pages 52 to 53 for lots of companions that bloom at the same time.

Another concept is to combine the large, witch hazel leaves with smaller leaves and different textures. Try the yuccas and Japanese yews, as shown below.

Witch hazel with some companions

Yucca (above, left) makes a good accent in front of a witch hazel. The vertical, spiky texture contrasts with the green leaves of the shrub. Plant yucca either by itself or in a group of three in front of the vine.

Japanese Yew (above, right) adds a different texture to the group. Plant the yew on either side of the yucca for year-round foliage and texture.

GROWING CONDITIONS

Light: Light shade to full sun

Water: Low. Witch hazel is native to moist stream banks. We have seen it living without irrigation, but it might not look at its best. For best results, water once every week or two. See pages 34 to 37 for more information.

Soil: Any fertile, well-drained soil that has been enriched with organic matter. Requires good drainage. See pages 28 to 31 for more information.

Hardiness: Zones 3 to 9

Propagation: Seeds or cuttings. Seeds are slow to germinate; cuttings are faster.

Pest Problems: Rare

PLANTING & MAINTENANCE

When to Plant: Witch hazel from containers can be planted at any time. Fall is best because they establish easier in cooler weather.

Trimming: If you want to control height, cut taller branches back to the trunk (or the ground). This reduces height while maintaining shape.

Fertilization: Low. Fertilize at planting time with a timed-release product. Less fertilizer is needed with the application of more organics. In the years after planting, fertilization needs vary, based on the nutrients in your soil. See pages 46 to 49 for more instructions.

Yucca

1ST

CHARACTERISTICS

Plant Type: Evergreen shrub.

Average Size: Easily maintained at sizes between 2 to 3 feet tall and equally as wide.

Growth Rate: Slow to medium

Leaf: Sword-like, elongated leaves 2 to 2 1/2 feet long by 1 inch wide with a sharp point. Blue green, bright green, or variegated.

Flower: Tall spikes (4 to 5 feet tall).

Origin: Southeast and southwest US.

Spacing: About 3 to 4 feet on center (measure from the center of each plant).

Cautions: Sharp edges, particularly on Spanish bayonet (*Yucca aloifolia).* Almost never damaged by deer.

Colors: White flower spike, 4 to 5 feet tall.

'Color Guard' yucca. When you first buy yuccas, they are usually about the size of this one. They form clumps as they grow, thickening like the one on the top of this page.

Hardy, dependable, and tough as nails. Provides dramatic accent in the garden. Easy to grow, but some have sharp stickers that can cut your hands. Easily wins a blue ribbon,* but be sure to wear heavy gloves while handling any sharp yuccas!

The only way you can kill this plant is to overwater it. Give it any other extreme, and it does quite well. Yuccas thrive in hot, sunny parking lots and in front of walls that reflect a lot of heat.

Regional Differences: None

Color Period: Blooms once in June with a tall (four to five feet), white flower spike. One spike per clump.

Buying Tips: All of the yuccas we have planted have done well. 'Bright Edge' has yellow along the edge of the leaves, while 'Color Guard' (pictured above and left) has yellow in the center of the leaf.

'Ivory Tower' yucca

**Blue ribbon plants are defined on page 12. For blue ribbon performance, follow the planting and maintenance guidelines on pages 30 to 49.*

Botanical Name: *Yucca filamentosa*

Family: Agavaceae

Companions: Use yucca as an accent in the garden to break up groups of plants with different colors or textures.

For color contrast, use this yucca with the darkest leaves you can find, like the loropetalum and purple heart, shown below.

Yucca with some companions

Loropetalum (above, left) is an evergreen shrub that has dark leaves that contrast well with the yellow-green leaves of the yucca. Plant the taller loropetalum behind the shorter yucca.

Purple Heart (above, right) is a low-growing, perennial groundcover that also contrasts well with the yellow-green yucca. Plant it in front of the taller yucca. All do well in light shade to full sun.

GROWING CONDITIONS

Light: Light shade to full sun

Water: Very low after establishment. Lives on rainwater alone, without supplemental water, in all but the most extreme conditions. See pages 34 to 37 for more information.

Soil: Yucca tolerates clay, but prefers a better soil. Best to plant it in fertile, well-drained soil that has been enriched with organic matter. Requires good drainage. See pages 28 to 31 for instructions.

Hardiness: Zones 4 to 9

Propagation: Root cuttings or division.

Pest Problems: Rare. A little aphid gets on the flowers occasionally. Leaf spots in wet weather.

PLANTING & MAINTENANCE

When to Plant: Yucca from containers can be planted at any time. Fall is best because they establish easier in cooler weather.

Trimming: Trim flower spike off after it fades. Be very careful of the stickers and spiky tips on this plant. Yuccas form clumps that can be divided every few years by digging them out of the ground, cutting the plants apart, and replanting the smaller pieces.

Fertilization: Low. Fertilize at planting time with a timed-release product. Less fertilizer is needed with the application of more organics. In the years after planting, fertilization needs vary, based on the nutrients in your soil. See pages 46 to 49 for more instructions.

**Lives on rainwater alone in all but the most extreme situations.*

Other Shrubs & Vines that Deserve Mention

Agave
Agave spp.

Agaves give a sculptural look to the landscape. Some do well in the south. *Agave americana var. photoamericana* grows as far north as zone 7. Others are tropical. Most have dangerous spines and thorns. Full sun. Very low water.

Anise, Yellow
Illicium parviflorum

The toughest of the native *Illicium* species, yellow anise is a wonderful, 8 foot, evergreen shrub with attractive foliage. Small yellow-green flowers open in May for several weeks. Tolerant of both wet and dry soils. Medium shade to morning sun. Low water. Zones 6 to 9.

Barberry, Japanese
Berberis thunbergii

Deciduous shrub noted for its thorny stems and red leaves. 'Crimson Pygmy' is the best-selling cultivar that provides beautiful foliage color. Larger barberries are tough and vigorous but are proving to be invasive in some parts of the country. Full sun to light shade. Low water. Zones 4 to 8.

Beautyberry, American
Callicarpa americana

Tough, deciduous, native shrub that produces an incredible berry display in purple or white. Grows 8 feet tall by 8 feet wide. Easy to grow. Large clusters of berries grow up and down the stems. Birds love them. Full sun to light shade. Low water. Zones 6 to 11.

Burning Bush
Euonymys alata

Burning bush lights up the landscape in fall. The name is appropriate because the foliage turns an intense bright red like few other plants. Dwarf form is best selection for home gardeners. Becoming invasive in more northern locales. Full sun to light shade. Low water. Zones 4 to 9.

Clematis
Clemantis spp.

Flowering vine. *C. armandii* is an excellent selection. The *C. x jackmanii* group have the largest and most beautiful flowers but suffer in the extreme heat of the deep south. Sweet Autumn clematis (*C. ternufolia*) should be avoided due to invasive character while *C. virginiana* is a native, fall flowering selection. Full sun to light shade. Medium water. Zones 5 to 9.

Daphne
Daphne odora

Incredible fragrance makes this a plant prized possession. However, it will die in a heart beat leaving us wondering what happened. Excellent drainage is a must. 3 to 4 feet tall. Keep it on dry side. Better suited to zones 6 to 7, but grows as far south as zone 9. Medium to light shade. Low water.

Firebush
Hamelia patens

If butterflies and hummingbirds are your thing then your garden must have a firebush even in the colder parts of zones 6 & 7 (treat as an annual). Tubular orange-red flowers for 3 to 4 months on 3 to 4 foot mounded shrubs. Likes water but needs good drainage. Full sun. Medium water. Zones 8 to 11.

Fothergilla
Fothergilla gardenii

Spectacular, native shrub with white flowers that open in spring for two weeks. Scalloped green leaves take on rich shades of yellow, orange, and burgundy in fall. 5 to 6 feet tall by 3 feet wide. Light shade to morning sun. Low water. Zones 4 to 9.

Fraser, Red-Tip Photinia
Photinia x fraseri

Glossy, green foliage with brilliant, red new growth on a fast growing shrub. Unfortunately, very prone to a leaf spot that will defoliate plants in our hot weather. Cleyera is a much better plant although it doesn't have the brilliant, red new growth. Full sun. Medium water. Zones 7 to 9.

Gardenia
Gardenia angustata

One of the best plants for summer fragrance. Evergreen foliage on 6 to 8 foot plants covered in white flowers for several months of the summer. Zones 8 to 10, often needs protection in zone 7. Insects and nutritional deficiencies are frequent problems. Light shade to morning sun. Medium water.

Golden Dewdrop
Duranta erecta

Butterfly and hummingbird magnet in the tropical south. Lavender blue flower panicles bloom almost all summer long. Dies to the ground in zone 8. Not hardy in zones 6 or 7. Range from 4 to 12 feet tall, depending on growing season. Full sun. Medium water. Zones 8 to 11.

**Blue ribbon plants are defined on page 12. For blue ribbon performance, follow the planting and maintenance guidelines on pages 33 to 48.*

Jackson Vine
Smilax smallii

In many parts of the south, this evergreen vine has attained a cult status, adorning every porch or arbor. Thorny on the lower stems and thornless above. 6 feet tall this vine starts slowly and then leaps out of the ground. Blue fruits in fall that birds love. Full sun to medium shade. Low water. Zones 6 to 10.

Japanese Andromeda
Pieris japonica

Beautiful, evergreen shrub with glossy foliage. White flower panicles open in spring for 2 to 3 weeks. Needs shade, even moisture and good drainage to thrive in the south. Some cultivars have brilliant red foliage on new growth. Medium to light shade. Medium water. Zone 4 to 7.

Jasmine, Asiatic
Trachelospermum asiaticum

The predominate, evergreen landscape groundcover for lower south. Green foliage on vigorously growing plants can cover a lot of ground quickly. Cold damage below 10 degrees or with late spring freezes after warm weather. Have not seen flowers on this species. Full sun to light shade. Low water. Zones 7b to 10.

Jasmine, Confederate
Trachelospermum jasminoides

Evergreen vine used extensively in the lower south for green foliage and fragrant, white flowers. The flowers open in late April and flower heavily for 4 to 6 weeks and then sporadically throughout the summer. Vines grow 12 feet to 20 feet tall with support. Full sun to medium shade. Medium water. Zones 8 to 10.

Laurel 'Otto Luken'
Prunus laurocerasus 'Otto Luyken'

Evergreen shrub that is excellent in masses or low hedges. Dark green foliage susceptible to Shot hole disease. 3 to 4 feet tall by 4 to 5 feet wide with small, white flowers in May. Must have good drainage to survive. Full sun to Medium shade. Medium water. Zones 6 to 8.

Ligustrum
Ligustrum japonicum

Evergreen, large shrub or small tree. Glossy green foliage on plants 6 to 12 feet tall. White flowers open in May and are quite fragrant, but some might say they stink. While not as invasive as the Chinese privet, some caution should be taken in planting profusely. Full sun to light shade. Medium water. Zones 7 to 10.

Mahonia
Mahonia bealei

Evergreen shrub known for its yellow flowers in winter followed by an amazing display of blue berries. Easily grown in shade with no pest problems. However, the birds love the fruits and gardeners are finding them popping up all over. Many states listing it as invasive. Medium to light shade. Low water. Zones 6 to 9.

Mountain Laurel
Kalmia latifolia

Evergreen shrub closely related to azaleas. Large, white, or pink flowers open for 2 to 3 weeks in spring. Slow growing; 6 to 12 feet tall but some dwarf selections available. Prefers moist, organic soil with good drainage. Medium to light shade. Low water (but at least once every 14 days). Zones 4 to 8.

Nandina
Nandina domestica

Comes in many shapes and sizes. Widely planted throughout the south. Larger growing nandinas spread both by root suckers and by birds dispersing berries. Look for dwarf nandina that produce few berries. Many states list it as invasive. Full sun to medium shade. Low water. Zones 6 to 9.

Oleander
Nerium oleander

Commonly-used in zones 8 to 11 for its durability and long bloom period. Grows about 6 feet tall in areas that freeze. Blooms for most of the warm season. Very toxic (can kill people), and attracts caterpillars that can completely defoliate it. Low water. Full sun.

Pittosporum
Pittosporum tobira

Widely planted, evergreen shrub in the lower south. Variegated or solid green leaves. 2 to 8 feet tall with equal spread. Tolerant of poor soils, but needs good drainage. Not reliably cold hardy below 10 degrees. Full sun to medium shade. Low water. Zones 8 to 10.

Podocarpus
Podocarpus macrophyllus

Often called the yew of the deep south, podocarpus has deep green foliage. Used as a large, evergreen hedge along the coastal regions and throughout Florida. Cannot tolerate wet soils. Winter damage below 10 degrees. Full sun to light shade. Medium water. Zones 8 to 10.

Other Shrubs & Vines that Deserve Mention

Pyracantha
Pyracantha coccinea

Brilliant, orange berry displays that ripen in September and persist for several months before being eaten by birds. Evergreen shrub growing 6 to 10 feet tall with small glossy foliage and thorny stems. Fireblight can be a problem. Full sun. Low water. Zones 5 to 9.

Quince, Flowering
Chaenomeles speciosa

Prized for its early spring floral display of white, pink, red or orange flowers. Deciduous shrub with thorny stems. 6 to 8 feet tall. Tough, durable plant is often first to bloom in spring. Flowers are visible for 2 to 3 weeks. Many different kinds available. Full sun. Low water. Zones 4 to 9.

Rhododendron
Rhododendron spp.

Large, evergreen shrubs with spectacular flowers for 2 to 3 weeks in May and June. More at home in the cooler, mountainous regions of the south. Need a moist, organic soil with good drainage. More heat tolerant selections are becoming available. Medium to light shade. Medium water. Zones 4 to 8.

Rosemary
Rosmarinus spp.

Fine garden plant whether you grow the upright form or spreading (prostrate) selections. Deep green, needle-like foliage with white markings. Neat plants that are highly aromatic. Lavender flowers in late winter to early spring. Needs good drainage. Full sun to light shade. Low water. Zones 7 to 9.

Sago Palm
Cycad circinalis

This plant is a cycad that is commonly grown in zones 8 to 11. Poisonous to both pets and humans. Getting cycad scale in tropical areas that could wipe it out. It eventually grows 10 feet tall, but that takes eons. Usually about 3 feet tall. Light shade to full sun. Low water.

Silverthorn
Eleagnus pungens

Large, evergreen shrub (8 to 12 feet tall) known for its fast growth and tough, unruly character. Shearing makes it grow faster, so it is best to let it grow naturally. There is concern over invasive potential of several of the *Eleagnus* species, so consider an alternative like wax myrtle for an evergreen screen. Full sun. Low water. Zones 6 to 10.

Sumac
Rhus typhina

Native shrub with outstanding fall color. Drought tolerant and prolific in its growth. Many consider this a weed. New introductions, especially ones with deeply divided foliage make great garden plants. 'Tiger Eyes' is a great cultivar for the home garden. Full sun to light shade. Low water. Zones 3 to 10.

Sweet Pepper Bush
Clethera alnifolia

Fragrant, native, deciduous shrub that attracts butterflies throughout much of the summer. Flowers of white, pink and red open in late June for 4 to 6 weeks. Fall color is golden yellow. 6 to 8 feet tall. Tolerant of moist soils. Full sun to light shade. Medium water. Zones 4 to 9.

Tea Olive
Osmanthus fragrans

Flowers are incredibly fragrant. Blooms heavily in spring and fall; sporadically in summer. In the lower south, makes an excellent large, evergreen, screen growing 10 to 15 feet tall. Plants may be damaged if temperatures fall below 10 degrees. Full sun to light shade. Medium water. Zones 7 to 10.

Thryallis
Galphimia gracilis

Thryallis is a wonderful, summer-blooming shrub for zones 9 to 11, but is working its way into zone 8 with our warming trend. Informal, spreading growth habit. Grows about 3 feet tall. Blooms for most of the summer and fall. Low water.

Thunbergia, Sky Vine
Thunbergia grandiflora

Evergreen vine grows 10 to 15 feet tall. Beautiful, sky blue flowers open in May and persist through the summer. Tropical in effect. May be damaged as temperatures drop below 10 degrees. Highly invasive in subtropical areas. Full sun to light shade. Medium water. Zones 8 to 11.

Turk's Cap
Malvaviscus arboreus

This plant is grown as a shrub or small tree in zones 8 to 11. It's best feature is the intensity of the flower color, particularly the red one. Grows about 3 feet tall in areas that don't freeze. Low water.

**Blue ribbon plants are defined on page 12. For blue ribbon performance, follow the planting and maintenance guidelines on pages 33 to 48.*

Viburnum 'Awabuki'
Viburnum awabuki

Evergreen shrub with white flowers in May. Nice, green foliage on fast growing plants. Bright red berries can be seen if good pollination occurs. 'Chindo' is a superior cultivar. Must have good drainage. Full sun to light shade. Medium water. Zones 8 to 9.

Viburnum, Burkwood
Viburnum x burkwoodii

Excellent, deciduous to semi-evergreen shrub with beautiful, fragrant spring flowers. 8 to 10 feet tall. Flowers appear pink to red in bud opening to a pure white emanating a heady fragrance in the garden. Blooms for 2 to 3 weeks in April. Full sun to light shade. Medium water. Zones 5 to 8.

Viburnum, Leatherleaf
Viburnum x rhytidophyllum

Coarse-textured, evergreen shrub that grows 8 to 10 feet tall. Foliage is quilted, dark green in color 8 inches long by 4 inches wide. Creamy white flowers open in April and are showy for 2 to 3 weeks followed by clusters of red berries in fall. Full sun to light shade. Medium water. Zones 5 to 8.

Viburnum, Sandankwa
Viburnum suspensum

An excellent hedge plant for zones 8 to 10. Takes sun or shade, which makes it useful for hedges that grow through areas of both light conditions. Easily maintained at sizes between 2 and 8 feet tall with a few trimmings each year. Low water. Medium shade to full sun.

Virginia Sweetspire
Itea virginica

Wonderful, native shrub that has beautiful drooping panicles of white flowers opening in May for 2 weeks. Shrubs are semi-evergreen growing 4 to 6 feet tall by 3 to 4 feet wide. Found along streambanks and is tolerant of wet soils. Prone to suckering. 'Henry's Garnet' and 'Merlot' have beautiful red foliage all year. Full sun to medium shade. Medium water. Zones 5 to 9.

Wintercreeper
Euonymys fortunei

Widely planted groundcover to small shrub depending upon cultivar selection. Very susceptible to Euonymus scale. Often grows out of control and has to be removed. Interesting foliage colors include plum-red and white and gold variegated forms. Full sun to medium shade. Medium water. Zones 5 to 9.

Wisteria, American
Wisteria frutescens

Native vine with beautiful lavender-purple flower panicles in late spring. Flowers are 4 to 6 inches long and last 2 to 3 weeks. Vines are more restrained than the very aggressive Japanese or Chinese wisterias (that are more commonly sold). Can be trained into small trees or attached to arbors and trellises. Full sun to light shade. Low water. Zones 5 to 9.

Wisteria, Japanese & Chinese
Wisteria floribunda, Wisteria sinensis

This plant is commonly used in the south, and one of the most destructive to our natural environment. It grows like kudzu in our native forests, killing trees and whatever other plants get in its way. Do not plant it! We have a native wisteria on this page that gives you the same look without the risk.

Chapter 5

Trees

✿ Trees are one of the easiest plants in your garden. Many require no maintenance at all other than a fall clean up of the fallen leaves.

✿ Plant trees to provide shade for your house. Houses with 50 percent of their roof shaded save up to 50 percent on their air conditioning bills.

✿ Trees also provide shade to the plants underneath, which saves over 50 percent of the water the plants need to grow.

✿ One of the most common gardening mistakes is choosing trees that outgrow their space. Check out tree size carefully before planting.

✿ Check out this bloom chart to see how you can plan seven months of color with flowering tress. The bloom times are approximate because they depend upon temperatures which vary from year to year.

Bloom Chart

Tree	Jan	Feb	Mar	Apr	May	June	July	Aug	Sept	Oct	Nov	Dec
Carolina silverbell				■								
Chaste tree						■	■	■	■			
Crapemyrtle							■	■	■			
Dogwood			■	■								
Magnolia						■	■	■	■			
Redbud				■								
Smoke tree				■	■							

Above and right: Pink dogwoods

1ST Arborvitae

CHARACTERISTICS

Plant Type: Evergreen tree.

Average Size: The original, native species is 50 to 70 feet tall by 10 to 15 feet wide. Most garden centers only stock cultivars, which range from 10 to 30 feet tall by 5 to 8 feet wide.

Growth Rate: Varies. 'Green Giant,' the best-selling cultivar, grows quickly. 'Holmstrup,' a smaller cultivar, grows slowly.

Leaf: Fan-shaped, bright green; long, pointed fingers on scale-like needles.

Flower: Insignificant

Origin: *Thuga occidentalis* is native to the eastern US. *Thuga plicata,* the western US.

Spacing: About 8 to 12 feet on center for the 'Green Giant' (measure from the center of each plant). 5 feet on center for smaller varieties if you want to create a solid wall. Stagger the plants for a solid effect rather than lining them up.

Cautions: Occasionally damaged by deer. The 'Holmstrup' arborvitae has a reputation for being less tasty to deer than the others, but we haven't witnessed it.

Colors: Leaves are a medium green.

Differences Between the Species: *Thuga plicata* are the taller arborvitaes like 'Green Giant.' Their form is looser than the smaller *Thuga occidentalis* as shown in the photos on this page.

Wonderful evergreen available in a large size range. Great plant for a vertical accent or screening. Very little maintenance; easily wins a blue ribbon.*

'Green Giant' arborvitae (left) grows 30 feet tall, while 'Emerald' arborvitae (right) grows 10 to 15 feet tall.The 'Emeralds' were recently planted at five feet on center. They will grow together to form a solid screen.

Arborvitae is a valuable accent plant because it provides a vertical growth habit and a textural contrast to many coarser-textured shrubs, like holly. It is quite similar in appearance to both cryptomeria and leyland cypress. Look at the close up of the cryptomeria on page 277 to see foliage differences - arborvitae has a flat leaf, while cryptomeria has small needles spirally arranged around a stem. Both cryptomeria and arborvitae offer superior performance, so the choice depends on which one you like better. Leyland cypress, on the other hand, is suffering from both leaf blight and canker after about 10 years in the ground, so we don't recommend it.

Regional Differences: None for zones six to eight

Color Period: Flower and berries are inconspicuous

Buying Tips: Arborvitaes come in sizes ranging from 10 to 70 feet tall, so you must know what size you want before going shopping. The native species is the tallest, and it is seldom sold because cultivars are better for color, growth rate, and smaller sizes. All of the cultivars we have tried have done well, so have confidence in your garden center's choices, even if they are different from these. 'Green Giant' is the best-selling cultivar, growing about thirty feet tall by twelve feet wide. 'Holmstrup' grows ten feet tall by two feet wide, and grows very slowly. 'Emerald' grows ten to fifteen feet tall by three to four feet across, and also grows quite slowly.

**Blue ribbon plants are defined on page 12. For blue ribbon performance, follow the planting and maintenance guidelines on pages 28 to 49.*

Companions: Arborvitaes are often used in groups, particularly for screening purposes. They are also frequently used alone as a vertical accent, as shown right. Be sure to buy the correct size arborvitae if you plan on using it in an area of limited space. Also, plant it several feet away from your house so that you will have room to clean the house.

When using arborvitaes with other plants, combine them with different textures, as shown below.

Arborvitae and some companions

Chinese Holly (above, left) is a great companion for the arborvitae because its texture is so different. It comes in many sizes, from three to thirty feet tall. Choose one that fits your space. Plant it in between the arborvitae and the yew.

Japanese Yew (above, right) adds a different texture to the group. Plant the yew in front of the two other plants since it only grows two to three feet tall. Plant them all in full sun.

**Only Thuga occidentalis is native to the south.*

GROWING CONDITIONS

Light: Full sun, at least 6 hours per day.

Water: Low after establishment. Likes water every week or two during the growing season, depending on its environment. See pages 34 to 37 for more information.

Soil: Grows in unimproved soil, including clay, provided the soil has not been compacted. Compaction occurs most commonly from heavy equipment working around a house under construction. Requires good drainage and could die without it. See pages 28 to 29 for instructions on improving drainage and pages 32 to 33 for information regarding tree planting.

Hardiness: *Thuga occidentalis,* zones 3 to 7. *Thuga plicata,* zones 4 to 8.

Propagation: Cuttings

Pest Problems: Bagworms. Arborvitae are more susceptible than cryptomeria but less than eastern red cedar.

PLANTING & MAINTENANCE

When to Plant: Arborvitaes from containers can be planted at any time. Fall is best because they establish easier in cooler weather. Likewise, fall is the best time for balled and burlapped arborvitaes.

Trimming: Remove any dead branches as needed. You may never need to trim this plant for the entire time you have it!

Fertilization: Low. Fertilize at planting time with a timed-release product. Less fertilizer is needed with the application of more organics. In the years after planting, fertilization needs vary, based on the nutrients in your soil. More fertilizer will cause arborvitaes to grow faster. See pages 46 to 49 for more information.

Carolina Silverbell

1ST

CHARACTERISTICS

Plant Type: Deciduous tree (loses its leaves in the winter).

Average Size: 20 to 30 feet tall by 15 to 25 feet wide. Occasionally, it grows as tall as 70 feet tall, but that is very unusual.

Growth Rate: Medium

Leaf: Oval to elliptical leaves, 4 to 5 inches long by 2 to 3 inches wide. Dark green on top and lighter green on the bottom. Slightly hairy on the bottom as well. Yellow fall color.

Flower: White, 1 inch long, drooping bells with a yellow center. 3 to 5 flowers in each cluster.

Origin: Southeastern US, from Virginia to Florida on the east side, and west to Oklahoma. These trees only occur naturally in ecosystems called Appalachian cove forests. They adapt well to suburban landscapes throughout the south.

Spacing: About 20 feet on center (measure from the center of each plant).

Cautions: Seldom damaged by deer.

Colors: White flowers. Leaves are green in summer and yellow in fall.

Outstanding, small, native tree for the home landscape. Beautiful spring flowers followed by dark green foliage make this an excellent selection for a woodland garden or small lawn tree. Nice fall color as well. Easily wins a blue ribbon* because of its ease of care.

Carolina silverbell underplanted with tulips

Silverbell produces a rounded, oval crown that is attractive as an understory planting or as a specimen in a small yard. In spring, the flower clusters of pure white jump out at you as you walk through the woods or see it in an open location. Blooming after the flowering cherries and dogwood, this tree provides an extension of spring color in our landscape. As a lawn tree, grass can be grown underneath, since the root system as not as extensive as many other trees. Dark gray bark with subtle stripping makes an attractive winter silhouette.

Regional Differences: None

Color Period: Blooms for two to three weeks starting in late March in zone eight, mid April in zone seven, and late April in zone six. Leaves usually turn yellow for about two weeks in fall, but this color change depends on temperatures and rainfall.

Buying Tips: If you can't find this tree at your local garden center, shop for it online.

**Blue ribbon plants are defined on page 12. For blue ribbon performance, follow the planting and maintenance guidelines on pages 28 to 49.*

Companions: Other spring-blooming, native plants, like azaleas, and woodland phlox, make excellent companions, as shown below.

Native Azaleas
Plant Profile: Page 202

Woodland Phlox
Plant Profile: Page 164

Carolina silverbell and some companions

Native Azaleas (above, left) usually bloom at the same time as the Carolina silverbell and do well in the shade beneath the tree. The azaleas grow from six to twelve feet tall. Plant them on either side of the taller tree, taking care that they stay in light shade.

Woodland Phlox (above, right) is another plant that blooms in early spring. Since the phlox stays low (about 12 to 16 inches tall), use it as a border for the Carolina silverbell and azaleas. It also works well as a groundcover under the tree. All of these plants do well in light shade.

GROWING CONDITIONS

Light: Light shade to full sun

Water: Low after establishment. Likes water every week or two during the growing season, depending on its environment. See pages 34 to 37 for more information.

Soil: Grows in unimproved soil, including clay, provided the soil has not been compacted. Compaction occurs most commonly from heavy equipment working around a house under construction. See pages 28 to 29 for instructions on improving drainage and pages 32 to 33 for information regarding tree planting.

Hardiness: Zones 4 to 8

Propagation: Seeds

Pest Problems: None serious

PLANTING & MAINTENANCE

When to Plant: Carolina silverbells from containers can be planted at any time. Fall is best because even container specimens establish easier in cooler weather. Balled and burlapped trees are best planted in fall.

Trimming: This tree seldom requires trimming, only occasionally to shape the crown.

Fertilization: Low. Fertilize at planting time with a timed-release product. Less fertilizer is needed with the application of more organics. In the years after planting, fertilization needs vary, based on the nutrients in your soil. See pages 46 to 49 for more information.

Chaste Tree, Vitex

1ST

CHARACTERISTICS

Plant Type: Deciduous tree or shrub (loses its leaves in the winter).

Average Size: 8 to 12 feet tall by 6 to 8 feet wide.

Growth Rate: Fast

Wind Tolerance: Unknown

Leaf: Small leaves in pairs on the stem. Dull, gray-green on top with whitish-gray on the bottom. Leaves have a fragrance when crushed. Fall color is yellow.

Flower: Beautiful, upright panicles, 12 to 18 inches tall by 6 inches wide. Slight fragrance.

Origin: Southern Europe (Mediterranean region) to Central Asia.

Spacing: About 8 to 12 feet on center (measure from the center of each plant).

Cautions: Juice or sap is an irritant, which can cause painful blisters. Bees frequent flowers in summer. Almost never damaged by deer.

Colors: Flowers are various shades of light blue, white, or pink. Leaves are green.

UNIVERSITY AWARDS

2001: Georgia Gold Medal Winner

2002: Mississippi Medallion Winner.

Chaste tree trimmed like a shrub at the home of Peggy Baker, Louisville, Mississippi.

An outstanding, small tree that blooms for three to five months with very little care. Great for butterflies. Easily wins a blue ribbon* for its high performance with very little care.

Chaste tree trimmed so the trunks show. Home of Melanie and Niles McNeel, Louisville, Mississippi.

Vitex or chaste tree is an outstanding, small, multi-stemmed tree for your butterfly garden. Beautiful panicles of light blue flowers attract hundreds of native butterflies throughout the three month bloom period. Provide full sun and good drainage, and watch it take off, blooming profusely from a very young age. This plant was found in most antebellum, southern landscapes, so it truly has a home in the south. The leaves are attractive, resembling Japanese maples without the red coloration.

Regional Differences: Does very well in zones seven through nine. Marginally hardy in zone six; may die to ground in a harsh winter but will re-grow from the roots. Luckily, it regrows quickly, reaching six feet tall in just one season.

Color Period: June through September. Deadheading keeps plants full of flowers, if you can reach them!

Buying Tips: All the chaste trees we have tried have done well. Several selections based on flower color are available in garden centers. 'Mississippi Blues' is an excellent deep blue selection; 'Abbeville Blue' and 'Shoal Creek' are good blue selections; 'Alba' and 'Silver Spire' have white flowers; and 'Rosea' has pink flowers.

**Blue ribbon plants are defined on page 12. For blue ribbon performance, follow the planting and maintenance guidelines on pages 28 to 49.*

Companions: Chaste tree is excellent for attracting butterflies, so pair with other butterfly-attracting plants, like butterfly bush (English butterfly series), abelia 'Rose Creek,' black-eyed Susans, and echinaceas. Both lantana and pentas are also butterfly favorites, so try layering them with vitex, as shown below.

Chaste tree and some companions

'Miss Huff' Lantana (above, left) is one of the few perennial lantanas that dependably comes back each spring in the south, blooming from about July until November. It reaches about three feet tall, so plant it in front of the taller chaste tree.

Pentas (above, right) are annuals that are amongst the best butterfly flowers. They bloom on and off from May until the first frost. Since they are shorter than both the lantana and the chaste tree, plant them as a front border.

GROWING CONDITIONS

Light: Full sun

Water: Low after establishment. Likes water every week or two during the growing season, depending on its environment. See pages 34 to 37 for more information.

Soil: Grows in unimproved soil, including clay, provided the soil has not been compacted. Compaction occurs most commonly from heavy equipment working around a house under construction. See pages 28 to 29 for instructions on improving drainage and pages 32 to 33 for information regarding tree planting.

Hardiness: Zones 4 to 9

Propagation: Seeds or cuttings

Pest Problems: None serious

PLANTING & MAINTENANCE

When to Plant: Chaste trees from containers can be planted at any time. Fall is best because they establish easier in cooler weather, but you are more likely to find them at your garden center in early spring, when they are blooming.

Trimming: Late winter to early spring. Thin out older canes to encourage new growth from the base. Blooms on new wood so prune before foliage emerges in the spring. Occasional deadheading will keep flowers coming over a longer period of time.

Fertilization: Medium. Fertilize at planting time and each spring with a timed-release product. Less fertilizer is needed with the application of more organics. See pages 46 to 49 for more information.

1ST Crapemyrtle

CHARACTERISTICS

Plant Type: Deciduous tree or shrub (loses its leaves in winter).

Average Size: Ranges from 3 to 25 feet tall; width varies from broad bushes to upright, vase-shaped trees. Check plant tags for a cultivar's mature size. For information on shrub crapemyrtles, see pages 214 to 215.

Growth Rate: Medium

Wind Tolerance: High

Leaf: Dark green, oval leaves to 4 inches long. Turns yellow, orange, or red in the fall.

Flower: Triangular clusters of crinkled flowers, some with conspicuous yellow stamens. Clusters measure up to 10 inches long by 5 inches wide.

Origin: China, Japan and Korea

Spacing: Varies with plant size. At maturity, plants should have ample space to stretch their limbs into unobstructed sun.

Cautions: Almost never damaged by deer. Flowers that drop on pavement can make it slippery.

Colors: Flowers are white and many shades of pink, red, and lavender. Leaves are green in spring and summer, turning yellow, orange, or red in the fall.

UNIVERSITY AWARDS

1998, 1999: Mississippi Medallion Winner, 'Natchez,' 'Tonto,' and 'Sioux.'

1996: Georgia Gold Medal Winner, 'Lipan,' 'Sioux,' 'Tonto,' and 'Yuma.'

One of the easiest and longest blooming trees in the south. Blooms for 90 days and follows with gorgeous, fall color. Requires very little care; even lives without irrigation. Almost never damaged by deer, but birds love it.

Crapemyrtles are one of the most common trees grown in the southern half of the country. Whether grown as a shrub or a small, multi-stemmed tree, crapemyrtle thrives in hot sun, and humid heat actually intensifies its bloom. Crapemyrtles come in many more sizes (three to thirty feet tall) than most other plants, so know the size you need before you buy. One of the most common mistakes in southern landscapes is planting crapemyrtles that outgrow their space. Crapemyrtles have a beautiful form naturally and don't take well to severe pruning. If you need a 10 foot tree, don't buy a 30 foot crapemyrtle. Most modern cultivars resist powdery mildew, once a persistent problem, and some bloom much longer than others.

Regional Differences: Easily grown throughout the south. A few varieties are not hardy in zone six, but these are not likely to be offered by local nurseries.

Color Period: Most varieties begin blooming in late June or early July. If early blooms are pruned off as they fade, many crapemyrtles continue to bloom until September. Leaves usually turn yellow, orange, or red for about two weeks in fall, but this color change depends on temperatures and rainfall.

Buying Tips: Varieties that bloom for three months or more include: red 'Centennial Spirit' (10 to 20 feet tall); light lavender 'Muskogee' (20 to 25 feet tall); and the white, best selling 'Natchez (20 to 25 feet tall).

**Blue ribbon plants are defined on page 12. For blue ribbon performance, follow the planting and maintenance guidelines on pages 28 to 49.*

Companions: Play up contrast by growing yellow daylilies or black-eyed Susans near red or lavender crapemyrtles. Crapemyrtles thrive in open lawns, or you can underplant them with dwarf daylilies, variegated liriope, or heat tolerant annuals, such as vinca or 'Profusion' zinnias.

For a low water garden, plant crapemyrtle with 'Ever Red Sunset' loropetalum and 'Rose Creek' abelia, as shown below. All three of these plants live without irrigation in all but the most extreme situations.

Crapemyrtle with some low water companions

'Ever Red Sunset' Loropetalum (above, left) is one of the few plants that offers year round color (from its leaves) with very little water. It grows six feet tall, so place it on either side of a taller crapemyrtle. Both plants thrive in sun.

'Rose Creek' Abelia (above, right) is a wonderful shrub that blooms for about six months during spring, summer, and early fall. It grows three to four feet tall, so put it in front of the crapemyrtle and the loropetalum.

GROWING CONDITIONS

Light: Full sun, at least 6 hours per day. The number one reason crapemyrtles don't flower is too much shade.

Water: Very low after establishment. Lives on rainwater alone, without supplemental water, in all but the most extreme conditions. See pages 34 to 37 for more information.

Soil: Any well-drained soil that is not extremely compacted.

Hardiness: Zones 6 to 10

Propagation: Cuttings

Pest Problems: Aphids often are controlled by natural predators, or you can spray infested plants with insecticidal soap. Japanese beetles often eat leaves, but feeding stops as the plants begin to bloom. Older varieties are sometimes weakened by powdery mildew.

PLANTING & MAINTENANCE

When to Plant: If you plant in summer when the plants are blooming, you will be sure of the color. If you plant in fall, however, it will be easier to establish the trees.

Trimming: Many crapemyrtles are radically over-pruned. In late summer, a single deadheading will encourage reblooming, and you can lop off old flower clusters in early winter. Do not top back plants to their trunks, regardless of what you see happening in your neighbor's yard. Mature crapemyrtles often look best when pruning is limited to removing twiggy suckers that spring up around the base of the plant.

Fertilization: Low. Fertilize at planting time with a timed-release product. Less fertilizer is needed with the application of more organics.

**Lives on rainwater alone in all but the most extreme situations.*

1ST Cryptomeria

CHARACTERISTICS

Plant Type: Evergreen tree

Average Size: The native species is 100 feet tall by 25 feet wide. Cultivars are smaller. The most popular one is 'Yoshino,' which grows 30 feet tall by 8 feet wide. An even smaller cultivar is 'Black Dragon,' which grows 10 feet tall by 4 feet wide.

Growth Rate: Medium to fast for the native species and most cultivars. 'Black Dragon' grows quite slowly.

Leaf: Needles are short, only 1/4 to 1/2 inch long. They are wrapped around a long stem.

Flower: Inconspicuous

Origin: Japan, China, and Korea

Spacing: About 8 to 10 feet on center (measure from the center of each plant) to create a privacy screen. Stagger plants instead of lining them up in a row if privacy is the goal.

Cautions: Occasionally damaged by deer.

Colors: Needles are green

Note: Cryptomeria look similar to arborvitae, eastern red cedar, and leyland cypress. Look at the close up of the cryptomeria on the opposite page and compare it with the arborvitae on page 268 to see foliage differences - arborvitae has a flat leaf, while cryptomeria has small needles spirally arranged around a stem. Check out the eastern red cedar on page 283. It has a tighter form than the cryptomeria. Cryptomeria, eastern red cedar and arborvitae offer superior performance (although the cedar has a few more problems), so the choice depends on which one you like better. Leyland cypress, on the other hand, is suffering from both leaf blight and canker after about 10 years in the ground, so we don't recommend it.

Wonderful, fast-growing evergreen that has fewer problems than the similar, eastern red cedar. Extremely easy to grow. Needs almost no care except for occasional water and fertilizer. Easily rates a blue ribbon.*

Cryptomeria is fairly common in the south for good reason. It is a strong, evergreen tree that naturally forms into a nice, pyramidal shape. This self-forming quality means less maintenance for you. While many trees need trimming to shape them when they are young, cryptomerias shape themselves. Although cryptomerias get bagworms like eastern red cedars, their infestations are so minor they seldom require spraying.

Regional Differences: In zone six and the northern part of zone seven, cryptomerias can get bronzing of some of the foliage if the temperatures drop too low. This bronzing goes away during the next growing season.

Color Period: Insignificant

Buying Tips: The native species grows quite tall (100 feet), which is taller than most people prefer. The most popular cultivar is 'Yoshino,' which grows 30 feet tall, and is a great choice for screening. 'Black Dragon' is a smaller, ten foot cultivar that grows quite slowly.

**Blue ribbon plants are defined on page 12. For blue ribbon performance, follow the planting and maintenance guidelines on pages 28 to 49.*

Companions: Plant cryptomerias with different colors and textures. Since it is evergreen, it is a good companion for deciduous trees (those that lose their leaves in winter). Crapemyrtle and chaste tree are both deciduous and our longest summer bloomers. Try the cryptomeria with them, as shown below.

Cryptomeria with some companions

Crapemyrtle (above, left) blooms for up to three months. Choose a bright pink one to contrast with the green of the cryptomeria and the purple of the chaste tree. Since so many different sizes of crapemyrtle's are available, choose the one that best fits your space. Be sure to plant it in full sun, at least six hours per day.

Chaste Tree (above, right) grows eight to twelve feet tall and blooms for a about three months in summer. Like the crapemyrtle, the chaste tree needs full sun, at least six hours per day.

GROWING CONDITIONS

Light: Light shade to full sun

Water: Low after establishment. Likes water every week or two during the growing season, depending on its environment. See pages 34 to 37 for more information. It is difficult to tell when these plants need water, so put them on a routine schedule.

Soil: Grows in unimproved soil, including clay, provided the soil has not been compacted. Compaction occurs most commonly from heavy equipment working around a house under construction. See pages 28 to 29 for instructions on improving drainage and pages 32 to 33 for information regarding tree planting.

Hardiness: Zones 5 to 8

Propagation: Seeds or cuttings

Pest Problems: Needle blight or bagworms occasionally. Usually not severe enough to spray for.

PLANTING & MAINTENANCE

When to Plant: Cryptomeria from containers can be planted at any time. Fall is best because they establish easier in cooler weather. Likewise, fall is the best time for balled and burlapped cryptomeria.

Trimming: Since cryptomerias grow into a nice, pyramidal form with no shaping, this tree seldom needs any trimming at all. Remove dead branches as needed.

Fertilization: Low. Fertilize at planting time with a timed-release product. Less fertilizer is needed with the application of more organics. In the years after planting, fertilization needs vary, based on the nutrients in your soil. See pages 46 to 49 for more information.

1ST Cypress, Bald

CHARACTERISTICS

Plant Type: Deciduous tree.

Average Size: 60 to 80 feet tall by 20 to 30 feet wide.

Growth Rate: Fast

Wind Tolerance: High. (Pond cypress has a low to medium wind tolerance.)

Leaf: Bright green, needle-like leaves arranged spirally around the stem; 1/2 to 3/4 inches long, very narrow needles.

Flower: Inconspicuous

Origin: Much of the US; from Delaware south to Florida on the east side, and Illinois south to Texas on the west side.

Spacing: About 40 feet on center (measure from the center of each plant).

Cautions: Almost never damaged by deer.

Colors: Flowers are inconspicuous. Leaves are green in summer and a beautiful shade of coppery orange in fall.

UNIVERSITY AWARDS

2004: Georgia Gold Medal Winner

1. *Fall color*
2. *Seeds*

One of the best trees for creating a strong, vertical statement in the landscape. Fast-growing, fine texture with a pyramidal growth habit make this a wonderful tree for the home landscape. Takes wet or dry situations well. Easily wins a blue ribbon* because of high performance with very little care.

Bald cypress in summer and fall

While most people assume that it needs a wet site to grow, bald cypress is tolerant of a wide variety of soil conditions. Once established, this tree can withstand long periods of drought. The strong, vertical growth habit helps to soften large, brick homes, and the needle-like leaves have such a soft look and feel in the landscape. Fall color is outstanding, with rich shades of copper standing out in the autumn sun. Since the leaves are so small, leaf litter is not a problem for the homeowner, and fallen leaves can be chopped up by the lawn mower or used as mulch in planting beds. In winter, this tree presents a wonderful silhouette, with a flared trunk, reddish-brown fibrous bark and pyramidal shape. New growth in spring is a wonderful yellow-green that radiates from the brown stems. All in all, bald cypress is an outstanding native tree for producing shade in a hurry.

Regional Differences: None

Color Period: Inconspicuous flowers in March and April. Leaves usually turn coppery orange for about two weeks in fall, but this color change depends on temperatures and rainfall.

Buying Tips: The original, native species, *Taxodium distichum*, is an excellent choice. 'Shawnee Brave' is a cultivar that is narrower (20 feet wide).

**Blue ribbon plants are defined on page 12. For blue ribbon performance, follow the planting and maintenance guidelines on pages 28 to 49.*

Resists Deer

Lives on Rain Water*

Attracts Birds

Southern Native

Avg. Weeks of Color

Botanical Name: *Taxodium distichum*

Family: Taxodiaceae

Companions: Since bald cypress is native and attracts birds, combine it with other natives that also attract wildlife. Bald cypress looks good with plants that have different textures, so look for natives that are coarser. Both wax myrtle and yaupon holly are native, attract birds, and have a coarser texture than the fern-like cypress. An added benefit of these three plants is that they grow without irrigation (after the initial establishment period) in all but the most extreme situations. All three of these plants need almost no maintenance at all! Combine them as shown below.

Bald cypress and some companions for a low water, low maintenance garden that attracts birds.

Yaupon Holly (above, left) grows 15 to 20 feet tall, so plant a few on either side of the much taller (60 to 80 feet) bald cypress.

Wax Myrtle (above, right) grows 10 to 15 feet tall in zones six through eight. Plant a group of three in front of the bald cypress. Plant them in full sun, so that all three do well.

**Lives on rainwater alone in all but the most extreme situations.*

GROWING CONDITIONS

Light: Full sun

Water: Adapts to wet or dry situations. Can take very low water situations after establishment. Lives on rainwater alone, without supplemental water, in all but the most extreme conditions. See pages 34 to 37 for more information about watering.

Soil: Tolerant of a wide range of soils. Great choice for sites with poor drainage.

Hardiness: Zones 4 to 10

Propagation: Seeds or cuttings

Pest Problems: Rare

PLANTING & MAINTENANCE

When to Plant: Bald cypress from containers can be planted at any time. Fall is best because they establish easier in cooler weather. Likewise, fall is the best time for balled and burlapped cypress trees.

Trimming: Trim only to shape trees when young or to lift the canopy. Lifting the canopy means trimming off the branches that are closest to the ground at the trunk. The green tree shown on the left (opposite page) has had its canopy lifted, while the orange tree on the right has not.

Fertilization: Low. Fertilize at planting time with a timed-release product. Less fertilizer is needed with the application of more organics. In the years after planting, fertilization needs vary, based on the nutrients in your soil. See pages 46 to 49 for more information.

Dogwood

1ST

CHARACTERISTICS

Plant Type: Deciduous tree (loses its leaves in the winter).

Average Size: 15 to 25 feet tall by 15 to 35 feet wide.

Growth Rate: Slow to medium

Wind Tolerance: High

Leaf: 4 to 6 inches long by 2 to 3 inches wide; oval with a pronounced point at end of leaf. Light green when emerging, changing to medium green or dark green depending upon exposure. Excellent fall color of rich red and purple.

Flower: Actual flowers are small yellow-green masses only 1/2 inch wide. The white, showy part we think are petals are truly bracts (modified leaves) and measure 4" across. The 4 showy bracts are arranged around the small flower cluster that opens in early April, often around Easter. They open before the foliage emerges at the ends of bare stems and are showy for 2 to 3 weeks.

Origin: Eastern United States, from New England to Florida, and west to Texas.

Spacing: 15 to 20 feet on center (measure from the center of each plant). Allow a similar margin between dogwoods planted near houses or larger shade trees.

Cautions: Sap or juice is an irritant, which can cause skin irritation or blisters. Occasionally damaged by deer.

Colors: Flowers are white, pink, and red. Leaves are green in spring and summer and offer excellent fall colors of rich red and purple.

Springtime in the south and dogwoods in bloom - the two go hand-in-hand. What better signal that spring has arrived than to see the beautiful white or pink floral display provided by our native dogwoods. These small, graceful trees are truly a four season hit: beautiful spring blooms; excellent summer foliage; brilliant fall color and fruit display; and a lovely winter silhouette. Rates a blue ribbon* for its ease of care.

Historic dogwood at Huntsville Botanical Garden

Dogwoods are excellent, small flowering trees for the home landscape, provided you follow a few simple guidelines - do not plant too deep, keep the weed trimmers and lawn mowers away from the trunk, and provide adequate moisture during times of drought. The dreaded dogwood anthracnose disease crippling native populations in the forest has not been a problem for the home gardener, provided you give your tree at least six hours of full sun - morning sun being preferable.

Regional Differences: None

Color Period: Blooms for two to three weeks, usually starting around March 15 in zone eight, April 1 in zone seven, and April 15 in zone six. Leaves turn red in fall for about two weeks.

Buying Tips: While original, native seedlings dot the eastern hardwood forest, homeowners are best served by buying a proven cultivar. Cultivars have been bred for flower color, vigor, growth habit, and disease resistance. 'Appalachian Spring' is the only dogwood that is resistant to the dreaded anthracnose to date. Other worthwhile selections include 'Cloud 9,' 'Barton,' 'Cherokee Chief' (red blooms), and *var. rubra* (pink blooms).

**Blue ribbon plants are defined on page 12. For blue ribbon performance, follow the planting and maintenance guidelines on pages 28 to 49.*

Attracts Birds

Attracts Butterflies

Southern Native

Avg. Weeks of Color

Botanical Name: *Cornus florida*

Family: Cornaceae

Companions: Dogwoods suffer when their shallow roots are disturbed, so partner them with long-lived azaleas, or simply stud the ground with daffodils or other little bulbs. Cover the area within two feet of the trunk with mulch to retain soil moisture and protect the tree from accidental bumps with lawn mowers or weed trimmers, which invite problems with pests.

Combine dogwoods with other native plants that bloom at the same time for a truly southern flower garden. Native azaleas and woodland phlox are both natives that bloom in spring with the daffodils. Combine them as shown below.

Dogwoods and some native companions that bloom at the same time

Native Azaleas (above, top) grow about six to twelve feet tall and bloom at the same time as dogwoods. Plant them on either side or in front of the taller dogwood.

Woodland Phlox (above, bottom) is another shade plant that blooms in early spring. Since the phlox stays low (about 12 to 16 inches tall), use them as the smallest plant in the grouping. All three plants do well in light shade.

**Lives on rainwater alone in all but the most extreme situations.*

GROWING CONDITIONS

Light: Light shade to full sun

Water: Medium after establishment. Likes water once or twice a week during the growing season, depending on its environment. Dogwoods live without irrigation all over southern forests. However, they prefer more moisture than nature provides. They particularly show stress after several drought years in a row, and we have had lots of reports of dead dogwoods in natural areas following 2 years of severe drought. Also, they will not tolerate poor drainage.

Soil: Grows in unimproved soil, including clay, provided the soil has not been compacted. Compaction occurs most commonly from heavy equipment working around a house under construction.

Hardiness: Zones 5 to 9

Propagation: Seeds or grafting

Pest Problems: Twig borers, anthracnose, powdery mildew, and root rots in poorly drained soil.

PLANTING & MAINTENANCE

When to Plant: Dogwoods from containers can be planted at any time. Fall is best because they establish easier in cooler weather. Likewise, fall is the best time for balled and burlapped dogwoods.

Avoid planting dogwoods too deep. They will not tolerate deep planting. See pages 32 to 33 for proper tree planting instructions.

Trimming: Occasionally, just to shape crown and thin out dead, diseased branches.

Fertilization: Medium. Fertilize at planting time and each spring with a timed-release product. Less fertilizer is needed with the application of more organics.

Eastern Red Cedar

CHARACTERISTICS

Plant Type: Evergreen tree

Average Size: The original native tree is 40 feet tall by 20 feet wide. Cultivars vary from 3 to 25 feet tall by 4 to 12 feet wide. Sizes of some specific cultivars are listed under 'Buying Tips' on this page.

Growth Rate: Fast

Wind Tolerance: The wind tolerance of the eastern red cedar is unknown. However, the southern red cedar, which has a similar form, has a low tolerance for wind.

Leaf: Narrow, scale-like needles; short, about 1 inch long.

Flower: Yellow flower is inconspicuous.

Origin: This tree has the largest native range of any plant in this book. It is native to the entire US with the exception of south Florida.

Spacing: About 6 to 10 feet on center (measure from the center of each plant), depending on cultivar.

Cautions: Slightly poisonous. Do not eat this plant. Sap or juice is a skin irritant to some. Pollen from flowers aggravates hay fever in some. Almost never damaged by deer.

Colors: Flowers are insignificant. Leaves are different shades of green, including blue-green, light green, and very dark green.

One of the most durable trees in the south, seen in abandoned fields and homesteads. Very low water. No ribbon because it gets a few pests.

Eastern red cedar is one of the most common trees in the south. It is native to all of the United States except south Florida. This adaptability to a large climate range shows that it is tough enough to take whatever adverse conditions the 21st century has in store for us except for bugs and floods. Unfortunately, this tree is susceptible to both bagworms and is a host of cedar apple rust (see "Pest Problems" in the right sidebar). And it will not tolerate wet soils. The easiest way to kill an eastern red cedar is to plant it in a spot with less-than-perfect drainage.

Regional Differences: None

Color Period: February to March. Yellow, inconspicuous flowers that aggravate hay fever bloom.

Buying Tips: Both the original, native species and the cultivars do equally as well. Most of the cultivars are smaller or a different shade of green. 'Canaertii,' which features the darkest green foliage, grows twenty feet tall by six to eight feet wide in a pyramidal shape. 'Emerald Sentinel,' a lighter shade of green, grows fifteen to twenty feet tall by six to eight feet wide. 'Blues Burkii,' with steel blue foliage, grows fifteen to twenty feet tall by eight to ten feet wide.

**Blue ribbon plants are defined on page 12. For blue ribbon performance, follow the planting and maintenance guidelines on pages 28 to 49.*

Attracts Birds

Lives on Rain Water *

Southern Native

Resists Deer

Botanical Name: *Juniperus virginiana*
Family: Cupressaceae

Companions: Eastern red cedars are often planted together to screen an area. Be sure to use the smaller cultivars described in 'Buying Tips' on the previous page if you want a screen less than twenty feet wide.

Since eastern red cedars grow to the ground, it is difficult to plant shrubs underneath. Other trees are the best companions. Eastern red cedar is evergreen, so it works well with trees that lose their leaves in winter. When mixing eastern red cedars with other trees, choose different textures, as shown below.

Eastern red cedar and some companions

Chinese Elm (above, left) exhibits a completely different texture than the cedar tree, so the two show up well together.

'Natchez' Crapemyrtle (above, right) is one of the tallest crapemyrtles, growing 20 to 30 feet tall. Like the pistache tree, it loses its leaves in the winter. Since the eastern red cedar is evergreen, it makes up for some of the color loss by both the pistache and the crapemyrtle in winter.

**Lives on rainwater alone in all but the most extreme situations.*

GROWING CONDITIONS

Light: Full sun

Water: Very low after establishment. Lives on rainwater alone, without supplemental water, in all but the most extreme conditions. Requires good drainage, and dies without it.

Soil: Grows in unimproved soil, including clay, provided the soil has not been compacted. Compaction occurs most commonly from heavy equipment working around a house under construction. See pages 28 to 29 for instructions on improving drainage and pages 32 to 33 for information regarding tree planting.

Hardiness: Zones 3 to 9

Propagation: Seeds or cuttings

Pest Problems: About 50% get bagworms, which can be severe. Spray in May with the least-toxic suggestion from your garden center. Also a host of cedar apple rust, which is only a problem if you grow this tree near fruit trees, like apples, crabapples, or even pyracantha.

PLANTING & MAINTENANCE

When to Plant: Eastern red cedar from containers can be planted at any time. Fall is best because they establish easier in cooler weather. Likewise, fall is the best time for balled and burlapped cedar trees.

Trimming: Eastern red cedars almost never require trimming, just to remove dead or wayward branches or to shape.

Fertilization: Low. Fertilize at planting time with a timed-release product. Less fertilizer is needed with the application of more organics. In the years after planting, fertilization needs vary, based on the nutrients in your soil. See pages 46 to 49 for more information.

1ST Elm, Chinese or Lacebark

CHARACTERISTICS

Plant Type: Deciduous tree (loses its leaves in the winter).

Average Size: 40 to 50 feet tall by 30 to 40 feet wide.

Growth Rate: Fast

Wind Tolerance: Drake elm (a cultivar of this elm, but far from the best one) has a low wind tolerance.

Leaf: Small, dark green, oval leaves with serrated margins measuring 2 inches long by 1 inch wide.

Flower: Inconspicuous but occurring late in the year.

Origin: China, Japan and Korea

Spacing: About 50 feet on center (measure from the center of each plant).

Cautions: Juice or sap can be a skin irritant. Seldom damaged by deer.

Colors: Flowers are insignificant. Leaves are green in spring and summer, turning yellow with red-orange hues in fall.

UNIVERSITY AWARDS

1995: Georgia Gold Medal Winner for 'Athena.'

An award-winning tree noted for its tough constitution. Performs well as a street tree handling adverse urban environments. This translates well for the homeowner who, with just a little care, can have a wonderful shade tree in a short period of time. Easily wins a blue ribbon.*

Chinese elm is an excellent, fast growing, shade tree for the home landscape. Dark green foliage with good fall color are fine attributes, but the exfoliating bark is the outstanding characteristic. The small leaves make fall clean-up a snap, and fast growth makes it an excellent selection for a new home void of trees. The choice of cultivars with rounded canopies or the striking vase shape of our beloved American elm provides great selections for homeowners.

Chinese elm is also known as Lacebark elm for good reason - as trees mature, the smooth bark begins peeling away exposing colors of varying hues of copper and orange.

Regional Differences: None

Color Period: Flowers in August, but blooms are inconspicuous. Leaves usually turn yellow with red-orange hues for about two weeks in fall, but this color change depends on temperatures and rainfall.

Buying Tips: Several excellent cultivars are available in local garden centers. 'Athena' has a rounded, broad-spreading crown growing 45 feet tall by 50 feet wide. 'Allee' has an upright spreading habit similar to the vase shape of the American elm. 'Bosque' is a selection demonstrating a central dominant trunk and fast growth. All three have grown well at the Huntsville Botanical Garden.

**Blue ribbon plants are defined on page 12. For blue ribbon performance, follow the planting and maintenance guidelines on pages 28 to 49.*

Attracts Birds   Lives on Rain Water*   Avg. Weeks of Color

Botanical Name: *Ulmus parvifolia*

Family: Ulmaceae

Companions: Lawns grow well under this tree. Groundcovers like pachysandra and vinca minor also do well.

Use this tree with other native trees to create a southern forest. Since lacebark elm loses its leaves in winter, it makes sense to surround it with evergreen trees. Since it attracts birds, using other trees that birds like will be the beginning of your own, personal, bird sanctuary! Magnolias and eastern red cedars are native trees that are evergreen and attract birds. They also feature textures that are quite different from the lacebark, making them ideal companion trees, as shown below.

Chinese elm and some native companions that attract birds

Eastern Red Cedar (above, left) grows about the same size as the elm (40 to 50 feet tall). Plant them on either side of the elm.

Magnolia Tree (above, right) is available in different sizes. The southern magnolia grows 60 to 80 feet tall, and the 'Little Gem' magnolia is considerably smaller, reaching about 40 feet tall. Use whichever one fits your space better. Either works well with the Chinese elm.

GROWING CONDITIONS

Light: Full sun

Water: Very low after establishment. Lives on rainwater alone, without supplemental water, in all but the most extreme conditions. See pages 34 to 37 for more information.

Soil: Grows in unimproved soil, including clay, provided the soil has not been compacted. Compaction occurs most commonly from heavy equipment working around a house under construction. See pages 28 to 29 for instructions on improving drainage and pages 32 to 33 for information regarding tree planting.

Hardiness: Zones 5 to 9

Propagation: Seeds or cuttings

Pest Problems: None serious; resistant to Dutch elm disease; not affected by elm leaf beetles or Japanese beetles.

PLANTING & MAINTENANCE

When to Plant: Elms from containers can be planted at any time. Fall to spring is best because they establish easier in cooler weather. Stick to the cooler months if you are planting a balled and burlapped tree.

Trimming: Prune to shape the canopy when young.

Fertilization: Low. Fertilize at planting time with a timed-release product. Less fertilizer is needed with the application of more organics. In the years after planting, fertilization needs vary, based on the nutrients in your soil. See pages 46 to 49 for more information.

**Lives on rainwater alone in all but the most extreme situations.*

1ST Ginkgo

CHARACTERISTICS

Plant Type: Deciduous tree (loses its leaves in the winter).

Average Size: 50 to 80 feet tall by 30 to 40 feet wide.

Growth Rate: Slow

Leaf: Very unusual, fan-shaped leaves measuring 2 to 3 inches long by 2 to 3 inches wide. They occur in clusters of 3 to 5 and are a rich emerald-green color, changing to vibrant golden yellow in fall.

Flower: Male and female flowers are on separate trees. Both are small and inconspicuous. However, you want to select a male plant, since the seeds of the female have a foul odor.

Origin: China

Spacing: About 40 to 50 feet on center (measure from the center of each plant).

Cautions: Poisonous. Do not eat this plant. Also, sap or juice can be a skin irritant. Odors from female seeds is objectionable (see 'Buying Tips,' right). Almost never damaged by deer.

Colors: Flowers are insignificant. Leaves are green in summer, turning golden yellow in fall.

A fall day in the presence of a golden ginkgo is truly evidence of nature's handiwork. To see a blanket of gold resting upon a fresh green carpet of grass looks more like a painting than something that nature provides. Rates a blue ribbon* because of its ease of care.

When choosing a ginkgo, make sure you buy a named cultivar, so you are positive you have a male tree. The smell from the seeds of a female is memorable and not in a good way. Growth habit and fall color are the basis for cultivar selection, and several make excellent choices. Ginkgos are slow growers but become large trees, so give them room to grow. If space is a factor, try 'Princeton Sentry,' a narrow, columnar tree that does not have a large spread. Ginkgos are not particular about soil and have proven to be excellent urban trees if given space to grow.

Regional Differences: None

Color Period: Inconspicuous flowers in March or April for two weeks. Leaves turn golden yellow for about two weeks in fall.

Buying Tips: Look for named cultivars when purchasing a ginkgo tree. All named cultivars are male and will insure that ten years from now you're not holding your nose as you leave your house. Excellent choices include 'The President' (from the Presidents home at University of Georgia), 'Princeton Sentry' (a very narrow form), 'Autumn Gold' and 'Golden Globe.' All have wonderful, golden yellow, fall color.

**Blue ribbon plants are defined on page 12. For blue ribbon performance, follow the planting and maintenance guidelines on pages 28 to 49.*

Botanical Name: *Ginkgo biloba*

Family: Ginkgoaceae

Companions: Ginkgo looks magnificent as a single specimen with a lawn growing beneath. The blanket of gold created by the falling leaves is a true, natural masterpiece.

GROWING CONDITIONS

Light: Full sun, at least 6 hours per day.

Water: Low after establishment. Likes water every week or two during the growing season, depending on its environment. See pages 34 to 37 for more information.

Soil: Grows in unimproved soil, including clay, provided the soil has not been compacted. Compaction occurs most commonly from heavy equipment working around a house under construction. See pages 28 to 29 for instructions on improving drainage and pages 32 to 33 for information regarding tree planting.

Hardiness: Zones 4 to 8

Propagation: Cuttings

Pest Problems: Rare

PLANTING & MAINTENANCE

When to Plant: Ginkgo trees from containers can be planted at any time. Fall is best because they establish easier in cooler weather. Likewise, fall is the best time for balled and burlapped ginkgos.

Trimming: Shape crown occasionally when tree is young. Remove lower branches to lift canopy as trees grow.

Fertilization: Low. Fertilize at planting time with a timed-release product. Less fertilizer is needed with the application of more organics. In the years after planting, fertilization needs vary, based on the nutrients in your soil.

1ST Hawthorn, Green

CHARACTERISTICS

Plant Type: Deciduous tree (loses its leaves in the winter).

Average Size: 20 to 30 feet tall by 15 to 25 feet wide.

Growth Rate: Medium

Leaf: 2 to 4 inches long by 3 inches wide; bright, emerald green, with prominent veins and yellow fall color.

Flower: Small, white flowers measuring 2 inches across; blooms in clusters at the ends of each stem.

Origin: Southeastern United States, from Maryland south to Florida, and west to Texas.

Spacing: About 15 to 20 feet on center (measure from the center of each plant).

Cautions: Thorny stems; seldom damaged by deer.

Colors: Flowers are white. Leaves are green in spring and summer and yellow to red in fall.

Hawthorn in fall or early winter

Truly outstanding clusters of bright red berries adorn the tree from October until February, when the birds swoop in and strip a tree in a day. A tough, native tree with beautiful, white flowers in spring and bright, red fruits in fall make this a winning choice for the home gardener. Easily wins a blue ribbon* because of its ease of care.

'Winter King' hawthorn is an excellent, small, flowering tree that needs no special care. The tree provides four seasons of interest with very showy, white flowers in spring, crisp emerald green foliage in summer, yellow fall color, and outstanding fruit display all winter. Also, the trunk has a wonderful exfoliating bark of creamy tan that adds to the winter interest.

Regional Differences: Hawthorns do best in zones six and seven. They experience some heat stress in zone eight, so plant them in light shade if you live that far south.

Color Period: Flowers open in late April to early May after leaves have emerged. They bloom for two weeks, putting on a good show after most other spring-flowering trees have finished blooming. Leaves usually turn yellow or red for about two weeks in fall, but this color change depends on temperatures and rainfall.

Buying Tips: The best green hawthorn is 'Winter King.' Generally, this will be the only choice in the garden center.

**Blue ribbon plants are defined on page 12. For blue ribbon performance, follow the planting and maintenance guidelines on pages 28 to 49.*

Attracts Butterflies | Attracts Birds | Lives on Rain Water * | Southern Native | Avg. Weeks of Color

Botanical Name: *Crataegus viridis*

Family: Rosaceae

Companions: Plant hawthorn with companions that bloom at the same time and complement its flowers, as shown below.

Green hawthorn and some companions

The 'Pink Knock Out' Rose (above, left) blooms on and off from spring until fall. Spring, when the hawthorn flowers, is one of the peak bloom times for this rose. It grows about four feet tall, so plant it in front of the tree, in an area where it will get sun.

'Rose Creek' Abelia (above, right) is a wonderful shrub that blooms for about six months during spring, summer, and early fall. It grows three to four feet tall, so put it on either side of the roses. And, like the roses, be sure it is positioned in a spot where it gets sun.

GROWING CONDITIONS

Light: Light shade to full sun. Plant in more shade in zone 8.

Water: Very low after establishment. Lives on rainwater alone, without supplemental water, in all but the most extreme conditions. See pages 34 to 37 for more information.

Soil: Grows in unimproved soil, including clay, provided the soil has not been compacted. Compaction occurs most commonly from heavy equipment working around a house under construction. See pages 28 to 29 for instructions on improving drainage and pages 32 to 33 for information regarding tree planting.

Hardiness: Zones 6 to 8

Propagation: Cuttings for 'Winter King.'

Pest Problems: Rust, but this hawthorn is the most resistant of all the *Crataegus.*

PLANTING & MAINTENANCE

When to Plant: Hawthorn from containers can be planted at any time. Fall is best because they establish easier in cooler weather. Likewise, fall is the best time for balled and burlapped hawthorns.

Trimming: Seldom needed. Occasionally trim to shape the crown, especially when the tree is young. Also, thin out dead, diseased branches throughout the life of the tree.

Fertilization: Medium. Fertilize at planting time and each spring with a timed-release product. Less fertilizer is needed with the application of more organics. See pages 46 to 49 for more information.

**Lives on rainwater alone in all but the most extreme situations.*

1ST Holly, Yaupon

CHARACTERISTICS

Plant Type: Evergreen tree

Average Size: 15 to 20 feet tall by 8 to 12 feet wide.

Growth Rate: Medium

Wind Tolerance: High

Leaf: 1 1/2 inches long by 1/2 inch wide. Oval with smooth sides. No spines, like most hollies.

Flower: Inconspicuous, greenish-white flowers in spring.

Origin: Southeast US

Spacing: About 10 to 15 feet on center (measure from the center of each plant).

Cautions: Poisonous. Do not eat this plant. Hollies attract quite a few bees when they bloom. Seldom damaged by deer.

Colors: Flowers are greenish-white, but inconspicuous. Leaves are dark green with a purple tinge. Berries are bright red.

UNIVERSITY AWARDS

2001: Mississippi Medallion Winner, 'Kathy Ann.'

Dwarf yaupon holly is used as a shrub, and covered on pages 220-221.

Outstanding, small, award-winning tree. Native evergreen that provides berries for birds. Needs no irrigation after establishment. Takes sun or shade. Extremely easy, so it rates a blue ribbon.*

Yaupon holly is the ideal small tree, having all the characteristics that most homeowners want. It grows quickly, is evergreen, attracts birds, needs little water, grows in sun or shade, adapts to a variety of soils, and seldom needs fertilizer or trimming. Not too many plants exhibit that many positive characteristics. However, yaupon holly looks different from the more common hollies we use for holiday decorations. Instead of the coarse leaves with spines, its leaves are smaller and smooth-sided. It looks best grown as a multi-stemmed tree, like a crape-myrtle, rather than with a single trunk. Its branches will grow to the ground, or you can trim off the bottom branches to expose the trunk. Let it grow into a natural form instead of attempting to trim it into a lollipop shape.

Regional Differences: Grows beautifully in zones seven to nine. In zone six, it can show winter damage if the temperatures dip below minus ten degrees.

Color Period: Blooms in about April with inconspicuous flowers. The berries give the most color. They appear in late October or early November.

Buying Tips: 'Folsom's Weeping' is the most popular weeping form. Favorite upright hollies that have the most fruit include 'Shadow's Female' and 'Kathy Ann.'

**Blue ribbon plants are defined on page 12. For blue ribbon performance, follow the planting and maintenance guidelines on pages 28 to 49.*

Attracts Birds Lives on Rain Water * Southern Native

Botanical Name: *Ilex vomitoria*

Family: Aquifoliaceae

Companions: Yaupon hollies are often planted in groups for screening. They also fit well with other native trees, like bald cypress and hawthorn.

For a low-water garden, combine yaupon holly with lantana and 'Hameln' fountain grass, as shown below.

Yaupon holly and some companions

'Miss Huff' Lantana (above, left) is one of the few perennial lantanas that dependably comes back each spring in the south, blooming from about July until November. Like the holly, it lives without irrigation, after it is established, in all but the most extreme situations. It reaches about three feet tall, so plant it in front of the taller holly tree.

'Hameln' Dwarf Fountain Grass (above, right) is a perennial grass that blooms from July until September with the lantana. It also lives on very little extra water. Since it reaches about two feet tall, plant it in front of the lantana.

GROWING CONDITIONS

Light: Light shade to full sun

Water: Very low after establishment. Lives on rainwater alone, without supplemental water, in all but the most extreme conditions. See pages 34 to 37 for more information.

Soil: Grows in unimproved soil, including clay, provided the soil has not been compacted. Compaction occurs most commonly from heavy equipment working around a house under construction.

Hardiness: Zones 7 to 10. In zone 6, it can show winter damage if the temperatures dip below -10 degrees.

Propagation: Seeds or cuttings

Pest Problems: Rare

PLANTING & MAINTENANCE

When to Plant: Hollies from containers can be planted at any time. Fall is best because they establish easier in cooler weather. Likewise, fall is the best time for balled and burlapped hollies.

Trimming: Yaupon holly seldom needs trimming. Let it grow into a natural form instead of attempting to trim it into a lollipop shape. It looks best grown as a multi-stemmed tree, like a crapemyrtle, rather than with a single trunk. Its branches will grow to the ground, or you can trim off the bottom branches to expose the trunk. Remove the suckers (small branches) that emerge from the bottom if you like.

Fertilization: Low. Fertilize at planting time with a timed-release product. Less fertilizer is needed with the application of more organics. In the years after planting, fertilization needs vary, based on the nutrients in your soil.

**Lives on rainwater alone in all but the most extreme situations.*

Magnolia, Southern & 'Little Gem'

1ST

CHARACTERISTICS

Plant Type: Evergreen tree

Average Size: 'Little Gem' is 20 to 30 feet tall by 10 to 15 feet wide. southern is 50 to 75 feet tall by 30 to 45 feet wide.

Growth Rate: Medium to fast

Wind Tolerance: High

Leaf: Leaves are dark, glossy green on top and rusty brown underneath. 'Little Gem' leaves measure 3 to 4 inches long by 1 to 2 inches wide. Southern magnolia's leaves reach 6 to 10 inches long by 3 to 5 inches wide

Flower: Large, white, fragrant flowers measure 3 to 4 inches wide on the 'Little Gem' and 8 to 12 inches wide on the southern. Red seeds, quite attractive to birds, appear in fall.

Origin: Southeastern United States, west to Texas.

Spacing: About 20 feet on center for 'Little Gem' and 25 to 30 feet on center for southern magnolias planted as a screen (measure from the center of each plant).

Cautions: Seldom damaged by deer. Bees love flowers.

Colors: White flowers. Leaves are green on top and rust on the bottom.

Summer in the south means the sweet smell of magnolia blossoms in the air. Large, southern magnolias dominate the landscape where planted. Give this tree room to grow, and you will be amply rewarded with beautiful flowers, intoxicating fragrances, bright red fruits, and glossy green foliage. Rates a blue ribbon* because of its ease of care.

Southern magnolia

Southern magnolia has become one of the most widely planted trees throughout the southern states. The thick, coarse texture of the magnolia stands tall as a testament to its strength and longevity. Southern magnolias still dot antebellum plantations and provide breathtaking beauty and fragrance when in bloom. Magnolias look best when the lower branches grow to the ground.

Color Period: Heavy flower production in May and June; blooms sporadically through rest of summer.

Buying Tips: Numerous cultivars are available, selected for uniform growth habit, size, and excellent leaf color, especially the presence of the rusty brown texture on the underside of the leaves. If planting more than one southern magnolia, it is best to plant a cultivar, so your trees will grow uniformly. Excellent choices include 'DD Blanchard,' 'Claudia Wannamaker,' 'Bracken's Brown Beauty,' and 'Cinnamon Twist.'

**Blue ribbon plants are defined on page 12. For blue ribbon performance, follow the planting and maintenance guidelines on pages 28 to 49.*

Attracts Birds

Lives on Rain Water*

Southern Native

9
Avg. Weeks of Color

Botanical Name: *Magnolia grandiflora, Magnolia grandiflora 'Little Gem'*
Family: Magnoliaceae

Smaller in stature than its older brother, 'Little Gem' is definitely not short on performance. Flowers, fragrance, and foliage are all beautiful in a dense, compact package.

'Little Gem' magnolia. Be sure to plant them at least eight to ten feet away from a building.

For the home landscape, 'Little Gem' magnolia is most often the best choice due to its smaller size and stature. The beautiful, dark green foliage with rusty brown undersides creates a thick screen or hedge, and the flower production on this Magnolia is fantastic, with flowers opening as late as November in some areas of the south. This is a perfect magnolia for creating an espalier on a large, brick wall or fence. Again, understand the full size before placing in the landscape, and you will be rewarded with years of beauty.

Color Period: Heavy flower production in May and June and then sporadically throughout rest of summer. Flowers still present on trees at the Huntsville Botanical Garden in September and early October.

Buying Tips: The 'Little Gem' is the southern magnolia sold as a 'dwarf.' While much smaller in stature than southern magnolia, it still can reach heights of 30 feet. Other dense, compact selections include 'Teddy Bear,' 'Alta,' and 'Greenback.'

**Lives on rainwater alone in all but the most extreme situations.*

GROWING CONDITIONS

Light: Light shade to full sun

Water: Very low after establishment. Lives on rainwater alone, without supplemental water, in all but the most extreme conditions. Loses some leaves in severe drought. See pages 34 to 37 for more information.

Soil: Grows in unimproved soil, including clay, provided that the soil has not been compacted. Compaction occurs most commonly from heavy equipment working around a house under construction.

Hardiness: Zones 6 to 9. Trees in zone 6 may experience winter burn.

Propagation: Cuttings

Pest Problems: Rare. Root rot can develop if plants are kept too wet.

PLANTING & MAINTENANCE

When to Plant: Magnolias from containers can be planted at any time. Fall is best because they establish easier in cooler weather. Likewise, fall is the best time for balled and burlapped magnolias.

Trimming: None necessary. Plants can be grown full to the ground or with a clear trunk.

Fertilization: Low. Fertilize at planting time with a timed-release product. Less fertilizer is needed with the application of more organics. In the years after planting, fertilization needs vary, based on the nutrients in your soil.

UNIVERSITY AWARDS

1997: Mississippi Medallion Winner, 'Little Gem.'

2000: Georgia Gold Medal Winner, 'Little Gem.'

Maple, Japanese

CHARACTERISTICS

Plant Type: Deciduous tree (loses its leaves in the winter).

Average Size: 15 to 20 feet tall by 10 to 20 feet wide.

Growth Rate: Slow, especially for grafted ones. Medium for seedlings.

Wind Tolerance: High

Leaf: Delicate leaves, 3 to 5 inches long by same width. Rich colors of green to deep burgundy available - all with excellent fall color.

Flower: Insignificant

Origin: Japan and Korea

Spacing: About 15 to 20 feet on center (measure from the center of each plant).

Cautions: Occasionally damaged by deer.

Colors: Leaves are available in rich colors of green to deep burgundy, all with excellent fall color.

UNIVERSITY AWARDS

2000: Mississippi Medallion Winner, 'Bloodgood' Japanese red maple.

2005: Georgia Gold Medal Winner, 'Glowing Embers.'

Japanese maple is a true aristocrat of the garden. Delicate, lacy, formal in appearance, Japanese maples exude an aura of importance and dignity as they take their place of prominence in the landscape. They are pickier than most trees, however, requiring really good drainage, more than average water, shallow planting, and no damage to the trunk. They miss a ribbon for these reasons.

Japanese maples are the most popular choice for what designers would call a specimen plant. Aristocratic, regal, and statuesque are all apt descriptions of how a Japanese maple fills a space. There are so many choices for one to make, with the first being whether you want an upright growing selection that makes a small tree or a weeping selection that fills a space from the top down. The next choice is color, as Japanese maples come in a wide variety of greens, rusts, and reds. Japanese maples, along with dogwoods, require more water than most of the trees in this book. And it sometimes leafs out before the last frost, which can weaken the tree. These trees are easily damaged from lawn mowers and weed trimmers hitting their trunks.

Regional Differences: None

Color Period: Insignificant flowers appear in April for about two weeks. Japanese maples with rust or burgundy leaves have color all season. All Japanese maples have fall color for about two weeks.

Buying Tips: Cultivar selection is immense: first choose color of foliage (red or green); then, decide on shape and mature size (upright forms or weeping selections). Excellent red foliage cultivars for the south include 'Bloodgood,' 'Emperor I,' and 'Moonfire.' Green foliage selections include 'Seiryu' and 'Glowing Embers.'

**Blue ribbon plants are defined on page 12. For blue ribbon performance, follow the planting and maintenance guidelines on pages 28 to 49.*

Companions: Many gardeners collect different Japanese maples and combine them in different areas of their gardens. Here are some of the many choices currently available.

Unidentified Japanese maple

'Moonfire' Japanese maple

'Golden Full Moon' Japanese maple

Red Japanese maple

Acer palmatum var. dissectum

**Japanese maples with leaves in colors other than green have color the longest.*

GROWING CONDITIONS

Light: Light shade to full sun

Water: Medium after establishment. Likes water once or twice a week during the growing season, depending on its environment. See pages 34 to 37 for more information.

Soil: Plant in any fertile, well-drained soil that has been enriched with organic matter. This tree cannot tolerate poor drainage.

Hardiness: Zones 5 to 8

Propagation: Seeds or grafts

Pest Problems: Rare

PLANTING & MAINTENANCE

When to Plant: Japanese maples from containers can be planted at any time. Fall is best because they establish easier in cooler weather. Likewise, fall is the best time for balled and burlapped maples. Take care to not to plant these trees too deep.

Trimming: Occasionally, just to shape crown and thin out dead, diseased and crossing branches.

Fertilization: Medium. Fertilize at planting time and each spring with a timed-release product. Less fertilizer is needed with the application of more organics.

'Oshi Beni' Japanese maple in summer.

Maple, Red and Sugar

1ST

CHARACTERISTICS

Plant Type: Deciduous tree

Average Size: Red maple is 40 to 60 feet tall by 30 to 40 feet wide. Sugar maple is 60 to 80 feet tall by 40 to 60 feet wide.

Growth Rate: Red maple is fast; sugar maple grows slowly.

Leaf: Red maple's leaves are medium green, measuring 3 to 5 inches long by 2 to 4 inches wide with 3 to 5 pointed lobes. Sugar maple's leaves are medium green leaves measuring 4 to 6 inches long by 3 to 5 inches wide; 3 to 5 pointed lobes (or tips) with deep indentations.

Flower: Both trees have insignificant flowers. However, the fruits of the red maple create a mess when they fall, unless the tree is one of the newer cultivars that don't produce seeds, like 'Brandywine.'

Origin: Red maple is native to the eastern United States - Maine south to Florida, west to a line from Minnesota south to Texas. Sugar maple is native to the eastern United States - Maine to Georgia, west to Texas.

Spacing: Red maples about 30 to 40 feet on center. Sugar maples about 40 to 50 feet on center.

Cautions: Occasionally damaged by deer.

Colors: Flowers are insignificant. Leaves are green in spring and summer. Fall leaf color is outstanding, with differing tints of yellow, orange, red, and purple.

UNIVERSITY AWARDS

2003: Mississippi Medallion Winner, 'Autumn Blaze,' a red maple.

Without a doubt, red maple is the most widely planted shade tree for new homeowners over the past twenty years. Excellent growth habit, fall color, and ease of care make this an easy choice for new tree plantings. For setting an October sky on fire, red maple is the tree of choice in the south. Easily wins a blue ribbon* for its high performance and ease of care.

Red maple is a perfect choice for one desiring to have an excellent shade tree in the shortest amount of time. Faster growing than the native oaks and sugar maple, red maple will reward the homeowner with a full canopy of shade without the problems associated with other, less desirable, 'fast' growing trees (such as limb breakage and split trunks from trees like Bradford pears). Fall color is outstanding, providing many variations of brilliant red - this tree has proven to be one of the most reliable producers of red fall color in the south.

Regional Differences: None for zones six to nine

Color Period: Insignificant flowers in March or April. Leaf color is outstanding for about two weeks in fall. Individual cultivars develop leaf color at different times in the fall.

Buying Tips: Numerous cultivars are available that have been selected for growth habit, vigor, and fall color. The proven cultivars are superior to the native species. You'll know it's a cultivar if it has another name after red maple. 'Red Sunset' (shown above and right) and 'October Glory' are two old, reliable cultivars. 'Brandywine' is a new male selection from the US National Arboretum that does not produce any bothersome seeds. Since individual cultivars will exhibit fall color at different times, plant more than one type for an extended fall color display.

*Blue ribbon plants are defined on page 12. For blue ribbon performance, follow the planting and maintenance guidelines on pages 28 to 49.

Botanical Names: *Acer rubrum* and *Acer saccharum*

Family: Aceraceae

Sugar maple is the tree you wish your grandfather had planted for you 50 years ago, so you could marvel at its magnificence today. It is an absolutely beautiful large shade tree for size, shape, and fall color. Rates a blue ribbon because it is easy to grow.

This tree needs space to truly shine, so be sure to give it room to grow. The fall foliage display of sugar maple is second to none, especially since we get such a tapestry of colors ranging from yellow to orange to red. Sugar maple is an excellent choice for a large shade tree in the home landscape, if you have the room for it to grow and the patience to let it mature. While it is very tolerant of neglect (that is, low water and fertilizer), the better care you provide as a young tree will enable it to grow faster and provide you with the large canopy you desire.

Regional Differences: None for zones six to nine. However, choosing a cultivar (like 'Caddo') for heat tolerance is desirable in zones eight to nine.

Color Period: Insignificant flowers for about two weeks in late March or April. Fall leaf color is outstanding with differing tints of yellow and orange for about two weeks, and red as shown on the opposite page.

Buying Tips: Cultivars of sugar maple are superior to one just labeled 'Sugar Maple' because they have better growth habits, vigor, and fall color. Look for an additional name of the tag. 'Commemoration,' 'Green Mountain,' 'Legacy,' and 'Bonfire' are excellent cultivars. 'Caddo' is a selection from Oklahoma that exhibits excellent wind and heat tolerance.

GROWING CONDITIONS

Light: Light shade to full sun

Water: Low after establishment. Likes water every week or two during the growing season, depending on its environment. Red maples live without irrigation but will lose leaves during droughts. See pages 34 to 37 for more information.

Soil: Grows in unimproved soil, including clay, provided the soil has not been compacted. Compaction occurs most commonly from heavy equipment working around a house under construction. See pages 28 to 29 for instructions on improving drainage and pages 32 to 33 for information regarding tree planting.

Hardiness: Zones 4 to 9

Propagation: Seeds or cuttings

Pest Problems: Leaf hoppers and twig borers can be troublesome.

PLANTING & MAINTENANCE

When to Plant: Maples from containers can be planted at any time. Fall is best because they establish easier in cooler weather. Likewise, fall is the best time for balled and burlapped maples.

Trimming: Prune to shape when young. Since maples are opposite branched, one often needs to train a central trunk from an area where two buds are growing from the same location.

Fertilization: Low. Fertilize at planting time with a timed-release product. Less fertilizer is needed with the application of more organics. In the years after planting, fertilization needs vary, based on the nutrients in your soil. See pages 46 to 49 for more information.

1ST Oak, Shumard and Willow

CHARACTERISTICS

Plant Type: Deciduous tree

Average Size: Shumard oak is 50 to 60 feet tall by 40 to 50 feet wide. Willow oak is 50 to 70 feet tall by 35 to 45 feet wide.

Growth Rate: Shumard oak is medium to fast. Willow oak is medium.

Leaf: Shumard oak's leaves are large, dark green leaves, 6 to 8 inches long by 4 to 5 inches wide with 7 to 9 pointed lobes. Willow oak's leaves are lance shaped, 3 to 5 inches long by 1/2 inch wide; resembles a willow leaf. Dark green in color changing to yellow-brown in fall.

Flower: Unlike most plants, these oaks have two different flowers, one male and another female. Both flowers appear on same tree. Male flowers are furry clusters; female flowers are small. Flowers emerge in spring and bloom for two weeks.

Origin: Shumard oak is native to the eastern US. Willow oak is native to most of the eastern United States, from New York south to Florida, and moving west to Texas, Missouri, and Oklahoma.

Spacing: About 60 feet on center (measure from the center of each plant).

Cautions: Slightly poisonous to some. Do not eat this plant. Acorns are eaten by deer.

Colors: Flowers are insignificant. Leaves are green in spring and summer. In fall, leaves fluctuate between brilliant red to brownish-red, depending on weather.

UNIVERSITY AWARDS

Superior rating in Auburn University Shade Tree Evaluation.

Wonderful, native oak with brilliant red, fall color. Excellent tree for a wide variety of soil types and tolerant of dry and windy sites. Fast growth and easy care are great attributes for a long-lived, blue ribbon* shade tree.

Far superior to pin oak in the landscape, shumard oak does not suffer from the unsightly chlorosis (leaf yellowing) that often plagues pin oak. This is a superior tree for street tree plantings in urban environments and as a large shade tree for the lawn. Foliage is much larger and coarser than willow oak, but it does develop brilliant reds to russet red-brown colors in the fall. Shumard oak is an excellent shade tree for the long haul - it will give you many years of outstanding service, providing cooling shade in summer, outstanding fall color, and a distinctive, statuesque form in the winter landscape. Shumard oaks provide a beautiful avenue of trees as one enters the Huntsville Botanical Garden.

Regional Differences: None

Color Period: Insignificant flowers for about two weeks in April. Leaves usually turn red to brownish-red for about two weeks in fall, but this color change depends on temperatures and rainfall.

Buying Tips: The native species is the only one available, and you can't go wrong with it. No cultivars have been developed yet.

**Blue ribbon plants are defined on page 12. For blue ribbon performance, follow the planting and maintenance guidelines on pages 28 to 49.*

2

Botanical Names: *Quercus shumardii, Q. phellos*
Family: Fagaceae

Willow oak is the most widely planted oak in the south, especially on commercial landscapes. Very easy to grow and tolerant of many different sites, so it rates a blue ribbon. One of the faster growing oak species, so mature trees can be obtained in a relatively short period of time.

Willow oak at Huntsville Botanical Garden

Excellent tree for the home landscape, especially for its fine texture and easy, fall clean up since the leaves are so small compared to other native oaks. Willow oak has a pyramidal growth habit when young, becoming rounded with age. The slick, silvery-gray bark is distinctive in winter and develops darker ridges and furrows as trees mature. Fall color is a golden brown - while not as striking as the rich reds of some oaks, it is attractive nonetheless. Homeowners looking for a large shade tree will be very pleased with the selection of willow oak.

Regional Differences: None

Color Period: Insignificant flowers for about two weeks in April. Leaves usually turn yellowish brown for about two weeks in fall, but this color change depends on temperatures and rainfall.

Buying Tips: The native species is widely available in garden centers. A few cultivars have been introduced, but we have not tested the benefits of these selections.

GROWING CONDITIONS

Light: Light shade to full sun

Water: Very low after establishment. Lives on rainwater alone, without supplemental water, in all but the most extreme conditions. See pages 34 to 37 for more information.

Soil: Grows in unimproved soil, including clay, provided that the soil has not been compacted. Compaction occurs most commonly from heavy equipment working around a house under construction. See pages 28 to 29 for instructions on improving drainage and pages 32 to 33 for information regarding tree planting.

Hardiness: Zones 5 to 9

Propagation: Seeds

Pest Problems: None serious, but some foliar diseases occur occasionally.

PLANTING & MAINTENANCE

When to Plant: Oaks from containers can be planted at any time. Fall is best because they establish easier in cooler weather. Likewise, fall is the best time for balled and burlapped oaks.

Trimming: Prune to shape when young to develop a well-shaped canopy. As the tree ages, it may be necessary to remove lower branches to raise the canopy.

Fertilization: Low. Fertilize at planting time with a timed-release product. Less fertilizer is needed with the application of more organics. In the years after planting, fertilization needs vary, based on the nutrients in your soil. See pages 46 to 49 for more information.

**Lives on rainwater alone in all but the most extreme situations.*

Palms

1ST

CHARACTERISTICS

Plant Type: Evergreen tree, although the needle palm is so short it is also considered a shrub.

Average Size: Varies by type

Wind Tolerance: The sabal palm has a very high tolerance for wind. It was judged the second strongest tree in the strongest hurricane on record (Camille) by Dr. Mary Duryea of University of Florida. The needle and European fan palm's wind tolerance in unknown.

Growth Rate: All four of these palms grow slowly, particularly at the northern limits of their temperature range.

Leaf: European fan palm's leaves are about 3 feet in diameter. Sabal palm's leaves grow 6 feet in diameter. Windmill palm leaves are 2 to 3 feet wide. Needle palm leaves are 3 feet wide.

Flower: Insignificant

Origin: Sabal and needle palms are native to the southeastern US. European fan palms are native to the Mediterranean region. Windmill palms come from China.

Spacing: About 5 to 10 feet on center (measure from the center of each plant).

Cautions: Sap is a skin irritant to some. European fan palms have sharp spines along the fronds. Windmill and needle palms are slightly spiny.

Colors: Flowers are insignificant. Leaves are different shades of green.

These are exceptionally easy palms for much of the south. Very low water. Easily win a blue ribbon.*

Needle palm, Rhapidophyllum hystrix

The needle palm (shown, above) is one of the most cold-hardy palms, doing well at Huntsville Botanical Garden (zone seven) for twenty years without any dieback. It provides a wonderful, large, evergreen mass of coarse texture in the 'Fern Glade,' and has required no maintenance at all! The name comes from the six-inch long, black needles that protrude from the leaf stalk that protect the plants seeds. These needles make the plant deer-proof, so this is an excellent choice for gardeners who are struggling to confound deer. It is a slow-growing, rather shrubby palm that only reaches about six to eight feet tall by four to eight feet wide.

Cold tolerance is more important for palms than for most other types of plants. If the new bud (growth emerging from the center) of the palm is killed, the entire plant dies. (Not so for most other plants. If the new growth dies on them, the roots still live.)

Palms are ideal candidates for containers, particularly European fan palms and windmill palms. They stay for many years in the same pot without the need for transplanting to a larger container.

Regional Differences: Dependable as far north as zone eight, although we have experiences with needle palms growing for years in zone seven.

Color Period: Insignificant

Buying Tips: These palms are becoming more available every year in southern garden centers. All of them grow slowly, so buy the largest one you can afford.

**Blue ribbon plants are defined on page 12. For blue ribbon performance, follow the planting and maintenance guidelines on pages 28 to 49.*

European Fan Palm (*Chamaerops humilis,* left). A slow-growing palm that looks shrub-like until it is old enough to develop a trunk. Single and multiple trunk specimens available.

Grows ten feet tall eventually, but very slowly. Very low water requirements after establishment. Light shade to full sun. Zones eight to eleven.

Sabal Palm (*Sabal palmetto,* right). State tree of both South Carolina and Florida. One of the most common native plants in the US. One of the best trees for tolerating high wind. Lives without irrigation after establishment. 'Boots,' or the rough-texture shown on the trunk, fall off as the palm ages and a smooth trunk remains. A serious disease (phytoplasma) has been reported in parts of Florida (see right sidebar, 'Pest Problems').

Eventually grows twenty to forty feet tall. Very slow grower. Full sun. Zones eight to eleven.

Windmill Palm (*Trachycarpus fortunei,* left*)* Does better in temperate zones than the tropics.

Slowly grows to 25 feet tall. Very low water requirements. Light shade to full sun. Zones eight to ten.

**Lives on rainwater alone in all but the most extreme situations. Sabal and needle palms are native to the south. The others are not.*

GROWING CONDITIONS

Light: Light shade to full sun for European fan palm, needle palm, and windmill palm. Full sun only for sabal palm.

Water: Very low after establishment. Lives on rainwater alone, without supplemental water, in all but the most extreme conditions.

Soil: European fan and sabal palms adjust to poor soil as long as it is well drained. Fertile, well-drained soil high in organic matter is best for needle and windmill palms.

Hardiness: Zones 8 to 11 for the European fan and sabal palm; 8 to 10 for windmill palm. 7B to 10B for needle palm.

Propagation: Seeds

Pest Problems: European fan palm is susceptible to scale, ganoderma, and potassium deficiency. Windmill palm is moderately susceptible to lethal yellowing. Sabal palms are susceptible to palmetto weevils, ganoderma, and phytoplasma, which is serious. Before planting, check out information at: http://flrec.ifas.ufl.edu/palm_prod/pdfs/Sabal-palmetto-Infected-with-Phytoplasma-in-Florida.pdf

PLANTING & MAINTENANCE

When to Plant: Palms can be planted at any time.

Trimming: Trim off the old fronds if they persist on the trunk after they turn brown. Don't pull them off, or you could damage the trunk.

Fertilization: European fan and sabal palms have a low need for fertilizer. Windmill and needle palms have a medium fertilization need. Fertilize at planting time with a timed-release product. Less fertilizer is needed with the application of more organics. In the years after planting, fertilization needs vary, based on the nutrients in your soil.

Pistache or Chinese Pistache

1ST

CHARACTERISTICS

Plant Type: Deciduous tree (loses its leaves in the winter).

Average Size: 30 to 40 feet tall by 20 to 30 feet wide.

Growth Rate: Fast

Leaf: Compound leaves measuring 12 inches long with even rows of 10 to 12 lance-shaped leaflets, 4 inches long by 1 inch wide.

Flower: Dioecious (meaning male and female flowers on separate trees) flowers are small, greenish in color but not very showy. Blue fruit clusters on female trees are enjoyed by birds.

Origin: China, Philippines

Spacing: About 30 to 40 feet on center (measure from the center of each plant).

Cautions: Seldom damaged by deer.

Colors: Flowers are small, greenish, and inconspicuous. Leaves are bright green in summer, with excellent red to orange to yellow fall colors. Fruit clusters are blue.

A medium-sized tree, it is a perfect solution for lot sizes that cannot take the larger sizes found in oaks and maples. A fast grower that requires little care, so it rates a blue ribbon.* Brilliant fall color that stops traffic.

Pistache literally sets the landscape on fire during the fall of the year. Its bright, red canopy cannot be ignored by those passing by this magnificent tree.

When faced with a site with poor soils, pistache fits the bill. Excellent plantings can be found along interstate interchanges and harsh urban environments. Once established, pistache can withstand prolonged droughts and is not bothered by insects or diseases. A little gangly when young, the canopy matures to a nice, rounded head with age.

Regional Differences: None

Color Period: April before foliage emerges, but the flowers are greenish and inconspicuous. Fruit clusters are blue and borne in fall. Leaves usually turn red, orange, or yellow for about two weeks in fall, but this color change depends on temperatures and rainfall.

Buying Tips: This tree is available in many garden centers.

**Blue ribbon plants are defined on page 12. For blue ribbon performance, follow the planting and maintenance guidelines on pages 28 to 19.*

Companions: Chinese pistache looks great planted alone in a lawn, which grows well underneath it. Groundcovers and small perennials or evergreen shrubs can be planted under canopy as well. Hostas and ferns are good choices for under this tree, as shown below.

Chinese pistache and some companions

Autumn Fern (above, left) is one of the few evergreen ferns. Since both the Chinese pistache and the hosta lose their leaves in winter, it makes sense to have an evergreen plant in this garden. The autumn fern grows two to two and a half feet tall, and likes shade.

Hosta 'Patriot' (above, right) is an outstanding hosta that grows 18 to 30 inches tall in shade. Its variegated leaves show up well in the shade. Since it is a similar size to the autumn fern, alternate clumps of both plants below the Chinese pistache tree.

GROWING CONDITIONS

Light: Light shade to full sun

Water: Low after establishment. Likes water every week or two during the growing season, depending on its environment. See pages 34 to 37 for more information.

Soil: Grows in unimproved soil, including clay, provided the soil has not been compacted. Compaction occurs most commonly from heavy equipment working around a house under construction. See pages 28 to 29 for instructions on improving drainage and pages 32 to 33 for information regarding tree planting.

Hardiness: Zones 6 to 9

Propagation: Seeds

Pest Problems: Rare

PLANTING & MAINTENANCE

When to Plant: Chinese pistache trees from containers can be planted at any time. Fall is best because they establish easier in cooler weather. Stick to the cooler months (fall to winter) if you are planting a balled and burlapped tree.

Trimming: Prune to shape when young to develop a well-shaped canopy. As the tree ages, remove dead branches as they occur.

Fertilization: Low. Fertilize at planting time with a timed-release product. Less fertilizer is needed with the application of more organics. In the years after planting, fertilization needs vary, based on the nutrients in your soil. See pages 46 to 49 for more information.

1ST Redbud, Eastern

CHARACTERISTICS

Plant Type: Deciduous tree (loses its leaves in the winter).

Average Size: 20 to 25 feet tall by 15 to 20 feet wide.

Growth Rate: Medium to fast

Wind Tolerance: Low

Leaf: Heart-shaped leaves measuring 4 to 6 inches long and wide. Medium green in color, with dull yellow as fall color.

Flower: Tiny, 1/2 inch across; tightly arranged all up and down the stem; rosy pink to lavender.

Origin: New York to Florida, west to Missouri and Texas.

Spacing: About 15 to 20 feet on center (measure from the center of each plant).

Cautions: Frequently damaged by deer.

Color: Flowers are pink to lavender and white. Leaves are medium green, turning yellow in fall.

UNIVERSITY AWARDS

2002: Georgia Gold Medal Winner, 'Forest Pansy,' 'Oklahoma,' and 'Texas' white redbuds.

Twisted 'Covey' or 'Lavender Twist' red bud.

Imagine a hillside dotted with rosy pink to lavender flowers popping out as the warm days of spring arrive. Redbuds are one of the first heralds of spring and offer a contrast to the predominant color of white we normally see in flowering trees. Excellent, small, native tree for naturalized settings that gives notice that spring is here. Very easy to grow, so it rates a blue ribbon.*

Eastern redbud is an excellent choice when a small flowering tree is needed. Tough, durable, and drought tolerant, this tree requires less water than both dogwoods and Japanese maples. New cultivars provide excellent choices for foliage color, growth habit, and flower color. For a dependable, tough, no-fuss, small flowering tree, one can't go wrong with Eastern redbud. The only negative is that redbuds are susceptible to pests after they reach about 25 years old. Most don't live to an old age but have very few problems in the first 25 years of life.

Regional Differences: Winter chilling promotes heavy bloom, so redbuds may not flower as profusely in the coastal South as they do in the rest of the region.

Color Period: Flowers for three to five weeks in March or April, before the leaves emerge.

Buying Tips: The original, native species is beautiful and a good choice. For white flowers, choose 'Alba.' 'Forest Pansy' is an excellent choice for burgundy foliage on new growth. 'Appalachian Red' has very dark pink flowers, and 'Covey' is an extraordinary weeping form.

**Blue ribbon plants are defined on page 12. For blue ribbon performance, follow the planting and maintenance guidelines on pages 28 to 49.*

Companions: Redbuds make great accent trees to plant along driveways, or they can be grown at the edge of a sunny yard. They make fine background plants for hydrangeas and other shrubs that grow in partial shade, or you can combine them with dogwoods and azaleas. Spanish bluebells are happy to grow in clumps near redbuds, as are small daffodils and other little, spring-flowering bulbs.

For a gorgeous, spring-flowering grouping, plant redbuds with dogwoods and woodland phlox, as shown below.

Redbud and some southern native companions

Dogwood Trees (above, left) not only bloom the same time as redbuds but are also native to the same forests in the south. Both trees are about the same height. Plant a redbud in the center of the group, with white dogwoods on either side, keeping at least 20 feet in between the trunks.

Woodland Phlox (above, right) is another native plant that blooms in early spring. Since the phlox stays low (about 12 to 16 inches tall), use them as a groundcover under all of the trees. Azaleas would work well under the trees also. Be sure to keep the dogwood and phlox in light shade.

**Lives on rainwater alone in all but the most extreme situations.*

GROWING CONDITIONS

Light: Light shade to full sun

Water: Very low after establishment. Lives on rainwater alone, without supplemental water, in all but the most extreme conditions. See pages 34 to 37 for more information.

Soil: Grows in unimproved soil, including clay, provided the soil has not been compacted. Compaction occurs most commonly from heavy equipment working around a house under construction.

Hardiness: Zones 5 to 9

Propagation: Seeds or grafts

Pest Problems: Canker, as it reaches 25 years of age.

PLANTING & MAINTENANCE

When to Plant: Redbuds from containers can be planted at any time. Fall is best because they establish easier in cooler weather. Likewise, fall is the best time for balled and burlapped redbuds.

Trimming: Occasionally, to shape crown and thin out dead, diseased branches.

Fertilization: Low. Fertilize at planting time with a timed-release product. Less fertilizer is needed with the application of more organics. In the years after planting, fertilization needs vary, based on the nutrients in your soil.

New growth on 'Forest Pansy'

Smoke Tree

1ST

CHARACTERISTICS

Plant Type: Deciduous tree or shrub (loses its leaves in the winter).

Average Size: 8 to 12 feet tall by 6 to 8 feet wide.

Growth Rate: Fast

Leaf: Oval leaves 3 to 4 inches long by 1 to 2 inches wide. Leaves are lime green, medium green, purple, or burgundy. Most leaves turn yellow in fall.

Flower: Light, airy, yellow-green spikes, 6 to 8 inches long. Fine hairs that give off a pinkish cast surround the flowers.

Origin: Southern Europe to China

Spacing: About 8 to 10 feet on center (measure from the center of each plant).

Cautions: Juice or sap is a skin irritant to some. Occasionally damaged by deer.

Colors: Yellow-green flowers are insignificant, but the fine, pinkish hairs surrounding the flower give it a marvelous, "smoky" hue. Leaves are lime green, medium green, purple, or burgundy. Most leaves turn yellow in fall.

1. 'Young Lady' smoke tree
2. 'Golden Spirit' smoke bush

What a contrast in textures on the same plant - the coarse texture of the foliage coupled with the light, airy flower panicles hovering like smoke over the leaves. Creates quite a picture in the landscape. Whether it is the blue-green foliage of the species or the rich, burgundy-purple leaves of numerous cultivars, smoke tree is bound to create a stir when seen in the landscape. Easy to grow, so it rates a blue ribbon.*

For dramatic, deep reds or purples in the landscape, smoke tree is hard to beat. This easy plant provides deep, rich color without the fuss of a Japanese maple. Smoke tree is best used in groupings at the back of the planting bed, providing a wonderful backdrop for both shrub and perennial plantings. Very drought tolerant once established and few pest problems make Smoke tree an easy plant to grow, even for a novice gardener. For those who like to use cut branches in flower arrangements, nothing has the visual effect of a long stem of purple smoke tree, whether in full flower or just in foliage.

Regional Differences: None

Color Period: Flowers in May to June for about three weeks. For the most color, plant a smoke tree with colored leaves for a full, six months of color. Most leaves turn yellow in fall for about two weeks.

Buying Tips: Several cultivars are available, with the burgundy and purple leaf forms being the most popular. 'Royal Purple' and 'Velvet Cloak' are two outstanding dark leaf forms. 'Grace' is another excellent cultivar noted for very large rosy pink flower panicles (over 12" tall). The foliage on 'Grace' changes from wine-red in spring to blue-green in summer to wonderful shades of yellow-orange-red in fall.

**Blue ribbon plants are defined on page 12. For blue ribbon performance, follow the planting and maintenance guidelines on pages 28 to 49.*

Botanical Name: *Cotinus coggygria*

Family: Anacardiaceae

Companions: Be sure to complement smoke tree with contrasting foliage colors and textures. The purple smoke tree selections are quite dramatic. Pair them with plants that have silvery-blue foliage, like butterfly bush or with a completely contrasting foliage (like the chartreuse of annuals like coleus and sweet potato vine).

'Gold Mound' spiraea is a shrub that gives that lime green color. Combine it with long-blooming 'Knock Out' roses for a bed that gives continuous color the entire growing season with very little care.

'Royal Purple' smoke tree and some companions

'Knock Out' Roses (above, left) bloom spring, summer, and fall, so they keep the bed in color for the entire growing season. Since 'Knock Outs' grow to about five feet tall, place them in front of taller smoke tree and behind shorter spiraea.

'Gold Mound' Spiraea (above, right) is a small shrub that blooms for a few weeks in May or June and sporadically throughout the summer. However, the lime foliage is the main reason to use it with the 'Royal Purple' smoke tree. The foliage remains this lime color from spring until the first frost.This spiraea grows about two feet tall, so use it as a front border around the taller smoke tree and roses. All three plants do well in sun.

GROWING CONDITIONS

Light: Full sun, at least 6 hours per day.

Water: Very low after establishment. Lives on rainwater alone, without supplemental water, in all but the most extreme conditions. See pages 34 to 37 for more information.

Soil: Grows in unimproved soil, including clay, provided the soil has not been compacted. Compaction occurs most commonly from heavy equipment working around a house under construction. This plant cannot take waterlogged locations. See pages 28 to 29 for instructions on improving drainage and pages 32 to 33 for information regarding tree planting.

Hardiness: Zones 5 to 9

Propagation: Seeds or cuttings

Pest Problems: Rare. Roots rot in poorly drained soils.

PLANTING & MAINTENANCE

When to Plant: Smoke trees from containers can be planted at any time. Fall is best because they establish easier in cooler weather. Likewise, fall is the best time for balled and burlapped smoke trees.

Trimming: Prune to shape as a large shrub or small tree - may need to thin out older canes every three to four years to encourage new shoots from the base.

Fertilization: Low. Fertilize at planting time with a timed-release product. Less fertilizer is needed with the application of more organics. In the years after planting, fertilization needs vary, based on the nutrients in your soil. See pages 46 to 49 for more information.

**Lives on rainwater alone in all but the most extreme situations.*

Other Trees that Deserve Mention

Ash, Green
Fraxinus pennsylvanica

Native, deciduous tree known for its vigorous growth. 50 to 60 feet tall with a rounded crown. Large, compound leaves that can be messy in the home landscape. 'Urbanite' and 'Emerald' are two of the best cultivars. Full sun to light shade. Low water. Zones 3 to 9.

Bamboo
Phylostachys spp.

Numerous species of fast growing and aggressively-spreading oriental plants. You must be careful in how you use bamboo in the landscape because it can take over your garden. Best used as a tall vertical accent planted in a container. Full sun to light shade. Low water Zones 7 to 10.

Birch, River
Betula nigra

Wonderful, native tree found growing along stream banks. 40 to 60 feet tall. Most often planted as a multi-stem specimen to show off the creamy-colored, exfoliating bark. More heat tolerant than White birch. 'Heritage' and 'Dura-Heat' best cultivars. Full sun to light shade. Low to medium water. Zones 4 to 9.

Black Gum, Black Tupelo
Nyssa sylvatica

Excellent, native tree for brilliant red fall color. Deep, glossy green foliage turns fire-engine red in autumn. Found along moist bottom lands, Black gum is adaptive to dryer sites. 40 to 50 feet tall. Slow growing but worth the wait. Full sun to light shade. Low water. Zones 4 to 9.

Bottlebrush Tree
Callistemon spp.

Small but attractive evergreen tree for zones 9 to 11. It is creeping into zone 8. Grows 6 to 15 feet tall. Full sun. Check with your county extension agent before buying because severe diseases are reported in some parts of Florida. Low Water.

Bradford Pear
Pyrus calleryana 'Bradford'

The most over-planted tree in the south. While attractive in flower and form, older trees are falling apart with the least provocation. Abundant fruit production is leading many states to list all flowering pears as invasive. Think long term and plant something else. Full sun. Low water. Zones 5 to 9.

Buckeye, Bottlebrush
Aesculus parvifolia

Excellent, native tree that grows like a large, multi-stemmed shrub. White flower panicles resembling a old-fashioned bottlebrush open in June for 2 to 3 weeks. 10 to 12 feet tall by an equal spread. Fall color is a golden yellow. Light shade to morning sun. Low water. Zones 4-9.

Buckeye, Flame
Aesculus pavia

Small, native tree. 15 to 20 feet tall. Brilliant red flower panicles open in mid spring and provide much needed nectar for migrating hummingbirds. Flowers visible for two weeks. Large fruit capsules ripen in October. Fall color is yellow. Full sun to medium shade. Low water. Zones 5 to 9.

Cedar, Deodar
Cedrus deodara

Handsome, needle-like evergreen. Pyramidal with almost weeping stem tips present a soft, lacy picture. Deep green to blue-green depending on selection. 40 to 60 feet tall. Damaged by temperatures below 5 degrees ('Shalimar' & 'Kashmir' most cold hardy). Full sun. Low water.

Cherry Laurel
Prunus caroliniana

Attractive, dependable tree. 40 feet tall. Sometimes pruned into a screen or hedge. Very sensitive to wind, one of the first to fall in any windstorm. Not recommended for areas that get hurricanes. Light shade to full sun. Zones 8 to 10a.

Cherry, Kwanzan
Prunus serrulata 'Kwanzan'

Spring blooming cherry tree flowering after Yoshino cherry. Large, double, deep pink flowers open after foliage has emerged. 25 to 30 feet tall. Needs supplemental water during drought. Borers and root rot diseases are significant problems. Full sun. Medium water. Zones 5 to 9.

Cherry, Okame
Prunus x incamp 'Okame'

First of the flowering cherries to bloom in spring with pink flowers lasting for 2 weeks. Trees will reach 20 to 30 feet tall with an upright to oval growth habit. Fall color is yellow to orange-red. US National Arboretum introduction - most cold hardy of the flowering cherries. Medium water. Zones 6-9

**Blue ribbon plants are defined on page 12. For blue ribbon performance, follow the planting and maintenance guidelines on pages 28 to 49.*

Cherry, Yoshino
Prunus x yedoensis

The most widely planted cherry tree in the south. Exquisite, white to pale pink flowers cover the tree in mid spring for 10 to 14 days. 15 to 20 feet tall. Not known for long life span (numerous insects and disease problems-not drought tolerant) Full sun. Medium water. Zones 5 to 8.

Crabapple Tree
Malus X

Large group of small spring flowering trees growing 15-25 feet tall by same spread. Numerous choices with flowers in white, pink and red. Flowers open for 10 to 14 days and are followed by excellent fruit displays in fall that birds love. Full sun. Low water. Zones 4-9.

Cypress, Leyland
x Cupressocyparis leylandii

Fast growing, evergreen that has been used extensively for large screens. However, several diseases are causing concern (needle blight and canker) on mature plants plus extended drought conditions are providing extra stress to plants. Consider Cryptomeria or Thuja instead. Full sun. Medium water. Zones 6 to 10.

Fringe Tree
Chionanthus virginicus

Spectacular, small native tree with pure white flowers in mid spring. Delicate petals resembling fringe are showy for 10 to 14 days. Clusters of deep blue fruits ripen in late summer and are a gourmet meal for songbirds. Yellow fall color. 15 to 20 feet tall. Light shade to morning sun. Low water. Zones 4 to 9.

Goldenrain Tree
Koelreuteria paniculata

Known for its spectacular floral display of bright yellow flowers in late May to early June. After flowering, dull brown fruit capsules cover the tree detracting from the bright green foliage. 30 to 35 feet tall by equal spread. Full sun. Low water. Zones 5 to 9.

Holly, Dahoon
Ilex cassine

Small, evergreen tree native to the coastal areas of the deep south and Florida. 15 to 25 feet tall. Red fruits in fall persist all winter. Not reliably cold hardy in zones 6 and 7. Best selections are hybrids with *Ilex opaca* (Foster holly). Full sun to medium shade. Medium water. Zones 7 to 10.

Jerusalem Thorn
Parkensonia aculeata

Evergreen in tropical areas. Deciduous in temperate zones. Fine-textured yellow flowers in spring for a few months. Easy to grow in areas that are warm enough, but have dangerous thorns. 15 to 30 feet tall. Very low water. Light shade to full sun. Zones 8b to 11.

Loquat
Eriobotrya japonica

Small, evergreen tree growing 15 to 20 feet tall. Thick, leathery, dark green leaves. Creamy white flowers followed by orange fruits. Flowers may open anytime from November to March depending on weather. Low water. Not cold hardy in zones 6 and 7. Full sun. Zones 8 to 11.

Magnolia, Tulip
Magnolia x soulangiana

Lovely, spring flowering trees that disappoint many because they don't bloom if there is a late frost. Tulip-shaped, pink blossoms. Look for late-spring blooming selections (Little Girl series, 'Alexandrinia') to minimize threat. 15 to 30 feet tall. Full sun. Low water. Zones 4 to 10.

Oak, Laurel
Quercus laurifolia

Fast-growing but relatively short-lived (40 years) oak for zones 8 to 10b. Native to the south. One of the most dangerous trees in areas susceptible to hurricanes because it grows quite large (50 to 70 feet tall) and falls quite easily, causing tremendous property damage in 70 to 80 mph winds. Light shade to full sun.

Oak, Live
Quercus virginiana

The most beautiful native oak for zones 8 to 11. Spreading growth habit. Very tolerant of wind. 40 to 50 feet tall by 50 to 60 feet wide. Evergreen, but drops a lot of leaves throughout the year. Light shade to full sun. Very low water.

Oak, Pin
Quercus palustris

Widely planted, fast growing oak tree with pyramidal growth habit when young. Develops a rounded crown with age. Leaves often persist through winter giving a messy, unkempt appearance. Prone to chlorosis in soils with high pH. 60 to 70 feet tall. Full sun. Low water. Zones 4 to 8.

Other Trees that Deserve Mention

Oak, Water
Quercus nigra

Acorns stain hardscape in fall and winter. One of the most dangerous trees for areas prone to hurricanes. Insurance companies are starting to charge higher premiums for houses that have these trees. 50 to 60 feet tall. Light shade to full sun. Zones 7 to 9b. Medium water.

Oak, White
Quercus alba

Fall color is fantastic on this huge, native oak. Too large for most residences. Leaves develop a deep red color before dropping. 60 to 80 feet tall by 50 to 60 foot spread. Relatively slow growing but very long-lived. Full sun. Low water. Zone 4 to 9.

Palm, Canary Island Date
Phoenix canariensis

One of the most beautiful palms for zones 9 to 11. Grows 60 feet tall in the desert, but only about 30 feet tall in areas of higher rainfall. Check with your local county extension agent before buying this expensive tree is prone to disease in some areas. High wind tolerance. Very low water.

Palm, Chinese Fan
Livistona chinensis

An excellent, slow-growing palm for zones 9b to 11. 30 feet tall by 8 to 12 feet wide. Medium-green fronds are 3 to 6 feet wide. Sharp thorns on stalks. Light shade to full sun. Low water.

Palm, Lady
Rhapis excelsa

A shrub-like palm for zones 9 to 11 that is sometimes used as a hedge. 6 to 8 feet tall by 5 to 6 feet wide. Dense to light shade - will not take full sun. Frequently used as an indoor plant. Easy to grow. Low to medium water.

Palm, Pindo
Butia capitata

A small palm that grows as wide as it is tall. 12 to 15 feet tall. Bluish-grey leaves. Orange fruit that is used to make jelly. Easy to grow. High wind tolerance. Low water. Light shade to full sun. Zones 8 to 9.

Palm, Pygmy Date
Phoenix roebelenii

One of the strongest palms in hurricanes. Small, only growing (slowly) to about 10 feet tall. Spines on stalks. Medium shade to full sun. Easy to grow. Very low water. Zones 9 to 11. Very high wind tolerance.

Palm, Saw Palmetto
Serenoa repens

Native palm that looks more like a shrub in temperate areas. Great plant to attract wildlife. Bees are attracted to the flowers and birds follow for the seeds. Zones 8 to 11. Light shade to full sun. Very low water. Very high wind tolerance.

Palm, Washingtonia
Washingtonia robusta

Commonly-planted palm that is not recommended. Attracts rats and lightening. Grows about 50 feet tall. Trunk breaks easily in wind storms, causing tremendous property damage. Dangerous thorns on stalks. Light shade to full sun. Very low water. Zones 9 to 11.

Pine, Loblolly
Pinus taeda

Fast-growing, evergreen tree widely planted for quick screens. Falls over easily in high winds. Reaches 60 feet tall. Make sure you have room for these trees - many regret that previous owners planted Loblolly as a quick fix and now they are having to remove them. Full sun. Low water. Zones 6 to 9.

Pine, White
Pinus strobus

The softest texture of any of the pines. Long, medium green needles are soft to the touch. Can be grown naturally or sheared. Better for cooler regions of zones 6 and 7 than further south. Must have good drainage - not drought tolerant. Full sun. Low to medium water. Zones 3 to 8.

Plum, Purple Leaf
Prunus x cistena

Small, spring-flowering tree planted more for its burgundy foliage than delicate white to light pink flowers. 15 to 25 feet tall. Same insect and disease problems that plague Flowering cherries. 'Newport' & 'Thundercloud' are good selections. Full sun. Low to medium water. Zones 5 to 8.

**Blue ribbon plants are defined on page 12. For blue ribbon performance, follow the planting and maintenance guidelines on pages 28 to 49.*

Podocarpus
Podocarpus gracilior

A beautiful, evergreen tree for zones 9 to 11. Round crown and dense branches have a fern-like appearance. 50 feet tall by 25 feet wide. Drops quite a bit throughout the year. Light shade to full sun. High wind tolerance. Low water.

Poplar, Yellow
Liriodendron tulipifera

First cousin to the southern magnolia (creamy yellow flowers in spring that resemble tulips), yellow poplar needs plenty of room - 70 to 90 feet tall. Can be messy in the home landscape. Drought tolerant but leaves shed early as a result. Full sun. Low water. Zones 4 to 9.

Sweet Gum
Liquidambar styraciflua

Native tree found growing along rivers and streams throughout the south. Fast growth reaching 50 to 60 feet tall with attractive, green leaves changing to hues of red, orange and purple in fall. Fruit capsules are a mess - especially in a small yard. Full sun to medium shade. Low water. Zones 5 to 9.

Sycamore
Platanus occidentalis

Very large, native tree with branches and stems of pure white in the upper canopy - incredible winter silhouette. 60 to 80 feet tall by equal spread. Leaves are large, fruit capsules are abundant and both are messy to clean up. Very tolerant of urban pollution. Full sun. Low water (but will drop leaves). Zones 4 to 9.

Walnut, Black
Juglans nigra

Large, native tree known for its beautiful wood, tasty nuts and the fact that few things can grow near it! Black walnut exudes a chemical that limits competition. Site it away from other plants and watch out for falling green baseballs that hide the tasty nuts. 60 to 80 feet tall. Full sun. Low water. Zones 4 to 9.

Willow, Weeping
Salix babylonica

Dramatic growth habit of pendulous branches. Fast growing. 30 feet tall. Quick fix for open site but not known for longevity. Be careful around septic systems - extensive root system can clog field lines. Great accent for lake or pond setting. Full sun. Low to medium water. Zones 6 to 8.

Right: Red maple and ginko leaves in fall.

Index

Index

I

J

K

L

M

Index

T

U

V

W

X

Y

Z